Continuities and Changes in Maya Archaeology: Perspectives at the Millennium

Continuities and Changes in Maya Archaeology: Perspectives at the Millennium

Edited by Charles W. Golden and Greg Borgstede

ROUTLEDGE
NEW YORK AND LONDON

Published in 2004 by
Routledge
29 West 35th Street
New York, NY 10001
www.routledge-ny.com

Published in Great Britain by
Routledge
11 New Fetter Lane
London EC4P 4EE
www.routledge.co.uk

Routledge is an imprint of the Taylor and Francis Group.

Printed in the United States of America on acid-free paper.

Library of Congress Cataloging-in-Publication Data
Continuities and changes in Maya archaeology : perspectives at the millennium/Charles W. Golden and Greg Borgstede, editors.
p. cm.
Includes bibliographical references and index.
ISBN 0-415-94413-9 (hardcover : alk. paper)
1. Mayas—Antiquities. 2. Mayas—Material culture. 3. Archaeology—Mexico—History—20th century. 4. Archaeology—Central America—History—20th century. 5. Mexico—Antiquities. 6. Central America—Antiquities. I. Golden, Charles W., 1972– II. Borgstede, Greg, 1972–
F1435.C77 2003
972.81′016—dc21 2003014008

To Maura and Karla, for their unfailing support

Contents

Notes on Contributors

Wendy Ashmore, Department of Anthropology, University of California-Riverside

Timothy Beach, School of Foreign Service, Georgetown University

Greg Borgstede, Department of Anthropology, University of Pennsylvania

Geoffrey E. Braswell, Department of Anthropology, University of California-San Diego

Marcello A. Canuto, Department of Anthropology, Yale University

T. Patrick Culbert, Department of Anthropology, University of Arizona

Nicholas P. Dunning, Department of Geography, University of Cincinnati

Kitty F. Emery, Curator of Environmental Archaeology, Florida Museum of Natural History, Gainesville

William L. Fash, Jr., Department of Anthropology, Harvard University

Antonia E. Foias, Department of Anthropology & Sociology, Williams College

Charles W. Golden, Department of Anthropology, University of Pennsylvania

Stephen D. Houston, Department of Anthropology, Brigham Young University

Takeshi Inomata, Department of Anthropology, University of Arizona

Matilde Ivic de Monterroso, Universidad del Valle de Guatemala

Alfonso Lacadena García-Gallo, Universidad Complutense de Madrid

K. Anne Pyburn, Department of Anthropology, Indiana University

Don S. Rice, Department of Anthropology, Southern Illinois University

Prudence M. Rice, Department of Anthropology, Southern Illinois University

Jeremy A. Sabloff, Director, University of Pennsylvania Museum of Archaeology and Anthropology

Robert J. Sharer, Department of Anthropology, University of Pennsylvania

Daniela Triadan, Department of Anthropology, University of Arizona

Lori E. Wright, Department of Anthropology, Texas A&M University

Jason Yaeger, Department of Anthropology, University of Wisconsin

PART 1
Introduction

1
Continuities and Changes in Maya Archaeology: An Introduction

CHARLES W. GOLDEN
GREG BORGSTEDE

To call an edited volume *Continuities and Changes in Maya Archaeology* seems overly ambitious at best and disingenuous at worst. It is beyond the scope of any one volume to encapsulate the entire field of Maya archaeology, covering the history of its past one hundred years, its current state, and its future prospects. But this volume is not an attempt to circumscribe and delimit the field. It is intended, instead, to highlight the diversity of methodologies, theoretical approaches, and interpretive frameworks that make up archaeology as practiced in the Maya area—extending from southern Mexico to western Honduras—at the beginning of the twenty-first century (figure 1.1). To this end, the volume includes contributions on "traditional" topics in archaeology, such as ceramics, sociopolitical organization, and epigraphy, as well as "innovative" topics, such as residue analysis, social context studies, and community studies, which highlight the theoretical and methodological diversity and fluidity of our discipline.

The beginning of the twenty-first century seems an opportune moment to take stock of the growth and development of a field that arose as an academic, institutionalized discipline at the beginning of the previous century. The roots of academic archaeology in the Maya area lie in the nineteenth century. Dilettantes, explorers, and gentlemen scholars brought forth the field in an era of continuing exploration and colonialism (e.g., Charnay

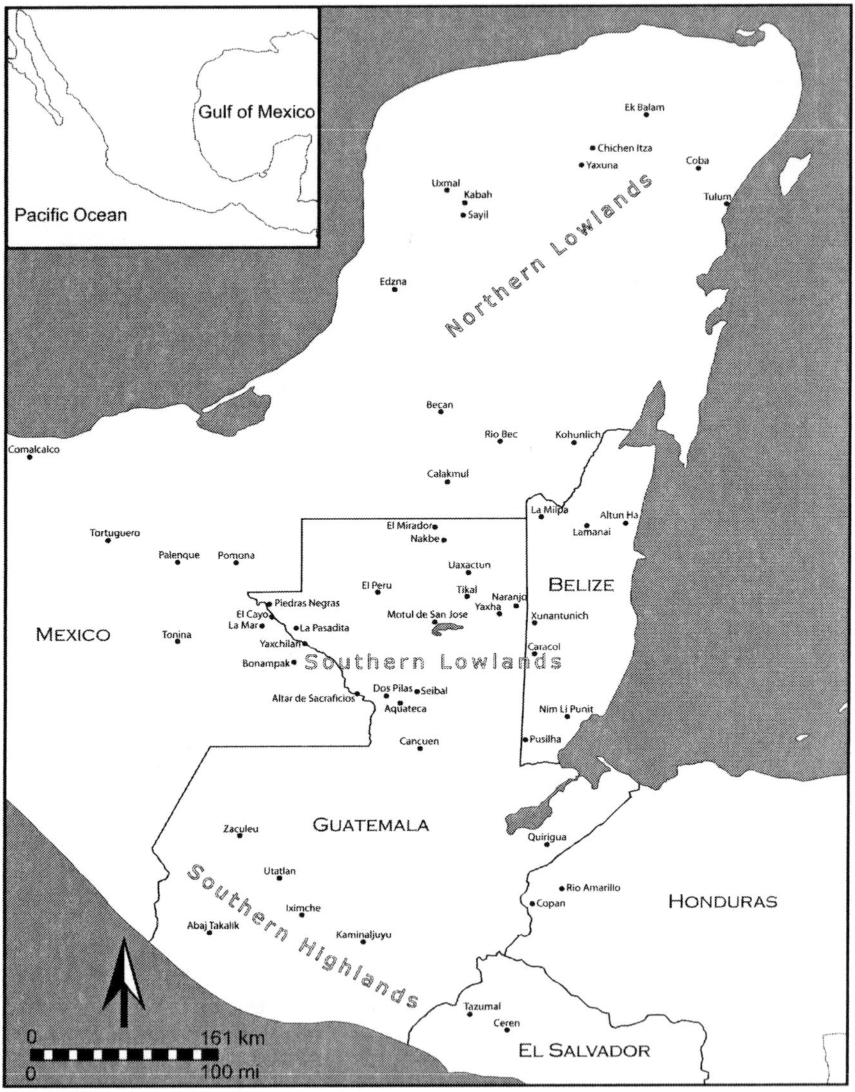

Fig. 1.1 Map of the Maya area showing major cultural zones and select archaeological sites.

1887; Stephens and Catherwood 1963 [1841], 1963 [1843]; Chambon 1994; see also Graham 2002). The end of the nineteenth century saw an initial proliferation of institutionally sponsored research in Mesoamerica, but this was minimal compared to what followed in the "classificatory-historical" period in the Maya area (see Willey and Sabloff 1993). As Mexican archaeologists initiated large-scale excavations of Pre-Columbian sites in central Mexico including Monte Alban, Xochicalco, and Teotihuacan, American institutions tended to focus on the cities of the Maya lowlands (Bernal 1980; Willey and Sabloff 1993). Excavations led by archaeologists from the Carnegie Institution of Washington continued for decades and covered the area from Yucatán to Honduras. Other institutions, including the University of Pennsylvania Museum of Anthropology and Archaeology, and the Peabody Museum of Harvard University, soon joined in this research (for an overview, see Black 1990; Schavelson 1989; Willey and Sabloff 1993) The doctoral programs of these university-based institutions not only helped to populate the field, they also encouraged the developing professionalism of archaeologists who would lead the discipline for the next quarter century.

The great interest in the Maya, within intellectual circles as well as among the broader public, drew more researchers and funding to Maya archaeology over the course of the twentieth century. This proliferation of archaeologists, and an enthusiastic public, required occasional assessments of the field as a whole. This need for a broad overview of the field has periodically resulted in the publication of large edited volumes dedicated to summarizing the "state of the art" of Maya archaeology. The most famous of these was the seminal *The Maya and Their Neighbors* (Hay et al. 1977 [1940]), which included both innovative scholarship in Maya archaeology, as well as a critique of the state of scholarship (Kluckhohn 1977 [1940] see also Sabloff in this volume).[1]

It is within this vein that we view *Continuities and Changes in Maya Archaeology: Perspectives at the Millenium*. As with *The Maya and Their Neighbors*, this volume is an attempt to take stock of the field of Maya archaeology, and to situate it within the wider scope of anthropological archaeology. The authors elaborate on the strengths and weaknesses of the discipline, and explore how archaeologists working in the Maya area can make contributions to a wider variety of publics—academic, popular, and political. Contributors consider not only the past and present, but also hypothesize on the future of various aspects of Maya archaeology. As the editors of this volume, we have elected to provide a relatively free forum to allow for debate and discussion. Our sole admonition to the authors was to offer statements that examine where the field stands in relation to the past, and its perceived future directions. We do not necessarily agree with all the interpretations put forward in this volume, but we acknowledge that the field can only grow and move forward in an environment of such open debate.

This volume provides a means of assessing Maya archaeology's contribution to anthropological archaeology and the influence of broader concerns—in anthropology, the social sciences, and political and social contexts—on Maya archaeology. As we have said, *Continuities and Changes in Maya Archaeology* is not an attempt to summarize or categorize the field of Maya archaeology. The diversity of the discipline precludes summary, which would be essentializing. In fact, it is the diversity of Maya archaeology—in its methodologies, theoretical approaches, practitioners, contexts, and knowledge—that is one of its greatest strengths and it is this diversity that the volume emphasizes. Following the conjunctive approach, a holistic, anthropological archaeology of the Maya consists of the insights drawn from all the data and perspectives available to us (Carmack and Weeks 1981; Fash and Sharer 1991; Taylor 1948). Following in the footsteps of *The Maya and Their Neighbors*, the goal of this volume is to provide points of discussion and debate that will advance our understanding and approaches to Maya archaeology.

The Contributions

This volume has been divided into four sections. In addition to the present chapter, the first section includes an introductory statement by Jeremy A. Sabloff, discussing a critical juncture in Maya archaeology—the critiques offered by Clyde Kluckhohn (1977 [1940]) and his student Walter Taylor (1948), and their aftermath. Sabloff suggests five directions in which Maya archaeology responded to this juncture, and the shifts it engendered (and continues to foster) within the field. His hopeful tone offers a pointed counter to the mid-century critiques of Kluckhohn and Taylor and highlights some important changes in Maya archaeology over the past fifty years.

The second section consists of contributions on the social, political, and ideological aspects of ancient Maya culture. These studies draw on analogies and developments in archaeology outside the Maya area. Authors examine, for instance, cross-cultural models of social organization and issues of landscape archaeology. In so doing, these chapters underscore Maya archaeology's continuing engagement with broader archaeological and anthropological theory.

Robert J. Sharer and Charles W. Golden discuss the various forms of Maya sociopolitical organization and how it has been interpreted based on the archaeological record. They reject the wholesale adaptation of cross-cultural models often applied to Maya polities, and instead build a picture of the polity that, while informed by similarities to other societies, is distinctly Maya. The intent is not to reject cross-cultural studies of political organization, but to avoid the reification of cross-cultural models.

Marcella A. Canuto and William L. Fash, Jr. develop the concept of the "community" in settlement pattern studies, suggesting that it can bridge the theoretical gap between elites and non-elites. Methodologically, they also see that a false dichotomy has been established at both ends of this elite/non-elite spectrum: (1) between the civic-ceremonial center and the polity of which it forms the center, and (2) between the household and larger population of which it is a component. They see research into the community as providing the methodological and theoretical link that can integrate multiple scales of organization.

Don and Prudence Rice examine the nature of "text-aided research" as it pertains to the reconstruction of Maya culture. They examine texts from Classic period inscriptions and Postclassic documents such as codices and colonial Spanish records. Using their research into the Colonial period Maya of the Petén as a case study, they seek to clarify the difference between "past" and "history," and challenge our preconceived notions that somehow these are one and the same. In so doing, they address a primary concern of many researchers, within and without Maya studies: Even with the abundance of textual data available to supplement our archaeological research, can we develop a picture of the "true" or "accurate" past?

Finally, Wendy Ashmore moves beyond settlement pattern studies to discuss the present and future of landscape archaeology in the Maya area. She sees landscape studies as the search for links between individual, society, and the world. Looking into the present and future of the discipline, Ashmore sees these links manifested in studies that expand on the fundamental definition of landscapes, that examine the often blurry boundaries between "natural" and "built" landscapes, and that offer a recognition of how time and human activity interact to constitute landscapes.

The third section—textual and material analysis—focuses on lithics, ceramics, zooarchaeology, bioarchaeology, and epigraphy. These categories of knowledge, common across regional specialties in world archaeology, provide a base for comparing advances in Maya archaeology with developments in other geographical and theoretical areas.

Stephen D. Houston and Alfonso Lacadena García-Gallo begin this section, addressing the history of an important defining characteristic of Maya studies—epigraphy. Although histories of the decipherment of Maya writing have been presented before (e.g., Coe 1992; Stuart 1992; Houston, Stuart, and Chinchilla 2001), here the authors focus on the present and future directions of epigraphy. They look at the "culture" of epigraphy and epigraphers as practiced in academic and popular circles, and they explore the promise and problems associated with integrating epigraphic data into broader interpretations of ancient Maya society.

Utilizing modern techniques, Nicholas P. Dunning and Timothy Beach address the role of environment in ancient Maya society. At issue is the nature of ancient Maya techniques for agricultural production and intensification, and the changing interpretations and theoretical approaches to the topic within Maya archaeology. As a more dynamic picture of the interaction between ancient Maya and their environment has emerged, so too has our understanding that agriculture as well as the environment were far more variable in time and space than we had previously believed.

Antonia Foias tackles the large problem of ceramic analysis in Maya archaeology—where it has come from and where it is going. Her brief history of the topic provides a much-needed assessment of the utility of current approaches to ceramic typology in the Maya area and where it may be headed. Much like lithic studies, ceramic analyses long focused on the development of typologies as the basis for site and regional chronologies. As Foias shows, however, the field of ceramic analysis has, in recent decades, made use of a wide variety of macroscopic, microscopic, chemical, art historical, and anthropological methods to provide us with a more complete picture of ancient Maya society.

Geoffrey E. Braswell examines the past and present of lithic studies in the Maya area, specifically the important role of the political economy of obsidian. He finds that before the 1970s lithic studies focused on typological analysis, but in that decade there was a "lithic revolution" during which Maya archaeologists began to focus on the economic implications of stone tools. Since then lithic studies have been a cornerstone of studies of Maya political economy—including issues of production, exchange, and extraction, among others.

Lori E. Wright, using specific case studies, underscores the importance of bioarchaeology in developing robust interpretations of burial remains and the social and political strategies they encode. Wright discusses three issues: (1) the reconstruction of life histories, (2) the development of skeletal biodistance studies, and finally (3) forensic analyses. Through these avenues of study she stresses that we can reconstruct more about social organization and heterogeneity, and group histories, including important processes such as migrations.

Kitty F. Emery highlights the important contributions made by zooarchaeology in interpretation and the future prospects for this field of study within the Maya area. She notes that despite a long history of zooarchaeological studies, it is only recently that such work has come to be incorporated into larger issues of ritual, economics, and politics. Emery believes that this shift forms the basis of a new "social zooarchaeology" that has much to contribute to Maya studies.

Finally, arguing that Maya archaeologists have for too long focused on the "big remains" found in tombs, caches, and other such contexts, Daniela Triadan and Takeshi Inomata develop an argument for the importance of small, or microscopic, artifact analysis. Their case study from the site of Aguateca, Guatemala, relies on residue analysis and activity area research, techniques that promise innovative and important insights into ancient life.

The final section of the volume—contemporary concerns—represents an important advance in the practice of Maya archaeology over the last twenty-five years. As archaeologists in the United States and elsewhere have struggled with the nature of their obligations to the descendant communities of the people they study, Mayanists are coming to an understanding that the practice of archaeology is firmly embedded in a social context that influences all aspects of archaeological practice. Jason Yaeger and Greg Borgstede begin this section with a historical examination of the relationship between archaeologists and contemporary Maya communities. They highlight how this relationship has not arisen in academic isolation, but has been influenced by broader developments in anthropology and social sciences more generally. They finish with a brief discussion of the implications of an "engaged" archaeology in the Maya area, and the importance of including alternate voices in the archaeological process.

K. Anne Pyburn begins with a look into the theoretical standpoint of Western archaeology, particularly in relationship to indigenous peoples, in a world of "posts" (post-modernism, post-colonialism, etc.). Taking a critical view of Maya archaeology and archaeologists she suggests a number of ways to rethink the context of anthropology in general and Maya archaeology in particular. Her broad-ranging argument contextualizes Maya archaeology within the wider arena of social sciences and humanities. She explores the issues surrounding modernity, post-modernity, objectivity, and subjectivity, particularly as these affect archaeological practice and modern communities in the Maya world.

Matilde Ivic de Monterroso analyzes the impact of a specific social development—the Guatemalan Peace Accords—on the practice of Maya archaeology within Guatemala. She argues for the importance of including nonarchaeological perspectives—particularly those of descendant communities—in academic discourse. More than this, Ivic looks at the other side of the coin to explore how descendant communities view the work of archaeologists.

The volume closes with a discussion by T. Patrick Culbert. This final chapter plays two roles. In the first place, Culbert examines his own experience over nearly fifty years in Maya studies, and his perceptions of the changes that have most affected the field. Second, he offers his interpretation of the state of the field as evident in some of the volume's chapters.

The Contributors

This volume grows out of a much larger project, an attempt by Drs. Houston and Sharer to bring together nearly two dozen scholars at the 99th Annual Meeting of the American Anthropological Association in Washington, D.C., in 2001. The current volume includes the work of most of those present in Washington, who have here contributed extended versions of their papers. This volume also incorporates a number of papers not presented at the original meeting, including those by Emery, Ivic, and Culbert.

Just as no single volume can hope to encompass the diversity of approaches within the field, this work is not representative of the diversity of archaeologists at work in the Maya area. Drs. Inomata, Lacadena, and Triadan, and Lic.Ivic notwithstanding, the contributors to *Continuities and Changes in Maya Archaeology* are from the United States, Canada, and Guatemala. Although attempts were made to include Honduran and Mexican, as well as additional Guatemalan, scholars, even this would not represent the range and diversity among archaeologists working in the region. Archaeologists and epigraphers come from Poland, Hungary, France, Spain, Britain, Australia, Guatemala, Mexico, El Salvador, Belize, Honduras, Canada, Japan, and the United States, among other countries, and provide a unique cauldron; a set of diverse cultural standpoints that continues to influence the development of Maya archaeology.

Moreover, apart from national affiliation, this volume is a production of non-Maya archaeologists concerning the field of Maya archaeology, and as such, it cannot "speak for" indigenous peoples. Although several contributions address issues related to indigenous positions and perceptions of archaeologists, none can speak in an "indigenous voice." Indeed, the question of what constitutes the indigenous voice and representation, particularly in relation to archaeological practice, is itself a subject of heated debate contested at professional meetings and political gatherings, and would constitute innumerable volumes (see Warren 1998; Montejo 2002).

Diversity as Strength

Finally, as stated above, the goal of this volume is not to define or delimit the extent of Maya archaeology but to engender discussion and debate—on the history, current state of the art, and future of the field. The current state of the art is as diverse as any geographical specialization in world archaeology, and we believe that the practice of archaeology in the Maya area has much to contribute to anthropological archaeology in general. We also believe, however, that the traditionally provincial focus of much Maya research remains an issue that archaeologists continue (by and large successfully) to struggle against. Only by drawing from research elsewhere in

Mesoamerica and around the world can Maya studies remain a vital aspect of anthropological archaeology.

In the end, the diversity of the discipline, far from being divisive, fosters cohesion as researchers attempt to incorporate the full breadth of data in conjunctive, holistic studies. Diversity does, however, challenge efforts at summation, as this volume clearly shows. Although various contributors have made attempts to envision the future of Maya archaeology, its diversity precludes any firm statements about that future. The only certainty, if the past is any indication, is that methodological, theoretical, and contextual advances will surprise and challenge practitioners as Maya archaeology moves rapidly into the next millennium.

Acknowledgments

First and foremost, we wish to thank Stephen Houston and Robert Sharer for sharing with us the opportunity to work on this project. We also thank the contributors, who endured numerous nagging e-mails. Finally, we thank Priti Gress, Karen Wolny, and Donna Capato at Routledge for their support of this book.

Notes

1. Mayanists have sometimes extended the scope of these volumes to include a wider Mesoamerican perspective, and a number of edited volumes have addressed issues of regional interaction (e.g., Hammond 1974; Hay et al. 1977 [1940]). These state-of-the-art volumes have also narrowed their focus to examine a temporal slice of Maya history (e.g., Sabloff and Henderson 1993) or have explored more specific topics within Maya archaeology, as with *Lowland Maya Settlement Patterns* (Ashmore 1981), *Function and Meaning in Classic Maya Architecture* (Houston 1998), and *Ancient Maya Women* (Ardren 2002). One of the most important of these volumes is *Classic Maya Political History* (Culbert 1991), which included early syntheses of archaeological and epigraphic data following the explosion of epigraphic decipherment of the 1980s.

References

Ardren, T. (ed.) (2002) *Ancient Maya Women*, New York: Alta Mira Press.

Ashmore, W. (ed.) (1981) *Lowland Maya Settlement Patterns*, Albuquerque: University of New Mexico Press.

Bernal, I. (1980) *A History of Mexican Archaeology*, London: Thames and Hudson.

Black, S. L. (1990) *Field Methods and Methodologies in Lowland Maya Archaeology*, Cambridge, MA: Harvard University Press.

Carmack, R. M., and Weeks, J. M. (1981) "The Archaeology and Ethnohistory of Utatlan: A Conjunctive Approach," *American Antiquity* 46:323–41.

Chambon, L. (1994) *Un Gascón en Mexico*, Mexico City: Mirada Viajera.

Charnay, D. (1887) *The Ancient Cities of the New World*, New York: Harper and Brothers.

Culbert, T. P. (ed.) (1991) *Classic Maya Political History: Hieroglyphic and Archaeological Evidence*, New York: Cambridge University Press.

Coe, M. (1992) *Breaking the Maya Code: The Last Great Decipherment of an Ancient Script*, New York: Thames and Hudson.

Fash, W. L., and Sharer, R. J. (1991) "Sociopolitical Developments and Methodological Issues at Copan, Honduras: A Conjunctive Perspective," *Latin American Antiquity* 2:166–87.

Graham, I. (2002) *Alfred Maudslay and the Maya: A Biography*, Norman: University of Oklahoma Press.

Hammond, N. (ed.) (1974) *Mesamerican Archaeology: New Approaches*, Austin: University of Texas Press.

Hay, C. L., Linton, R. L., Lothrop, S. K., Shapiro, H. L., and Vaillant, G. C. (eds.) (1977 [1940]) *The Maya and Their Neighbors: Essays on Middle American Anthropology and Archaeology*, New York: Dover.

Houston, S. D. (ed.) (1998) *Function and Meaning in Classic Maya Architecture*, Washington, DC: Dumbarton Oaks.

Houston, S. D., Chinchilla, O., and Stuart, D. (eds.) (2001) *The Decipherment of Ancient Maya Writing*, Norman: University of Oklahoma Press.

Kluckhohn, C. (1977 [1940]) "The Conceptual Structure in Middle American Studies," in C. Hay, R. Linton, S. K. Lothrop, H. L. Shapiro, and G. C. Vaillant (eds.), *The Maya and Their Neighbors: Essays on Middle American Anthropology and Archaeology*, pp. 41–51, New York: Dover.

Montejo, V. (2002) "The Multiplicity of Mayan Voices: Mayan Leadership and the Politics of Self-Representation," in K. Warren and J. Jackson (eds.), *Indigenous Movements, Self-Representation, and the State in Latin America*, pp. 123–48, Austin: University of Texas Press.

Sabloff, J. A., and Henderson, J. S. (1993) *Lowland Maya Civilization in the Eighth Century A.D.*, Washington, DC: Dumbarton Oaks.

Schavelson, D. (1989) "History of Mesoamerican Archaeology at the Crossroads: Changing Views of the Past," in *Tracing Archaeology's Past*, A. Christenson (ed.), pp 107–112. Carbondale: Southern Illinois Press.

Stephens, J. L., and Catherwood, F. (1963 [1841]) *Incidents of Travel in Central America, Chiapas, and Yucatán*, New York: Dover.

Stephens, J. L., and Catherwood, F. (1963 [1843]) *Incidents of Travel in Yucatán*, New York: Dover.

Stuart, G. (1992) "Quest for Decipherment: A Historical and Biographical Survey of Maya Hieroglyphic Investigation," in E. Danien and R. J. Sharer (eds.), *New Theories on the Ancient Maya*, pp. 1–63, Philadelpia: University Museum Press.

Taylor, W. W. (1948) *A Study of Archaeology*, American Anthropologist Memoir, no. 69 3(2), Washington, DC: American Anthropological Association.

Warren, K. B. (1998) *Indigenous Movements and Their Critics: Pan-Maya Activism in Guatemala*, Princeton: Princeton University Press.

Willey, G. R., and Sabloff, J. A. (1993) *A History of American Archaeology*, San Francisco: W. H. Freeman.

2
Looking Backward and Looking Forward: How Maya Studies of Yesterday Shape Today

JEREMY A. SABLOFF

In the middle of the past century, Clyde Kluckhohn (1940) and his student Walter W. Taylor (1948) launched energetic and caustic assaults on Maya studies, in general, and A. V. Kidder and the Carnegie Institution of Washington's Maya program, in particular. Ironically, at a time when Mayanists might have been celebrating the coming of age of their field with the publication of Sylvanus Morley's (1946) massive 520-page synthesis, *The Ancient Maya*, they found themselves under vigorous attack.

Here are just a few examples of this onslaught. First from Kluckhohn (1940:42–3):

> I should like to record an overwhelming impression that many students in this field are but slightly reformed antiquarians.
>
> . . . There seems a great deal of obsessive wallowing in detail of and for itself.
>
> Authors of research monographs ought to make it plain . . . that they have given such amplitude of detail only toward the end of elucidating such and such larger questions. And from time to time in any field there should appear books or articles on a somewhat higher level of abstraction, which suggest the pertinence of various constellations of data to the primary problems of human interaction. It is the candid opinion of this writer that such efforts by Middle American specialists have been pitifully few.

> I suspect that unless archaeologists treat their work quite firmly as part of a general attempt to understand human behavior they will, before many generations, find themselves classed with Aldous Huxley's figure who devoted his life to writing a history of the three-pronged fork.

In regard to Mesoamerican studies, Kluckhohn (1940:51) further notes: "Factual richness and conceptual poverty are a poor pair of hosts at an intellectual banquet."

Taylor (1948:57) specifically targets the research of the Carnegie Institution of Washington:

> And so it goes. Carnegie has sought and found the hierarchal, the grandiose. It has neglected the common, the everyday. And even within its chosen segment of Maya culture, it has produced data for the most part in a narrowly descriptive range.

In criticizing the Kaminaljuyu, Guatemala, project, Taylor (1948:58) argues that the project:

> would seem to have been a very worthy project and one which might give promise of some well-grounded conclusions upon cultural manifestations, their modifications, and their sequence. But the road to Hell and the field of Maya archaeology are paved with good intentions.

Additionally, Taylor (1948:59) states:

> . . . It may be concluded that both the field work and the publications of the Carnegie are weighted overwhelmingly toward the hierarchical. They have hardly touched, and then only incidentally, the cultural remains of the common Maya. But even within the hierarchical culture, the emphasis has not been to construct a picture of how the Maya hierarchy lived: what they did and where, how, and with what.

I would argue that in many respects, explicitly, implicitly, or in effect, Maya studies over the past five decades have been a massive response to the criticisms that Kluckhohn and Taylor leveled against the field in the 1940s.

Now, we all know that every self-respecting archaeologist divides things into three categories—early, middle, late or Preclassic, Classic, Postclassic, for instance—but since I am an administrator at the moment, hopefully I can get away with discussing this massive response in five parts, instead of three:

1. New emphasis on non-elite
2. Research that moves beyond the description of the elite
3. Concern with method and theory

4. Connecting the ancient Maya to broad comparative studies of pre-industrial civilizations
5. Relating the ancient Maya to the historic and modern Maya and drawing understandings from historic writings and current studies

In discussing the general nature and import of some of these five approaches, I should emphasize that my intent is not to review the past fifty years of Maya studies in a short introductory chapter. Rather, in responding to the editors' charge, I plan to very briefly examine those aspects of the history of Maya studies, and especially in archaeology, that may help us illuminate the paths that the field may take in the early years of the new millennium.[1]

Although one could argue at great length about the merits of the Kluckhohn–Taylor critique, as many archaeologists have,[2] it is clear that the emphasis in Maya studies from the latter part of the nineteenth century until the middle of the twentieth *was* heavily weighted toward the ruling elite.[3] However, the nearly total absorption with things elite in the ancient Maya world began to change, as we are all aware, in the 1950s and 1960s, as some scholars, led by Gordon Willey, turned their attention away from the temples and the palaces to the remains of the non-elite and especially the houses of commoners and farmers. For example, on the basis of their research on settlement patterns in the Belize River Valley, Willey et al. (1965) were able to infer that the mounds they were excavating were the remains of perishable houses lived in for long periods of time. The importance of this research cannot be overemphasized. In this regard, Wendy Ashmore and I (Sabloff and Ashmore 2001:14) have recently contended that if "one were asked what has been the single most critical theoretical or methodological innovation in archaeology since World War II, a strong argument could be made for settlement pattern studies."

More than forty-five years ago, in the lead article of the October 1956 issue of the *American Anthropologist,* Willey (1956) published one of the key written pieces in Maya studies—and in American archaeology, for that matter—an article entitled "The Structure of Ancient Maya Society." In this article and other writings, Willey clearly showed that the study of the Maya "peasantry" had to be an integral part of any consideration of the development of ancient Maya civilization. Willey's pioneering research was soon followed up by a host of important settlement pattern projects, perhaps most significantly by the field project initiated by the University of Pennsylvania Museum and the government of Guatemala at Tikal (see Coe 1965 for an overview).

While the Tikal fieldwork followed some of the tenets of the traditional elite approach, it imbedded them in a much broader settlement context. The

Tikal research between 1956 and 1970 successfully challenged the traditional conception of peaceful astronomer-priests living in splendid isolation in their jungle setting, and helped stimulate the emergence of a much more complex model that saw the ancient Maya as an urban civilization supported by varied agricultural techniques, broadly similar to a general model of preindustrial civilization throughout the ancient world of Egypt, Mesopotamia, the Indus, and China that scholars were developing at the same time.

Also at this time, the emerging decipherment of Maya hieroglyphic writing led to the revolutionary understandings of political complexity in Classic times that have come to the fore in recent years (see Martin and Grube 2000). The growth of knowledge of Maya written history, coupled with detailed archaeological work in both elite and non-elite households, has in turn led to rich and nuanced understandings of the lifeways of Maya rulers and their relationships with urban developments. The exciting research in—and under—the Copan Acropolis, the Copan urban zone, and throughout the Copan Valley is just one example of the fruitfulness of combined archaeological, ecological, and epigraphic research and the insights that such approaches have provided into the development of both ancient Maya rulers and commoners/farmers alike (e.g., Fash 2002).

A host of recent and current research projects show that Mayanists have utilized, and are utilizing, the latest technical and methodological advances in the field and have been and are contributing to them, as well. These researches have provided important new insights into the changing Pre-Columbian environment, agriculture and diet, economics and trade, social organization, politics and religion, cosmology, and ideology (see Weeks 2002 for a number of bibliographic examples).

Another clear trend over the second half of the twentieth century has been a growing consideration and understanding of the ancient Maya as a Mesoamerican civilization, and its embeddedness in the broad Mesoamerican system from early formative times to the Spanish Conquest some three thousand years later. In contrast to the isolationism of the traditional model, in recent decades Mayanists have gained better understandings of the complex relationships among the Maya and their near and far neighbors to the north and south and the two-way influences in economics, politics, and religion.

Research in recent decades, in part stimulated by the pioneering fieldwork by the late Bill Andrews at Dzibilchaltun (see Andrews IV and Andrews V 1980), also has led to a greater scholarly appreciation of both the Northern Maya Lowlands and the Postclassic period as key components of research on the ancient Maya. Moreover, the Postclassic is now seen as a time of continued Maya development and not decline, as it previously had been viewed. There also has been growing attention to sixteenth-century cultural continuities and discontinuities and the importance and utility of historical sources for providing significant insights into ancient Maya culture. The same can be said for the continuities and discontinuities between historic Maya peoples in Yucatán and the highlands and their modern descendants and the importance of understanding the cultures of modern Maya peoples for illumination of aspects of ancient Maya lifeways.

Finally, as Mayanists have slowly begun to appreciate the relevance and relatedness of their studies to the modern world, we have begun to see a new balance between—on one hand—the ongoing emphasis and interest in the collapse of Classic Maya civilization and—on the other hand—a rising appreciation for the long-term sustainability of large urban centers throughout the Southern Lowlands over more than a millennium. The sustainability of ancient population densities far in excess of modern densities, in spite of all the advances in technology and mechanized agriculture, clearly has relevance to modern concerns with sustainable agriculture for peasant communities today within contexts of long-term tropical rainforest conservation (see Rice and Rice 1984; also see Atran and Ucan Ek' 1999, among others). Mayanists have contributed to new understandings in this area and have much more to contribute, I believe, in the future.

Let me close by further commenting on the future, in relation to what lessons the recent history of Maya archaeology might have for Mayanists in this new decade of the twenty-first century (also see Marcus 1995). Let me make three (back to orthodoxy here) predictions. The first is almost a sure bet, the second is somewhat chancier, and the third puts me in a place I have been many times before—out on a limb!

Number one is that building on the base of the Tikal project and the great success of more recent collaborative archaeological/epigraphic projects with both urban/rural and elite/non-elite foci, such as the Copan and Petexbatun projects of the 1980s and 1990s, we will see many more such productive undertakings in the coming decade (Bell, Canuto, and Sharer in press; Demarest 1997).

Number two is a terminological argument that I have made for more than fifteen years (Sabloff 1985, 1990), which has garnered little or no support from my colleagues. However, given the tremendous new understandings of the complex middle and late Preclassic developments throughout the Maya area, and given the growing insights into the Terminal Classic and Early Postclassic developments that new research in the Northern Lowlands are revealing, my crystal ball has begun to glow brighter with the prediction that the old Preclassic–Classic–Postclassic chronology will prove not only to be outmoded, but also a hindrance to richer and more productive insights into the nature of ancient Maya civilization over a period of three millennia.

Number three is a lesson from the intellectual trend in the second half of the twentieth century toward a more holistic and systemic consideration of Pre-Columbian Maya culture. An appreciation of the trend from the traditional emphasis on the Maya elite to a much broader interest in commoners and artisans and their households, the middle or working classes (see Marcus 1998), if you will, provides the basis for a difficult, but crucial, prediction for Maya studies in the new millennium: Namely, the expansion of perspective from elite to non-elite, while admirable, is not yet complete and will not be until there is new and comparable attention to the heretofore invisible lower class, which I believe is coming. This prediction involves intellectual as well as methodological challenges, but ones that I feel can be overcome. Until new light is cast on what might be called the marginal peoples of ancient Maya civilization, questions such as "Who supplied all the labor for transport and building?", "Who supplied the labor for long-distance movement of goods over land and over water?", "Were there migrant agricultural laborers?", and "What was the role of slavery?" will not be fully answered.

In relation to the latter, for instance, it is clear from historical sources that the Maya elite at the time of the Spanish Conquest in Yucatán regularly bought and sold slaves. Nancy Farriss (1984:25) states, for example: "Slaves had been one of Yucatán's principal exports in Pre-Columbian times, and slave taking a major incentive for border warfare in the region." Ralph Roys (1943:35) also points out:

> A large slave traffic existed both for export and domestic labor. Slaves were employed for heavy manual labor, working on farms and in the fishing industry, as carriers on the road and as paddlers in the trading canoes. They were also useful in domestic service. . . .

Roys (1943:34) additionally notes the possibility that a stratum of serfs, who were situated in the social hierarchy between the slaves and commoners, existed in Pre-Conquest Yucatán.

How far back in time does this practice go? Did it play critical economic, social, and ideological roles? Answers to such questions will allow Mayanists to overcome their still incomplete and partial views of the ancient Maya and to expand their understandings of the pre-industrial world. The field continues to have a too top-heavy emphasis on the upper tiers of Maya society that needs to be redressed.

I am heartened by the incredible progress that Maya studies have made since World War II and how inapplicable most of the Kluckhohn–Taylor critiques of the 1940s would be today. Scholars of ancient Maya civilization now not only draw on the contributions of archaeologists studying complex societies elsewhere in the Americas and the Old World, but they are in turn making substantial contributions to such topics as household archaeology and landscape studies, in particular, and to archaeological theory and method, in general. Despite all these advances in understanding the ancient Maya, I am nevertheless chastened by the contentious challenges that still confront the field, many of which are discussed in the chapters that follow, and daunted by what remains to be accomplished.

Notes

1. I am grateful to Professor Joyce Marcus for her helpful comments on an earlier draft of this chapter.
2. I was taken aback, for example, some years ago, when I chaired a session at the 50th anniversary meeting of the Society for American Archaeology and many of the major figures in the field were asked to reflect on *A Study of Archaeology.* How raw some scholars nerves still were on this question nearly forty years after its publication!
3. The research of Oliver R. Ricketson and Edith B. Ricketson (1937) and Robert Wauchope (1934, 1938) were significant exceptions.

References

Andrews IV, E. W., and Andrews V, E. W. (1980) *Excavations at Dzibilchaltun, Yucatán, Mexico,* Middle American Research Institute, Publication 48, New Orleans: Tulane University.

Atran, S., and Ucan Ek', E. (1999) "Classification of Useful Plants by the Northern Petén Maya (Itzaj)," in C. D. White (ed.), *Reconstructing Ancient Maya Diet,* pp. 19–59, Salt Lake City: University of Utah Press.

Bell, E. B., Canuto, M. A., and Sharer, R. J. (eds.) (in press) *Understanding Early Classic Copan,* Philadelphia: University Museum Publications.

Coe, W. R. (1965) "Tikal: Ten Years of Study of a Maya Ruin in the Lowlands of Guatemala," *Expedition* 8: 5–56.

Demarest, A. A. (1997) "The Vanderbilt Petexbatun Regional Archaeological Project, 1989–1994: Overview, History, and Major Results of a Multidisciplinary Study of the Classic Maya Collapse," *Ancient Mesoamerica* 8(2): 209–27.

Farriss, N. M. (1984) *Maya Society under Colonial Rule: The Collective Enterprise of Survival,* Princeton: Princeton University Press.

Fash, W. L. (2002) *Scribes, Warriors, and Kings: The City of Copan and the Ancient Maya,* revised ed., New York: Thames and Hudson.

Kluckhohn, C. (1940) "The Conceptual Structure in Middle American Archaeology," in C. L. Hay et al. (eds.), *The Maya and Their Neighbors,* pp. 41–51, New York: D. Appleton-Century.

Marcus, J. (1995) "Where Is Lowland Maya Archaeology Headed?" *Journal of Archaeological Research* 3: 3–53.

———(1998) "Maya Commoners: The Stereotype and the Reality." Unpublished Manuscript in the possesion of the author.

Martin, S., and Grube, N. (2000) *A Chronicle of Maya Kings and Queens,* New York: Thames and Hudson.

Morley, S. G. (1946) *The Ancient Maya,* Stanford: Stanford University Press.

Rice, D. S., and Rice, P. M. (1984) "Lessons from the Maya," *Latin American Research Review* 19 (3): 7–34.

Ricketon, O. G., and Ricketson, E. B. (1937) *Uaxactun, Guatemala, Group E, 1926–1937,* Publication 477, Washington, DC: Carnegie Institution of Washington Publication.

Roys, R. L. (1943) *The Indian Background of Colonial Yucatán,* Publication 548, Washington, DC: Carnegie Institution of Washington.

Sabloff, J. A. (1985) "Ancient Maya Civilization: An Overview," in C. Gallenkamp and R. E. Johnson (eds.), *Maya: Treasures of an Ancient Civilization,* pp. 34–44, New York: Henry M. Abrams.

———(1990) *The New Archaeology and the Ancient Maya,* New York: W. H. Freeman.

Sabloff, J. A., and Ashmore, W. (2001) "An Aspect of Archaeology's Recent Past and Its Relevance in the New Millennium," in G. Feinman and T. D. Price (eds.), *Archaeology at the Millennium: A Sourcebook*, pp. 11–32, New York: Kluwer Academic/Plenum.

Taylor, W. W. (1948) *A Study of Archaeology*, Memoirs of the American Anthropological Association, 69, Menasha, WI: American Anthropological Association.

Wauchope, R. (1934) *House Mounds of Uaxactun, Guatemala*, Publication 436, Washington, DC: Carnegie Institution of Washington.

———(1938) *Modern Maya Houses*, Publication 502, Washington, DC: Carnegie Institution of Washington.

Weeks, J. M. (2002) *Maya Civilization 1996–2000: A Bibliographic Guide*, Lancaster, CA: Labyrinthos.

Willey, G. R. (1956) "The Structure of Ancient Maya Society: Evidence from the Southern Lowlands," *American Anthropologist* 58: 777–82.

Willey, G. R., Bullard, W. R., Glass, J. B., and Gifford, J. C. (1965) *Prehistoric Maya Settlement Patterns in the Belize Valley*, Papers of the Peabody Museum, 54, Cambridge, MA: Harvard University.

PART 2
Reconstruction of the Social, Political, and Ideological

3
Kingship and Polity: Conceptualizing the Maya Body Politic

ROBERT J. SHARER
CHARLES W. GOLDEN

In an attempt to escape the provincialism for which Mayanists have long been accused (e.g., Kluckhohn 1940), over the past several decades archaeologists have drawn models of political organization from outside Mesoamerica to better situate the Classic period Maya within a more general anthropological discourse on political complexity (Adams and Smith 1981; Coe 1957; Sabloff 1986; Sanders 1981:365–9). The application of such comparative models began at a time when reconstructions of Maya political systems were based almost entirely on archaeological and ethnohistorical evidence. Recent archaeological and epigraphic research has greatly enriched our knowledge of Classic Maya political systems. While the unprecedented availability of information from deciphered Classic period texts concerning individual Maya kings, dynasties, polities, intrapolity alliances, and warfare has revolutionized our understanding of Maya political affairs, we emphasize that the full potential of this historical information is only realized by its use in conjunction with archaeological and collateral data sets (Fash and Sharer 1991).

The increased information provided by such multiple data sets allows us to examine our current understanding of Classic Maya political systems and the issues raised by the application of cross-cultural models to the study of Maya political organization. Insofar as these models allow cross-cultural comparison, they remain valuable, since they contribute to the anthropological study of political systems and facilitate discussion across the anthropological subfields. But the value of such comparisons is greatly diminished if in their application they submerge the unique facets of ancient Maya society (Marcus 1983, 1995; Sharer 1991, 1993).

Cross-cultural comparisons must avoid the tendency to reify models.[1] In the Maya case, such comparisons usually minimize the diversity of political organization across time and space (Marcus 1995). Moreover, the application of a model developed through the culturally specific observation and interpretation of other societies has an adverse effect on the model itself. Each model is based on a specific culture, which itself has unique traits that gave rise to the model. When the specifics of Maya cultural patterns and processes are pressed to fit into such a framework, this can redefine the model itself, potentially making it inappropriate for the culture to which it was originally developed.

Saying this, we do not seek to return to an era of myopic studies, and do not propose an exclusive focus on the Southern Maya Lowlands without comparative perspectives. Rather, we seek models of Maya political systems based on archaeological and historical data that also allow cross-cultural comparisons. We believe this can be done by identifying the specific features of a Maya-based model that parallel features of models based on other societies without assuming a wholesale identity between such frameworks. In other words, the model of a Maya-based polity would comprise individual attributes, some of which may be similar to features of non-Maya-based models, but these attributes would be combined in ways unique to Maya polities. By favoring this analytical approach, we do not seek to refute all cross-cultural models on a point-by-point basis. At the same time, however, our approach reveals the problematic aspects of several currently popular cross-cultural models.

There is general agreement that the Classic Maya lowlands was dominated by a series of separate state-level polities, exhibiting considerable variability in scale and other characteristics across space and time. Given such variability, we cannot hope to cover the development of Maya politics in all areas, incorporating over three thousand years of Maya history. Rather we focus in this chapter on the kingship and polities of the Maya Classic period (c. A.D. 250–900) in the Southern Lowlands encompassing Tabasco, portions of Chiapas the southern Yucatán Peninsula, the Petén of Guatemala, Belize, and western Honduras.[2] Our emphasis is on the political process in the Maya lowlands throughout the course of the Classic period, exploring briefly beyond these artificial boundaries to examine the origins and endpoints of Classic period political systems to offer a dynamic picture of kingship and the Maya body politic through time.

Current Comparative Models of Maya Political Organization

In recent decades two cross-cultural models have come to dominate discussions of the organization of Classic period lowland Maya polities: the *galactic polity model* (often associated with "theater states") and the *segmentary state model.*[3] Both are "weak" state models, positing the lack of a truly stratified and hierarchically organized political system, and emphasize power based on the control of people rather than control of territory. In contrast to these two popular weak state models is an alternative view that posits the Maya polity as a "strong" or "unitary" state, with a stratified and hierarchical organization and an emphasis on political boundaries and territoriality.

There have been several thorough reviews of the debate concerning the utility of a segmentary state model in Maya studies, and we refer our readers to these for an overview of such positions (Canuto 2002; Chase and Chase 1996; Fox et al. 1996). Suffice it to say that we find that the segmentary state model—developed on the basis of ethnographic studies in Africa—offers few, if any, attributes comparable to ancient Maya polities. In fact, there appears to be no evidence for segmentary lineages or segmentary states in Classic period Maya society (see also Marcus 2003).

As John W. Fox et al. (1996:798) rightly point out, segmentation does not exist in any absolute sense (see also Southall 1991). Segmentation represents a political potential: Segmentation emerges when opposition external to the maximal lineage is ebbing, and segmentation decreases toward unity when opposition external to the maximal lineage is on the rise (Kuper 1982:80; Sahlins 1961). The key to identifying segmentary polities archaeologically, therefore, is to establish that social, political, and economic roles are predicated on the ability to trace lineage through a common ancestry, and replicated at several scales within the polity such that the potential exists for segments to split off and emerge as new maximal units.

A similar situation is true for identifying galactic polities, a model based on Southeast Asian political systems, which are composed of a "central place surrounded by autonomous satellites in turn adjoining similar galactic structures" (Tambiah 1976:113). The galactic polity is developed as a cosmogram, or a *mandala*, in which the division of the world politically, and architecturally, is a matter of scale rather than kind. Great kings are merely larger versions of petty princes. The palaces of political centers are models of the universe and are replicated on a smaller scale in the courts of outlying nobles.

In the case of the Maya, although the architecture of major and minor centers, and even smaller rural patio groups, may certainly reflect notions of cosmology (see Ashmore and Sabloff 2002; Tourtellot et al. 2002), they are not merely scalar replicas of one another. Maya royal palaces, together with royal tombs and inscribed monuments associated with Maya kings, defined the capitals of Maya polities, and stand uniquely apart from the residences, burials, and carved memorials of even the highest-ranking nobility. Polity capitals maintained their status over long periods of time and were recognized as primate centers by the Maya in their texts, as indicated by the use of emblem glyphs that allow us to identify kings, capitals, and polities (Marcus 1976; Mathews 1991). In contrast, within each polity there are lesser sites without these characteristics that comprise a hierarchy of secondary centers (Folan et al. 1995; Marcus 1973). The same contrasts are apparent for the political roles of the king vis-à-vis the nobility (Inomata and Houston 2001).

Although the power and fortunes of kings shifted over time, one thing seems glaringly true of Maya polities and their capitals—contrary to the expectations of the galactic polity model, roles were not merely replicated on multiple levels at primate and subordinate centers. The *k'uhul ajaw*, "holy lord" or "divine king," lived in a polity capital and ruled over a complex political pyramid composed of numerous title-holders who could not replicate his role (figure 3.1). Some of these secondary lords lived in the capital as part of the royal court; others lived in lesser centers where they maintained authority on behalf of their king, the *k'uhul ajaw.*

This does not mean that these Maya states did not share some attributes comparable to the galactic polity or other organizational models based in other societies. The galactic polity model and the theater state model (Geertz

Fig. 3.1 Panel 3 from Piedras Negras, as reconstructed by Mary Louise Baker. Probably the finest sculpted representations of a Maya royal court. Ruler 4 of Piedras Negras presides over his seated subordinates. Each of these lords is named and titled. To the right stand young lords, including the royal heir and a youth who would go on to rule the site of La Mar. To the left are visiting lords, including an individual named as a ruler of Yaxchilán, who is unknown in the inscriptions of that site (courtesy of the University of Pennsylvania Museum.neg NC35-19374).

1980) both stress the importance of performance in ritual, dance, warfare, and statecraft to define the authority wielded by individual kings (e.g., Demarest 1992; Inomata 2001a; Johnston 2001; Schele and Miller 1986; Webster 1998, 2000). It is clear that Maya kings also used performance in similar roles to reinforce their authority (see, e.g., Houston 2001; Houston and Taube 2000; Inomata 2001a; Schele and Freidel 1991; Schele and Miller 1986; Stuart 1996, 1998a; Taube 1988, 1998). The subordinate nobility were, in turn, dependent on their successful performance of expected roles in similar, albeit lesser, displays often linked directly with the performances of the primate ruler. We note, however, that performance in these roles was only one means used by Maya kings to define their authority.

Also reminiscent of the "weak" state model, in some cases subordinate Maya lords were able to break away from their former overlords and form new independent polities (Anaya 2001; Demarest et al. 1997; Houston 1993; Marcus 1992; Martin and Grube 2000). At first glance, such episodes appear to recall the process of segmentation as described by the segmentary state model. A number of new dynastic rulers emerged over the course of the Early Classic, when the dynastic political landscape was relatively open, so that the fissioning of royal houses may have occurred with relatively little negative effect on the authority of the original royal house. Such may very well be the case for the dynasties of Yaxchilán and Palenque (Houston et al. 2003).[4] But unlike segmentary lineage fissioning, in these Early Classic period cases fissioning did not occur at the state margins (cf. Johnston 2001:374), but at locations relatively distant from the parent political body and in areas where similar political systems were absent.

Once the political landscape had been filled in, at the end of the Early Classic and in the Late Classic, such fissioning events are notable for their rarity and for their drama. Perhaps none are more famous than the emergence of dynastic rulers at Quirigua and Dos Pilas as those polities emerged from under the suzerainty of the Copan and Tikal dynasties, respectively. But contrary to the expectations of the segmentary state model, these Late Classic period polities fissioned when external pressures were peaking. In other words, the emergence of new polities came not in the absence of external threats to the royal family at the parent centers, but rather as a result of threats to, and hostile actions against, the parent centers.

The founding kings of both Quirigua and Dos Pilas appear to have been sponsored by the rulers of Tikal. According to textual evidence, Quirigua was founded under the authority of Copan's founding king in A.D. 426–427 (Schele 1991; Stuart and Schele 1986; Martin and Grube 2000:216). Recent archaeological evidence suggests that the founder of the Copan dynasty may have been from Tikal (Sharer 2003). A little over a century later Calakmul and its allies began moving against Tikal (Houston 1993; Looper 1999;

Martin and Grube 2000:56, 219). Evidence of architectural and monumental destruction suggests Copan may have been attacked about the same time as Calakmul's initial moves against Tikal (c. A.D. 554–564; Sharer in press), but the agent responsible for this destruction at Copan is not yet identified. Within a few years of the Dos Pilas founding (A.D. 648) by its Ruler I, apparently from Tikal, Calakmul attacked Dos Pilas and seemingly coerced its ruler to join its alliance against Tikal. Finally, there is textual evidence suggesting Calakmul may have been behind Quirigua's successful uprising against Copan in A.D. 737, resulting in Quirigua breaking away from Copan and gaining its independence (Looper 1999; Martin and Grube 2000; Sharer 1988). By the Terminal Classic period (after c. A.D. 800), some smaller centers had clearly fissioned off from large primate centers—as in the case of the rulers of Ixlu and Jimbal laying claim to the dynastic titles of Tikal (Marcus 1976; Martin and Grube 2000:53)—but by this time systemic failure had already wracked the primate Classic polities.

When we examine the source materials for some of these models applied to the Classic period, we can see other serious problems. The segmentary state model, as applied in the Maya area, relies on highland Guatemalan and Yucatecan ethnographic and ethnohistoric analogy for positing kinship as a fundamental organizing principle of the Classic Maya polity. However, because the interpretations of these Post-Conquest documents are themselves problematic, the ethnohistoric and ethnographic data pose serious hazards in application to the Classic period Maya. In fact, Matthew Restall's (1998) recent interpretations of colonial documents indicate that although lineage organization was central to the development of political authority in Late Postclassic and Colonial Yucatán, "both [district] and [lineage] were built upon territorial access to cultivable lands thus revealing the territorial underpinnings of community and lineages" (Restall 1998:49).

Such an interpretation resonates with recent models of Classic period social organization that place emphasis not on lineage, but rather on social hierarchies and corporate groups that have as their focus "houses" as physical structures or places on the landscape (Gillespie 2000a; 2000b; Houston 1998:521; Inomata and Houston 2001:9–10).[5] Several aspects of a house-based society fit remarkably well with information, derived from archaeological and epigraphic sources, about Maya kings and dynasties. For example, the house presents a locus for a corporate body organized by their shared residence, subsistence, means of production, origin, ritual actions, or metaphysical essence, all of which entail a commitment to a corpus of house property, which in turn can be said to materialize the social group (Gillespie 2000c:1–2; see also Lévi-Strauss 1982).[6] One can find material evidence for most, if not all, of these attributes from the recent excavations of exceptionally well-preserved artifacts at the Aguateca royal palace (Inomata

2001b; Inomata and Stiver 1998; Ponciano et al. 1998). Kinship may still represent a significant part of the construction of the social group, but it is inseparable from the spatial component.[7]

The importance of territoriality implicit in such a house-based model provides a definite contrast to both the galactic polity and theater state models, both derived from studies of Southeast Asian polities, and often applied in the Maya area. In those "weak" states the source of authority stems from control over networks of human relations and labor, rather than physical control of territory (Demarest 1992:151; Geertz 1980:24; Tambiah 1976:120). A house society model does not deny the need to control labor and human relations, but fundamental to labor and human relations is territorial control. Recent research provides evidence for territorial control as an important component of Maya polities (see Marcus 1992). Maya rulers were concerned with the control of territory *and* people, unlike the rulers of galactic polities and theater states who were primarily occupied with the control of people. Epigraphic studies demonstrate that ruling titles are significantly based on a description of territoriality. Conquests are frequently described using toponyms that specify a location within the polity (e.g., Lakamha' within the Palenque realm; see Martin and Grube 2000:160; Palka 1996), and captives are named with regard to their place of origin (e.g., "He of Mutul"; see Stuart and Houston 1994).

As we have mentioned, work by Restall (1998) shows that political authority in Late Postclassic and Colonial Yucatán was based on territorial access to cultivable lands. It is apparent that this must have been even more important in Classic times, since productive land was scarce in many regions. This became increasingly true as populations increased throughout the Classic period (see Dunning and Beach in this volume; also Brenner et al. 2001; Culbert et al. 1990; McAnany et al. 2002:128). This, again, stands in contrast to the Southeast Asian origins of the galactic polity, where land was abundant and the population relatively sparse (Tambiah 1976:120).

The Bases of Authority in Maya Polities

To understand the form and integrative mechanisms of Classic Maya polities, we must understand the nature and meaning of authority for the Maya, and not draw a priori notions of authority from cross-cultural models. Since lineage and other kin-based relationships were not the bases of authority for Classic Maya rulers (Chase and Chase 1996; Marcus 2003), the foundations of power clearly lay elsewhere. The Classic Maya were no more, and no less, warlike than people in other preindustrial states, and there is no question that Maya kings possessed and used coercive power in the same manner as kings of many other states. The most vivid representations of the life and death power held by Maya rulers are the scenes of bound and tortured captives on the Bonampak murals, or carved on monuments and stairways (Marcus 1974). As David Webster (2002:99) states, "Wars were fought for land, for slaves, to avenge insults and punish theft, and to control trade routes and the sources of various valued products." Military power was fundamental to the dynamic relationships that existed between Classic Maya polities, and a major factor responsible for the waxing and waning of individual polities over time (Demarest 1996; Sharer 1991).

In contrast to the exercise of military power across political boundaries, there are few explicit depictions of such naked power that refer to the authority of Maya kings over their own subjects. Diego de Landa (1978:39) provides some evidence for the enforcement of social sanctions during the Colonial period, but we have no similar evidence to reconstruct how the rulers of Classic Maya polities policed the populace. Warfare, however, does act within political frontiers to reinforce the community through the wide-scale participation of commoners and the nobility in battle. At the end of the Postclassic and during the beginning of the Colonial period, in both the highlands and lowlands, large numbers of non-elites participated in warfare (see descriptions of warfare in de Landa 1978:50–1; Recinos 1999:86). Although we lack similar direct evidence for the Classic period, indirect evidence for the participation of commoners in Classic period warfare does exist in the hieroglyphic record. The timing of warfare events as recorded on dozens of monuments follows the schedule not merely of the wet and dry season—a necessity for moving a military force no matter who was involved—but of the complexities of the agricultural cycle. Thus, it would seem that at least some people involved in these warfare activities had to return to their fields to weed and tend their crops (Child 1999). It seems unlikely that Maya lords would have been so constrained. With the possible exception of the vivid battle scene in the Bonampak murals (Ruppert et al. 1955:Fig. 28), the common Maya soldier is not obvious in the formal scenes of warfare created by Classic period artists, but commoners almost certainly provided the bulk of any military force.

Coercion, too, need not have been military, but could also have taken the form of exclusion from exchange systems under the control of Maya kings. Much of the wealth represented by elite status markers, such as finely painted polychrome vessels, were produced by elite artists, and the distribution of their work was very likely to have been controlled by rulers (see Foias in this volume for an extended discussion). The *k'uhul ajaw* also controlled the output of sculptors. Thus, the rulers of Piedras Negras allowed their artists to sculpt some of the fine pieces of representational art at El Cayo, and the king of Yaxchilán similarly supported a number of his subordinate nobles with panels carved by the same sculptors who produced the texts and images

Fig. 3.2 El Cayo Altar 4. The band of glyphs below the seated figure includes the name of the sculptor, Siyaj Chan Ahk, whose other titles indicate that he is a *ch'ok ajaw*, young lord, from Piedras Negras (drawing by Peter Mathews from Mathews 1998:117). At least two other sculptors from Piedras Negras were responsible for the creation of monuments at Piedras Negras (Martin and Grube 2000:153).

of the paramount ruler (figure 3.2; Martin and Grube 2000:153). The ability to restrict access to the artists capable of producing these potent symbols of authority in ceramic, stone, and other media represented a significant weapon in the political arsenal that Classic Maya rulers used to control their subordinates.

We infer the basis of authority within Maya polities from a variety of sources, ranging from the harnessing of labor and resources for monumental constructions to supernatural associations portrayed on monuments. Manipulation of this belief system provided another potent source of power for Maya rulers. The degree of power held by Maya rulers also varied according to the fortunes and misfortunes of their reigns. Of course, in the Maya world view the successes or failures of kings were reflections of supernatural powers, tied closely to the cycles of time, which controlled human events.

In addition to physical coercion, therefore, here we will explore some aspects of this ideological dimension of Maya royal power. Although it may seem that such ideological power is fundamentally different from coercive power as exercised through physical means such as warfare, in the Maya worldview the threat of supernatural sanctions could be as real and as effective a means of social control. In particular, we focus on the role of moral authority as a basis for the power of Maya kings, and the relationship of this authority to Maya concepts of time. The morality of a ruler, and the incorporation of notions of morality into the state formation, have been long recognized by anthropologists, and indeed they are fundamental to the models of the galactic polity and the theater state (Tambiah 1976:22).[8]

By morality we do not mean Western notions of morality as defined by Old World religious traditions or contemporary society. "Morality" is present in every society in the basic sense that there are generally agreed on notions circulating within that society which define "correct" and "incorrect" behavior. There is no necessary relationship of morality to "authority," but for the Maya, among other cultures, notions of so-called correct behavior were apparently fundamental to the practice of royal authority.[9] The authority of the ruler was, therefore, based on the shared view among both rulers and the ruled in the sanctions that gave rulers the rights to exercise authority over their subjects (*sensu* Weber 1969:215).[10] During the Classic period, the moral authority of rulers was based on a Maya world view that included the responsibility of kings to maintain the world order by successfully engaging and appeasing the supernatural powers that controlled the destiny of the universe through time.[11]

Well after the downfall of Maya divine kings, in fifteenth-century Yucatán, cycles of time, such as the twenty-year K'atun, were established in named locations. So, for example, according to *The Book Chilam Balam of Chumayel*, "The Katun is established at Ichcaanzihoo" (Roys 1967:152). Moreover, there is a materiality to these periods of times, which were equated with stones, and perhaps marked by the placement of stone monuments. Quoting again from the *Chilam Balam*, "12 Ahau. The stone was taken at Otzmal. 10 Ahau. The stone was taken at Zizal" (Roys 1967:142). These Postclassic examples reflect continuity with the earlier Classic Maya association of stone monuments with periods of time. The royal monuments of the Classic era were material expressions of time and reinforced the moral authority of rulers, defined by Maya concepts of correct and incorrect behavior.

In many parts of Mesoamerica, the ethnographic and ethnohistoric data indicate that a person's destiny, and their nature as moral or amoral beings, were, and are, defined by the day of birth (Monaghan 1998). The notion of

Fig. 3.3 The Katun 5 Ahau, as depicted in the Chilam Balam of Chumayel. "Harsh is its face, harsh its tidings, to the ruler . . . It is the opossum chieftain, the fox chieftain. . . . The blood-sucking chieftain, the avaricious ones of the town" (from Roys 1967:153, courtesy of University of Oklahoma Press).

temporality and morality is also in evidence during the Colonial period. In but one of many examples from *The Book of Chilam Balam of Chumayel*, the K'atun 5 Ahau is described as a lord whose destiny and moral status are defined by its face, "Harsh is its face, harsh its tidings, to the ruler" (figure 3.3). This harsh face brings with it governance by morally bankrupt lords, "It is the opossum chieftain, the fox chieftain . . . The blood-sucking chieftain, the avaricious ones of the town" (from Roys 1967:153). These amoral lords were "the two-day occupant of the throne, the two-day occupant of the mat" (Roys 1967:152–3).

During the Classic period the relationship between time, person, place, and materiality was explicitly related to the *k'uhul ajaw*.[12] The dedication of monuments—particularly those bearing the portrait of the king—was rhetorically equated with the creation of a moment in time (see Stuart 1998a). Moreover, Classic period rulers were not only responsible for the establishment of temporal cycles, they themselves were rhetorically equated with units of time. They often bore regnal names that included some version of the *k'inich ajaw* ("sun-faced" or "sun-eyed" lord) title.[13] Some inscriptions make explicit the link between the ruler's face and the nature of the day, where the ruler's portraits appear within the cartouche of the day Ajaw, substituting for the standard logograph (Stuart 1996, 1998).

These relationships between body, time, place, and morality have a long history in the Maya area, and provide insight into the need for Maya lords to maintain their physical composure in order to maintain a moral temporal state, not merely for themselves, but for society as a whole. Maya rulers had themselves portrayed on monuments and polychrome vessels as ideally controlled moral beings, and we may assume that their public personae were similarly restrained. Debased displays of terror, drunkenness, or lewd acts denoted behavior associated with animals, captives shorn of their rank and composure, and supernatural beings among others (Houston 2001). The linkage between self and image made such depictions particularly potent political symbols (see Geertz 1980:129–30).

Debased, immoral behavior was dangerous for Maya rulers who were in fierce competition with their peers in other polities and also with the subordinate nobility—including siblings—ideally subsumed within their own polity. The claims to authority by Maya kings lay, in part, in their ability to distinguish themselves as uniquely other, and their ability to locate themselves, and the polity, within an ideally and definitively moral place in time. This was a kind of authority not directly accessible to competing members of the nobility (see Houston et al. 2003). The ever-present danger was that they might make the wrong connections and be identified as the Classic period equivalents of illegitimate "two-day occupants of the throne." Instead, it was vital for Maya kings to emphasize their connections to the revered past(s) such as that associated with dynastic founders, who were often from a distant place.[14]

In practice, however, the dynasties of many Maya polities were plagued by disruptions in the royal house (see Martin and Grube 2000), and the need of individual Maya rulers to legitimate their personal dynastic ties may explain the ever more complex historical references made on monuments. Some of these inscriptions extend dynastic history back to the beginnings of the current baktun cycle and beyond, into what appears to the modern reader as a mythical past. At Palenque, for example, a glyphic panel in the Temple of the Inscriptions begins with a relatively contemporary date of 9.9.0.0.0 (A.D. 613), then jumps 1,246,826 years and 270 days into the past to record the accession of an ancestral deity. The inscription subsequently jumps forward to a date that would be the equivalent of a day in A.D. 4772 (Schele and Mathews 1998:106–7). At the site of Quirigua, Stelae D and F record dates that extend tens, even hundreds, of millions of years into the past (Martin and Grube 2000:221; Sharer 1991:34–6, 39–41, 1994:571).

K'inich Janaab' Pakal I at Palenque and K'ak' Tiliw Chan Yoaat ("Cauac Sky") at Quirigua were two rulers who had to overcome tremendous obstacles in maintaining their legitimacy. At Palenque, Pakal ascended to the throne in the wake of nearly a century of problematic dynastic succession and military defeat (Martin and Grube, 2000:158–62; Schele and Mathews 1998:95). At Quirigua, K'ak' Tiliw Chan Yoaat had waged a successful war against his former overlord at Copan, resulting in the beheading of the latter. Subsequently, K'ak' Tiliw Chan Yoaat went to great efforts to make good his claim to be the legitimate dynastic successor not only of Quirigua, but of Copan as well (Fash and Stuart 1991; Martin and Grube 2000:219; Sharer 1990:107).

Thus, we see the recording of events of such tremendous time-depth not as an attempt at passive myth making, but as part of the efforts of Maya rulers to both reaffirm and reform the nature of their right to rule. Such chronological gymnastics were fundamentally important for the production of a culturally legitimate history needed to provide the proper context for the dedication of monuments and architecture (see Stuart 1998). Furthermore, Classic period rulers did not merely exist within, or move through, time. As David Stuart (1996:165) indicates, on the basis of epigraphy and iconography, rulers of Classic period polities "were themselves embodiments of time and its passage." That their monuments were inseparable from their fundamental selves (Houston and Stuart 1998:90; Stuart 1996:160–5) reinforced the connection between person and monuments such that these inscribed objects "served the related purpose of manifesting individual time periods and of embodying the royal self" (Stuart 1996:168).[15] This rationale also helps explain why such monuments were monopolized by Maya rulers until the bases of royal power began to erode at the end of the Late Classic: Although some may have possessed the artists or artistic skills to do so, no one but the king possessed the moral authority to be commemorated by texts and portraits on these famous standing stones.[16]

Political Integration

We have proposed that temporally based moral authority within a specific Maya context modeled as a house society may provide a basis for understanding the ideological source and practice of power exercised by Maya kings. But this is not the whole story, for the ideological source and practice of power do not explain the organization of Maya polities—the mechanisms of integrating the top of the political hierarchy with the subordinate nobility and the vast body of commoners. With regard to the nobility, the notion of the moral authority of the *k'uhul ajaw* counters the notion of weak states such as galactic polities, in which the rulers of "subordinate centers had less *need* for the affiliation with the capital center than the [rulers of the] capital center had for affiliation with [their] subordinates, and there was a large potential pool of usurpers for each capital" (Demarest 1992:151; see also Johnston 2001:373). In fact, we find that in Classic period society the authority of subordinate nobility was largely dependent on their ability to derive status via association with the supreme font of Maya moral authority in the person of the *k'uhul ajaw*.

In Maya terms, moral authority implies a social contract that the ruler must be able to fulfill on the one hand, and in which the subordinates are bound to participate if they are in turn to be obeyed by those beneath them in the social hierarchy (Houston et al. 2003). In the Late Preclassic as the institution of the *k'uhul ajaw* emerged, there was a more direct relationship between the king and his subjects, with fewer intermediate officials than documented for the Classic period. Smaller populations and smaller polity size may have made the direct application of moral authority from the ruler to the ruled possible. However, as time passed, populations increased, and the political ambitions of Maya kings burgeoned, direct rule over the entire populace by a single ruler without intermediaries may have become untenable.

As lowland population increased during the Classic period, the political landscape filled in and the nature of integration between different levels of the political system changed in a variety of ways. Although all Classic Maya polities are in some sense defined by divine kingship as an institution, the modes of integrating that institution with the rest of the body politic differed between polities for reasons of physical size, geography, population densities, historical relationships with other polities, and royal strategy (Smith and Berdan 1996:8; Houston et al. 2003).

By the Late Classic period, Maya texts make it clear that the number of subordinate nobility had increased dramatically. Texts make reference to persons bearing titles such as *ajaw* ("lord"), *ch'ok ajaw* ("young lord"), *sajal* (perhaps "he who fears"), *a-k'uh-hu:n* (a scribal title), *y-ajaw-k'ak* ("the fire's lord"), among others. *Ajaw* and *sajal* title bearers might be further subdivided by the addition of the *ba-* ("head") prefix. Thus, individuals within a polity who were the head-*sajal* were ranked above all others holding the *sajal* title by itself (Houston and Stuart 2001).

In return for their services, subsidiary nobility often received the benefits of status ascribed through textual and iconographic representation on monuments, carved by scribes whose work was controlled by, and the prerogative of, the ruler. These negotiated symbols of status were realized differently at different sites. In most cases, subordinates are shown only in the company of their king. But as royal power declined, some subordinates are represented without their overlords. At Palenque, for instance, the *sajal* Chak-Zutz' is accorded his own epigraphic program within the site center emphasizing his inherited status, without reference to the paramount (Schele 1991; Villela 1993).

At Copan, on the other hand, inscriptions associated with the residences of secondary elites are concerned with the interconnections of these subordinates to the *k'uhul ajaw* (Fash and Stuart 1991; Martin and Grube 2000; Villela 1993). In the Yaxchilán polity, subordinates such as *sajal* are depicted both at Yaxchilán proper and at subsidiary centers such as La Pasadita and Laxtunich, often in scenes depicting war captives (Golden 2003; Golden et al. 1998; Mathews 1988; Schele and Freidel 1990:295). They are most often depicted in subordinate positions to the *k'uhul ajaw* and are never depicted individually at the capital of Yaxchilán itself.

Subordinate nobility within the Piedras Negras polity occupy a highly visible position in the monumental programs of both Piedras Negras proper and its subsidiary centers. At the site of El Cayo, several monuments were commissioned by *sajal* subject to the rulers of Piedras Negras, and make textual references to participation in ceremonies with the paramount ruler of Piedras Negras. Furthermore, the monuments at El Cayo were carved by sculptors under the direct control of the ruler of Piedras Negras, and who were responsible for monuments at the paramount center as well (Schele 1991; Martin and Grube 2000:153). Parrot Chaak, for instance, the ruler of the site of La Mar in the late eighth century is depicted on his own monuments as well as on Stela 12 from Piedras Negras, delivering captives as tribute to his overlord (Houston et al. 1999). He is also mentioned on Throne 1 from Piedras Negras and is depicted as a child on Panel 3 (Martin and Grube 2000:153).[17]

Participation with the ruler in activities of sociopolitical import (e.g., warfare, auto-sacrifice, or dancing) provided a fundamental source of prestige and political power for these subordinate nobility. Tribute was paid by the subordinate nobility as by a client to a patron, in anticipation of reciprocity. Although inherited status was certainly a major factor in social ranking, it provided only the potential—a potential that could only be realized through subordination to, and participation with, the *k'uhul ajaw*.

Economic Integration

The economics of Classic period Maya polities are poorly understood at best (McAnany 1992). It is difficult to say with any certainty what constituted the full range of materials that were traded across political boundaries during the Classic period, and how all aspects of trade were incorporated into the political economy. A broad spectrum of luxury goods, in addition to necessities such as salt, were traded over long distances in late Pre-Conquest Yucatán (Roys 1943), and there is no reason to doubt that trade during the Classic period was any less vigorous (see Aliphat 1994; Andrews and Mock 2002; Braswell 2002; Foias in this volume). Indeed, some sites such as Chunchicmil in the Northern Lowlands, or Cancuen at the junction of the

Petén and Alta Verapaz, Guatemala may have acted as "trade nodes," where rulers derived much of their power through their control over the trade and production of raw materials and finished products (see Barrientos et al. 2001; Dahlin and Ardren 2002; Kovacevich et al. 2001).

Even if, as some would argue, bulk foodstuffs were not traded over long distances, this does not imply that the control of these foodstuffs was not part of state apparatus, or that there was a disjunction between the political and economic infrastructure (cf. Demarest 1992:143, 146). Archaeological evidence suggests the presence of centralized marketplaces immediately adjacent to royal palace compounds at both Tikal (Jones 1996) and Quirigua (Sharer 1988:56). The ability of the ruling sectors of society to limit access to some foods, creating what has been described at Caracol as a "palace diet" clearly implies some control over the provision of foodstuffs as part of state apparatus (e.g., Chase et al. 2001; Emery in this volume; Whittington and Reed 1997; Wright in this volume).

Though trade in bulk foodstuffs is not portrayed prominently in text or visual media, the delivery of food as tribute is. These include prestige food items such as tamales and prestige goods such as cacao, both shown on vessels (see Foias in this volume). Apart from food, the nobility, and especially the royalty of Maya polities, were the recipients of trade goods that formed many of the most obvious markers of their status (e.g., quetzal feathers, jade, and spondylus). The very nature of such elite trade goods, of course, is that they are not readily reproduced within the consumer's domain. Such goods are continually removed from circulation, whether through breakage or through ritual disposal (e.g., burials and caches). Moreover, an increasingly conspicuous secondary elite would have siphoned off a greater percentage of these limited resources as time passed in return for their continued service to their overlord.

It is not clear that there was any single system of organizing the production of status markers in the Classic period political economy. Some particularly fine ceramic pieces are signed by artists who were members of the nobility (Foias in this volume; Inomata 2001b; Muñoz and Golden 2001; Reents-Budet 1994) and may be the product of what Joseph W. Ball (1993) calls "palace schools." Evidence at Aguateca suggests that many of the finely incised bones found in the rapidly abandoned ruins of the royal palace were produced by the residents of that palace, who were themselves members of the royal family (Inomata 2001b). Many of the beautifully worked items of jade and other precious materials that constituted markers of status, however, were made by humble craftspeople whose work was apparently alienated from them (e.g., Kovacevich et al. 2001)

Although locally produced versions of long-distance status markers may very well have increased in frequency during the Late Classic (Rathje 1973) in order to fill some of the ever-increasing demand, some items could simply not be replicated. Maintaining a steady supply was imperative in a society where the display of power was embodied by such items as jade and feather-worked costumes, and was essential to the authority of the ruler. To draw once more on the example of late Pre-Conquest Yucatán, trade often continued to flow unabated across the boundaries of warring areas. In fact, the cessation of trade between regions did, at times, provide the basis for the initiation of warfare (Roys 1943).

Warfare, in some sense, bridged the gap between political and economic practice. It brought in tribute and was fundamental to the political economy of Classic period polities, but the effects of warfare on economic processes may have been ambivalent. Successful military exploits would have resulted in economic benefit for both king and polity through the acquisition of tribute, resources, territory, and new subjects that could be redistributed as wealth. Even small-scale "inexpensive" raids, though, probably reinforced the territorial boundaries of polities. Political actions intended to control trade routes and territorial access, actions such as warfare and the construction of defensive sites along political frontiers, acted to ensure royal authority when successful.[18] The demands of offensive and defensive warfare created alliances between polities, such as Calakmul and Caracol (Ferguson 1994; Reyna 1994:149). Warfare, though, is also expensive, creating costs for the polity in people and materials that may have outstripped any material or territorial gains (Cohen 1984:353).

But even "costly" battles, couched explicitly in economic terms, were important because of their consequences for royal authority. Destruction of the enemy may be expensive in the short term, but it would have reduced the need for warfare in the long term by eliminating threats to royal power. Indeed, after a series of successful battles in the eighth century, the rulers of Tikal revived the power of their polity and were never again threatened by their long-time adversaries at Calakmul (Martin and Grube 2000). But ultimately such victories were not enough to ensure the stability and prosperity of lowland Maya kingdoms, or to prevent their decline at the end of the Classic period (Demarest et al. 1997). One dramatic example comes from the Yaxchilán polity, where evidence of dynastic rule disappeared shortly after a final victory over their rivals at Piedras Negras in A.D. 808 (Stuart 1998b).

Reconstructing Kingship and Polity

The most important characteristic underlying all that we have addressed in this chapter about Maya polities is that they varied considerably across space and through time. The particularities of administration, organization, and implementation of the Classic polity differed from place to place and changed dramatically over the centuries even within the same polity. That said, recent advances in research do make it possible to generalize about some things that characterize many, if not most, Classic period lowland Maya polities, making possible the trial formulation of a model for these polities.

These Maya polities were not organized around a particular individual as the king, or even the royal court of the king (cf. Demarest 1992; Johnston 2001; Inomata and Houston 2001), but rather around the institution of divine kingship as embodied by the *k'uhul ajaw*. The performances of individual *k'uhul ajaw* could dramatically alter the fortunes of a polity for better or worse, even resulting in the polity's dissolution. But polities could clearly withstand the loss of the ruler, and even the cessation of a dynasty, so long as the office of *k'uhul ajaw* was retained, and the figure who claimed that position was able to demonstrate a legitimate moral authority through connections with the appropriate moment in time—connections perhaps backed up by the use of force to eliminate competing historical narratives and narrators. Just such a scenario was realized in the Naranjo polity when a new line of divine kings was installed after the old dynasty had been extinguished by warfare (Martin and Grube 2000:72–7).

The *k'uhul ajaw* was a ruler sanctioned as the successor by his ancestors, predecessors who could be invoked in the present. The "holy lord" was also conceived of and created as the embodiment of time itself—but in particular, a specific time or times chosen to formulate a history and to mold a present that was appropriately auspicious. The ruler performed in acts of sacrifice, dance, warfare, the dedication of stelae, caches, and buildings, among other activities in order to make these temporal connections essential to success as measured by supernatural favor and material benefits—material benefits that enriched not only the king, but all those who participated in the systems of trade, tribute, and redistribution that focused around the king.

Although the *k'uhul ajaw* was the paramount ruler atop a hierarchy within the polity, we can see that between polities there was heterarchy, and that some of the *k'uhul ajaw* were more paramount than others. The rulers of the polities of Calakmul and Tikal waged their political struggle across the lowlands through the centuries and, in so doing, dominated, cajoled, negotiated with, allied with, and eliminated the rulers of other polities. The rulers of regional powers such as Yaxchilán, Piedras Negras, Palenque, Copan, and Dos Pilas, among many others, practiced their own versions of these power politics resulting in the expansion and contraction of their range of authority over time, giving the appearance of political fluctuations similar to that evident in the galactic polities of Southeast Asia.

But the combination of archaeological and epigraphic evidence indicates that Maya kings exercised a degree of territorial and administrative control that is more typical of "strong state" organizations. Furthermore, the kings of the paramount powers of Calakmul and Tikal exercised some authority or dominance over the rulers bearing the title of *k'uhul ajaw* at other centers. However, it is important to understand that even these most potent of Maya states did not truly *incorporate* these less powerful polities into their realm. Thus, although the ruler of Caracol may have been allied with, and likely subordinate to, the ruler of Calakmul in a series of wars waged against the rulers of Tikal, the polity of Caracol was never incorporated into the political and economic apparatus of Calakmul. If Dos Pilas was founded by a branch of the Tikal dynasty as part of the Tikal polity, soon thereafter it broke away under the auspices of the ruler of Calakmul and established itself as an independent dynasty, never integrated in any real sense into the Calakmul polity.

On the other hand, secondary centers ruled by *ajaw*, *sajal*, and other nobles subordinate to a *k'uhul ajaw* residing in a polity capital were truly integrated into the political and economic structure of that polity. Thus, La Pasadita was part and parcel of the polity ruled from Yaxchilán, and La Mar and El Cayo formed part of an integrated political system governed from Piedras Negras, just as Rio Amarillo and Quirigua (prior to A.D. 737) constituted part of the Copan polity.

The polity itself was defined by its territorial extent, which, like the authority of the individual ruler, expanded and contracted over time. But it is imperative to make the distinction between the extent of the authority of the ruler and the extent of territorial control held by the polity as a collective political organization. Some Classic Maya lowland polities, like Copan, appear to have been at their maximum extents in the Early Classic period, when interpolity competition was far less violent than in later times (Marcus 1992). But most polities clearly reached their maximum populations (Rice and Culbert 1990), and in some cases even their most extensive territorial boundaries, toward the end of the Late Classic period when the role and authority of the *k'uhul ajaw* were increasingly vulnerable due to a variety of social and environmental stresses (see Sabloff and Andrews 1986; Webster 2002), and when the subordinate nobility was increasingly able to access prerogatives that had once belonged only to the *k'uhul ajaw*. Thus, the political processes that had allowed for the growth of many large, lowland polities carried the seeds for their own destruction, as an expanding cadre of subordinates siphoned off the authority and wealth once monopolized by the *k'uhul ajaw*, leading ultimately to the demise of the institution of divine kingship

Finally, this chapter began with an examination of cross-cultural models and their applicability to the Maya, and we wish to close with a brief synopsis of what we see as the role of such models in Maya archaeology, and how we see Maya archaeologists making a contribution to the anthropological study of political complexity in general. This review of current conceptions about Classic Maya polities shows that holistic models derived from a culturally specific context should not be applied cross-culturally. To do so is to inordinately burden the model, the culture from which the model was derived, and all subsequent cultures to which the model is applied, with problematic associations.[19]

We can, however, apply specific attributes derived from culturally specific contexts, or even specific models, such as the concept of "moral authority" or the "house society." Their application to the Classic period lowland Maya is useful if they do not stipulate how specific social and cultural forms are realized in practice. In this way, such models facilitate cross-cultural contrast and comparison without the drawback of universal models. As but one example, when Stanley J. Tambiah and Clifford Geertz discuss the central moral figure of the ruler in Southeast Asia, they are talking about moral authority as based on the specific cultural contexts present in Southeast Asian society. In order to facilitate comparison between Southeast Asian and Maya ruling authority, we must examine the nature, distribution, and application of moral authority in Classic period Maya society. For the Buddhist kingdoms of Southeast Asia, the moral authority of the ruler was based on a morality shared by all members of society. Thus, the moral ruler was an exemplar for society as a whole. The same was not true in the Hindu kingdoms, where the morality of the ruler was applicable to the ruler, but not to members of other castes within society (Tambiah 1976:22; see endnote 9).

If we are to better understand the nature of moral authority in Maya kingdoms, we must similarly determine whether the morality of the ruler was the same as that of society as a whole. In this chapter we have suggested that, in a general, there was a shared moral code among rulers and the ruled within Classic period Maya society, so it would seem that for this specific characteristic the Buddhist kingdoms of Southeast Asia provide a better candidate for cross-cultural comparison than do the Hindu kingdoms. But, in fact, this assertion remains a likely hypothesis that needs to be tested further in the Maya case. We know far too little about Classic Maya non-elites and, in particular, their beliefs and practices that formed reciprocal bonds with Maya kings (Canuto 2002; Yaeger 2000). We also have to remember that moral authority is only one component in understanding the bases and practices of Classic period Maya kingship and polity.

In this chapter we have explored the shortcomings of applying cross-cultural models from whole cloth to the Maya (or elsewhere around the world). At the same time, we have tried to demonstrate how we can stitch together the threads of more specific models that match what we know about Maya kingship and polity from the combined array of historical and archaeological data now available to us. This allows us to identify the relevant and applicable elements of cross-cultural models and form a coherent picture of Classic period Maya polities. These elements incorporate notions of power, authority, process, performance, and other concepts that are applicable in many cultures, but that were combined in unique and dynamic ways in the Classic Maya lowlands. In so doing, Maya archaeologists can draw from and contribute to discussions of political processes in all complex societies, while maintaining a clear perspective on the unique historical development of kingship and polities in the Classic period.

Notes

1. Although somewhat dated, Claude Lévi-Strauss (1963:277–345) presents a valuable discussion of the interplay between cultures and cultural models.
2. For readers interested in the poltical organization of other periods or other portions of the Maya area, we refer them to the following: Carmack (1981); Chase and Rice (1985); de Landa (1978); Farriss (1984); Hill (1998); Jones (1998); Masson (2001); Recinos (1999); Restall (1998); Robinson (1998); Sachse (2001); Tedlock (1985).
3. *Galactic polity* (see Tambiah 1976) and *theater state* (see Geertz 1980) are often used interchangeably in Maya studies to describe the similarity between Maya and Southeast Asian polities (see Demarest 1992). Although it is true that both Clifford Geertz (1980) and Stanley J. Tambiah (1976) are in many instances discussing overlapping concepts in many of the same polities, it is important to differentiate between their two models. This difference stems from their research emphases. Geertz's (1980) theater state model is concerned with describing a semiotic system that constructs notions of rulership and that rulers used as a basis for their authority. Symbols of rulership and performance are also central to Tambiah's (1976) galactic polity; however, his focus lies more in discerning the social and political structures, as well as the historical origins in Hindu and early Buddhist kingdoms, that underlie the symbolic construction of the polity in Southeast Asia.
4. The establishment of some dynasties, such as that at Copan, during the Early Classic period is not relevant to the case of fissioning since these instances appear to represent the imposition of "foreigners" as dynastic founders (Sharer et al. 1999; Stuart 2000).
5. For more thorough reviews of current research into the nature of house societies, see Carsten and Hugh-Jones (1995) and Joyce and Gillespie (2000). Houston and McAnany (2003) have recently raised some pertinent concerns regarding the application of the House Society model to Classic period society. We recognize the validity of many of their concerns, and this chapter has addressed similar issues associated with the application of totalizing cultural models to the Classic period Maya. Houston and McAnany also suggest that a royal court model may be more appropriate to the uppermost stratum of Classic Maya society than a House Society model. However, we feel that concepts of the royal court and House Society are not mutually exclusive. Indeed, we hold that both are useful, particularly if the house concept operated broadly within Maya society, applicable to all social strata, whereas, by definition, a court society was restricted to the ruling "houses" in each polity. Maya royal *houses* were almost certainly more restrictive in their membership than royal *courts*, and could express continuity over time with past members defined by blood, marriage, and fictive ties to the current members. Courts, in contrast, are defined in relation to the royal center, but can have a broader membership that includes all or most members of a royal house, including many non-royal officials and personages (see Inomata and Houston 2001).
6. The *house society model* is more effective cross culturally than the *galactic polity model* because it does not define the particular formations, structures, and processes at work within a society. The house society model posits a structural form whose realization in practice is culturally and historically contingent.
7. Classic period inscriptions from both monuments and ceramics make clear that statements referring to an individual as the "Nth" successor to the dynastic founder of a polity do not necessarily refer to statements of descent, but rather to statements of legitimate institutional

succession. Those statements of lineal descent that are made typically refer only to parents, grandparents, and children with more distant members of the matriline or patriline conspicuously absent but for a few cases. The inscriptions also provide direct and indirect evidence of royal successions that depart from a simple father-to-son pattern, including the succession of royal siblings, women, and usurpers (Martin and Grube 2000).

8. Similarly, Emile E. Durkheim (1976 [1915]:62) states that "a religion is a unified system of beliefs and practices relative to sacred things, that is to say, things set apart and forbidden—beliefs and practices which unite into one single moral community called a Church, all those who adhere to them." If instead of a "church" per se, we substitute a political figure as the central focus of a moral community, we close in on something more akin to the Maya or Southeast Asian examples. In these cases, the ruler comports him or herself—and is constructed in practice by those who render obeisence to them—as a moral focus for the community. The community constructs the ruler as an ideal being and it is the function of the ruler to fulfill this role.
9. Indeed, within our own society the right to rule of a president or of any elected official is based on a moral judgment regarding their representation of "we the people" loosely defined as the political constituents of the country. Elected officials who are not deemed morally competent to participate in the government (e.g., they are guilty of "high crimes and misdemeanors") may be censured or removed from office.
10. In Weber's terms, the performance of the moral Maya ruler affords both "traditional" and "charismatic" authority (Weber 1969:215).
11. Tambiah (1976) notes that one of the most significant differences between Hindu kingdoms and Buddhist kingdoms in Asia lies in their different application of morality to the king and society. For Hindu kingdoms, based on a notion of caste distinctions, there is a different *dharma* for each caste, and thus the king represents and acts on a morality that is fundamentally different from that of other members of society. The moral ruler acts within a moral schema appropriate to rulership, but necessarily not to society as a whole. For the Buddhist rulers, the king was constructed as the exemplar of moral behavior for all of society, such "that the dharma of kingship becomes the encompassing code that reigns over society and political economy, which are not separable" (Tambiah 1976:22). For further development of the notion of moral authority among the Maya kings, we must begin to draw out this distinction for the Maya.
12. Again emphasizing the relationship between time and the body, on a panel found in the vicinity of Palenque, Mexico, for instance, one date is said to be at the back of another (Stuart 1990). At other sites, full figure glyphs on monuments show the various temporal cycles as burdens carried by deified numbers (see Aveni, 2001:30).
13. At Piedras Negras, a common title was *k'in ajaw*, with *k'in* signifying both "sun" and "day" as a period of time.
14. As but one non-Maya example for comparison, David Sutton (1998:173–94) makes eminently clear in his study of national and local identities on the island of Kalymnos, Greece, that oral history—even the history embodied by personal names—may indeed be considered as property. In such instances, the associations with named ancestors and places may have very real effects on notions of property and politics even in modern Europe. The same is true in Tambiah's discussion of the galactic polity.
15. The indivisibility of self and image is, again, reminiscent of the construction of rulership in Southeast Asia, where Geertz (1980:130) states that "to visualize was to see, to see to imitate, and to imitate to embody."
16. Cross-culturally rulers often derive their authority from revered ancestors, or from living personages whose origins are distant in space, time, or both (Helms, 1988, 1998). In Mesoamerica these connections are often phrased in terms of royal origins in places such as Tollan, The "Place of Cattails" (Boone 2000; Gillespie 1989; Stuart 2000; López Austin and López Lujan 2000; Recinos 1999:171–3; Roys 1967:88–98; Tedlock 1985:167–76). David Stuart (2000) has provided strong evidence that for Classic period rulers the Place of Cattails was, in fact, the central Mexican capital of Teotihuacan.
17. Panel 3 from Piedras Negras is, without a doubt, the most complex sculptural depiction of the idealized relationship of subordinate nobles with the *k'uhul ajaw* in a courtly setting. *Sajal* are arranged before the throne of Ruler 4 in rank order, with visiting *ajaw* and young lords of Piedras Negras arranged in intermediary positions before the sovereign.

18. Much of the fighting between the polities of Yaxchilán and Piedras Negras, for instance, may have taken place as skirmishes along their frontiers, where defensible sights such as La Pasadita seem to have been imposed on the landscape as a means of controlling overland access and trade routes, and helped to enforce centralized royal authority (Aliphat 1994; Anaya 2001; Golden 2003).
19. Indeed, Geertz's theater state was intended as a culturally and historically specific model, wherein the rulers of Balinese kingdoms wielded the symbols of their authority in very particular ways because "they were what there was" (Geertz 1980:136). What can be generalized from Geertz's work is the conception of symbolic practice as a mode of rulership and domination.

References

Adams, R. E. W., and Smith, W. D. (1981) "Feudal Models for Classic Maya Civilization," in W. Ashmore (ed.), *Lowland Maya Settlement Patterns*, pp. 335–50, Albuquerque: University of New Mexico Press.

Aliphat, M. M. (1994) *Classic Maya Landscape in the Upper Usumacinta River Valley*, unpublished Ph. D. thesis, Department of Archaeology, University of Calgary.

Anaya Hernandez, A. (2001) *Site Interaction and Political Geography in the Upper Usumacinta Region during the Late Classic: A GIS Approach*, British Archaeological Reports, International Series 994, Oxford: BAR.

Andrews, A. P., and Mock, S. B. (2002) "New Perspectives on the Prehispanic Maya Salt Trade," in M. A. Masson and D. A. Freidel (eds.), *Ancient Maya Political Economies*, pp. 307–34, Walnut Creek, CA: Alta Mira Press.

Ashmore, W., and Sabloff, J. A. (2002) "Spatial Orders in Maya Civic Plans," *Latin American Antiquity* 13(2): 201–16.

Aveni, A. (2001) "Time, Number, and History in the Maya World," *KronoScope* 1(1/2): 29–62.

Ball, J. W. (1993) "Pottery, Potters, Palaces, and Polities: Some Socioeconomic and Political Implications of Late Classic Maya Ceramic Industries," in J. A. Sabloff and J. S. Henderson (eds.), *Lowland Maya Civilization in the Eighth Century A.D.*, pp. 243–72, Washington, DC: Dumbarton Oaks.

Barrientos, T., Demarest, A., Bishop, R., and Fahsen, F. (2001) "Redescubriendo Cancuen: Nuevos Datos sobre un Sitio Fronterizo Entre las Tierras Bajas y el Altiplano Maya," in J. P. Laporte and H. Escobedo (eds.), *XIV Simposio de Investigaciones Arqueológicas en Guatemala*, pp. 569–88, Guatemala City: Instituto de Antropología e Historia de Guatemala.

Boone, E. H. (2000) "Venerable Places of Beginnings: The Aztec Understanding of Teotihuacan," in D. Carrasco, L. Jones, and S. Sessions (eds.) *Mesoamerica's Classic Heritage*, pp. 371–96, Boulder: University of Colorado Press.

Braswell, G. E. (2002) "Praise the Gods and Pass the Obsidian?: The Organization of Ancient Economy in San Martín Jilotepeque, Guatemala," in M. A. Masson and D. A. Freidel (eds.), *Ancient Maya Political Economies*, pp. 285–306, Walnut Creek, CA: Alta Mira Press.

Brenner, M., Leyden, B., and Binford, M. W. (2001) "Recent Sedimentary Histories of Shallow Lakes in the Guatemalan Savannas," *Journal of Paleolimnology* 4(3): 239–52.

Canuto, M. A. (2002) *A Tale of Two Communities: Social and Political Transformation in the Hinterlands of the Maya Polity of Copan*, unpublished Ph.D. thesis, University of Pennsylvania.

Carmack, R. M. (1981) *The Quiché Mayas of Utatlan*, Oklahoma City: University of Oklahoma Press.

Carsten, J., and Hugh-Jones, S. (eds.) (1995) *About the House: Leví-Strauss and Beyond*, New York: Cambridge University Press.

Chase, A. F., and Chase, D. Z. (1996) "More than Kin and King: Centralized Political Organization among the Late Classic Maya," *Current Anthropology* 37(5): 803–10.

Chase, A. F., and Rice, P. M. (1985) *The Lowland Maya Postclassic*, Austin: University of Texas Press.

Chase, A. F., Chase, D. Z., and White, C. D. (2001) "El Paisaje Urabano Maya: La Integración de los Espacios Construidos y La Estructura Social en Caracol, Belice," in A. C. Ruiz, J. I. Ponce de León, and C. Martínez Martínez (eds.), *Reconstruyendo La Ciudad Maya: El Urbanismo en las Sociedades Antiguas*, pp. 95–122, Madrid: Sociedad Española de Estudios Mayas.

Child, M. (1999) "Classic Maya Warfare and its Sociopolitical Implications," paper presented at the 1999 Palenque Mesa Redonda, June.
Coe, M. D. (1957) "The Khmer Settlement Pattern: A Possible Analogy with That of the Maya," *American Antiquity* 22: 409–10.
Cohen, R. (1984) "Warfare and State Formation: Wars Make States and States Make Wars," in R. B. Ferguson (ed.), *Warfare, Culture and Environment*, pp. 329–58, New York: Academic Press.
Culbert, T. P., Levi, L. J., and Cruz, L. (1990) "Lowland Maya Wetland Agriculture," in F. S. Clancy and P. D. Harrison (eds.), *Vision and Revision in Maya Studies*, pp. 115–24, Albuquerque: University of New Mexico Press.
Dahlin, B. H., and Ardren, T. (2002) "Modes of Exchange and Regional Patterns: Chunchucmil, Yucatán," in M. A. Masson and D. A. Freidel (eds.), *Ancient Maya Political Economies*, pp. 249–84, Walnut Creek, CA: Alta Mira Press.
de Landa, D. (1978) *Yucatán Before and After the Conquest.* New York: Dover.
Demarest, A. A. (1992) "Ideology in Ancient Maya Cultural Evolution: The Dynamics of Galactic Polities," in A. A. Demarest and G. W. Conrad (eds.), *Ideology and Pre-Columbian Civilizations*, pp. 135–58, Santa Fe: School of American Research Press.
———(1996) "Closing Comment," *Current Anthropology* 37(5): 821–4.
Demarest, A. A., O'Mansky, M., Wolley, C., Tuerenhout, D. V., Inomata, T., Palka, J., and Escobedo, H. (1997) "Classic Maya Defensive Systems and Warfare in the Petexbatun Region," *Ancient Mesoamerica* 8: 229–53.
Durkheim, E. (1976 [1915]) *Elementary Forms of Religious Life*, London: Allen and Unwin.
Farriss, N. M. (1984) *Maya Society under Colonial Rule: The Collective Enterprise of Survival*, Princeton: Princeton University Press.
Fash, W. L., and Sharer, R. J. (1991) "Sociopolitical Developments and Methodological Issues at Copan, Honduras: A Conjunctive Perspective," *Latin American Antiquity* 2: 166–87.
Fash, W. L., and Stuart, D. S. (1991) "Dynastic History and Cultural Evolution at Copan, Honduras," in T. P. Culbert (ed.), *Classic Maya Politica History: Hieroglyphic and Archaeological Evidence*, pp. 147–79, Cambridge, UK: Cambridge University Press.
Ferguson, R. B. (1994) "The General Consequences of War: An Amazonian Perspective," in S. P. Reyna and R. E. Davis (eds.), *Studying War: Anthropological Perspectives, War and Society*, Vol. 2, pp. 85–111, Langhorne, PA: Gordon and Breach.
Folan, W. J., Marcus, J., and Miller, W. F. (1995) "Verification of a Maya Settlement Model through Remote Sensing," *Cambridge Archaeological Journal* 5(2): 277–83.
Fox, J. W., Cook, G. W., Chase, A. F., and Chase, D. Z. (1996) "Questions of Political and Economic Integration: Segmentary versus Centralized States among the Ancient Maya," *Current Anthropology* 37(5): 795–801.
Geertz, C. (1980) *Negara: The Theatre State in Nineteenth-Century Bali*, Princeton: Princeton University Press.
Gillespie, S. D. (1989) *The Aztec Kings: The Construction of Rulership in Mexican History*, Tucson: University of Arizona Press.
———(2000a) "Maya 'Nested Houses': The Ritual Construction of Place," in R. Joyce and S. D. Gillespie (eds.), *Beyond Kinship: Social and Material Reproduction in House Societies*, pp. 135–60, Philadelphia: University of Pennsylvania Press.
———(2000b) "Rethinking Ancient Maya Social Organization: Replacing 'Lineage' with 'House,'" *American Anthropologist* 102(3): 467–84.
———(2000c) "Beyond Kinship: An Introduction," in R. Joyce and S. Gillespie (eds.), *Beyond Kinship: Social and Material Reproduction in House Societies*, pp. 1–21, Philadelphia: University of Pennsylvania Press.
Golden, C. W. (2003) "The Politics of Warfare in the Usumacinta Basin: La Pasadita and the Realm of Bird Jaguar," in M. K. Brown and T. Stanton (eds.), *Ancient Mesoamerican Warfare*, Walnut Creek, CA: Alta Mira Press.
Golden, C. W., Barrientos, T., Hruby, Z., and Muñoz, R. (1998) "La Pasadita: Nuevas Investigaciones en un Sitio Secundario en la Region del Usumacinta," in J. P. Laporte and H. L. Escobedo (eds.), *XII Simpósio de Investigaciones Arqueológicas en Guatemala, 1998*, pp. 435–54, Guatemala City: Museo Nacional de Arqueología y Etnología.
Helms, M. W. (1988) *Ulysses' Sail: An Ethnolgraphic Odyssey of Power, Knowledge, and Geographical Distance*, Princeton: Princeton University Press.

———(1998) *Access to Origins: Affines, Ancestors, and Aristocrats*, Austin: University of Texas Press.

Hill, R. M. II (1998) "Los Otros Kaqchikeles: Los Chajomá Vinak," *Mesoamerica* 35: 229–54.

Houston, S. D. (1993) *Hieroglyphs and History at Dos Pilas: Dynastic Politics of the Classic Maya*, Austin: University of Texas Press.

———(1998) "Finding Function and Meaning in Classic Maya Architecture," in S. D. Houston (ed.), *Function and Meaning in Classic Maya Architecture*, pp. 519–38, Washington, DC: Dumbarton Oaks.

———(2001) "Decorous Bodies and Disordered Passions: Representations of Emotion among the Classic Maya," *World Archaeology* 33(2): 206–19.

Houston, S. D., Escobedo, H., Child, M., Golden, C., and Muñoz, R. (2003) "Moral Community and Settlement Transformation among the Classic Maya: Evidence from Piedras Negras, Guatemala," in M. Smith (ed.), *The Social Construction of Ancient Cities*, pp. 65–93, Washington, DC: Smithsonian Institution Press.

Houston, S. D., Escobedo, H., Hardin, P., Terry, R., Webster, D., Child, M., Golden, C., Emery, K., and Stuart, D. (1999) "Between Mountains and Sea: Investigations at Piedras Negras, Guatemala, 1998," *Mexicon* XXI(1): 10–12.

Houston, S. D., and McAnany, P. A. (2003) "Bodies and Blood: Critiquing Social Construction in Maya Archaeology," *Journal of Anthropological Archaeology* 22(1): 26–41.

Houston, S. D., and Stuart, D. (1996) "Of Gods, Glyphs and Kings: Divinity and Rulership among the Classic Maya," *Antiquity* 70: 289–312.

———(1998) "Ancient Maya Self: Personhood and Portraiture in the Classic Period," *RES* 33: 72–101.

———(2001) "Peopling the Classic Maya Court," in T. Inomata and S. D. Houston (eds.), *Royal Courts of the Ancient Maya*, pp. 54–83, Boulder: Westview Press.

Houston, S. D., and Taube, K. (2000) "An Archaeology of the Senses: Perception and Cultural Expression in Ancient Mesoamerica," *Cambridge Archaeological Journal* 10(2): 261–94.

Inomata, T. (2001a) "King's People: Classic Maya Courtiers in a Comparative Perspective," in T. Inomata and S. D. Houston (eds.), *Royal Courts of the Ancient Maya: Volume 1, Theory, Comparison and Synthesis*, pp. 27–53, Boulder: Westview Press.

———(2001b) "The Power and Ideology of Artistic Creation: Elite Craft Specialists in Classic Maya Society," *Current Anthropology* 42(3): 321–49.

Inomata, T., and Houston, S. D. (2001) "Opening the Royal Maya Court," in T. Inomata and S. D. Houston (eds.), *Royal Courts of the Ancient Maya: Volume 1, Theory, Comparison, and Synthesis*, pp. 3–23, Boulder: Westview Press.

Inomata, T., and Stiver, L. R. (1998) "Floor Assemblages from Burned Structures at Aguateca, Guatemala: A Study of Classic Maya Households," *Journal of Field Archaeology* 25(4): 431–52.

Johnston, K. J. (2001) "Broken Fingers: Classic Maya Scribe Capture and Polity Consolidation," *Antiquity* 75(288): 373–81.

Jones, C. (1996) *Tikal Report No. 16: Excavations in the East Plaza of Tikal*, Philadelphia: University Museum Press.

Jones, G. D. (1998) *The Conquest of the Last Maya Kingdom*, Stanford: Stanford University Press.

Joyce, R., and Gillespie, S. D. (eds.) (2000) *Beyond Kinship: Social and Material Reproduction in House Societies*, Philadelphia: University of Pennsylvania Press.

Kluckhohn, C. (1940) "The Conceptual Structure in Middle American Studies," in C. L. Hay, R. L. Linton, S. K., Lothrop, H. L. Shapiro, and G. C. Vaillant (eds.), *The Maya and Their Neighbors: Essays on Middle American Anthropology and Archaeology*, pp. 41–51, New York: Dover.

Kovacevich, B., Barrientos, T., Demarest, A., Callahan, M., Bill, C., Sears, E., and Moran, L. (2001) "Produccion e Intercambio en el Reinado de Cancuen," in J. P. Laporte and H. Escobedo (eds.), *XIV Simposio de Investigaciones Arqueológicas en Guatemala*, pp. 589–609, Guatemala City: Instituto de Antropología e Historia de Guatemala.

Kuper, A. (1982) "Lineage Theory: a Critical Retrospect," *Annual Review of Anthropology* 11: 71–95.

Lévi-Strauss, C. (1963) *Structural Anthropology*, New York: Basic Books.

———(1982) *The Way of the Masks*, Seattle: University of Washington Press.

Looper, M. G. (1999) "New Perspectives on the Late Classic Political History of Quirigua, Guatemala," *Ancient Mesoamerica* 10(2): 263–80.

López Austin, A., and López Lujan, L. (2000) "The Myth and Reality of Zuyúa: The Feathered Serpent and Mesoamerican Transformations from the Classic to the Postclassic," in

D. Carrasco, L. Jones, and S. Sessions (eds.), *Mesoamerica's Classic Heritage*, pp. 21–86, Boulder: University of Colorado Press.

Marcus, J. (1973) "Territorial Organization of the Lowland Classic Maya," *Science* 180: 911–16.

———(1974) "Iconography of Power among the Classic Maya," *World Archaeology* 6(1): 83–94.

———(1976) *Emblem and State in the Classic Maya Lowlands*, Washington, DC: Dumbarton Oaks.

———(1983) "Lowland Maya Archaeology at the Crossroads," *American Antiquity* 48: 454–88.

———(1992) "Dynamic Cycles of Mesoamerican States," *National Geographic Research and Exploration* 8(4): 392–411.

———(1995) "Where Is Lowland Maya Archaeology Headed?" *Journal of Archaeological Research* 3(1): 3–53.

———(2003) "Recent Advances in Maya Archaeology," *Journal of Archaeological Research* 11(2): 71–148.

Martin, S., and Grube, N. (2000) *Chronicle of the Maya Kings and Queens: Deciphering the Dynasties of the Ancient Maya*, London: Thames and Hudson.

Masson, M. (2001) *In the Realm of Nachan Kan: Postclassic Maya Archaeology at Laguna De On, Belize*, Boulder: University of Colorado Press.

Mathews, P. (1988) *The Sculpture of Yaxchilan*, unpublished Ph.D. thesis, Yale University, New Haven.

———(1991) "Classic Maya Emblem Glyphs," in T. P. Culbert (ed.), *Classic Maya Political History: Hieroglyphic and Archaeological Evidence*, pp. 19–29, Cambridge, UK: Cambridge University Press.

———(1998) "Una Lectura de un Nueuo Monumento de El Cayo, Chiapas, y sus Implicaciones Políticas," in S. Trejo (ed.), *Modelos de Entidades Políticas Mayas: Primer Seminario de las Mesas Redondas de Palenque*, pp. 113–129. Mexico City: INAH.

McAnany, P. A. (1992) "A Theoretical Perspective on Elites and the Economic Transformation of Classic Period Maya Households," in S. Ortiz and S. Lees (eds.), *Understanding Economic Process*, pp. 85–103, Lanham, MD: University Press of America.

McAnany, P. A., Thomas, B. S., Morandi, S., Peterson, P. A., and Harrison, E. (2002) "Praise the Ajaw and Pass the Kakaw: Xibun Maya and the Political Economy of Cacao," in M. A. Masson and D. A. Freidel (eds.), *Ancient Maya Political Economies*, pp. 123–39, Walnut Creek, CA: Alta Mira Press.

Monaghan, J. (1998) "The Person, Destiny and the Construction of Difference in Mesoamerica," *RES* 33: 137–46.

Muñoz, A. R., and Golden, C. W. (2001) "Ceramic Innovation and Elite Competition at Piedras Negras Guatemala," paper presented to the 100th Annual Meeting of the American Anthropological Association, Washington, DC.

Palka, J. (1996) "Sociopolitical Implications of a New Emblem Glyph and Place Name in Classic Maya Inscriptions," *Latin American Antiquity* 7(3): 211–27.

Ponciano Alvarado, E., et al. (1998) "Aguateca: Evidencias de un Abandonado Repentino en el Clásico Tardío," in J. P. Laporte and H. L. Escobedo (eds.), *XII Simposio de Investigaciones Arqueológicas en Guatemala*, pp. 685–98, Guatemala City: Instituto de Antropología e Historia.

Rathje, W. L. (1973) "Classic Maya Development and Denoument: A Research Design," in T. P. Culbert (ed.), *The Classic Maya Collapse*, pp. 405–54, Albuquerque: University of New Mexico Press.

Recinos, A. (1999) *Memorial de Solola, Anales de los Kaqchikeles y Titulo de los Senores de Totonicapan*, Guatemala City: Editorial Piedra Santa Arandi.

Reents-Budet, D. (1994) *Painting the Maya Universe: Royal Ceramics of the Classic Period*, Durham, NC: Duke University Press.

Restall, M. (1998) *Maya Conquistador*, Boston: Beacon Press.

Reyna, S. P. (1994) "Predatory Accumulation and Religious Conflict in the Early 19th Century Chad Basin," in S. P. Reyna and R. E. Davis (eds.), *Studying War: Anthropological Perspectives, War and Society*, Vol. 2, pp. 127–55, Langhorne, PA: Gordon and Breach.

Rice, D., and Culbert, T. P. (eds.) (1990) *Historical Contexts for Population Reconstruction in the Maya Lowlands*, Albuquerque: University of New Mexico Press.

Robinson, E. J. (1998) "Organización del Estado Kaqchikel: el Centro Regional de Chitak Tzak," *Mesoamerica* 35: 49–71.

Roys, R. (1943) *The Indian Background of Colonial Yucatán*, Publication 613, Washington, DC: Carnegie Insitution of Washington.

———(1967) *The Book of Chilam Balam of Chumayel*, Norman: University of Oklahoma Press.

Ruppert, K., Thompson, J. E. S., and Prouskouriakoff, T. (1955) *Bonampak, Chiapas, Mexico.* Washington: Carnegie Institution of Washington.

Sabloff, J. A. (1986) "Interaction among Maya Polities: A Preliminary Examination," in C. Renfrew and J. F. Cherry (eds.), *Peer Polity Interaction and Socio-Political Change*, pp. 109–16, Cambridge, UK: Cambridge University Press.

Sabloff, J. A., and Andrews, E. W. IV (eds.) (1986) *Late Lowland Maya Civilization: Classic to Postclassic*, Albuquerque: University of New Mexico Press.

Sachse, F. (2001) "The Martial Dynasties, the Postclassic in the Maya Highlands," in N. Grube (ed.), *Maya: Divine Kings of the Rainforest*, pp. 356–71, Cologne: Könemann Verlagsgesellschaft.

Sahlins, M. D. (1961) "The Segmentary Lineage: An Organization of Predatory Expansion," *American Anthropologist* 63 (2): 322–45.

Sanders, W. T. (1981) "Classic Maya Settlement Patterns and Ethnographic Analogy," in W. A. Ashmore (ed.), *Lowland Maya Settlement Patterns*, pp. 351–69, Albuquerque: University of New Mexico Press.

Schele, L. (1991) "An Epigraphic History of the Western Maya Region," in T. P. Culbert (ed.), *Classic Maya Political History: Hieroglyphic and Archaeological Evidence*, pp. 72–101, New York: Cambridge University Press.

Schele, L., and Freidel, D. (1990) *A Forest of Kings: The Untold Story of the Ancient Maya*, New York: Morrow.

———(1991) "The Courts of Creation: Ballcourts, Ballgames, and Portals to the Maya Otherworld," in D. R. Wilcox and V. L. Scarborough (eds.), *The Mesoamerican Ballgame*, pp. 289–315, Tucson: University of Arizona Press.

Schele, L., and Mathews, P. (1998) *The Code of Kings*, New York: Touchstone.

Schele, L., and Miller, M. E. (1986) *The Blood of Kings: Dynasty and Ritual in Maya Art*, Fort Worth: Kimbal Art Museum.

Sharer, R. J. (1988) "Quirigua as a Classic Maya Center," in E. H. Boone and G. R. Willey (eds.), *The Southeast Classsic Maya Zone*, pp. 31–65, Washington, DC: Dumbarton Oaks.

———(1990) *Quirigua: A Classic Maya Center and its Sculptures.* Durham, NC: Carolina Academic Press.

———(1991) "Diversity and Continuity in Maya Civilization: Quirigua as a Case Study," in T. Culbert (ed.), *Classic Maya Political History*, pp 180 198, Cambridge, UK: Cambridge University Press.

———(1993) "The Social Organization of the Late Classic Maya: Problems of Definition and Approach," in J. A. Sabloff and J. S. Henderson (eds.), *Lowland Maya Civilization in the Eighth Century A.D.*, pp. 91–110, Washington, DC: Dumbarton Oaks.

———(1994) *The Ancient Maya*, 5th ed., Stanford: Stanford University Press.

———(2003) "Tikal and Copan Dynastic Founding," in J. A. Sabloff (ed.), *Tikal: Dynasties, Foreigners, and Affairs of State*, pp. 319–393, Santa FE: School of American Research Press.

———(in press) "External Interaction at Early Classic Copan," in E. B. Bell, M. Canuto, and R. J. Sharer (eds.), *Understanding Early Classic Copan*, Philadelphia: University of Pennsylvania Museum.

Sharer, R. J., Fash, W. L., Sedat, D. W., Traxler, L. P., and Williamson, R. (1999) "Continuities and Contrasts in the Early Classic Architecture of Central Copan," in J. K. Kowalski (ed.), *Mesoamerican Architecture as Cultural Symbol*, pp. 220–49, Oxford: Oxford University Press.

Smith, M. E., and Berdan, F. F. (1996) "The Postclassic Mesoamerican World System," *Current Anthropology* 41(2): 283–86.

Southall, A. (1991) "The Segmentary State: From the Imaginary to the Material Means of Production," in N. Claessen and P. van de Welde (eds.), *Early State Economics*, pp. 75–96, New Brunswick, NJ: Transaction.

Stuart, D. (1990) "A New Carved Panel from the Palenque Area," *Research Reports on Ancient Maya Writing* 32.

———(1996) "Kings of Stone: A Consideration of Ancient Stelae in Maya Ritual and Representation," *RES* 29–30: 148–71.

———(1998a) "'The Fire Enters His House': Architecture and Ritual in Classic Maya Texts," in S. D. Houston (ed.), *Function and Meaning in Classic Maya Architecture*, pp. 373–426, Washington, DC: Dumbarton Oaks.

Stuart, D. (1998b) "Una Guerra entre Yaxchilán y Piedras Negras," in H. L. Escobedo and S. D. Houston (eds.), *Informe Preliminar No. 2, Segunda Temporada 1998*, pp. 389–392, Guatemala City: Proyecto Arqueologico Piedras Negras.

———(2000) "'The Arrival of Strangers': Teotihuacan and Tollan in Classic Maya History," in D. Carrasco, L. Jones, and S. Sessions (eds.), *Mesoamerica's Classic Heritage*, pp. 465–514, Boulder: University of Colorado Press.

Stuart, D., and Houston, S. D. (1994) *Classic Maya Place Names Studies*, Pre-Columbian Art and Archaeology, 33, Washington, DC: Dumbarton Oaks.

Stuart, D., and Schele, L. (1986) "Yax-K'uk'-Mo', the Founder of the Lineage of Copan," *Copan Notes* 6.

Sutton, D. E. (1998) *Memories Cast in Stone: The Relevance of the Past in Everyday Life*, New York: Berg.

Tambiah, S. J. (1976) *World Conqueror and World Renouncer*, Cambridge, UK: Cambridge University Press.

Taube, K. (1988) "Classic Maya Scaffold Sacrifice," in E. P. Benson and G. G. Griffin (eds.), *Maya Iconography*, pp. 331–51, Princeton: Princeton University Press.

———(1998) "Jade Hearth: Centrality, Rulership, and the Classic Maya Temple," in S. Houston (ed.), *Function and Meaning in Classic Maya Architecture*, pp. 427–78, Washington: Dumbarton Oaks.

Tedlock, D. (1985) *Popol Vuh*, New York: Simon & Schuster.

Tourtellot, G., Wolf, M., Smith, S., Gardella, K., and Hammond, N. (2002) "Exploring Heaven on Earth: Testing the Cosmological Model at La Milpa, Belize," *Antiquity* 76(293): 633–34.

Villela, K. D. (1993) *The Classic Maya Secondary Tier: Power and Prestige at Three Polities*, unpublished M.A. thesis, University of Texas.

Weber, M. (1969) *Basic Concepts in Sociology*, New York: Greenwood Press.

Webster, D. (1998) "Classic Maya Architecture: Implications and Comparisons," in S. D. Houston (ed.), *Function and Meaning in Classic Maya Architecture*, pp. 5–48, Washington, DC: Dumbarton Oaks.

———(2000) "The Not So Peaceful Civilization: A Review of Maya War," *Journal of World Prehistory* 14(1): 65–119.

———(2002) *The Fall of the Ancient Maya: Solving the Mystery of the Maya Collapse*, New York: Thames and Hudson.

Whittington, S. L., and Reed, D. M. (eds.) (1997) *Bones of the Maya: Studies of Ancient Skeletons*, Washington, DC: Smithsonian Institution Press.

Yaeger, J. (2000) "The Social Construction of Communities in the Classic Maya Countryside," in M. A. Canuto and J. Yaeger (eds.), *The Archaeology of Communities: A New World Perspective*, pp. 123–42, London: Routledge.

4

The Blind Spot: Where the Elite and Non-Elite Meet

MARCELLO A. CANUTO
WILLIAM L. FASH, JR.

As early as 1904, Franz Boas succinctly described Anglo-American anthropology's innate dualism: "We find in anthropology two distinct methods of research . . . the *historical method* which endeavors to reconstruct the actual history of mankind, [and] the *generalizing method* which attempts to establish the laws of its development" (Boas 1974 [1904]:24; our italics). Insofar as Maya archaeology has belonged to this intellectual tradition, it too has engaged in a century-long struggle between historical and generalizing tendencies. The study of Classic Maya sociopolitical integration has long been riven by this polemic, as research has tended to produce either unitary models based on the history of polity centers or segmentary models generalized from settlement analysis. This struggle of Boasian proportions has fostered the proliferation of other dichotomies as well, such as political versus domestic economy, monumental versus residential architecture, political center versus rural hinterland, that have inhibited a holistic study of mechanisms of sociopolitical integration in Classic Maya society.

As we enter a new century of anthropologically informed research on the Classic Maya, scholars have increasingly sought to undermine any tendency toward dichotomy. Modern research has begun to replace reified heuristic categories with contextual, emic, and phenomenological approaches to Classic Maya sociopolitical complexity that untie the historical-generalizing knot. Therefore, as we stand at the threshold of a second century of research, we have begun to question these once naturalized dichotomies and blaze a "third way" that merges these unnecessarily estranged endeavors which Boas always recognized as related.

Variability or Methodology?

Throughout the last century, research theories and models of Classic Maya society became increasingly more complex and nuanced (for a detailed review of such developments, see Fash 1994). In general, research on Classic Maya society expanded in scope and captured a greater variety of its forms. In terms of Classic Maya sociopolitical organization, however, this development resulted in a myriad of contradictory models. Associating these contradictions with the broader scope of Maya archaeology, Arthur Demarest (1996:821) claimed, "The principle source of disagreement, although not the only one, about modeling ancient Maya political organization arises from the fact that the scholars are deriving and/or testing their models using different segments of the range of Maya state forms." Demarest further noted that these differences reflected the "protean nature of Maya social and political formations" (1996:821) and should be understood as indicative of the range of coöccurring political forms during the Classic period.

Although some of these models did focus on different "segments" of Classic Maya society, we posit that disagreement regarding Maya sociopolitical organization and integration also derived from another equally important axis of variation—the specialization of research method. It is perhaps a truism to claim that Classic Maya archaeology developed a battery of ever more intricate archaeological research methods, such as site-based excavations, regional survey (Bullard 1960, 1964; Hammond 1975; Leventhal 1981; Schortman 1993; Sharer and Coe 1979; Willey, Bullard, and Glass 1955; Willey, Leventhal, and Fash 1978; Willey et al. 1965), household archaeology (de Montmollin 1989; Drennan 1988; Fash 1983b; Freidel 1983; Kurjack and Andrews 1976; Pollock et al. 1962; Puleston and Callender 1967; Wilk and Ashmore 1988), landscape studies (Adams 1980; Fedick and Ford 1990; Sanders 1977; Hall and Viel in press), epigraphy (Berlin 1958; Marcus 1976; Mathews 1985; Proskouriakoff 1960), and iconography (Coe 1978; Reents-Budet 1994). However, this trajectory of increased methodological specialization also fostered the development of narrower, more contingent research designs that more precisely focused on specific scales of Classic Maya society—for example, single households, rural populations, elite compounds, royal palaces, administrative buildings, public spaces. In other words, besides the expanding scope of Maya studies, the ever more precisely honed research methods exacerbated the divide between historical and generalizing approaches by developing models designed to interpret specific scales of Classic Maya society.

This trend has been manifest in the last several decades of research at Copan where contradictory models of Classic Maya political organization developed from research efforts with different methodological scales of analysis. Overall, research at Copan was designed to conform to Walter Taylor's (1948) conjunctive approach since "archaeology (including settlement studies), epigraphy, iconography, and architectural restoration—in combination can provide more information than any single discipline could provide in isolation" (Fash and Sharer 1991:172; see also Fash 2002; Canuto, Sharer, and Bell in press). Therefore, research at Copan involved both a *series* as well as a *concurrence* of research efforts whose interrelated but separate research designs were designed to overlap in scope. In fact, to the extent that these multiple research efforts focused on the Copan polity, they were studying the same *segment* (*sensu* Demarest 1996) of Classic Maya society. However, despite their common focus, they still gave rise to distinct models of the polity's sociopolitical organization (Agurcia 1996, 1997; Andrews and Fash 1992; Fash 1983b, 1988; B. Fash et al. 1992; W. Fash et al. 1992; Freter 1994, 1996; Gonlin 1993, 1994; Hendon 1987, 1989; Leventhal 1979; Rue 1987; Sanders 1989; Sanders and Webster 1988; Sharer, Miller, and Traxler 1992; Sharer et al. 1999; Viel 1999; Webster 1985; Webster and Freter 1990a, 1990b; Webster and Gonlin 1988; Willey, Leventhal, and Fash 1978; Williamson 1996; Wingard 1996).

It remains important to emphasize here that the development of contradictory models is neither an indictment of the multidisciplinary approach at Copan, nor a critique of the specific models developed. A nascent and fast-evolving discipline like archaeology should eschew apodictic posturing by tolerating some degree of chronic debate. However, it seems incumbent to explore the source of this contradiction. In the case of Copan, the larger research enterprise was designed to balance separate efforts targeting different scales of analysis of the same Classic period polity. This effort resulted in the development of concurrent top-down and bottom-up approaches that engendered disparate models. If the contradiction results from distinct research methods, the resolution lies in the development of a different research method rather than in the disproof of one model over another.

From Contradiction to Integration

At Copan, top-down research methods that focused on large-scale archaeological units, such as the Acropolis, Las Sepulturas, and various other secondary centers, developed the *civic-ceremonial center* and the *polity* as the basic scales of analysis (see Agurcia 1996, 1997; Andrews and Fash 1992;

Ashmore 1991; Bell, Canuto, and Sharer in press; Fash 1983b, 1988; B. Fash et al. 1992; Fash and Sharer 1991; W. Fash et al. 1992; Sanders and Webster 1988; Viel 1999; Sharer, Miller, and Traxler 1992; Sharer et al. 1999; Traxler 2000; Williamson 1996). In general, the emphasis on these units focused research on questions of political history, organization, and factionalism. In fact, these efforts adopted a historical approach that developed a *unitary state* model emphasizing the establishment and decline of the Copan dynasty.

Conversely, research methods at Copan that emphasized smaller archaeological units of analysis—such as the patio group, house structures, and activity areas—tended to establish the *household* as the unit of analysis through which all interaction and organization were modeled. In fact, this method extrapolated the household's organizational template onto the rest of the Classic Copan *population.* The generalizing of a household-based imprimatur for all society (see Netting, Wilk, and Arnould 1984; Rathje 1983; Webster 2001; Wilk and Rathje 1982) highlighted the internal redundancy, loose integration, and dissolutive tendency of the Copan polity (see Freter 1988, 1994, 1996; Gonlin 1993, 1994; Rue 1987; Sanders 1989; Sanders and Webster 1988; Webster 1985; Webster and Freter 1990a, 1990b; Webster and Gonlin 1988; Willey, Leventhal, and Fash 1978; Wingard 1996). Consequently, these bottom-up research methods resulted in a *segmentary state* model for Classic period Copan that emphasized the socioeconomic autonomy of households and the fragmentary nature of the Maya political system.

In the case of Copan research, these divergent theories spawned an irresolvable debate about Copan's sociopolitical development, organization, and decline (for instance, compare Bell, Canuto, and Sharer in press with Webster, Freter, and Gonlin 2000). Therefore, there is a need to bridge these top-down and bottom-up approaches by focusing on a form of sociopolitical organization that mediates between the realms of kin and king. Such a study can only be successful when targeting a scale of organization where political and social units intersect. We suggest that the application of a community-scale research method in archaeology achieves this integration because it focuses on a unit of analysis that represents both the physical location and social context for all forms of supra-household interaction (see Canuto 2002; Yaeger 2000a; Yaeger and Canuto 2000) as well as localized polity-wide interaction.

Stated in the terminology and framework of traditional research methods: Between the political civic-ceremonial center and the overall polity, or between the social household and population, exists a middle-scale unit of sociopolitical organization that integrates the regional with the local, the political with the social. The "community," as both a regional and local context of interaction, proves pivotal to the understanding of how a multiscalar polity was integrated. It represents the locale—both figurative and literal—where the elite and non-elite would have met. Since a community research method integrates multiple scales of organization, its archaeological study requires the combination of traditionally distinct research methods such as center-based excavation, regional survey, and household archaeology that avoid the development of one-sided models. It is our contention that a community research method best recognizes the complexities inherent to the Classic period Maya polity.

The Community Research Method

Two paradigms have defined community studies in Maya archaeology. The most popular paradigm has been the *natural community*, which treats the community as an empirical entity, real and observable (Hollingshead 1948). The second paradigm, the *constituted community*, deemphasizes spatial and physical dimensions, focusing on the development and maintenance of social groups, that is, community identity.

The Paradigm of the Natural Community

In terms of archaeology, the natural community paradigm defines the community according to visible criteria such as spatial discreteness, residential nucleation, and even a shared material culture; it uses the same criteria traditionally used to define an archaeological "site" (Yaeger and Canuto 2000). Within this paradigm, several different approaches have developed to interpret the role and function of the community: normative, processual, and historical-developmental.

The normative approach sees the community as a static social entity. Drawn largely from Robert Redfield's (1955) ethnographic work on the "little community," the community was interpreted as a bounded, homogeneous, social isolate that presupposed its self-sufficiency and integrity as a social group. In other words, the community encompassed the entire scope of its members' lives with little need for external interaction. Studies in archaeology that adopted and then operationalized this bounded, static, and normative interpretation favored methods that *recognized* rather than *interpreted* the community. As a result, archaeology focused more on the existence, definition, and description of the institution, and less on its creation, maintenance, alteration, and manipulation. In Maya archaeology this normative approach attempted to characterize the typical community of the past, that is, "*the* prehispanic Maya community" (de Borhegyi 1956; Coe 1965; Willey 1955).

The development of Processual Archaeology changed the course of community studies in Maya research. Processualism treated the community less like an "object" of study, and more like a microcosm where larger dynamics could be observed and hypotheses about evolution of social organization could be assessed (see Flannery 1976; Hill 1970; Johnson and Earle 1987; Kolb and Snead 1997; Longacre 1970; Rogers and Smith 1995; Schwartz and Falconer 1994; Wills and Leonard 1994; Wilson 1999). This reassessment in archaeology was consistent with a broader methodological shift in the social sciences that now saw the community as "a *method* of observation and exploration, comparison, and verification. It is not the study of a community, communities, or *the* Community" (Arensberg and Kimball 1965:30).

In terms of method and research scope, processualism amplified the scope of archaeological research through the development of large-scale settlement pattern studies that expanded the repertoire of analytical units—such as activity areas, households, settlement clusters, catchment zones, and landscapes (see Johnson 1977; Parsons 1972; Roper 1979; Sanders 1956). As a result of settlement pattern research and the ensuing household archaeology, the community came to be seen as part of a settlement hierarchy—a scale of social organization achieved by a broad set of processes. More specifically, processual studies treated the community as a social response to environmental forces, that is, as a "natural ecological community" (Sanders 1981:362).

These approaches are limited because the community, as a social group, becomes a "black box" whose development and maintenance are assumed to be functional and adaptive in nature. Furthermore, they involve a uniformitarian bias that interprets the community as a timeless form of human organization divorced from its local context. Mindful of these limitations, Eric R. Wolf (1986) criticized these approaches for developing "billiard ball" models of the community. He suggested that the community was an intrinsic element of a much larger regional system, and therefore a product of a historical trajectory. Developing his historical-developmental framework, he claimed that distinct historical and regional conditions would contribute to the development of different *kinds* of communities (Wolf 1955). In other words, he turned the focus of research away from the specific community per se and onto the regional and historical context within which community integration could be assayed. This approach has been rarely adopted in Maya archaeology, despite its diachronic perspective.

Overall, the natural community paradigm's focus on empirically observable attributes appeals to an archaeological reliance on spatial and material evidence, that is, the site (Trigger 1967; Sanders 1981; Willey 1968). Importantly, the materialist bias of this paradigm is, in fact, bolstered by Maya ethnography that has repeatedly averred that the community represents a meaningful and important sociologically definable group (*sensu* Fox 1967:168) among the Maya (Redfield 1955; Reina 1965; Tax 1941; Tozzer 1907; Vogt 1969; Wisdom 1940; Wolf 1957, 1990). Therefore, archaeological studies adopting a natural community paradigm do indeed focus on a salient social institution that likely played a critical role in the development of the sociopolitical complexity of Classic Maya society.

The Paradigm of the Constituted Community

This paradigm deëmphasizes the spatio-physical dimension and defines the community as an *idea* rather than a place. Consequently, it emphasizes the development and maintenance of social groups, that is, community identity. In fact, although members of "imagined communities" need not interact with one another on a daily basis, they can conceive of themselves as unitary—such as diaspora, ethnic, worker, or national communities (Anderson 1991). The community is a socially constituted group that depends on the practice of its individual members for its perpetuation (Cunningham 1973; Bourdieu 1973, 1977, 1990; Giddens, 1984)—that is, community members "think themselves into difference" (Cohen 1985:117). However, an unmitigated adoption of the constituted community paradigm runs the risk of altogether sublimating the phenomenal dimension of community to the ideological. In fact, the "sense of place" (Feld and Basso 1996) represents the fundamental context for the formation of collective experience, shared history, and common identity. As such, community derives from collective actions undertaken throughout space, engendered by and capable of reconstructing its physical dimension.

In Maya studies, the constituted community paradigm has been increasingly adopted (see Canuto 2002; Canuto and Yaeger 2000; Demarest 1992; Joyce 1991; Marcus 1992; Schortman and Nakamura 1991; Yaeger 2000a). These studies, some more explicitly than others, recognize that a community is more complex than just a "correspondence between a socially interacting group, a bounded territory, economy, political, reproductive pool, intergenerational education, desires and sentiments" (Isbell 2000:249). Yaeger (2000a) and Canuto (2002) have interpreted the role of the "local community" in the Classic Maya lowlands by applying Cheney's views on the interplay of space and action, as wells as Pierre Boudieu's (1973, 1977, 1990) practice-oriented approach.

Jason Yaeger (2000a, 200b), interpreting the local community of the Xunantunich hinterlands, isolated three types of practices that developed community identity: those activities undertaken by everyone in the social group that provided a sense of communal belonging, those that helped members create local affiliations, and those that connected members of the local group to the larger polity. Marcello Canuto (2002) modified this model to accommodate for a more diachronic perspective of the Copan hinterlands. He introduced the temporal dimension of these practices—that is, the degree to which they were repetitious, episodic, or irregularly undertaken—in order to account for *change* in community practice and identity over time.

Both studies attempted to develop material indices and then provide confirmation for the developing and shifting allegiances of the middle-scale and smaller local communities in relation to their larger centers. These efforts, therefore, dovetail with broader models, such as Joyce Marcus's *dynamic model* (Marcus 1992) and Demarest's *galactic polity* (1992), which focus on the spatially amorphous polity as a larger community constituted by the integration of multiple scales of social and political organization.

Although Marcus's work is based on purely Maya analogies, and Demarest's relies on comparisons with Southeast Asian polities, both see a relatively weak development of control over land and resources in the outlying areas of Classic Maya "capitals." In Demarest's view, the power of the ruler of any Maya polity derived in large measure from his own charisma, and his ability to draw in the populace from his domain through public performances, and the redistribution of goods. In other words, much of Maya kingship was founded on the rulers' ability, in the immortal words of Clifford Geertz, to "make in-equality enchant" (Geertz 1980). Actual control of land and of the labor of what has been vaguely termed the "supporting population" was minimal, with tribute being the main economic resource the ruler could command. These models point out that the smaller local communities between the major capitals (from the secondary and tertiary centers, down to the smaller villages, and hamlets) played a key role in the political fortunes of the great Classic Maya centers such as Copan.

The study of the sense of place and the role of the phenomenal world in the constitution of imagined communities also have been advanced by epigraphy. The pioneering work of Heinrich Berlin (1958) in identifying the *emblem* glyphs of major Classic Maya centers was followed by an innovative and enlightening reconstruction of Classic period political geography in Marcus's *Emblem and State in the Classic Maya Lowlands* (1976). Therein, the citation of emblems was shown to reflect, in perhaps imperfect but certainly consistent measure, the political hierarchy of the sites with hieroglyphic inscriptions. Among the more interesting findings was that site size did not always reflect political power, indicating that the inscriptions could provide fine-grained indications of the constitution and power of particular sociopolitical groups at precise points in time.

More recently, David Stuart and Stephen Houston (1994) have further elucidated the Classic Maya conception of their own space by studying actual geographic place names, rather than names of kingdoms or their patron gods. In many cases, the toponyms may refer to purely supernatural realms, whereas in others they do seem to be references to real-world places. In Mesoamerica more broadly, of course, place names very often do have supernatural or otherwordly referents, with Coatepec being but one well-known example. Therefore, we must not forget the importance of pilgrimage to sacred (presumably in some sense "supernatural") places throughout ancient

Mesoamerica, including the Maya lowlands (Kubler 1985). This is another realm wherein archaeologists and epigraphers can identify, locate, and investigate places that attracted commoners and elites alike, serving to bridge the gap between them (Stuart and Fash in press).

It seems clear that the corpus of geographic information, as a font of emic knowledge, holds great potential in the identification of actual locations within and between the major centers. More important, as socially and politically constituted markers, these places reflect how the elites, who used and recorded them in their texts, segmented, delineated, and defined—that is, constituted—larger communities such as kingdoms, realms, and lands. This information, therefore, provides Maya archaeologists the opportunity to see how communities outside the center interacted with the royal family, and other members of the elite, by associating communities and their actors with toponyms, and their real-world as well as supernatural aspects.

Ethnicity provides another venue for the study of imagined communities. One fascinating wrinkle in Classic Maya studies is the realization that many commoners may not have been Maya-speaking at all (Canuto 2002; Gerstle 1987; Schortman 1993; Sharer 1979). Thus, we have a new source of inspiration for modeling the cleavages between elites and commoners, and the importance as well as the forms by which the elites in ancient "Maya" societies could "think themselves into difference." Maya polities may prove to be more multiethnic than the old monolithic views of them had allowed, with burial practices and food production (along with the sophisticated new bone chemistry analyses) being more reliable indicators of ethnicity than the mere presence of imported ceramics, other elite craft goods, or "international" styles of architecture and sculpture.

Overall, the constituted community paradigm is not limited to social groups defined by strict sociospatial phenomena. This paradigm orients archaeology toward the practices underpinning the constitution of any social group—even those strictly defined by physical phenomena. This paradigm sees the "polity" as an imagined community whose members—vis-à-vis the "local community"—interact in an empirically more loosely defined space marked by a broader variety of materials and physical cues. The local community, however, is also seen as integrated by practices that operate at a local level and result in more empirically manifest phenomena.

Community Approaches at Copan

Although not dominant in the past decades, some archaeological efforts at Copan have adopted community-based research designs (Canuto 2002; Fash 1983a; Freter 1994). Initially developed using the natural community paradigm, the latest efforts have also adopted the practice-oriented paradigm. Taken together, however, these models provide a holistic view of Copan's sociopolitical development by attempting to determine the role of this middle-level unit of organization and identity.

Natural Community Paradigm

Expansion of Harvard's settlement research throughout the Copan pocket (figure 4.1) by William Fash allowed for the recognition of "specific social/geographical units . . . among the Late Classic settlements of the Copan pocket" (Fash 1983a:268). This research noted the existence of larger settlement clusters composed of smaller "minimum residential units" (single mounds), "group residential units" (mound groups), and larger residential sites (figure 4.2). These larger clusters showed a regularity in architectural composition and spatial organization that established them as a distinct settlement scale less complex than the elite compound but larger than a residential group. As such, they represented a form of social organization intermediate to the individual household and the monumental center. The recognition of these units as well as their ubiquity throughout the Copan pocket led to their subsequent inclusion in a model for the Copan polity.

Using ethnographic and ethnohistoric sources, Fash (1983a:282) suggested that these clusters represented the Classic period equivalent of the *sian otot* unit of contemporary Chortí, that is, the local community. Once interpreted as local communities, their relative homogeneity throughout the pocket indicated that their development "was simply the result of the same factors producing the notable population increases in the bottomlands . . . [resulting] in more homogeneous groupings, where the majority of the families could be traced to two or more lineages that first colonized that particular [Copan] pocket sector" Fash (1983a:282). Given this developmental model, it was suggested that the Copan polity was integrated by lineage ties and a feudal form of land ownership that eventually led to its decentralization and fragmentation.

David Webster and AnnCorrine Freter (Freter 1988, 1994; Webster and Freter 1990a, 1990b) expanded settlement research to the hinterlands outside the Copan pocket. This work recovered a widely distributed rural settlement composed of several spatially limited clusters of sites (figure 4.3). Freter claimed that these clusters represented autonomous rural communities: "A period of rural out-migration and rural community formation occurred subsequent to the collapse of the Copan ruling elite structure" (Freter 1994:169). Freter treated the community as the result of adaptive (functional) behaviors of the smaller units of the rural population: "The remaining sizeable population [outside the Copan pocket] responded more gradually to systemic problems, forming small rural communities . . . complete with secondary elite positions, and rural administrative centers" (Freter 1994:161).

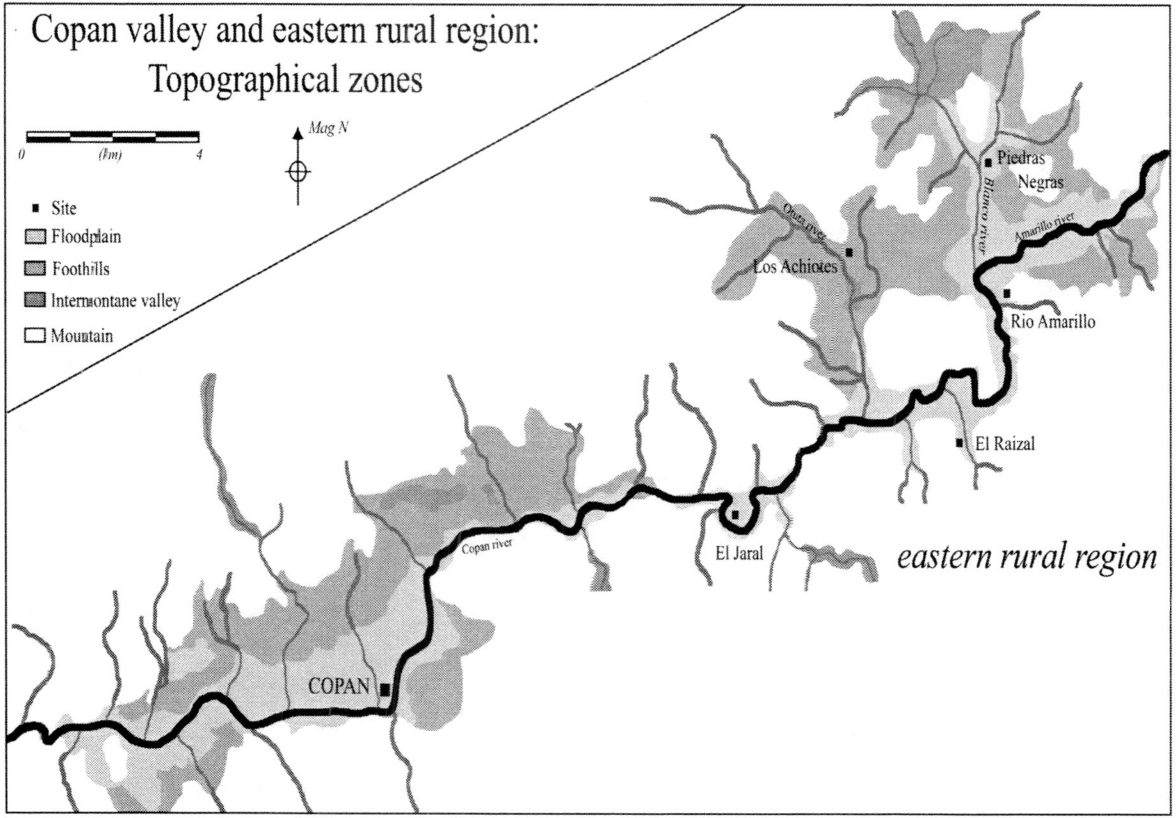

Fig. 4.1 Map of the Copan Valley (courtesy of M. Canuto).

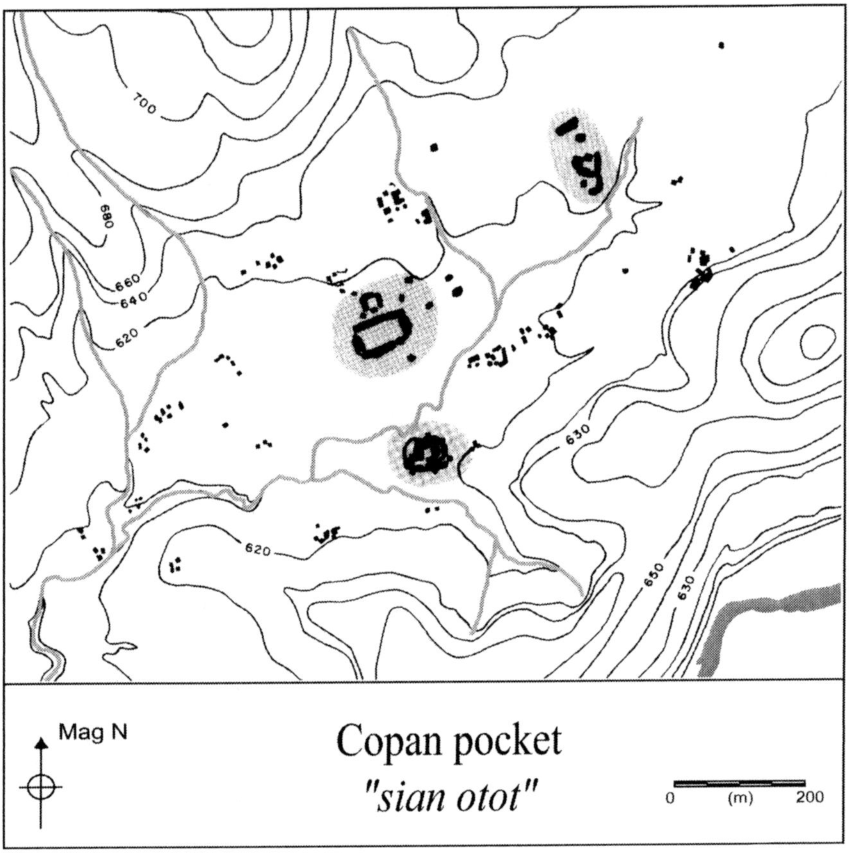

Fig. 4.2 The Copan pocket *sian otot* (from Fash 2002: Figure 97).

Although grave doubts remain regarding her dating of this out-migration (Anovitz et al. 1999; Braswell 1992; Braswell et al. 1996; Cowgill and Kintigh 1997; Freter 1992, 1993; Webster, Freter, and Gonlin 2000; Webster, Freter, and Rue 1993), Freter did recognize the existence of an intervening, middle-scale unit of organization as a function of natural population growth patterns throughout the rural regions. Freter (1994) and others (Hendon 1991; Sanders 1989; Sanders and Webster 1988) treated the development of these communities as evidence for a segmentary lineage form of sociopolitical integration between Copan's urban and rural populations. This system's centrifugal nature resulted in the constant hiving off of smaller social groups that established autonomous localized lineage communities at a distance from the polity center.

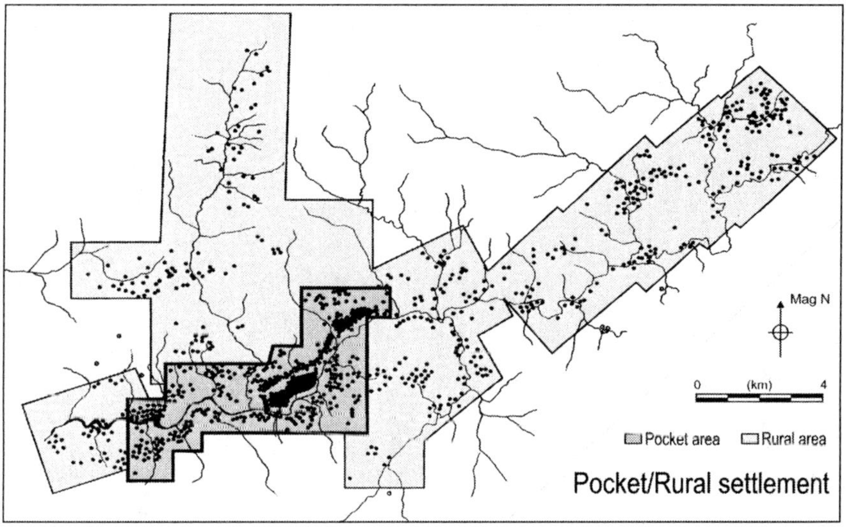

Fig. 4.3 Communities of the Copan hinterlands (from Webster, Freter, and Gonlin 2000: Figure 3-1).

Canuto (2002, in press) undertook the latest phase of community-scale research at Copan. Building on the results of previous research, he focused on the Copan hinterlands to determine the nature and degree of supra-household organization among the rural populations of the Copan valley. Canuto focused on two rural *sian otot* communities—Los Achiotes and El Raizal—that were equivalently sized and located in similar neighboring valleys (figure 4.4). Los Achiotes was occupied in the Late Preclassic period (300 B.C.–A.D. 50), whereas El Raizal was founded during Classic Copan's apogee (A.D. 500–800). Because the occupation of these two communities did not overlap, Canuto (2002, in press) compared them as unrelated exemplars of Copan's local communities.

Despite their similar size and environmental settings, they differed according to fundamental empirical categories such as settlement pattern, spatial organization, architecture, material goods, and even the placement of special deposits. Canuto claimed that the rural community of the Late Preclassic period differed from its Classic period equivalent because of cultural and historical differences of their members (Canuto 2002, in press). In other words, the local community at Copan was not just the outgrowth of a feudal system of land ownership based on lineage affiliation, nor was it solely a response to demographic pressures and environmental degradation. By claiming that the community *responded to* and thereby *reflected*

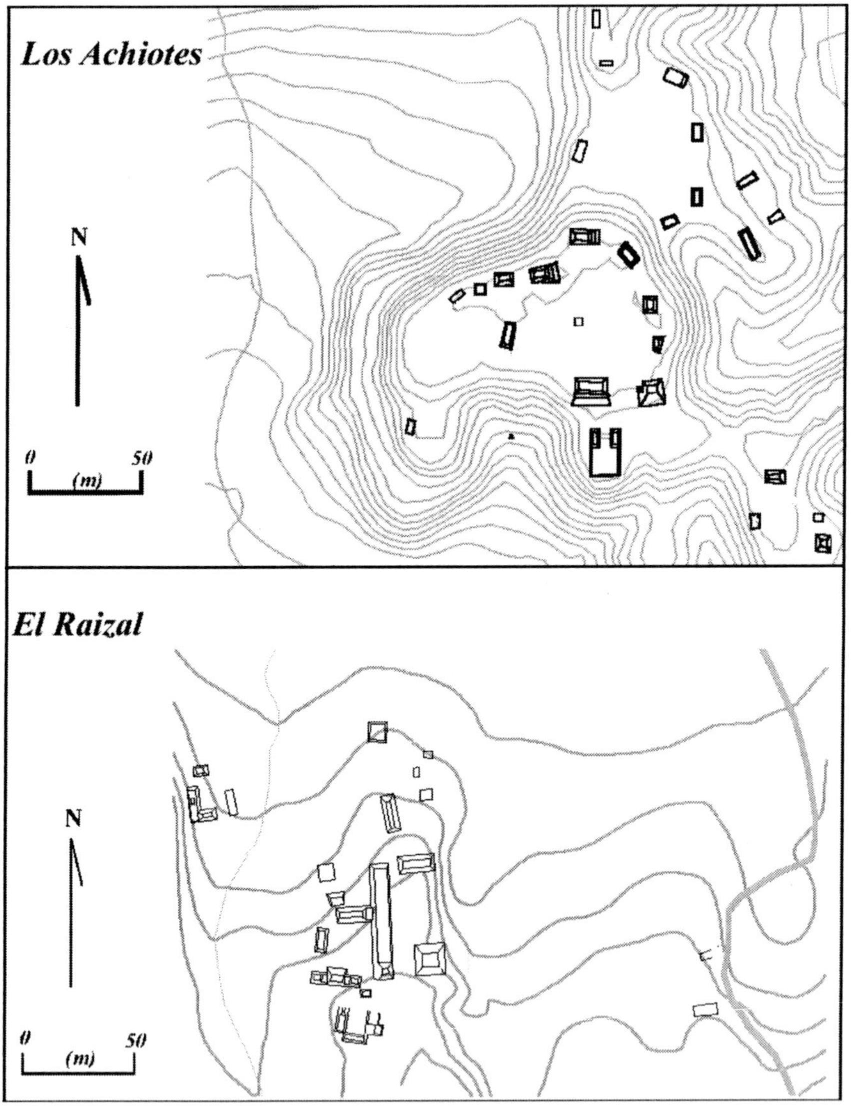

Fig. 4.4 The Communities of Los Achiotes and El Raizal (courtesy of M. Canuto).

changes in the sociopolitical and ecological landscape of the Copan polity, Canuto favored Wolf's (1955, 1957) "historical-developmental" perspective associating community form with its historical and cultural conditions.

He interpreted the community forms recognized by previous research efforts in Copan as highly contingent on their specific sociopolitical landscapes. Canuto suggested that various types of community in the Copan Valley—that is, the pre-dynastic communities like Los Achiotes, the *sian otot* of the Copan pocket, and the Late Classic rural communities like El Raizal—corresponded to changes in the sociopolitical complexity of the Copan Valley. In other words, his application of the natural community paradigm led to the conclusion that the Copan Valley saw the development of multiple *types* of local communities, all of which had embedded within them patterns that reflected the level of the Copan Valley's sociopolitical complexity.

Constituted Community

Application of the constituted community paradigm at Copan has focused on the modeling of practices integrating the local community to a larger political entity (Canuto 2002, in press), the constitution and social delineation of larger imagined communities, like the polity through the use and distribution of toponyms (Fash and Davis-Salazar in press; B. Fash et al. 1992; Fash 2002), and the potential development of ethnic communities in the Copan Valley (Canuto 2002; Gerstle 1987).

Canuto's study of two rural communities—Los Achiotes and El Raizal—showed how the material and empirical differences between the two related to subtle variations in the prominence of certain practices of local group affiliation. Los Achiotes dates to the Late Preclassic, preceding Copan's dynastic expansion by several centuries. The material record suggests that the inhabitants of this earlier community undertook daily practices such as cooperative farming and similar household activities that effectively minimized interfamily differentiation. These practices were a daily reinforcement and reproduction of a locally based sense of practical solidarity. Less frequent—more episodic—practices involved the construction of public architecture (a ballcourt) and participation in public rituals. These functioned to enhance a sense of commonality throughout the community. Finally, members of Los Achiotes occasionally interacted with external groups as evinced by the presence of a ballcourt and the importation of few foreign goods. Moreover, there was no exclusivity in either the access to and distribution of the few foreign goods throughout the community. It appears that these interactions were irregular and only reinforced local community identity.

Soon after the founding of the Copan dynasty, the hinterland community of El Raizal was established. Members of this community undertook different daily household routines that enforced the notion of household rather than community identity. Furthermore, group-affirming periodic practices were removed from communal space altogether and either embedded within limited-access household spaces (such as caches and special deposits) or surrendered entirely to the Copan polity (such as the ballgame since El Raizal had no ballcourt; Fox 1996). The frequency and nature of regional interaction also changed: One family enjoyed a more frequent interaction with the regional polity than the rest of the families in the community. The more frequent interaction with the regional polity of this family undermined their membership with the local group while enhancing their affiliation to an imagined regional community centered in Copan's Acropolis.

At Los Achiotes, local affiliation was maintained by a host of shared daily activities, enforced through periodic practices of communal action, and then made manifest on the rare occasions where extracommunity interactions took place in the community. Life in the community involved an almost continuous multiscalar enforcement of local group identity. At El Raizal, community-affirming activities were either absorbed into the kin-based household or politicized by the elite and made into politywide events (see Pauketat 2000). These changes resulted in an attenuated local community identity among the members of El Raizal who were segmented by other polity-based identities.

Since the differences between these two communities coincide chronologically with the development of dynastic rule at Copan, the practice-based approach suggests that major changes in Classic Maya society were related to the manipulation of various forms of community affiliation. The politically fragmented nature of the region in the Late Preclassic period did not foment a broad politically imagined community beyond that of local groups. Therefore, the local community identity of Los Achiotes would have been highly salient. With the rise of the Copan dynasty, the influence of a regional polity interfered with the salience of local group identity. In its place, the polity provided an imagined affiliation to a larger entity for some families that, in turn, isolated others into expressing a greater degree of household autonomy. In other words, the differences between Los Achiotes and El Raizal suggest that the decline of local community identity, the rise of household autonomy, and the empowerment of rural families (or houses, *sensu* Lévi-Strauss 1982) coincide with the development of an "imagined" polity community during the Classic period that undermined local group affiliation.

These conclusions are consistent with discoveries from the Copan Acropolis that attest to the development of a broad sociopolitical unit whose membership extended to local communities throughout the Copan Valley. The case has been made that the toponyms on one prominent structure of the Copan Acropolis (Structure 10L-22A; figure 4.5) may represent the

Fig. 4.5 Structure 10L-22A, Copan Acropolis and toponyms (from Fash 2002: Figures 84 and 85).

names of communities that participated in the royal council. Placed in a prominent spot on the Acropolis, where it could be viewed by the populace gathered in either the Great Plaza, or the Plaza of the Hieroglyphic Stairway, Structure 22A was decorated with ten large mat (*pop*) designs, which are believed to name the structure as the *Popol Otot*, or *Popol Nah*, a reading supported by the roof elements that provide the same meaning. Placed between the mat signs were nine toponymic glyphs, seated atop each of which was a human figure, hypothesized to be the representative to the council, from that particular locality.

Prudently, our epigrapher colleagues continue to believe that many if not all the names on the Copan structure are supernatural abodes (Stuart and Houston 1994:57). However, the archaeological discovery and documentation of one of the Structure 22A toponyms on the facades of two different structures at an elite residential compound south of the Acropolis (Andrews and Fash 1992) would seem to imply that these toponyms are in some sense "claimed," if not physically occupied, by important houses (*sensu* Lévi-Strauss 1982; Gillespie 2000), or whole communities. Furthermore, it is certainly noteworthy that one of the most often cited toponyms is translated as the "black water place." Vernon Scarborough (1993, 1996), Nicholas Dunning (Dunning et al. 1999), and others have shown that reservoirs and *aguadas* were important in the ancient Maya landscape. In this case, iconography and settlement/geography studies complement each other nicely in the investigation of the use and control of water resources (Fash and Davis-Salazar in press; Lucero and Fash in press; Scarborough 1998), which modern-day Maya still use as a form of defining, and integrating, their communities (Vogt 1969).

Apart from local and polity communities, another potentially factionalizing force in Classic period Copan would have been the constitution of *ethnic communities* whose members lived dispersed throughout the polity. Possibly working against the development of a single polity affiliation, ethnic factions are suggested by several independent lines of evidence. Robert Sharer (1979) and Edward Schortman (1993) have succeeded in showing that although the royal center of Quirigua was "Classic Maya" in every material sense (including some of the largest hieroglyphic stelae ever created), the surrounding population of the lower Motagua Valley was not. Similarly, in the case of Copan both the ceramics and architecture indicate that much of the valley population was non-Maya (Bill 1997; Canuto 2002; Gerstle 1987; Willey et al. 1994; Manahan 2000; Viel 1993) in and around the Copan Acropolis for centuries.

Recently, Kathryn Josserand (2002) proposed a thought-provoking model to explain polities such as Copan and Palenque, on the westernmost geographic margin of the Maya lowlands. She pointed out that royal houses and other elites of medieval Europe all adopted the language, dress, architecture, food, and even the furniture of the French, regardless of their own country, language, and customs of the commoners who supported their lavish lifestyles. If equivalent, the development of a political community throughout the Classic period could also have had overtones of cultural transformation. That is, efforts to integrate the polity through the constitution of an imagined community based on not just political affiliation but also cultural similarity might have accelerated the decline of local group identities in the surrounding communities. Concurrently, this process might have also galvanized into existence equivalent factions constituted by other ethnicities. In this regard, the Copan polity might have been wracked by the factionalism of ethnic communities that cleaved through "natural" local communities.

Conclusions

The study of the community as the crucible of past interaction conflates regional, local, and domestic scales of analysis and therefore bridges the widening paradigmatic divide in archaeology. Therefore, the community approach demonstrates how research of the Classic Maya can avoid theoretical provincialism that foments a contentment with either historical or generalizing views of the past. In fact, the community paradigms thus far employed in Maya archaeology have enriched and nuanced the models of sociopolitical integration.

At Copan the combination of paradigms postulates that the Classic period was an arena of multiple, imagined communities varying according to scale and sociospatial manifestation that were competing for social salience and political sway over the Copan population. Contradictory strategies of selective inclusion and access exploited local economic systems, kin relations, and even ethnic affiliations vying for control over people's primary affiliation. In this model, therefore, some strategies were unitary in scope, whereas others were segmentary in effect. The contradiction of the unitary versus segmentary models developed for Copan has not been resolved in favor of one over the other. Rather, that debate has been superceded by a broader multiscalar model that sees the Classic period polity of Copan as a combination of various scales of community constituted and manipulated by a series of constantly shifting practices.

We began our discussion with the prophetic observation of the father of our field Boas who helped us define the origin of the deep theoretical divide within modern Maya archaeology. We noted that this difference was reflected in the contradictory models of Classic Maya sociopolitical integration. We claimed that this contradiction was partly based on the specialization of methodology that limited the scope of research and handicapped the resulting theoretical models. We hope to have shown how through a community approach, multiscalar phenomena (such as the Classic period Maya polity) can be integrated into a single practice-oriented model that is neither paradigmatically historical nor generalized.

References

Adams, R. E. W. (1980) "Swamps, Canals, and the Location of Ancient Maya Cities," *Antiquity* 54: 206–14.

Agurcia F. R. (1996) "Rosalila, El Corazón de la Acrópolis: El Templo del Rey-Sol," *Yaxkin* 14: 5–18.

———(1997) "Rosalila, an Early Classic Maya Cosmogram from Copan," *Symbols:* 32–7.

Anderson, B. (1991) *Imagined Communities: Reflections on the Origin and Spread of Nationalism,* London: Verso.

Andrews, E. W. V., and Fash, B. (1992) "Continuity and Change in a Royal Maya Residential Complex at Copan," *Ancient Mesoamerica* 3: 63–87.

Anovitz, L. M., et al. (1999) "The Failure of Obsidian Hydration Dating: Sources, Implications, and New Directions," *Journal of Archaeological Science* 26(7): 735–52.

Arensberg, C. M., and Kimball, S. T. (eds.) (1965) *Culture and Community*, New York: Harcourt Brace.

Ashmore, W. (1991) "Site-planning principles and concepts of directionality among the ancient Maya," *Latin American Antiquity* 2(3): 199–226.

Bell, E. E., Canuto, M. A., and Ramos, J. (2000) "El Paraíso: Punto Embocadero De La Periferia Sudeste Maya," *Yaxkin* 19: 41–75.

Bell, E. E., Canuto, M. A., and Sharer, R. J. (in press) "Introduction" in E. Béll, M. Canuto, and R. Sharer (eds.), *Understanding Early Classic Copan*, Philadelphia: University Museum Press.

Berlin, H. B. (1958) "El Glifo "Emblema" En Las Inscripciones Mayas," *Journal De La Societé Des Américanistes* 47: 111–19.

Bill, C. R. (1997) *Patterns of Variation and Change in Dynastic Period Ceramics and Ceramic Production at Copan, Honduras*, unpublished Ph.D. dissertation, Department of Anthropology, Tulane University, New Orleans.

Boas, F. (1904) "The History of Anthropology," *Science* 20: 513–24.

Bourdieu, P. (1973) "The Berber House," in M. Douglas (ed.), *Rules and Meaning: The Anthropology of Everyday Knowledge*, pp. 98–110, Hammondsworth, UK: Penguin.

———(1977) *Outline of a Theory of Practice*, Cambridge UK: Cambridge University Press.

———(1990) "Appendix: The Kabyle House: Or the World Reversed," in P. Bourdieu (ed.), *The Logic of Practice*, pp. 271–83, Stanford: Stanford University Press.

Braswell, G. E. (1992) "Obsidian-Hydration Dating: The Coner Phase, and Revisionist Chronology at Copan, Honduras," *Latin American Antiquity* 3(2): 130–47.

Braswell, G. E., Glascock, M. D., and Neff, H. (1996) "The Obsidian Artifacts of Group 10L-2, Copan: Production, Exchange and Chronology," paper presented at the 61st Annual Meeting of the Society for American Archaeology, New Orleans, LA.

Bullard, W. R., Jr. (1960) "Maya Settlement Pattern in Northeastern Petén, Guatemala," *American Antiquity* 25(3): 355–72.

———(1964) "Settlement Patterns and Social Structures in the Southern Maya Lowlands during the Classic Period," *XXXV Congreso Internacional de Americanistas* 1: 279–87.

Canuto, M. A. (2002) *A Tale of Two Communities: The Role of the Rural Community in the Socio-Political Integration of the Copan Drainage in the Late Preclassic and Classic Periods*, unpublished Ph.D. dissertation, Department of Anthropology, University of Pennsylvania, Philadelphia.

———(in press) "The Rural Settlement of Copan: Changes through the Early Classic," in E. Bell, M. Canuto, and R. Sharer (eds.), *Understanding Early Classic Copan*, Philadelphia: University of Pennsylvania Museum Press.

Canuto, M. A., Sharer, R. J., and Bell, E. E. (in press) "Understanding Early Classic Copan: A Classic Maya Center and Its Investigation," in E. Bell, M. Canuto, and R. Sharer (eds.), *Understanding Early Classic Copan*, Philadelphia: University of Pennsylvania Museum Press.

Canuto, M. A., and Yaeger, J. (eds.) (2000) *The Archaeology of Communities: A New World Perspective*, London: Routledge.

Coe, M. D. (1965) "A Model of Ancient Community Structure in the Maya Lowlands," *Southwestern Journal of Anthropology* 21(2): 97–114.

———(1978) *Lords of the Underworld: Masterpieces of Classic Maya Ceramics*, Princeton: Princeton University Press.

Cohen, A. P. (1985) *The Symbolic Construction of Community*, London: Routledge.

Cowgill, G. L., and Kintigh, K. W. (1997) "How Random Error in Dates Increase Apparent Lengths of Intervals," paper presented at the 62nd Annual Meeting of the Society for American Archaeology, Nashville, TN.

Cunningham, C. (1973) "Order in the Atoni House," in R. Needham (ed.), *Right and Left: Essays on Dual Symbolic Classification*, pp. 204–38, Chicago and London: University of Chicago Press.

de Borhegyi, S. F. (1956) "The Development of Folk and Complex Cultures in the Southern Maya Area," *American Antiquity*: 343–56.

de Montmollin, O. (1988) "Settlement Scale and Theory in Maya Archaeology," in N. J. Saunders and O. de Montmollin (eds.), *Recent Studies in Pre-Columbian Archaeology*, pp. 63–104, BAR International Series, 421, Oxford: British Archaeological Reports.

———(1989) *Settlement Survey in the Rosario Valley, Chiapas*. Papers of the New World Archaeological Foundation, no 57. Provo: BYU Press.

Demarest, A. A. (1992) "Ideology in Ancient Maya Cultural Evolution," in A. A. Demarest and G. W. Conrad (eds.), *Ideology and Pre-Columbian Civilizations*, pp. 135–57, Santa Fe: School of American Research Press.
———(1996) "Closing Comment," *Current Anthropology* 376(5): 820–4.
Drennan, R. D. (1988) "Household Location and Compact Versus Dispersed Settlement in Prehispanic Mesoamerica," in R. R. Wilk and W. A. Ashmore (eds.), *Household and Community in the Mesoamerican Past*, pp. 273–93, Albquerque: University of New Mexico Press.
Dunning, N., et al. (1999) "Temple Mountains, Sacred Lakes, and Fertile Fields: Ancient Maya Landscapes in Northwestern Belize," *Antiquity* 73(281): 650–60.
Fash, B., and Davis-Salazar, K. (in press) "Copan Water Ritual and Management: Imagery and Sacred Place," in L. L. Lucero and B. W. Fash (eds.), *Pre-Columbian Water Management: Ideology, Ritual, and Power*, Tucson: University of Arizona Press.
Fash, B. W., et al. (1992) "Investigations of a Classic Maya Council House at Copan, Honduras," *Journal of Field Archaeology* 19: 419–42.
Fash, W. L. (1983a) "Deducing Social Organization from Classic Maya Settlement Patterns: A Case Study from the Copan Valley," in R. L. Leventhal and A. L. Kolata (eds.), *Civilization in the Ancient Americas*, pp. 261–88, Albuquerque and Cambridge: University of New Mexico Press and Peabody Museum of Archaeology and Ethnology, Harvard University.
———(1983b) "Reconocimiento y Excavaciones En El Valle," in *Introducción a La Arqueología De Copan, Honduras*, Vol. 1, pp. 229–469, Proyecto Arqueológico Copan, Tegucigalpa: Instituto Hondureño de Antropología e Historia, Secretaría de Estado en el Despacho de Cultura y Turismo.
———(1988) "A New Look at Maya Statecraft from Copan," *Antiquity* 62: 157–69.
———(1994) "Changing Perspectives in Maya Civilization," *Annual Review of Anthropology* 23: 181–208.
———(2001) *Scribes, Warriors and Kings: The City of Copan and the Ancient Maya*, London: Thames and Hudson.
———(2002) "Religion and Human Agency in Ancient Maya History: Tales for the Hieroglyphic Stairway," *Cambridge Archaeological Journal* 12(1): 5–19.
Fash, W. L., and Sharer, R. J. (1991) "Sociopolitical Developments and Methodological Issues at Copan, Honduras: A Conjunctive Perspective," *Latin American Antiquity* 2: 166–87.
Fash, W. L., et al. (1992) "The Hieroglyphic Stairway and Its Ancestors: Investigations of Copan Structure 10L-26," *Ancient Mesoamerica* 3: 105–15.
Fedick, S. L., and Ford, A (1990) "The Prehistoric Agricultural Landscape of the Central Maya Lowlands: An Examination of Local Variability in a Regional Context," *World Archaeology* 22: 18–33.
Feld, S., and Basso, K. H. (1996) *Senses of Place*, Santa Fe: School of American Research.
Flannery, K. V. (ed.) (1976) *The Early Mesoamerican Village*, New York: Academic Press.
Fox, J. (1996) "Playing with power: Ballcourts and Political Ritual in Southern Mesoamerica," *Current Anthropology* 37:483–509.
Fox, R. (1967) *Kinship and Marriage*, London: Penguin.
Freidel, D. A. (1983) "Political Systems in Lowland Yucatán: Dynamics and Structure in Maya Settlement," in E. Z. Vogt and R. M. Leventhal (eds.), *Prehistoric Settlement Patterns: Essays in Honor of Gordon R. Willey*, pp. 375–86, Albuquerque and Cambridge: University of New Mexico Press and Peabody Museum of Archaeology and Ethnology, Harvard University.
Freter, A. (1988) *The Classic Maya Collapse at Copan, Honduras: A Regional Settlement Perspective*, Department of Anthropology, College Park: Pennsylvania State University.
———(1992) "Chronological Research at Copan: Methods and Implications," *Ancient Mesoamerica* 3: 117–33.
———(1993) "Obsidian-Hydration Dating: Its Past, and Future Application in Mesoamerica," *Ancient Mesoamerica* 4: 285–303.
———(1994) "The Classic Maya Collapse at Copan, Honduras: An Analysis of Maya Rural Settlement Trends," in G. M. Schwartz and S. E. Falconer (eds.), *Archaeological Views from the Countryside*, pp. 160–76, Washington and London: Smithsonian Institution Press.
———(1996) "Rural Utilitarian Ceramic Production in the Late Classic Period Copan Maya State," in A. G. Mastache et al. (eds.), *Arqueología Mesoamericana: Homenaje a William T. Sanders II*, pp. 209–29, Mexico: Instituto Nacional de Antropología e Historia, Mexico.
Geertz, C. (1980) *Negara: The Theater State in Nineteenth Century Bali*, Princeton: Prnceton University Press.

Gerstle, A. (1987) "Ethnic Diversity and Interaction at Copan, Honduras," in E. J. Robinson (ed.), *Interaction on the Southeast Mesoamerican Frontier: Prehistoric and Historic Honduras and El Salvador*, Vol. 2, pp. 328–56, BAR International Series, 327, Oxford: British Archaeological Reports.

Giddens, A. (1984) *The Constitution of Society: Outline of the Theory of Structuration*, Berkeley: University of California Press.

Gillespie, S. D. (2000) "Rethinking Ancient Maya Social Organization: Replacing 'Lineage' With 'House,'" *American Anthropologist* 102(3): 467–84.

Gonlin, N. (1993) *Rural Household Archaeology at Copan, Honduras*, Department of Anthropology, College Park: Pennsylvania State University.

———(1994) "Rural Household Diversity in the Late Classic Copan, Honduras," in G. M. Schwartz and S. E. Falconer (eds.), *Archaeological Views from the Countryside*, pp.177–97, Washington and London: Smithsonian Institution Press.

Hall, J., and Viel, R. (in press) "The Early Classic Copan Landscape: A View from the Preclassic, " in E. Bell, M. Canuto, and R. Sharer (eds.), *Understanding Early Classic Copan*, Philadelphia: University of Pennsylvania Museum Press.

Hammond, N. (1975) "Maya Settlement Hierarchy in Northern Belize," *Contributions to the University of California Archaeological Research Facility* 27: 40–55.

Hendon, J. A. (1987) *The Uses of Maya Structures: A Study of Architecture and Artifact Distribution at Sepulturas, Copan, Honduras*, unpublished Ph.D. dissertation, Department of Anthropology, Harvard University, Cambridge.

———(1989) "Elite Household Organization at Copan, Honduras: Analysis of Activity Distribution in the Sepulturas Zone," in S. MacEachern, D. J. W. Archer, and R. D. Garvin (eds.), *Household and Communities: Proceedings of the 21st Annual Chacmool Conference*, pp. 371–80, Archaeological Association, University of Calgary.

———(1991) "Status and Power in Classic Maya Society," *American Anthropologist* 93: 894–918.

Hill, J. N. (1970) *Broken K Pueblo: Prehistoric Social Organization in the American Southwest*, Anthropological Papers, 18, Tucson: University of Arizona.

Hollingshead, A. B. (1948) "Community Research: Development and Present Condition," *American Sociological Review* 13: 136–55.

Isbell, W. H. (2000) "What We Should Be Studying: The 'Imagined Community' and the 'Natural Community,'" in M. Canuto and J. Yaeger (eds.), *The Archaeology of Communities: A New World Perspective*, pp. 243–66, London: Routledge.

Johnson, A. W., and Earle, T. K. (1987) *The Evolution of Human Societies*, Palo Alto: Stanford University Press.

Johnson, G. (1977) "Aspects of Regional Analysis in Archaeology," *Annual Review of Anthropology* 6: 479–508.

Josserand, K. (2002) "Classic Maya Social Interaction and Linguistic Practice: Evidence from Hieroglyphic Inscriptions and Mayan languages," in V. Tiesler Blos, R. Cobos, and M. G. Robertson (eds.), *La Organización Social Entre los Mayas Prehispánlcos, Coloniales y Modernos, Memoria de la Tercera Mesa Redonda de Palenque*, pp. 355–372, México City and Merida: Instituto Nacional de Antropologia e Historia and Universidad Autónoma de Yucatán.

Joyce, R. A. (1991) *Cerro Palenque: Power and Identity on the Maya Periphery*, Austin: University of Texas Press.

Kolb, M. J., and Snead, J. E. (1997) "It's a Small World After All: Comparative Analysis of Community Organization in Archaeology," *American Antiquity* 62(4): 609–28.

Kubler, G. (1985) "Pre-Columbian Pilgrimages in Mesoamerica," in E. P. Benson (ed.), *Fourth Palenque Round Table, 1980*, pp. 313–6, San Francisco: Pre-Columbian Art Research Institute.

Kurjack, E. B., and Andrews, E. W. V. (1976) "Early Boundary Maintenance in Northwest Yucatan, Mexico," *American Antiquity* 41(3): 318–25.

Leventhal, R. M. (1979) *Settlement Patterns at Copan, Honduras*, unpublished Ph.D. dissertation, Harvard University, Ann Arbor: University Microfilms.

———(1981) "Settlement Patterns in the Southeast Maya Area," in W. Ashmore (ed.), *Lowland Maya Settlement Patterns*, pp. 187–209, Albuquerque: University of New Mexico Press.

Lévi-Strauss, C. (1982) *The Way of the Masks*, Seattle: University of Washington Press.

Longacre, W. A. (1970) *Archaeology as Anthropology: A Case Study*, Anthropological Papers of the University of Arizona, No. 17, Tucson: University of Arizona Press.

Lucero, L. L. and Fash B. (eds.) (in press) *Pre-Columbian Water Management: Ideology, Ritual, and Power*, Tucson: University of Arizona Press.

Manahan, K. (2000) *After the Fall: Examining the Nature of the Classic Maya Collapse of Copan, Honduras*, report submitted to the Foundation for the Advancement of Mesoamerican Studies Inc.

Marcus, J. (1976) *Emblem and State in the Classic Maya Lowlands: An Epigraphic Approach to Territorial Organization*, Washington, DC: Dumbarton Oaks.

———(1992) "Dynamic Cycles of Mesoamerican States," *National Geographic Research and Exploration* 8(4): 392–411.

Mathews, P. (1985) "Maya Early Classic Monuments and Inscriptions," in G. R. Willey and P. Mathews (eds.), *A Consideration of the Early Classic Period in the Maya Lowlands*, pp. 5–54, Institute for Mesoamerican Studies, Albany: State University of New York at Albany.

Netting, R. M., Wilk, R. R., and Arnould, E. J. (eds.) (1984) *Households: Comparative and Historical Studies of the Domestic Group*, Berkeley: University of California Press.

Parsons, J. R. (1972) "Archaeological Settlement Patterns," *Annual Review of Anthropology* 1: 127–50.

Pauketat, T. R. (2000) "Politicization and the Community in the Pre-Columbian Mississippi Valley," in M. Canuto and J. Yaeger (eds.), *The Archaeology of Communities: A New World Perspective*, pp. 16–43, London: Routledge.

Pollock, H. E. D., Roys, R. L., Proskouriakoff, T., and Smith, A. L. (1962) *Mayapán, Yucatán, Mexico*, Publication 619, Washington, DC: Carnegie Institution of Washington.

Proskouriakoff, T. (1960) "Historical Implication of a Pattern of Dates at Piedras Negras," *American Antiquity* 25: 454–75.

Puleston, D. E., and Callender, D. W. (1967) "Defensive Earthworks at Tikal," *Expedition* 9(3): 40–8.

Rathje, W. L. (1983) "To the Salt of the Earth: Some Comments on Household Archaeology Among the Maya," in E. Z. Vogt and R. M. Leventhal (eds.), *Prehistoric Settlement Patterns: Essays in Honor of Gordon R. Willey*, pp. 23–34, Albuquerque and Cambridge: University of New Mexico Press and Peabody Museum, Harvard University.

Redfield, R. (1955) *The Little Community: Viewpoints for the Study of a Human Whole*, Chicago: University of Chicago Press.

Reents-Budet, D. (1994) *Painting the Maya Universe: Royal Ceramics of the Classic Period*, Durham, NC: Duke University Press.

Reina, R. E. (1965) "Town, Community, and Multicommunity: The Theoretical Implications of a Guatemala Case," *Estudios De Cultura Maya* V: 361–90.

Rogers, J. D. and Smith, B. D. (eds.) (1995) *Mississippian Communities and Households*, Tuscaloosa: University of Alabama Press.

Roper, D. C. (1979) "The Method and Theory of Site Catchment Analysis: A Review," in M. B. Schiffer (ed.), *Advances in Archaeological Method and Theory*, Vol. 2, pp. 119–40, New York: Academic Press.

Rue, D. J. (1987) "Early Agriculture and Early Postclassic Occupation in Western Honduras," *Nature* 326: 285–6.

Sanders, W. T. (1956) "The Central Mexican Symbiotic Region," *Viking Fund Publications in Anthropology* 23: 115–27.

———(1977) "Environmental Heterogeneity and Evolution of Lowland Maya Civilization," in R. E. W. Adams (ed.), *Origins of Maya Civilization*, pp. 287–98, Albuquerque: University of New Mexico.

———(1981) "Classic Maya Settlement Patterns and Ethnographic Analogy," in W. Ashmore (ed.), *Lowland Maya Settlement Patterns*, pp. 351–69, Albuquerque: University of New Mexico Press.

———(1989) "Household, Lineage, and the State in 8th-Century Copan," in D. Webster (ed.), *House of the Bacabs, Copan: A Study of the Iconography, Epigraphy, and Social Context of a Maya Elite Structure*, pp. 89–105, Washington, DC: Dumbarton Oaks.

Sanders, W. T., and Webster, D. L. (1988) "The Mesoamerican Urban Tradition," *American Anthropologist* 90: 521–46.

Scarborough, V. L. (1993) "Water Management in the Southern Maya Lowlands: An Accretive Model for the Engineered Landscape," in V. L. Scarborough and B. L. Isaac (eds.), *Economic Aspects of Water Management in the Prehispanic New World*, pp. 17–69, Research in Economic Anthropology, Supplement 7, Greenwich, CT: JAI Press.

———(1996) "Reservoirs and Watersheds in the Central Maya Lowlands," in S. Fedick (ed.), *Managed Mosaic: Ancient Maya Agriculture and Resource Use*, pp. 304–14, Salt Lake City: University of Utah Press.
———(1998) "Ecology and Ritual: Water Management and the Maya," *Latin American Antiquity* 9(2): 135–59.
Schortman, E. M. (1993) "Archaeological Investigations in the Lower Motagua Valley, Izabal, Guatemala: A Study in Monumental Site Function and Interaction," in *Quirigua Reports*, Vol. 3, University Museum Monograph, 80, Philadelphia: University of Pennsylvania Museum of Archaeology and Anthropology.
Schortman, E. M., and Nakamura, S. (1991) "A Crisis of Identity: Late Classic Competition and Interaction on the Southeast Maya Periphery," *Latin American Antiquity* 2(4): 311–36.
Schwartz, G. M., and Falconer, S. E. (eds.) (1994) *Archaeological Views from the Countryside*, Washington and London: Smithsonian Institution Press.
Sharer, R. J. (1979) *Quirigua Reports Papers 1 to 5*, Philadelphia: University Museum Press.
Sharer, R. J., and Coe, W. R. (1979) "The Quirigua Project: Origins, Objectives and Research in 1973 and 1974," in *University Museum Monograph*, Vol 37, pp. 1–11, Philadelphia: University Museum Press.
Sharer, R. J., Miller, J. C., and Traxler, L. P. (1992) "Evolution of Classic Period Architecture in the Eastern Acropolis, Copan: A Progress Report," *Ancient Mesoamerica* 3: 145–59.
Sharer, R. J. et al. (1999) "Early Classic Architecture Beneath the Copan Acropolis," *Ancient Mesoamerica* 10: 3–23.
Stuart, D. S., and Fash, W. L. Jr. (in press) "Classic Maya Pilgrimage: Archaeological and Epigraphic Evidence," in J. Carlson (ed.), *Pre-Columbian Pilgrimage: A Conference at Dumbarton Oaks*, Washington, D.C.: Dumbarton Oaks Research Library and Collection.
Stuart, D., and Houston, S. D. (1994) *Classic Maya Place Names*, Studies in Pre-Columbian Art and Archaeology, 33, Washington, DC: Dumbarton Oaks.
Tax, S. (1941) "World View and Social Relations in Guatemala," *American Anthropologist* 43: 27–42.
Taylor, W. W. (1948) *A Study of Archaeology*, Memoirs of the American Anthropological Association, 69, Menasha, WI: American Anthropological Association.
Tozzer, A. M. (1907) *A Comparative Study of the Mayas and the Lacandones*, London: Macmillan.
Traxler, L. P. (2000) "The Royal Court of Early Classic Copan," in T. Inomata and S. D. Houston (eds.), *Royal Courts of the Ancient Maya*, Boulder: Westview Press.
Trigger, B. G. (1967) "Settlement Archaeology—Its Goals and Promise," *American Antiquity* 32(2): 149–60.
Viel, R. H. (1993) *Evolución De La Cerámica De Copan, Honduras*, Tegucigalpa: IHAH.
———(1999) "The Pectorals of Altar Q and Structure 11: An Interpretation of the Political Organization at Copan, Honduras," *Latin American Antiquity* 10(4): 377–99.
Vogt, E. Z. (1969) *Zinacantan: A Maya Community in the Highlands of Chiapas*, Cambridge, MA: Harvard University Press.
Webster, D. L. (1985) "Recent Settlement Survey in the Copan Valley, Honduras," *Journal of New World Archaeology* 5: 39–51.
———(2001) "Spatial Dimensions of Maya Courtly Life: Problems and Issues," in T. Inomata and S. D. Houston (eds.), *Royal Courts of the Ancient Maya, Volume I: Theory, Comparison, and Synthesis*, pp. 130–67, Boulder: Westview Press.
Webster, D. L., and Freter, A. (1990a) "The Demography of Late Classic Copan," in T. P. Culbert and D. Rice (eds.), *Precolumbian Population History in the Maya Lowlands*, pp. 37–62, Albuquerque: University of New Mexico Press.
———(1990b) "Settlement History and the Classic Collapse at Copan: A Redefined Chronological Perspective," *Latin American Antiquity* 1: 66–85.
Webster, D. L., Freter, A., and Gonlin, N. (2000) *Copan: The Rise and Fall of an Ancient Maya Kingdom*, Fort Worth: Harcourt Brace.
Webster, D. L., Freter, A., and Rue, D. J. (1993) "The Obsidian-Hydration Dating Project at Copan: A Regional Approach and Why It Works," *Latin American Antiquity* 4(4): 303–24.
Webster, D. L., and Gonlin, N. (1988) "Household Remains of the Humblest Maya," *Journal of Field Archaeology* 15: 169–90.
Wilk, R. R., and Ashmore, W. (eds.) (1988) *Household and Community in the Mesoamerican Past*, Albuquerque: University of New Mexico Press.

Wilk, R. R., and Rathje, W. L. (1982) "Household Archaeology," in R. Wilk and W. Rathje (eds.), *Archaeology of the Household: Building a Prehistory of Domestic Life*, pp. 617–40, Special Issue of American Behavioral Scientist (July/August) 25(6).

Willey, G. R. (1955) "The Maya Community of Prehistoric Times," *Archaeology* 8(1): 18–25.

———(1968) "Settlement Archaeology: An Appraisal," in K.C. Chang (ed.), *Settlement Archaeology*, pp. 208–26, Palo Alto: National Press Books.

Willey, G. R., Bullard, W. R., and Glass, J. B. (1955) "The Maya Community of Prehistoric Times," *Archaeology* 8: 18–25.

Willey, G. R., Bullard, W. R., Glass, J. B., and Gifford, J. C. (1965) *Prehistoric Maya Settlements in the Belize Valley*, Papers of the Peabody Museum of Archaeology and Ethnology, Vol. 54, Cambridge, MA: Harvard University.

Willey, G. R., Leventhal, R. M., Demarest, A. A., and Fash, W. L. (eds.) (1994) *Ceramics and Artifacts from Excavations in the Copan Residential Zone*, Papers of the Peabody Museum of Archaeology and Ethnology, Vol. 80, Cambridge, MA: Harvard University.

Willey, G. R., Leventhal, R. M., and Fash, W. L. (1978) "Maya Settlement of Copan Valley," *Archaeology* 31(4): 32–43.

Williamson, R. V. (1996) "Excavations, Interpretations, and Implications of the Earliest Structures beneath Structure 10L-26 at Copan, Honduras," in *Eighth Palenque Round Table 1993*, pp. 169–75, San Francisco: Pre-Columbian Art Institute.

Wills, W. H., and Leonard, R. D. (eds.) (1994) *The Ancient Southwestern Community*, Albuquerque: University of New Mexico Press.

Wilson, D. J. (1999) *Indigenous South Americans of the Past and Present: An Ecological Perspective*, Boulder: Westview Press.

Wingard, J. D. (1996) "Interaction between Demographic Processes and Soil Resources in the Copan Valley, Honduras," in S. Fedick (ed.), *The Managed Mosaic: Ancient Maya Agriculture and Resource Use*, pp. 207–35, Salt Lake City: University of Utah Press.

Wisdom, C. (1940) *The Chorti Indian of Guatemala*, Chicago: University of Chicago Press.

Wolf, E. R. (1955) "Type of Latin American Peasantry: A Preliminary Discussion," *American Anthropologist* 57: 452–71.

———(1957) "Closed Corporate Peasant Communities in Mesoamerica and Central Java," *Southwestern Journal of Anthropology* 13: 1–18.

———(1986) "The Vicissitudes of the Closed Corporate Peasant Community," *American Ethnologist* 13: 325–29.

———(1990) "Distinguished Lecture: Facing Power—Old Insights, New Questions," *American Anthropologist* 92(3): 586–96.

Yaeger, J. (2000a) *Changing Patterns of Social Organization: The Late and Terminal Classic Communities at San Lorenzo, Cayo District, Belize*, unpublished Ph.D. dissertation, Department of Anthropology, University of Pennsylvania, Philadelphia.

———(2000b) "The Social Construction of Communities in the Classic Maya Countryside," in M. A. Canuto and J. Yaeger (eds.), *The Archaeology of Communities: A New World Perspective*, pp. 123–42, London: Routledge.

Yaeger, J., and Canuto, M. A. (2000) "An Introduction to the Archaeology of Communities," in M. A. Canuto and J. Yaeger (eds.), *The Archaeology of Communities: A New World Perspective*, pp. 1–12, London: Routledge.

5
History in the Future: Historical Data and Investigations in Lowland Maya Studies

DON S. RICE
PRUDENCE M. RICE

In his essay "A Poetic for History" (Dening 1991, 1996), anthropologist/historian Greg Dening offers an "old joke that the world will not end with either a bang or a whimper. Instead, it will simply sink under the weight of old *National Geographic* magazines" (1996:46). If the "cargo" of *National Geographic* is large, Dening notes, "the sum total of the cargo of all the interpretive encounters of our world is immense" (ibid.).

Dening's use of the term "cargo" comes from his notion that events and objects of the past are a burden to, and embedded in, all of the moments that follow. In this sense, there is little remove from the cargo borne by the Yearbearers of the Maya calendar or the *cofradías* in Maya ethnography (Vogt 1969). As archaeologists we all have a role in preserving and perpetuating the burden of Maya history, but in doing so we make cultural artifacts of the past into social realities of the present. Ceramic vessels, codices, figurines, stelae—"marked with meaning upon the occasion of their origins . . . are translated into something else for the moments they survive" (Dening 1996:46). They may become aesthetic objects, (meta-) narratives, or anthropological arguments.

Increasingly anthropologists and historians are aware of this "double entendre," that histories are the past being made into the present. We do not create the past, and the past and our reconstructions of it are not the same. We create histories from products of the past, and these histories bind the past and the present together, a point to which we will return in the close of this chapter. In this sense history is "texted past" (Dening 1992:5, 1996:41–3); the past is "text-able." Our role in this volume on continuities and contentions in Maya archaeology is to discuss briefly those cultural artifacts of the Maya past that are both texted-past and text-able, and the roles they can play in archaeological investigations.

Sources of Textual Relics

Four major types or sources of textual artifacts have informed our historical narratives of the pre-conquest lowland Maya. These differ in their abundance and accessibility to modern scholars, and in the spatial, substantive, and temporal discontinuities among them.

(1) Maya hieroglyphic inscriptions of the Classic period provide a unique corpus of information about political history, making the Maya historical record different from those of other pre-hispanic groups in the Western Hemisphere. Stunning developments in decipherment during the last two decades of the twentieth century have resulted in readings for approximately sixty percent of the five-hundred or so regularly-used glyphs and signs in this logosyllabic system (Martin and Grube 2000:11; see also Houston, et al. 2001; Coe 1992).

These texts provide information on the accomplishments of the royal dynasties of the Maya, including births, genealogies, marriages, deaths, kingly triumphs vis-à-vis other sites and dynasties, and performance of an untold variety of rituals. Surviving examples are found carved or painted on free-standing monuments (stelae and altars), tomb walls, murals, stone panels, and wooden lintels of palace and temple buildings. Painted pottery vessels often display brief texts, the so-called "Primary Standard Sequence" (Coe 1978:13; Grube 1991; Reents-Budet 1994), which are simple statements about who owned the vessel. No Classic period versions of the later painted "books" known as codices survive.

Classic period inscriptions largely convey what Hammond has called "winners' history" (1991:2) rather than "proctological history" (Cohn 1980), a populist history written from the bottom up. Thus these texts have very specific referents and scope. Unlike the written records of some other archaic states, Maya texts provide little information on quotidian or economic affairs.

(2) A second source of textual information consists of indigenous texts of the Postclassic and Colonial periods, of which several kinds have survived. One is the codex, a "book" made of long strips of the beaten bark of a fig

tree (*Ficus cotonifolia*), sized with a lime wash, and folded accordion-style. Each "page" had hieroglyphic texts, tables, and illustrations written in black pigment with red, blue, and other color highlights.

Only four of these books are known today, a consequence of the Spanish conquerors' zealous burning of these artifacts in an effort to rid the Maya area of the "superstitions and lies of the devil" (de Landa, in Tozzer 1941:169). The surviving codices, all dating to the Postclassic period, are probably copies of earlier versions and are named for the places where they were found or now reside: Dresden (Vienna), Tro-Cortesianus or Madrid (Spain), Pérez or Peresianus (Paris), and Grolier (the Grolier Club in New York). All treat "predictive astronomy," that is, tables predicting the astronomical events and cycles governing ritual, rather than dynastic histories. The dates and origins of all three are subject to debate, although prototype astronomical tables may go back to the middle eighth century (Justeson 1989:76).

Perhaps the most important category of late native documents are the so-called "prophetic histories" collectively known as the "books of the *chilam b'alams*." Compilations of oral and probably codical traditions originally delivered by the spokesman or speaker (*chilan, chilam*) of the jaguar priest (*b'alam*), these books were committed to writing during the Colonial period by educated Maya who had been trained to write in Yukatekan using characters of the Spanish alphabet, as part of their religious instruction. Some sixteen of these books survive and are known today by the names of the Yucatán towns in which the manuscripts were found, as for, example, the *chilam b'alam of Chumayel* (figure 5.1).

The texts of these books address astrological and medical matters, but they also record history as the Maya (re-)constructed it, which is to say it is based on recurring cycles of twenty-year periods known as *k'atuns*. References to Christianity and post-conquest affairs indicate that extant versions of most of these books date between 1824 and 1837 (Edmonson 1979:9). The richly metaphorical language of these books is not prose but poetry, "a highly charged and allusive language that stresses the quality of time over its factual content" (Farriss 1987:577), making interpretation difficult, perhaps intentionally. In addition, the texts incorporate references to long-standing socio-ethnic rivalries between the two major elite lineages of the Postclassic Northern Lowlands, the Xiw and the Itzá. *The Book of Chilam Balam of Chumayel* (Roys 1967; Edmonson 1986) favors the Xiw of western Yucatán and repeatedly mentions symbolically significant defeats of the Itzá, while *The Book of Chilam Balam of Tizimin* (Edmonson 1982) presents an idealized account of the Itzá.

These characteristics have made it difficult for scholars to assess the credibility of these books for reconstructing event histories of the Late Classic and Postclassic periods. Sylvanus G. Morley (1915:199) noted that the texts

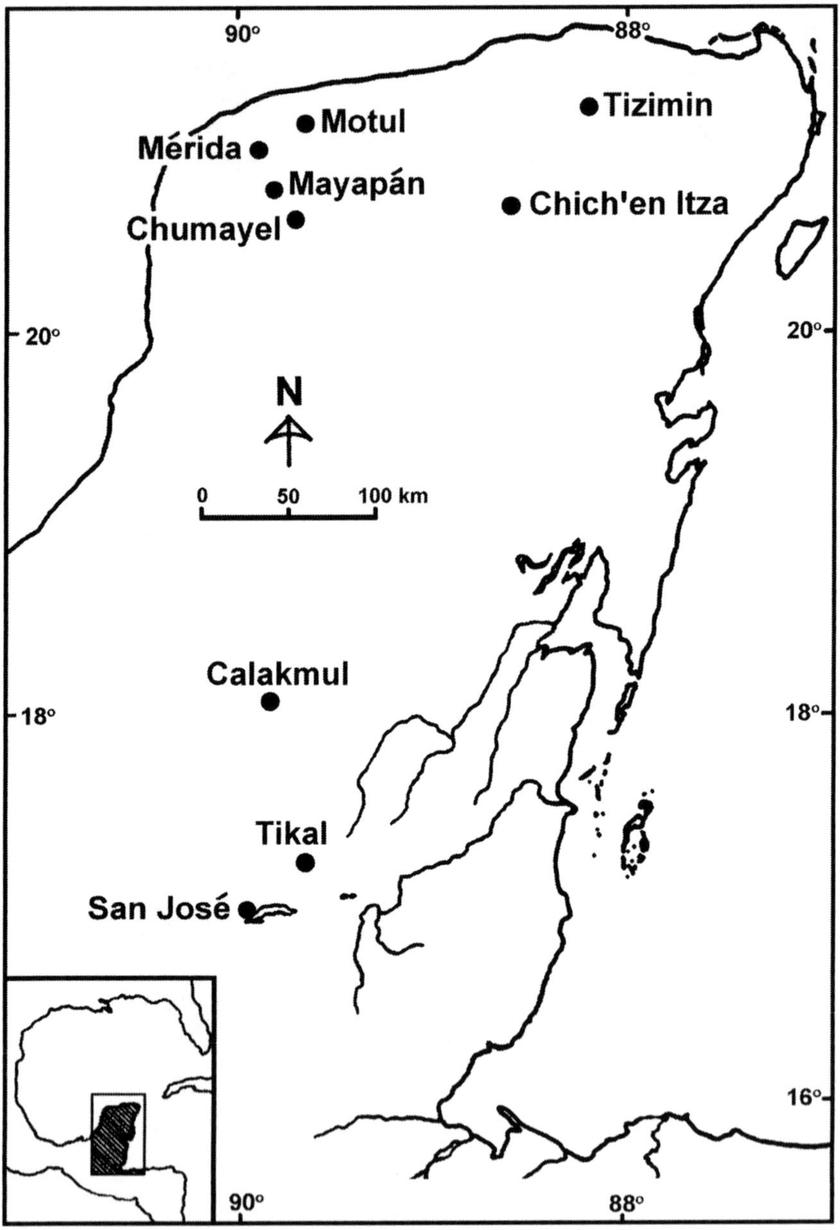

Fig. 5.1 Sites and towns mentioned in text.

"exhibit a similarity of detail which is little short of remarkable, and it is highly indicative of their reliability," concluding that there was "in fact little doubt" that the temporal cycles presented in these documents were "literal translations of Maya historical codices" (Morley and Brainerd 1956:255). Later researchers approached these documents with a healthy dose of skepticism. Munro Edmonson (1982:xvi) considered the books of the *chilam b'alams* to be "essentially mythological as they relate to the Classic period" although reasonably trustworthy from the tenth century onward. More recently, Linda Schele and others (Schele and Mathews 1998; Milbrath and Peraza Lope 2002; Rice in press) have proposed more direct interpretations relating to the Classic period.

(3) A third category of textual sources on Maya history consists of accounts and administrative records kept by Spanish officials, priests, and soldiers about their experiences during and after conquest and colonization of the lowlands. Spanish control over the Maya was established militarily, in part, but also by means of forced conversion to Catholicism, and members of the Franciscan Order left substantial records of their activities at the churches and missions they established in the peninsula.

Scholars commonly note, however, that such European documents impose their own biases on modern-day reconstructions. They report primarily what the Spaniards thought the Maya were doing, or what their Maya informants selectively chose to mention to them. European-based sociopolitical models—specifically those pertaining to a society such as existed in post-medieval Europe—were applied to the Maya, and indigenous forms of organization were misunderstood, ignored, or contorted to fit a Western mindset. Data on Maya demography and social structure, particularly after the "pacification" of Maya communities by the Spaniards, can be equally confused by the impact of European diseases, the founding of missions and forced relocation of populations (the 1552 declaration of *reducción*, or congregación), and the institutions of *encomienda* and *repartimiento.*

(4) A fourth category of textual information comes from various Maya-Spanish and Maya-English dictionaries. Some of these vocabularies were compiled in the Colonial period, most notably the late sixteenth-century Yukatekan *Diccionario de Motul* (Martínez Hernández 1929), while others date from as late as the nineteenth and twentieth centuries, such as the *Diccionario Maya Cordemex* (Barrera Vásquez et al. 1980) and the *Diccionario Español-Maya* (Solís Alcalá 1949). Most recently, the trilingual *Itzaj Maya-Spanish-English Dictionary* (Hofling and Tesucún 1998) records the language of the last speakers of Itzaj Maya in San José, Petén, Guatemala. These and other dictionaries provide insights into native categorizations of daily life. Many Colonial period words survived into modern times and some can be traced back to titles recorded in Classic period hieroglyphic

inscriptions (see Roys 1957, 1972; Marcus 1993:128–30; Restall 1997:24–9; Rice in press).

The Archaeological Role of Textual Artifacts

These textual products of the Maya past play at least two major roles in the conduct of archaeology in the Maya region—two ways in which texts are "texted" in our historical narratives of the Maya. First, the details of Maya texts can inform the recovery and interpretation of archaeological data from sites and deposits that are contemporaneous with the writings (see Kepecs and Kolb 1997). With advances in decipherment of hieroglyphic texts and increasing attention to native texts and Colonial documents in European script, Maya archaeology is moving toward "text-aided" archaeology. Often called "historical archaeology," this sub-field is a multi- and inter-disciplinary endeavor in which written and material records are evaluated, one against the other, to illuminate events and circumstances of the past (visit http://www.ncf.edu/andrews for a working bibliography of "Historical Archaeology in the Maya Area" compiled by Tony Andrews).

From the perspective of our use of the term "history" here, as an exegesis of relics of the past in the present, the unfortunate implication of the term "historical archaeology" is that history equals writing and that societies without writing are ahistorical. Such a position is untenable and more than a matter of semantics as the boundaries between the disciplines of anthropology and history continue to blur. Nonetheless, it is the case that we arrive at deeper, fuller reconstructions and explanations when we can consider Maya and Spanish descriptions of ethnographic moments, and Maya and Spanish reconstructions of and theories of history, together with more traditional artifacts of lesser voice. Space constraints do not permit us to review the numerous studies by Mayanist colleagues that are ethnohistorical in this regard, but let us offer an example of research from our own Proyecto Maya-Colonial which we believe demonstrates productive synergy between contemporaneous textual and non-textual data.

Proyecto Maya-Colonial

We have spoken and written about the structure and outcomes of Proyecto Maya-Colonial in many venues and so we will only give a brief summary here. The Proyecto is a long-term archival and archaeological investigation of the development of Postclassic (ca. A.D. 950–1525) and Early Historic (A.D. 1525–1700) period Maya society in the central part of the Department of Petén, in northern Guatemala (Rice 1981, 1986; Rice and Rice 1984, in press; Rice and Rice 1985; Rice, Rice, and Jones 1993). The project is guided by a model of Late Postclassic indigenous Maya lineage distributions

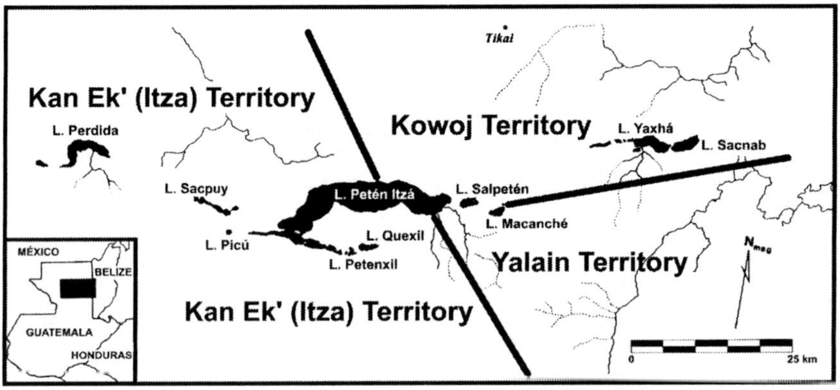

Fig. 5.2 17th century lineage territories in the Central Petén lakes region.

and political relations proposed by Grant Jones (1998), based on his analyses of sixteenth through eighteenth century Spanish documents from the Achivo General de Indias in Sevilla, Spain, and the Archivo General de Centroamérica in Guatemala City, Guatemala. With careful reading these documents yield information on the names, locations, and affiliations of towns and regional settlements, the names and titles of rulers of these places, and the political territories the Spaniards encountered around the lakes region of Petén.

Jones proposed the existence of three distinct administrative provinces, each controlled by a principal lineage or lineages from regional "capitals," centered on the Lake Petén Itzá region at the close of the seventeenth century (figure 5.2). The three territorial divisions of this social and political system were: the Kowoj province, encompassing the north shore of Lake Petén Itzá to the basins of lakes Yaxhá and Sacnab; the Yalain province, extending east from the eastern end of Lake Petén Itzá and incorporating lakes Salpetén and Macanché; and the Kan Ek' province, around the southern and western shores of Lake Petén Itzá, including the basin of Lake Sacpuy to the west (with the Kan Ek' and their allies known to the Spaniards as the Itzá).

The boundaries of these provinces shifted over time as a result of changing relations between the Kowoj, Yalain, and Itzá. By comparing Maya matronyms and patronyms from post-conquest baptismal and other records, Jones has been able to hypothesize the degree of interaction between these groups, in particular the marked isolation of the Kowoj that is consistent with other evidence for enmity between this group and the Yalain and Itzá (1998:75–81).

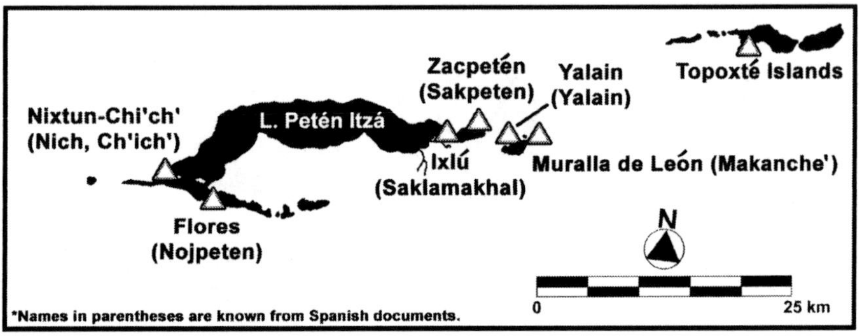

Fig. 5.3 Historic period sites investigated by Proyelto-Maya colonial.

Proyecto Maya-Colonial was designed as a comparative investigation of historically known sites in these territories. Through archaeological surveys, surface collections, and test excavations the project confirmed the presence of Postclassic and Historic period occupation at twenty-two locations in the central Petén lake basins. Once that universe was defined, we embarked on a program of extensive clearing and excavation of structures and open spaces at sites of major occupation in the three proposed lineage territories: Zacpetén at the margin of the western Kowoj and Yalain territories; Ixlú and Yalain in the Yalain territory; and Nixtun Ch'ich' in the Kan Ek' territory (figure 5.3). Fieldwork was designed to obtain data on the structure and histories of these towns, and to isolate architectural and artifactual markers of political identities in these territories. Only the work at Nixtun Ch'ich' has yet to be initiated.

At Zacpetén, the historically known site of Sakpeten, the presence of architectural "temple assemblages" suggests strong cultural and historical connections between this Petén site and the Yucatecan city of Mayapán (see figure 5.1) excavated by the Carnegie Institution of Washington in the 1950s (Proskouriakoff 1962:90–1, fig. 2). These architectural complexes are present at Tipuj in Belize, and at the Topoxté Islands (Bullard 1973; Rice 1986; Johnson 1985), Muralla de León (Rice and Rice 1981), Zacpetén (Pugh 2001a, 2002; D. Rice 1981, 1986, 1988), and Ixlú (Rice et. al. 1998). This distribution is consistent with archival data on Kowoj settlement locations (see figure 5.3).

Together with the presence of temple assemblages elsewhere in the purported Kowoj territory, these lend credence to the seventeenth century Petén Maya Kowoj lineage claim of genealogical descent from Mayapán, as documented by Jones (D. Rice 1986; D. Rice, P. Rice, and T. W. Pugh 1998; Pugh 2001a, 2001b, 2002). Temple assemblages, conspicuous caching of pairs of human skulls, and the presence of Topoxté ceramics in association with assemblage architecture give us a complex of markers by which to identify Kowoj. The incorporation of earlier components of Postclassic architecture into the Sakpeten temple assemblages is indication that the Kowoj came late to the region, as late as the fifteenth century, and encroached upon Yalain territory. The presence of a fortification at the northern end of the Zacpetén peninsula, artifacts suggesting armaments, and numerous deposits of human bone all lend credence to Spanish descriptions of endemic warfare in the region at the close of the seventeenth century, in large part prompted by the arrival of the Kowoj.

Archival accounts refer to a port town of Saklamakhal on the isthmus between lakes Petén Itzá and Salpetén, which was contested by the Yalain, Kowoj, and Itzá in the late seventeenth century. Spaniards noted it as a Yalain town, occupied briefly by the Kowoj, with the Itzá later taking control for several years following the Spanish conquest in 1697. Archaeological work at the site of Ixlú (Saklamakhal) and at what we believe to be the historically known town of Yalain in the Lake Macanché basin revealed shared architectural plans (facing "open halls" across plazas), distinctive ceramic pastes (Cecil 2001a, 2001b), and caches of human skulls in lines, all apparent indicators of the Yalain and their territory. A late temple assemblage and a small central shrine in the main plaza of Ixlú, with cached paired skulls around it, one pair overlying earlier Yalain skull lines, are intrusive constructions and interments consistent with the interval of Kowoj occupation. These data confirm archival accounts that Saklamakhal was a contested site in the late seventeenth century, occupied briefly by the Kowoj just before the Spanish conquest.

Our thus-far limited investigations in the Kan Ek' territory focused upon the site of Nixtun Ch'ich' on the Candelaria Peninsula, south of the Ensenada San Jerónimo at the western end of Lake Petén Itzá, opposite the Tayasal peninsula. Both George Cowgill (1963) and Arlen Chase (1983) had reported the presence of architecture and ceramics on the peninsula, but prior to Proyecto Maya-Colonial's surveys this large site was unmapped and unnamed. The site lies in what was the late seventeenth-century territory of Chak'an Itzá, the northern of five provinces (four directional quadrants plus the island capital of Nojpeten) of the Kan Ek', each with paired, hierarchically ranked rulers, that made up the Itzá kingdom (Jones 1998:93). Each of the surrounding provinces was also represented in one of the four residential quadrants or wards of Nojpeten and Chak'an Itzá may have been associated with the principal temple on Nojpeten (Jones 1998:99).

When Franciscan friar Andrés de Avendaño y Loyola (1987) made his second trip to Nojpeten in 1696, he traveled from Campeche through the territory of Chak'an Itzá, arriving at what he identified as the principal settlement of the province, Nich, on shore of Lake Petén Itzá, in sight of Nojpeten. Nich is also known in other sources as Ch'ich', reflecting, we believe, the location of this small "community" relative to the larger site of which it is a part (*nich* means 'flower, sprout, child [of father]' in Yukatekan Maya, suggesting an "offspring" of a larger parent settlement). Avendaño identified Nich as the principal western port of the lake and described the town as comprising ten "houses" (Jones 1998:192). Thirty Postclassic structures, including oratorio-style buildings arranged in several groups, lie east of the western-most of three ditch-wall complexes that cut the Nixtun peninsula north-south, and a number of Postclassic buildings are also built upon the surface of that fortification wall.

Spanish descriptions suggest that eastern structures at the site may constitute the village of Ch'ich', visited by Avendaño y Loyola in January of 1696, but captured and occupied by Spanish soldiers by early 1697. We believe, but cannot yet demonstrate, that General Martín de Ursúa y Arismendi camped in the highest groups of the monumental core of Nixtun-Ch'ich', overlooking the peninsula, while preparing to launch his attack on Nojpeten to the east. The presence of gunflints in three structures partially-cleared in 1996 at Nixtun-Ch'ich', and a clay pipe-stem found in surface collections elsewhere (which dates 1650–1680 on the basis of its stem bore diameter) speak to the presence of Spaniards at the site, while a pair of the ditch-wall fortifications on the peninsula correspond to Spanish details of Maya resistance during the military encampment and conquest.

Jones has documented that the Kan Ek' lineage asserted their descendants came from the Terminal Classic and Early Postclassic (A.D. 750–1200) site of Chichén Itzá in the northern Yucatán peninsula (see figure 5.1), and the lineage head of the Kan Ek' at the time of the Spanish conquest in 1697 claimed genealogical descent from that site. Consistent with this interpretation, and with recorded Itzá relations with the Chichén Itzá region, the mapped and tested architectural forms at Nixtun-Ch'ich' suggest similarities to the site of Chichén Itzá in northern Yucatán. Shared features include bench structures, formal open halls, raised shrines, and architectural sculpture. Of particular interest in such comparisons, however, are the large I-shaped ballcourt complexes found at both Chichén Itzá and Nixtun-Ch'ich'.

The Great Ballcourt at Chichén Itzá dates to the early Terminal Classic Period (Wren and Schmidt 1991). The upper and lower Temples of the Jaguar on its eastern wall are embellished with relief carvings celebrating warfare and sacrifice. The art of the upper temple depicts rites by the leaders of the Itzá and "wars of conquest that gave them the right to rule" (Schele and Mathews 1998:254), and one mural illustrates the "conquest" of a village that has been interpreted as being in Petén (Miller 1977). In the South Temple that bounds the I-shaped court, one of the piers (C4) depicts the founding lineages, including Kan Ek', the lineage name and ruler title associated with the Itzá of Guatemala's Lake Petén Itzá region (Schele and Mathews 1998:244–245, 254). A carved disk from Chichén refers to an "Aj Joltun Balam, Petén, Itzamal Ajaw," further reinforcing suggestions of relations between the Itzá and the Petén area (ibid.:354n4).

The ballcourt at Nixtun-Ch'ich' has not yet been excavated, but it is similar in size and structure to that at Chichén. This isomorphism, the shared architectural features of other building forms, and the presence at Nixtun-Ch'ich' of serpent and raptor limestone architectural adornments (Pugh 1996) common at Chichén are among cultural artifacts that supplement chronologically and substantively the textual data upon which Jones based his *The Conquest of the Last Maya Kingdom* (1998). These, as well as Spanish documentation of the community of Nixtun-Ch'ich' and its occupation by Itzá and Spaniards, are the touchstones for a different, but as yet unwritten history of the Itzá in Petén.

Classic Maya Political Organization

A second role of Maya self-reporting in texts is as metaphor or model in archaeologists' analogical reasoning. Analogical reasoning is a type of inferential argument used in many science, social science, and humanities fields, in which "one thing is inferred to be similar to another thing in a *certain respect* on the basis of the known similarity between things in *other respects*" (Webster's Encyclopedic Unabridged Dictionary of the English Language 1989:53; emphases ours). The role of analogical reasoning received a great deal of attention among American archaeologists during the 1960s through mid 1980s (e.g., Ascher 1961; Gould and Watson 1982; Wylie 1985; see also Lyman and O'Brien 2001), as processual arguments were frequently based on efforts to "read" the archaeological record through ethnographic analogy.

The various debates resulted in something called "the New Analogy" and called attention to certain criteria that distinguished appropriate from inappropriate analogies. Appropriateness could be assessed by scientific parsimony, justifiability, reliability, validity, and especially continuity. In particular, the most appropriate and credible archaeological analogies are specific rather than general, and are grounded in known cultural continuities, a process known as the "Direct-Historical Approach" (Wedel 1938). This approach confers the advantage of greater "prior probability" that a given analogy is correct because of known relationships between the past and present societies (Salmon 1982). Although analogical reasoning has sometimes been overdone—what Wobst (1978) called "the tyranny of the ethnographic record"—a direct-historical approach has been the basis for much of our Petén work, using analogies between the material and non-material culture of the early Colonial period Maya in northern Yucatán, and retrodicting it to Postclassic and Classic period occupations of the Petén lakes period.

The second author has recently completed a reconstruction of Classic period political organization based on a Direct-Historical Approach and using multiple kinds of textual evidence, including Classic period glyphic texts and iconography, the books of the *chilam b'alams*, and ethnohistoric writings (Rice in press). All support the position, which we first argued some years ago (Rice, Rice, and Jones 1993) and which was originally proposed by Munro Edmonson in 1979, that the Classic period Maya shared the same type of geo-politico-ritual organization that structured the Postclassic and Early Colonial period lowland Maya. This political organization is based on the *may*, a cycle of approximately 256 of our Gregorian years. These 256-year cycles are actually composed of thirteen *k'atuns*, the *k'atun* being a period of 20 *tuns*, or roughly 20 Gregorian years.

In this model, large Classic cities had the distinction, by analogy with Postclassic Mayapán, of seating the *may*, and as such held the title *siyaj k'an*, "born of heaven" (Edmonson 1979, 1982, 1986). In other words, what are now recognized as large regional capitals such as Tikal and Calakmul (see figure 5.1), with "overlordship" (to use Martin and Grube's term; 2000) over smaller centers, would have been seats of the *may*. The smaller centers within the territory dominated by the *may* seat/capital were ritual seats of each of its thirteen constituent *k'atuns*. During the Postclassic and Early Colonial periods, the *k'atun* seats were not only ritual centers, home of the jaguar priest or *b'alam*, but they also controlled tribute rights, land titles, and appointments to public office within the realm for the 20-year duration. Because *k'atun* seats wielded considerable political and economic power, towns competed vigorously, sometimes violently, for the privilege of seating the *k'atun*.

The importance of the regular celebration of *k'atun*-endings among the Classic Maya is best known from Late Classic Tikal. There, a series of architectural complexes, known as twin-pyramid groups, incorporated carved dated stelae-altar pairs depicting the ruler commemorating the end of the *k'atun* (Jones 1969). Similar period-ending celebrations are known at numerous sites in central Petén, and indeed throughout the Maya lowlands, beginning in the Late Preclassic (Rice in press).

But *k'atun* celebrations are only one clue to a Classic *may*-based political organization. The review of monument dates, iconography, architectural programs, and other evidence, plus a Direct Historical Approach grounded in the Postclassic Maya books of the *chilam b'alams*, reveals substantial correspondences with multiple elements of *may*-type political structure. In particular, among the early Colonial period Maya, the momentous occasion of the ending of one *may* and the beginning of another was celebrated with great ceremony. The *Book of Chilam Balam of Chumayel* (Edmonson 1986), describes these celebrations as ritually structured, historico-mythological "dramas" of multiple "acts." The ceremony of the turning of the *may* in 1539 in Mérida took place in thirteen "acts" (recall thirteen *k'atuns* in a *may*), modeled after the ceremony for ending the *k'atun*, and included the following:

1. A counterclockwise procession through the towns of the *k'atun/may* realm or around the town itself, in a symbolic ordering of space.
2. Seating: the new jaguar priest of the *k'atun/may* takes his place in the cycle seat.
3. Seating of the Yearbearers.
4. Another ceremonial procession, this time to measure the land and confirm land titles.
5. The "counting" or ranking of the mats (symbolic seats of authority) and declarations of candidacy for priesthoods, governor, and other officials.
6. Sacrifice.
7. A ceremonial feast and ritual riddling, or "interrogation," to prove rulers' legitimacy.
8. Announcement of the prophecy for the upcoming *k'atun/may* by the "speaker" of the jaguar priest.
9. Auto sacrifice (bloodletting) by the priesthood, represented on Classic stelae by bloodletting and "scattering."
10. Commemoration of the Ancestors by erection of a carved stela. This was an important Classic component that lasted into Late Postclassic times: at least thirteen sculptured stelae are known from Mayapán, and when Bishop de Landa asked the natives about them, they replied that "they were accustomed to erect one of these stones every twenty years." In Late Colonial times, a cross was erected.
11. Recitation or verification of the calendrical basis of the current place in mythic time.
12. Farce and 13. Sermon—In the Colonial Period these last included a "morality play" about various sins and a review of past history.

At least five, and possibly eight or more, acts of these ceremonies are of particular significance for retrodicting these rituals into the Classic period: the ceremonial processions; the seating of the *k'atun* and the Yearbearers; sacrifice and bloodletting; examination and feast; the prophecy for the incoming *k'atun*; and the erection of a cross, pole, or stela.

Note the splendor and range of these calendrical ceremonies, which involve several days of processions, speeches, feasting, drinking and dancing, and were carried out in some form or another for the turning of every New Year, which falls within every quarter-, half-, and full-20-year *k'atun* completion, which fall within every 52-year Calendar Round completion, within every 256-year *may* completion, and within every 400-year *bak'tun* completion. All told, they give new credence to the idea of the Classic Maya as a "theater-state."

The Future of Texted Past in Maya Studies

As we ponder the future of text-aided research in Maya studies, it is legitimate to consider whether or not Mayanists are poised to uncover new textual artifacts. Few would say no. So much of the Maya lowlands is unexplored and unmapped, and such a small percentage of sites has been investigated, and those on a cursory level, that the likelihood of finding texts on new Classic period architecture and monuments is high, if only archaeologists can get to them before looters do. We are somewhat less sanguine about the promise of recovering unknown texts on more perishable materials, such as codices and records from the Spanish era. Certainly there are likely to be documents in archives, libraries, museums, and in private hands that scholars are not aware exist. It is more likely still, however, that there are known documentary materials whose value to Maya studies has not yet been realized because the right questions have not been asked of them. For us, the future of text-aided research lies in part in such discoveries.

We have implied, but not yet stated, that the majority of textual artifacts that inform our archaeological practices and reasoning are themselves historical narratives and, like all histories, are not unbiased records of reality; all histories are written with a purpose and can be consciously manipulated. As we *did* state in our opening comments, these artifacts bind the past to the present in that they speak of people or events past for a specific end in the present of their creation, and we in turn bind those pasts to our own purposes, our own narratives, in our own present. "Relics of what happened in the past are cultural artifacts of the moments that produce them, but they also become cultural artifacts of all the moments that give them permanence" (Dening 1996:43). When dealing with Maya and/or Spanish texts as cultural artifacts, regardless of period, the "double entendre of history," of which we spoke, becomes more complex still. The textual threads comprise a spiraling helix, history and archaeology, pasts and presents.

Grant Jones's monumental effort to research and write *The Conquest of the Last Maya Kingdom* (1998), against which we play our own archaeological data, has demonstrated to us that histories, like cultures, require ethnographic descriptions of their forms, structures, and functions on multiple levels. The future of text-aided research in Maya studies is not simply the recovery and use of written histories, it is in pursuing an anthropology of history. It is in this process of ethnohistory, of attempting to understand the conceptions of the past by both the native and the foreigner, in parsing out the details of the helix, where we believe the real excitement of text-aided archaeological research lies.

Ultimately, what we as archaeologists seek are combinations of descriptive and chronological data that when interpreted from a particular theoretical perspectives fit into satisfyingly conclusive—or at least minimally plausible—narratives of the events and processes of change in prehistory. We strive to write "academic" or "scientific" histories, "accurate" event histories, distanced from contemporary cultural and political biases. Being accurate can be an elusive goal, however. We approach interpretation of cultural artifacts influenced by our own implicit or explicit theories of the past, as well as current debates and motivations. That histories are factual pasts is a myth upon which many academic oxen have been gored (cf. Dening 1992, 1996; Windschuttle 1999, 2003) and we must always keep this in mind in our reading and writing of histories.

Rather, our realities are built from textual and material artifacts, tempered by our understandings of historical consciousness, our presuppositions, and the questions we bring to inquiry. That these understandings change over time is responsible for the revisions of narratives and the intellectual arguments that mark the history of Mayanist archaeology. We expect no less in the future. As romantic positivists we will all continue to rise to the challenge of making "history news" with an "exposure" or a "revelation" that creates fleeting notoriety, funds our projects, and fills the pages of those everduring *National Geographic* magazines.

References

Ascher, R. M. (1961) "Analogy in Archaeological Interpretation," *Southwestern Journal of Anthropology* 17: 317–25.

Avendaño y Loyola, Fray A. de (1987) *Relation of Two Trips to Petén: Made for the Conversion of the Heathen Ytzaex and Cehaches*, F. E. Comparato (ed.), C. P. Bowditch, and G. Rivers (trans.), Culver City: Labyrinthos.

Barrera Vásquez, A., et al. (1980) *Diccionario Maya Cordemex: Maya-Español, Español Maya*, Merida: Ediciones Cordemex.

Boone, E. H. (1992) "Pictorial Codices of Ancient Mexico," in R. Townsend (ed.), *The Ancient Americas: Art from Sacred Landscapes*, pp. 197–209, Chicago: University of Chicago Press.

Bullard, W. R. (1973) "Postclassic Culture in Central Petén and Adjacent British Honduras," in T. P. Culbert (ed.), *The Classic Maya Collapse*, pp. 221–41, Albuquerque: University of New Mexico Press.

Cecil, L. G. (2001a) *Technological Styles of Late Postclassic Slipped Pottery from the Central Petén Lakes Region, El Petén, Guatemala*, unpublished Ph.D. dissertation, Department of Anthropology, Southern Illinois University, Carbondale.

———(2001b) "Developing Technological Styles of Petén Postclassic Slipped Pottery with Regard to Clay Mineralogy," in I. Druc (ed.), *Archaeology and Clays*, pp. 107–21, International Series 942, Oxford: BAR.

Chase, A. F. (1983) *A Contextual Consideration of the Tayasal-Paxcaman Zone, El Petén, Guatemala*, unpublished Ph.D. dissertation, Department of Anthropology, University of Pennsylvania, Philadelphia.

Chase, D. Z. (1992) "Postclassic Maya Elites: Ethnohistory and Archaeology," in D. Z. Chase and A. F. Chase (eds.), *Mesoamerican Elites, an Archaeological Assessment*, pp. 118–34, Norman: University of Oklahoma Press.

Coe, M. D. (1978) *Lords of the Underworld*, Princeton: Princeton University Press.

———(1992) *Breaking the Maya Code*, New York: Thames and Hudson.

———(1989) "The Hero Twins: Myth and Image," in J. Kerr (ed.), *The Maya Vase Book*, Vol. 1, pp. 161–84, New York: Kerr Associates.

———(1992) *Breaking the Maya Code*, New York: Thames and Hudson.

Cohn, B. S. (1980) "History and Anthropology: The State of Play," *Comparative Studies in Society and History* 22:198–221.

Cowgill, G. L. (1963) *Postclassic Period Culture in the Vicinity of Flores, Petén, Guatemala*, unpublished Ph.D. dissertation, Department of Anthropology, Harvard University, Cambridge.

Dening, G. (1991) "A Poetic for Histories: Transformations that Present the Past," in Aletta Biersack (ed.), *Clio in Oceania*, pp. 347–80, Washington, DC: Smithsonian Institution Press.

———(1992) *Mr. Bligh's Bad Language: Passion, Power, and Theatre on the Bounty*. Cambridge: Cambridge University Press.

———(1996) *Performances*, Chicago: University of Chicago Press.

Edmonson, M. S. (1979) "Some Postclassic Questions about the Classic Maya," in M. G. Robertson and D. C. Jeffers (eds.), *Tercera Mesa Redonda de Palenque*, Vol. IV, pp. 9–18, Palenque, Chiapas, Mexico: Pre-Columbian Art Research Center. {Reprinted in J. A. Graham (ed.), *Ancient Meosamerica, Selected Readings* [2nd ed., 1981], pp. 221–8, Palo Alto, CA: Peek Publications.}

———(1982) *The Ancient Future of the Itzá: The Book of the Chilam Balam of Tizimin*, Austin: University of Texas Press.

———(1986) *Heaven Born Merida and Its Destiny: The Book of Chilam Balam of Chumayel*, Austin: University of Texas Press.

Farriss, N. M. (1987) "Remembering the Future, Anticipating the Past: History, Time, and Cosmology among the Maya of Yucatán," *Comparative Studies in Society and History* 29: 66–93.

Gould, R. A., and Watson P. J. (1982) "A Dialogue on the meaning and use of analogy in 5 ethno archaeological reasoning," *Journal of Anthropological Archaeology* 1(4): 355–81.

Grube, N. (1991) "An Investigation of the Primary Standard Sequence on Classic Maya Ceramics," in M. G. Robertson (ed.), *Sixth Palenque Round Table, 1986*, pp. 223–32, Norman: University of Oklahoma Press.

Hammond, N. (1991) "Introduction," in T. P. Culbert (ed.), *Classic Maya Political History. Hieroglyphic and Archaeological Evidence*, pp. 1–18, Cambridge, UK: Cambridge University Press and School of American Research.

Hanson, C. A. (1995) "The Hispanic Horizon in Yucatán: A Model of Franciscan Missionization," *Ancient Mesoamerica* 6: 15–28.

Hofling, C. A., and Tesucún, F. (1998) *Itzaj Maya-Spanish-English Dictionary*, Salt Lake City: University of Utah Press.

Houston, S. D. (2000) "Into the Minds of Ancients: Advances in Maya Glyph Studies," *Journal of World Prehistory* 14(2): 121–201.

Houston, S. D., Robertson, J., and Stuart, D. (2000) "The Language of Classic Maya Inscriptions," *Current Anthropology* 41(3): 321–56.

Houston, S. D., Chinchilla, O., and Stuart, D. (eds.) (2001) *The Decipherment of Ancient Maya Writing*, Norman: University of Oklahoma Press.

Johnson, J. K. (1985) "Postclassic Maya Site Structure at Topoxte, El Petén, Guatemala," in A. Chase and P. Rice (eds.), *Lowland Maya Postclassic*, pp. 151–65, Austin: University of Texas Press.

Jones, C. (1969) *The Twin-Pyramid Group Pattern: A Classic Maya Architectural Assemblage at Tikal, Guatemala*. Unpublished Doctoral Dissertation, University of Pennsylvania, Philadelphia.

Jones, G. D. (1998) *The Conquest of the Last Maya Kingdom*, Stanford: Stanford University Press.

Justeson, J. S. (1989) "Ancient Maya Ethnoastronomy: An Overview of Hieroglyphic Sources," in A. Aveni (ed.), *World Archaeoastronomy*, pp. 76–129, Cambridge, UK: Cambridge University Press.

Kepecs, S., and Kolb, M. J. (eds.) (1997) "Special Issue: New Approaches to Combining the Archaeological and Historical Records," *Journal of Archaeological Method and Theory* 4(3/4).

Kerr, J. (1992) "The Myth of the Popol Vuh as an Instrument of Power," in E. C. Danien and R. J. Sharer (eds.), *New Theories on the Ancient Maya*, pp. 109–21, Symposium Series, Vol. 3, Philadelphia: The University Museum, University of Pennsylvania.

Lyman, R. L., and O' Brien, M. J. (2001) "The Direct Historical Approach, Analogical Reasoning, and Theory in Americanist Archaeology," *Journal of Archaeological Method and Theory* 8(4): 303–42.

Marcus, J. (1993) "Ancient Maya Political Organization," in J. A. Sabloff and J. S. Henderson (eds.), *Lowland Maya Civilization in the Eighth Century* A.D., pp. 111–83, Washington, DC: Dumbarton Oaks.

Martin, S., and Grube, N. (2000) *Chronicle of the Maya Kings and Queens. Deciphering the Dynasties of the Ancient Maya*, London: Thames and Hudson.

Martínez Hernández, A. (1929 [1585]) *Diccionario de Motul: Maya-Español*, Merida: Talleres de la Compañaí Tipográfica Yucateca.

Milbrath, S., and Peraza Lope, C. (2002) "Revisiting Mayapan, Mexico's Last Maya Capital," *Ancient Mesoamerica* 13: 21–48.

Miller, A. G. (1977) "Captains of the Itzá: Unpublished Mural Evidence from Chichén Itzá," in N. Hammond (ed.), *Social Process in Maya Prehistory: Studies in Honour of Sir Eric Thompson*, pp. 197–225, London: Academic Press.

Morley, S. G. (1915) *An Introduction to the Study of the Maya Hieroglyphs*, Bureau of American Ethnology, Bulletin 57, Washington, DC: Smithsonian Institution.

———(1917) "The Historical Value of the Books of Chilam Balam," *Journal of the Archaeological Institute of America* XV(2): 195–214.

Morley, S. G., and Brainerd, G. W. (1956) *The Ancient Maya* (3rd ed.), Stanford, CA: Stanford University Press.

Perry, R., and Perry, R. (1988) *Maya Missions, Exploring the Spanish Colonial Churches of Yucatán*, Santa Barbara, CA: Espadana Press.

Proskouriakoff, T. (1962) "Civic and Religious Structures of Mayapan," in H. E. D. Pollock, R. L. Roys, T. Proskouriakoff, and A. L. Smith (eds.), *Mayapan, Yucatán, Mexico*, Publication 619, pp. 87–163, Washington, DC: Carnegie Institution of Washington.

Pugh, T. W.(1996) "Excavaciones en estructura 188," in D. Rice, P. Rice, R. Sanchez, and G. Jones (eds.), *1996 Proyecto Política del Siglo XVII en el Centro del Peten: Informe Preliminar*, pp. 206–224, Guatemala City: DEMOPRE.

Pugh, Timothy W. (2001a) *Architecture, Ritual, and Social Identity at Late Postclassic Zacpetén, Petén, Guatemala: Identification of the Kowoj*, unpublished Ph.D. dissertation, Department of Anthropology, Southern Illinois University, Carbondale.

———(2001b) "Flood Reptiles, Serpent Temples, and the Quadripartite Universe: The *imago mundi* of Late Postclassic Mayapán," *Ancient Mesoamerica* 12: 247–58.

———(2002) "Remembering Mayapán: Kowoj Domestic Architecture as Social Metaphor and Power," in M. O'Donovan (ed.), *The Dynamics of Power*, Center for Archaeological Investigations Occasional Paper no. 30, pp. 301–23, Carbondale: Southern Illinois University.

Reents-Budet, D. (1994) *Painting the Maya Universe: Royal Ceramics of the Classic Period*, Durham, NC: Duke University Press.

Relaciones de Yucatán (1898–1900) Incluidas en la colección de documentos inéditos relativos al descubrimiento, conquista y organización de las antiguas posesiones españoles de ultramar, 2nd series, Vols. 11 and 13, Madrid.

Restall, M. (1997) *The Maya World: Yucatec Culture and Society, 1550–1850*, Stanford, CA: Stanford University Press.

Rice, D. S. (1981) "Zacpetén: A Postclassic Center in the Central Petén, Guatemala," paper presented at the 46th Annual Meeting of the Society for American Archaeology, San Diego, CA.

———(1986) "The Petén Postclassic: A Settlement Perspective," in J. A. Sabloff and E. W. Andrews, V. (eds.), *Late Lowland Maya Civilization: Classic to Postclassic*, pp. 301–44, Albuquerque: University of New Mexico Press.

Rice, D. S. (1988) "Classic to Postclassic Maya Household Transitions in the Central Petén, Guatemala," in R. Wilk and W. Ashmore (eds.), *Household and Community in the Mesoamerican Past*, pp. 227–48, Albuquerque: University of New Mexico Press.

Rice, D. S. and Rice, P. M. (1981) "Muralla de Léon: A Lowland Maya Fortification," *Journal of Field Archaeology* 8(3): 271–88.
Rice, D. S. and Rice, P. M. (1984) "Collapse to Contact: Postclassic Archaeology of the Petén Maya," *Archaeology* 36: 45–51.
———(in press) "Seventeenth-century Maya Political Geography and Resistance in Central Petén, Guatemala," in R. Alexander and S. Kepecs (eds.), *The Postclassic- to Spanish-Era Transition in Mesoamerica: Archaeological Perspectives*, Albuquerque: University of New Mexico Press.
Rice, D. S., Rice, P. M., and Jones, G. D. (1993) "Geografía política del Petén central, Guatemala, en el siglo XVII: la arqueología de las capitales mayas," *Mesoamérica* 14(26): 281–318.
Rice, D. S., Rice, P. M., and Pugh, T. W. (1998) "Settlement Continuity and Change in the central Petén Lakes Region: The Case of Zacpetén," in A. Ciudad Ruiz, et al. (ed.), *Anatomía de una civilización: Aproximaciones interdisciplinarias a la cultura maya*, Publication 4, pp. 208–52, Madrid: Sociedad Española de Estudios Mayas.
Rice, P. M. (in press) *Maya Political Science: The Political Organization of the Lowland Maya*, Austin: University of Texas Press.
Rice, P. M., and Rice, D. S. (1985) "Topoxte, Macanche, and the Central Petén Postclassic," in A. Chase and P. M. Rice (eds.), *The Lowland Maya Postclassic: Questions and Answers*, pp. 186–203, Austin: University of Texas Press.
Roys, R. L. (1957) *The Political Geography of the Yucatán Maya*, Publication 613, Washington, DC: Carnegie Institution of Washington.
———(1967 [1933]) *The Book of Chilam Balam of Chumayel*, Norman: University of Oklahoma Press.
———(1972 [1943]) *The Indian Background of Colonial Yucatán*, Norman: University of Oklahoma Press.
Salmon, M. H. (1982) *Philosophy and Archaeology*, New York: Academic Press.
Schele, L., and Mathews, P. (1998) *The Code of Kings: The Language of Seven Sacred Maya Temples and Tombs*, New York: Scribners.
Scholes, F. V., and Roys, R. L. (1968) *The Maya Chontal Indians of Acalan-Tixchel: A Contribution to the History and Ethnography of the Yucatán Peninsula* (2nd ed.), Norman: University of Oklahoma Press.
Smith, V. G. (1984) "Izapa Relief Carving. Form, Content, Rules for Design, and Role in Mesoamerican Art History and Archaeology," in *Studies in Pre-Columbian Art and Archaeology*, no. 27, Washington, DC: Dumbarton Oaks.
Solís Alcalá, E. (1949) *Diccionario Español-Maya*, Merida.
Stuart, D. (1996) "Kings of Stone: A Consideration of Stelae in Ancient Maya Ritual and Representations," *RES* 29/30: 148–71.
Tedlock, D. (1985) *Popol Vuh. The Definitive Edition of the Mayan Book of the Dawn of Life and the Glories of Gods and Kings*, New York: Simon & Schuster.
———(1992) "The Popol Vuh as a Hieroglyphic Book," in E. Danien and R. J. Sharer (eds.), *New Theories on the Ancient Maya*, pp. 229–40, Symposium Series, Vol. 3, Monograph 77, Philadelphia: University Museum, University of Pennsylvania.
Thompson, J. E. S. (1972) "A Commentary on the Dresden Codex, a Maya Hieroglyphic Book," *Memoirs of the American Philosophical Society*, no. 93, Philadelphia.
Tozzer, A. M. (ed.) (1941) *Landa's Relación de las cosas de Yucatán. A Translation*, Papers of the Peabody Museum of Archaeology and Ethnology, no. 28, Cambridge, MA: Harvard University.
Vogt, E. Z. (1969) *Zinacantan: A Maya Community in the Highlands of Chiapas*, Cambridge, MA: Belknap Press of Harvard University Press.
Webster's Encyclopedic Unabridged Dictionary of the English Language (1989) New York: Gramercy Books.
Wedel, W. (1938) "The Direct-Historical Approach in Pawnee Archaeology," *Smithsonian Miscellaneous Collections*, Vol. 97, no. 7, Washington, DC: Smithsonian Institution Press.
Windschuttle, K. (1999) "A Critical Survey of the Recent Literature on Postmodernism in History," Paper present to the conference on *Turning Points in Historical Thinking: A Comparative Perspective*, Student University of New York, Buffalo, August 21, 1999. [http://www.sydneyline.com/Critical%20Survery%20Postmodernism.htm].
———(2003) "The State of the Discipline of History," *Capitalism Magazine*, February 5, 2003. [http://capmag.com/article.asp?ID=2375]. An excerpt from the Afterword of the second

edition of *The Killing of History: How Literary Critics and Social Theorists are Murdering Our Past*, 1997, Fress Press, New York; paper back edition, 2000, Encounter Books, San Francisco.

Wobst, H. M. (1978) "The Archaeo-Ethnology of Hunter-gatherers or the Tyranny of the Ethnographic Record in Archaeology," *American Antiquity* 43(2): 303–309.

Wren, L. H., and Schmidt, P. (1991) "Elite Interaction during the Terminal Classic Period: New Evidence from Chichén Itzá," in T. P. Culbert (ed.), *Classic Maya Political History: Hieroglyphic and Archaeological Evidence*, pp. 199–225. Cambridge, UK: Cambridge University Press and School of American Research.

Wylie, A. (1985) "Between Philosophy and Archaeology," *American Antiquity* 50(2): 478–90.

6
Ancient Maya Landscapes

WENDY ASHMORE

> The beauty of the sculpture, the solemn stillness of the woods, disturbed only by the scrambling of monkeys and the chattering of parrots, the desolation of the city, and the mystery that hung over it, all created an interest higher, if possible, than I had ever felt among the ruins of the Old World. (Stephens 1969 [1841]:119–20)

As the brief epigram suggests, the captivating words of John Lloyd Stephens distilled a sense of landscape at the city of Copan and at other Maya locales for fascinated Euro-American readers more than 150 years ago. So did marvelous drawings and paintings by his traveling companion, Frederick Catherwood. These and other evocative renderings, before and since, yield an enduringly dramatic frame within which outsiders think about ruined Maya cities and their ancient occupants.

In counterpoint, archaeologists writing a century later approached Maya landscapes more systematically, as *environments*, via theory and methods of scientific inquiry dominating archaeology in this country. As fundamentally informative as ecological analyses continue to be, they are increasingly complemented by inferences of social and symbolic meanings in landscapes, among the Maya and other peoples. More and more often, theoretical and operational definitions emphasize landscapes as socially constituted and inscribed with social meaning. In this regard, Maya studies mirror wider trends, in archaeology, interpretive models, and underlying social theory.

Because theoretical definitions of landscape have received lengthy consideration in numerous contexts (e.g., Anschuetz et al. 2001; Hirsch and O'Hanlon 1995; Knapp and Ashmore 1999), I treat them here only in passing. Focus instead goes to the state of Maya landscape studies by the close of the twentieth century, and then to three emergent shifts in operational definitions. That is, the goal of the chapter is to examine how analysts now approach Maya landscapes, as articulation between individual, society, and the world. The pertinent shifts are (1) expanding the physical extent of what comprises landscapes, (2) blurring boundaries between "natural" and "built" landscapes, and (3) recognizing more deeply the roles of time and human activity in constituting landscapes.

Archaeologies of Landscape

Denis Cosgrove (1998 [1984]:1) characterizes the "idea of landscape" as

> a way of seeing that has its own history, but a history that can be understood only as part of a wider history of economy and society [since the Renaissance].... The landscape idea emerged as a dimension of European elite [i.e., landowner] consciousness at an identifiable period in the evolution of European societies: it was refined and elaborated over a long period during which it expressed and supported a range of political, social, and moral assumptions and became accepted as a significant aspect of taste.

Succinctly put, *landscape* was a word "originally coined in the emergent capitalist world of western Europe by aesthetes, antiquarians and landed gentry—all men" (Bender 1993:1–2). For most Euro-Americans of Stephens's time, however, landscape was not recognized consciously as a social construct; rather, the term held strong, somewhat romantic implications for designating simply *nature*, "untainted by human presence" (Spirn 1996:111). Even overtly modified expanses were quickly renaturalized in popular thought, as illustrated dramatically in perceptions of Yosemite and other places, shortly after U.S. landscape architect Frederick Law Olmsted had actively reshaped them for greater public health and enjoyment. After World War I, Carl Sauer (1925) formally distinguished "cultural" landscapes from "natural" ones. Still, the notion of landscapes as pristine nature, unsullied environment, remains frequent in the United States, among scholars as well as the Euro-American public, in part a continuing legacy of Enlightenment thought (Kirch 2000:315).

By the mid-twentieth century, archaeologists in the United States viewed landscapes principally through currents of theory and method relating humans to their ambient environment, especially Julian Steward's cultural ecological studies and Gordon Willey's settlement pattern research. Indeed, these two bodies of work are commonly cited as major sources shaping American archaeology as a whole (e.g., Billman 1999; Sabloff and Ashmore 2001). Both were significant foundations for positivist, processualist ideas in the "New Archaeology," which broadly paralleled coeval thinking in the "New Geography." From a research vantage in both disciplines, landscapes and other kinds of space were objects to be measured and compared, analyzed and interpreted via powerful statistical models in which the land remained a neutral and passive object, occupied and used by people but otherwise relatively detached from them.

In studying landscapes, archaeologists based in the United States have tended to invoke theory from economic geography, ecology, and anthropology, to examine general principles in the social and economic dimensions of land use (e.g., central place theory, optimal foraging theory). As variant and partial contrast, historical ecology relates changes and constancies in landscape form to histories of human decision making, of historically contingent strategies for relating to the land (e.g., Crumley 1994). Location and distribution of material resources figure importantly in all the foregoing, if with growing attention now as well to monuments and rock art or other symbolic markings, and to landscapes materializing ideology or meaning. Those who explore the latter rely on social theory with a more explicitly humanistic cast, frequently drawing attention to etymology of the term landscape, from Dutch *landschap*, designating a seventeenth-century genre of scenic painting commissioned by wealthy landowners. Although U.S.-based archaeologists focus on strands of social theory different from (if overlapping) those invoked in landscape studies elsewhere, widening exploration is evident, in perspectives such as practice theory, structuration, and Marxist thought (for fuller reviews, see Anschuetz et al. 2001; Ashmore 2003; Fisher and Thurston 1999).

Today, in short, definitions of and approaches to studying landscape vary most notably in the degree to which they implicate human presence and involvement, in the ways human involvement can be understood from landscape traces, and by extension, in identifying the traces most pertinent for study. For some, landscape remains approximately equivalent to environment; as such, landscape may also retain some notion of pristine nature, conceptually remaining relatively detached from humankind. For other analysts, however, and I believe these are in the majority, landscape exists *only* through human involvement. Landscapes are "taskscapes," places of meaning, and complex palimpsests of human interaction with the land. In the sections that follow, I accept the general theoretical position that landscapes presuppose some degree of human involvement, and advocate changes in those operational aspects of definitions that actively shape thinking about and conducting research concerning landscapes, specifically those of the ancient Maya world.

Late Twentieth-Century Perspectives on Ancient Maya Landscapes

Turning to the study of ancient Maya landscapes, one can certainly discern the shaping force of the broad tendencies just described. Additionally critical since the late 1980s has been the emergence of a *conjunctive approach* to studying the Maya past (e.g., Fash and Sharer 1991; Stone 2002b:7, 10). The latter is explicitly interdisciplinary and encourages conjoining multiple theoretical and methodological perspectives, especially those of archaeology, iconography, and epigraphy, while drawing critically as well from ethnography and ethnohistory. The result highlights a still maturing rapprochement between scientific approaches that had dominated anthropological archaeology, and humanistic studies associated more closely with art history, literature, and history (Diehl 1984). This rapprochement, in fact, marks a return to the importance attached to humanistic perspectives in Maya studies in the late nineteenth and early twentieth centuries (e.g., Stone 2002b:11). At the same time, analysis and interpretation recognize more explicitly the impact of interactions between the Maya and neighboring societies, over the documented span of human presence (e.g., Carrasco, Jones, and Sessions 2000).

To illustrate economic themes, by the end of the last century, cultural ecology had become well established for yielding critical insights into landscape as environment, principally its resources and risks. Perceived resource deficiencies of the Maya lowlands instigated multiple, long-standing debates, especially about the role of environment in the rise and "collapse" of Classic society (e.g., Sabloff 1973; Sanders 1977). For characterizing ancient Maya use of environment and resources, seemingly unassailable models of ancient swidden farmers eventually gave way to evidence supporting other, more complex models recognizing peasants with a mosaic of quite diverse strategies for food procurement and production (e.g., Fedick 1996). David Webster (2002) situates these strategies within a framework of historical ecology, toward a discussion of factors contributing to the Classic collapse. Not only do Maya (or any) landscapes provide sustenance, of course: They also encompass the abrupt violence of hurricanes, volcanic eruptions, floods, and earthquakes, as well as the quieter perils of drought (e.g., Gunn and Folan 2000; Sheets 2002). Moreover, the same environmental traits may incorporate both hazard and benefit, as when long-term soil productivity succeeds initially destructive volcanism, or when the patchiness of resources stimulates exchange, alliance, or conquest (Rice 1993).

Since the 1970s, new interests in ancient Maya landscapes, and those of neighboring societies, have emerged from two principal sources, and from their synergistic convergence. One is the study of ancient astronomy, and the relation of celestial bodies and their movements to human activities and places on earth. The other is the revolutionary set of advances in text decipherment and iconographic study. Readings for Maya words and images about their world have come to light at an exhilarating pace, if also sometimes a dizzying one. Maya geography and the names of its constituent places and creatures are newly available for comprehending society, world view, politics, and—encompassing it all—landscape. Interpretive models drawn from linguistic (especially semiotic and discourse) and performance theories inform inferences about how landscapes and other kinds of space were conceptualized and infused with social life (e.g., Reese-Taylor and Koontz 2001).

Whatever the variables under study, a consideration of Maya landscapes relates intimately to studies elsewhere in Native America, especially here to understanding landscapes of ancient Olmec, Zapotec, and Aztec societies (e.g., Carrasco 1991). In a conference held at Dumbarton Oaks, now classic interpretations of varied Mesoamerican sites and landscapes were expressed in terms of world views (Benson 1981). Then and since, Anthony Aveni (1980), Johanna Broda (1982), Davíd Carrasco (1991), John Carlson (1981), and others have identified with increasing detail relations between astronomy, ritual, world view, and landscapes of the Maya, and other societies in Mesoamerica.

Linda Schele, her colleagues, and students have dramatically transformed views about landscapes of the Maya and their neighbors, especially highlighting inferences that the celestial and terrestrial landscapes map the story of creation (e.g., Freidel et al. 1993; Koontz et al. 2001; Schele and Mathews 1998; Stone 2002a), as do landscapes of many non-Western societies of the world (e.g., Richards 1999; Sofaer et al. 1989; Taçon 1999). More generally, conjunctive approaches to Maya landscapes continue to merge iconographic and epigraphic study with archaeological research. A central theme in many of these studies is landscapes' shaping of the social and political order, particularly the legitimization of royal authority (e.g., Ashmore 1991; Brady and Ashmore 1999; Looper 1995; Reese-Taylor 2002; Ringle 1999; Wren et al. 2001).

Ancient Maya Landscape in the New Millennium

As indicated earlier, I perceive three key changes emerging in operational definitions of Maya landscape: (1) expanding the physical extent of what comprises landscapes, (2) blurring boundaries between "natural" and "built" landscapes, and (3) recognizing more deeply the roles of time and human activity in constituting landscapes. All three shifts arise from combinations of factors cited earlier, both from within Maya studies and from broader theoretical trends in landscape inquiry. I advocate continued, explicit expansion of all three as a means of reaching a fuller understanding of Maya landscapes and society.

Physical Extent

Whereas mountains, plains, and water sources are certainly fundamental physical elements of which a landscape is made, it is now equally clear that Maya landscapes are incomplete without including the sky—especially the night sky—and the watery underworld. Until recently analysts have tended to look only at the middle world, the earth's surface, the most conventional and accessible of the set. Anthony Aveni, Linda Schele, David Freidel, and others have made it clear that positions of the stars and planets forecast the fate of Maya wars, alliances, and other strategic events, in addition to the aforementioned mapping of the story of creation (Aveni 1992, 2002; Freidel et al. 1993). Building from these bases, Kathryn Reese-Taylor (2002) argues further that landscapes of civic precincts were then laid out to map that creation on the ground, such that processions among public spaces recreated the acts of creation commemorated in specific buildings (compare Ringle 1999). Moreover, with respect to such public activities, the observation that texts recognize the evening appearance of Venus more frequently than the morning appearance hints at a quite specific conscious choice favoring a more "impressive cosmic backdrop to grace the ritual stage" (Aveni 2002:17). In addition, the hierophanies of changing light offered celestial punctuation, accentuating messages rendered more continuously in stone and stucco, in buildings and sculpture, as with the dying winter sun's descent into the Temple of Inscriptions and Pakal's tomb at Palenque (Schele 1977), or the summer's solstice sunrise prolonged illumination of a statue of Bird Jaguar III in Structure 33, Yaxchilan (Tate 1985:99–100), or the equinox sunset emergence of a shadowy serpent along the north stair of Chichén Itzá's Castillo (Schele and Kappelman 2001:43–4).

Below the earth, too, Maya landscape extends seamlessly from its more mundane components into a supernatural realm; in this direction, the transition is effected through caves and other cavities penetrating the earth. For the Maya and many other peoples, the earth's surface is a cayman afloat in a primordial sea. Ample evidence of such an arrangement is identified from subterranean waters within caves, as well as in the visible links between earth and water at *cenotes*, lakeshores, and coastlines. The ancient Maya, like their descendants today, do homage to the earth lord through rituals enacted in cave interiors (e.g., Bassie-Sweet 1996; Brady and Ashmore 1999; Stone 1995). Where no natural caverns exist, the imperative remains, and frequently the Maya create surrogates, as tunnels or lagoons (e.g., Brady and Veni 1992). Prehispanic tunnels are documented in such places as the highland Quiché capital of Gumaarcaj (Utatlán; Brady 1991) and exist in oral tradition for places as mutually distant as Xunantunich, Quirigua, and Copan. Like the sky, then, the subterranean world is integral to Maya landscapes.

Blurred Boundaries

The second change noted is the merging of natural landscape and constructed worlds (e.g., Bradley 1993; Richards 1996; Tuan 1977). Architecture and monuments are commonly treated as metaphors for the natural world. For example, a Classic Maya plaza set with portrait stelae is a "forest of kings" (e.g., Schele and Freidel 1990), a funerary temple with its internal tomb stands metaphorically as mountain and sacred cave, and a ballcourt embodies death, rebirth, and connections to the underworld (e.g., Gillespie 1991). What we recognize less often is the reciprocal transformation of expressive metaphor back into natural feature. In fact, the question remains as to whether the Maya or their neighbors would make such a categorical status distinction at all. At non-Maya Cholula, for example, the Great Pyramid was known as the "manmade mountain" (*Tlachihualtepetl*) at the time of the Spanish Conquest; a potent symbolic and visual focus of the Cholultec landscape, it inspired local contention that "if anyone attacked the holy city, the pyramid would burst open, and flood waters would wash away the attackers" (McCafferty 2001:307). After some 2,500 years of sequential construction and modification, the Cholula pyramid and the spring above which it rose were recognized simultaneously as central to what we call "natural" and "built" landscapes.

For Maya and other Mesoamerican societies, both natural and built landscapes provide key and mutually equivalent routes between the middle world and the upper and under-worlds. As caves and other cavities lead into the watery underworld, so mountains lead toward the sky (e.g., Gillespie 1993). Each thereby also constitutes an *axis mundi*, whose location centers a place in the world (Brady and Ashmore 1999; Eliade 1959). The Maya labeled constructed plazas glyphically as places of water, out of which built mountains arose (e.g., Looper 1995; Schele and Mathews 1998). Schele and Kappelman (2001) assert that bodies of water adjoining an identifiable "Snake Mountain" (*Coatepec* or *Coatepetl*, sometimes paired or merged with a "Sustenance Mountain") were essential ingredients for establishing any Mesoamerican civic center in antiquity, including those of the Maya (see also Brady and Ashmore 1999). Together, water and mountain provided a spatial framework identifying each place specifically as Tollan, the mythic "place of reeds," and thereby bestowing localized divine sanction for rulership and acts of warfare and sacrifice. Building and rebuilding the key features necessary to ground and center the place often acknowledged tacitly the need for human construction and engineering. In some cases, evidence confirms that myth and legend required such construction; although the divine mandate for founding Aztec Tenochtitlan is particularly famous, the iconography of built mountains at Maya places like Uaxactun, Tikal, or Toniná, together with early evidence of water management, supports the inference of similar imperatives (Schele and Kappelman 2001; compare Gillespie 1993).

Even from an outside, Western perspective, as cited earlier for Yosemite and other of Olmsted's engineered places, a carefully *constructed* cultural landscape is subsequently *naturalized.* Over time, if not immediately, buildings, monuments, and open spaces become accepted as part of the natural landscape. The physical process of naturalization, or ruin formation, is illustrated tangibly in many places. At Copan, for instance, the northwest corner of the Acropolis west court has been left to grade visibly (west to east) from tree-covered rise, to cleared ruin, to reconsolidated building. Ethnographic evidence among the Maya and other peoples indicates, moreover, that as implied by the Cholula case above, a *social* process of naturalization also pertains, for residents as well as visitors: The metaphorical, architectural landscapes have "always been there" and thereby merge with the "natural world" (Ashmore and Knapp 1999; Barrett 1999; Bradley 1993).

Time and Human Activity

The first two changes expanded Maya landscapes to embrace sky, earth, and underworld, and to accord equal standing to constructed and natural features as landscape constituents. Together, these changes imply a third: More than spatial juxtaposition is required to combine all the elements of natural and built worlds into what residents or observers define as a landscape. To integrate these components into a whole, it takes human action, and maintaining a coherent and orderly landscape is accomplished in individual and social memory (e.g., Ingold 1993; Schama 1995; Van Dyke and Alcock 2002). Indeed, Julian Thomas (2001) considers landscape to exist only as it is disclosed through experience, while Barbara Bender defines landscape as "*time materialized.* Or, better, *Landscape is time materializing:* landscapes, like time, never stand still" (Bender 2002:S103, emphasis in original).

Like people elsewhere, the Maya unite landscape elements by incorporating time and human activities, creating a resilient spatial matrix of experience, memory, and meaning. People move across and through the land, marking it with buildings and monuments, communicating with it by planting, harvest, and ritual. People also monitor the movements of the heavens, and engage in a dialogue of prediction and response to changes in weather. We all do these things repetitively with the passing days, seasons, years, and generations. In other words, people act together with each other and with other creatures, to create a landscape thoroughly suffused with life. The Maya, like other people, join with creatures around them to perform and enact the world, and to imbue it with meaningful social memories.

Among the Maya of Zinacantan, for example, Evon Vogt (1992) and others describe ritual circuits, pilgrimages through the landscape, paying respects at primordial places by conducting rituals and repeating proper verbal accounts, thereby ensuring that the meanings and importance of these mountaintops, caves, and other places continue. As already hinted, ethnographers, archaeologists, and epigraphers write about both ancient and modern Maya reenacting creation in the landscape. The Maya do so by repeatedly establishing the four-sided universe in buildings, cloth, and fields; by repeatedly recounting human histories and genealogy; by repeatedly reading the cosmic creation story in the stars and planets; and by fitting historically "unique" events into the overall picture (e.g., Freidel et al. 1993; Hanks 1991; compare Basso 1996). Through these steps, people create an encompassing landscape that is both orderly and meaningful. Just as Reese-Taylor (2002) outlines the relation of processions to reenacting creation within Maya civic precincts, so Julia Kappelman (2001), Kent Reilly (2002), and David Grove (1999) unite the natural topography and built environment and *actions within them* within a landscape of creation and political legitimization at Izapa and Olmec La Venta, respectively. These materializations of creation are artistic tropes that define poetics of space, and structure worlds of both space and meaning (e.g., Reese-Taylor and Koontz 2001).

Water, too, was critical for ritual acts and reenactment of creation, as well as for quotidian economic needs. Some aspects of this were cited earlier, with respect to the combination of water and mountain as crucial ingredients for establishing a new civic center. At Maya Tikal, Vernon L. Scarborough (1998) notes that the largest *aguadas* or reservoirs were positioned at approximately cardinal points, and thereby helped define a landscape structured by the four appropriate corners. Like *cenotes* farther north and water-filled caves elsewhere, the Tikal *aguadas* also were portals to the watery underworld. Rituals and offerings at such water places are clear in archaeological evidence from Chichén Itzá to Copan (e.g., Coggins 1984; Davis-Salazar 2001), and were significant landscape nodes for asserting social order among neighbors and political control by rulers (e.g., Scarborough 1998). Indeed, Lisa Lucero (1999:44) argues that it "was ideological association with water purification, in addition to the control of reservoirs, that provided Maya rulers the foundation on which to build and maintain their power."

Moreover, the shimmering mirrorlike surface of the water plausibly lent itself to divination: Karl Taube (1992) describes mirrors as implements for divination, and goes on to note that in Mesoamerica and the Southwest, mirrors were widely equated with supernatural caves. Mirrors and caves are linked metaphorically through water; all have characteristics of visual or physical transition, and reflection. For all the foregoing reasons, then, the reservoirs and other bodies of water were arguably potent ingredients of the landscape, whose varied social roles were inscribed in social memory both visually and *by the various actions performed at them.*

In addition, the sounds and smells and colors experienced in moving through the landscape reinforce memories—and the sense of a world in order (e.g., Tuan 1977). Taube and others have called attention to the importance of brilliant red in the colors of Classic civic buildings; he, Andrea Stone, and Simon Martin each have written of the wildness of the forest beyond the city's edge, and the importance of contrast between built and wild portions of the overall landscape (Martin 2001:170–1; Stone 1992; Taube 1998, in press). Creating landscape, then, requires enveloping it in appropriate and meaningful colors. Some colors are already in place, in the forest; people are responsible for the balance. In either case, all become part of the natural or naturalized landscape.

Attending to a different sensory dimension, that of sound, James Brady describes the annual rush of water from the cave beneath the main pyramid at Dos Pilas (Brady and Ashmore 1999). Still today, the sudden thunderous din signals the arrival of the rainy season, making a dramatic clamor that, in antiquity, for all within inescapable earshot, proclaimed how much power and authority the king atop that pyramid held over the rains, the seasons, the food supply, and their general welfare. Comparable harnessing of aural effects was evident in non-Maya Chalcatzingo, where the carved image of a ruler occupies the place at which wind issues noisily from the mountain on which the image resides (Brady and Ashmore 1999). In both locales, humans "conspired" with what analysts distinguish as "nature" to enact the phenomena, to tell and retell their meaning, and thereby to inscribe their memory indelibly on the landscape.

Similarly, people's actions contribute to animating individual buildings and other constructions, to completing their creation as living things. Indeed, David Carrasco (1982, 1991) prefers the term "ritual or ceremonial landscape" to sacred geography, because the former emphasizes the role of human actions in constituting the landscape (see also Broda 2000). At a smaller spatial scale, burials set in the domestic or civic landscape, beneath a house floor or in a temple's tomb, complete and "ensoul" the buildings involved (e.g., Gillespie 2000; McAnany et al. 1999). And as already cited, processions bring civic landscapes to life (Reese-Taylor 2002; Ringle 1999). In short, buildings, fields, water, sky, and landscape—all become whole and alive because of the actions people perform through time and across space.

Closing Remarks

To understand landscapes better, then, analysts need to continue expanding the definition of the domain under study, to accord with the scope of landscape forms and meanings amid which the ancient Maya lived. In short, the Maya created these landscapes, from the sky to the underworld, by drawing on natural and "naturalized" elements, then by repeatedly animating the whole through what they saw, heard, and did there. And as analysts, we need as well to continue drawing on diverse theoretical and methodological vantages to gain textured insights into how people have engaged with the landscape, constituting its form and meaning, and being shaped by landscape in return.

Certainly, physical landscapes have changed since Classic Maya peoples lived in them. Landforms have shifted in response to both natural processes and human behavior. Paths, fields, and ephemeral pilgrimage sites have become even more elusive than are the ruined buildings and spaces that mark the built landscape. Meanings inscribed on the land are commonly partly or wholly decoupled from the social memories that would relate stories about their significance. But the same people left tantalizing hints by which we can learn about their landscapes—in hieroglyphic data, in iconography, in archaeological data, and in the beliefs and practices of today's Maya peoples. And methods and theories for recovering evidence on these subjects grow steadily in diversity and sophistication. Stephens and Catherwood captivated observers 150 years ago with their portrayals of Maya landscapes. In the next 150 years, understandings of these landscapes will doubtless advance in ways we are only beginning to envision.

Acknowledgments

Partial antecedents of this chapter were presented at UCLA and UCR, and to the 2001 American Anthropological Association, and in a contribution for *Mesoamerican Archaeology* (Ashmore in press). For encouragement and critiques, I am grateful as Chelsea Blackmore, Greg Borgstede, Jim Brady, Jane Buikstra, Carole Crumley, Clark Erickson, Ginny Ebert, Scott Fedick, Charles Golden, Julia Hendon, Steve Houston, Rebecca Huss-Ashmore, Rosemary Joyce, Angela Keller, Bernard Knapp, Richard Leventhal, Lynn Meskell, Tom Patterson, Bob Preucel, Dominique Rissolo, Jerry Sabloff, Bob Sharer, and Karl Taube.

References

Anschuetz, K. F., Wilshusen, R. H., and Scheick, C. L. (2001) "An Archaeology of Landscapes: Perspectives and Directions," *Journal of Archaeological Research* 9: 157–211.

Ashmore, W. (1991) "Site-planning Principles and Concepts of Directionality among the Ancient Maya," *Latin American Antiquity* 2: 199–226.

————(2003) "Social Archaeologies of Landscape," in L. Meskell and R. W. Preucel (eds.), *Blackwell Companion to Social Archaeology*, Oxford: Blackwell.

————(in press) "Classic Maya Cultural Landscapes and Settlement," in J. A. Hendon and R. A. Joyce (eds.), *Mesoamerican Archaeology*, Oxford: Blackwell.

Ashmore, W., and Knapp, A. B. (eds.) (1999) *Archaeologies of Landscape: Contemporary Perspectives*, Oxford: Blackwell.

Aveni, A. F. (1980) *Skywatchers of Ancient Mexico*, Austin: University of Texas Press.

———(ed.) (1992) *The Sky in Mayan Literature*, Oxford: Oxford University Press.

———(2002) "Reaching for the Stars: Linda Schele's Contributions to Maya Astronomy," in A. Stone (ed.), *Heart of Creation: The Mesoamerican World and the Legacy of Linda Schele*, pp. 13–20, Tuscaloosa: University of Alabama Press.

Barrett, J. (1999) "The Mythical Landscapes of the British Iron Age," in W. Ashmore and A. B. Knapp (eds.), *Archaeologies of Landscape: Contemporary Perspectives*, pp. 253–65, Oxford: Blackwell.

Bassie-Sweet, K. (1996) *At the Edge of the World: Caves and Late Classic Maya World View*, Norman: University of Oklahoma Press.

Basso, K. H. (1996) *Wisdom Sits in Places: Landscape and Language among the Western Apache*, Albuquerque: University of New Mexico Press.

Bender, B. (1993) "Introduction: Landscape—Meaning and Action," in B. Bender (ed.), *Landscape: Politics and Perspectives*, pp. 1–17, Oxford: Berg.

———(2002) "Time and Landscape," *Current Anthropology* 43, Supplement: S103–12.

Benson, E. P. (ed.) (1981) *Mesoamerican Sites and World-Views*, Washington DC: Dumbarton Oaks.

Billman, B. R. (1999) "Settlement Pattern Research in the Americas: Past, Present, and Future," in B. R. Billman and G. M. Feinman (eds.), *Settlement Pattern Studies in the Americas: Fifty Years Since Virú*, pp. 1–5, Washington DC: Smithsonian Institution Press.

Bradley, R. (1993) *Altering the Earth: The Origins of Monuments in Britain and Continental Europe*, Edinburgh: Society of Antiquaries of Scotland.

Brady, J. E. (1991) "Caves and Cosmovision at Utatlán," *California Archaeologist* 18(1): 1–10.

Brady, J. E., and Ashmore, W. (1999) "Mountains, Caves, and Water: Ideational Landscapes of the Ancient Maya," in W. Ashmore and A. B. Knapp (eds.), *Archaeologies of Landscape: Contemporary Perspectives*, pp. 124–45, Oxford: Blackwell.

Brady, J. E., and Veni, G. (1992) "Man-made and Pseudo-karst Caves: The Implications of Subsurface Geologic Features within Maya Centers," *Geoarchaeology* 7: 149–67.

Broda, J. (1982) "Astronomy, Cosmovision, and Ideology in Prehispanic Mesoamerica," in A. F. Aveni and G. F. Urton (eds.), *Ethnoastronomy and Archaeoastronomy in the American Tropics*, pp. 81–110, Annals of the New York Academy of Sciences 385, New York.

———(2000) "Calendrics and Ritual Landscape at Teotihuacan: Themes of Continuity in Mesoamerican 'Cosmovision,"' in D. Carrasco et al. (eds.), *Mesoamerica's Classic Heritage: From Teotihuacan to the Aztecs*, pp. 397–432, Boulder: University of Colorado Press.

Carlson, J. (1981) "A Geomantic Model for the Interpretation of Mesoamerican Sites: An Essay in Cross Cultural Comparison," in E. P. Benson (ed.), *Mesoamerican Sites and World-Views*, pp. 143–215, Washington DC: Dumbarton Oaks.

Carrasco, D. (1982) *Quetzalcoatl and the Irony of Empire*, Chicago: University of Chicago Press.

———(ed.) (1991) *To Change Place: Aztec Ceremonial Landscapes*, Niwot: University Press of Colorado.

Carrasco, D., Jones, L., and Sessions, S. (eds.) (2000) *Mesoamerica's Classic Heritage: From Teotihuacan to the Aztecs*, Boulder: University Press of Colorado.

Coggins, C. C. (1984) "The Cenote of Sacrifice: A Catalogue," in C. C. Coggins and O. C. Shane III (eds.), *Cenote of Sacrifice: Maya Treasures from the Sacred Well at Chichén Itzá*, pp. 23–165, Austin: University of Texas Press.

Cosgrove, D. E. (1998 [1984]) *Social Formation and Symbolic Landscape*, Madison: University of Wisconsin Press.

Crumley, C. L. (1994) "The Ecology of Conquest: Contrasting Agropastoral and Agricultural Societies' Adaptation to Climatic Change," in C. L. Crumley (ed.), *Historical Ecology: Cultural Knowledge and Changing Landscapes*, pp. 183–201, Santa Fe: SAR Press.

Davis-Salazar, K. (2001) *Late Classic Maya Water Management at Copan, Honduras*, unpublished Ph.D. dissertation, Harvard University.

Diehl, R. A. (1984) "Current Directions and Perspectives in Mesoamerican Cognitive Archaeology," *Latin American Research Review* 19: 171–81.

Eliade, M. (1959) *The Sacred and the Profane: The Nature of Religion*, translated by Willard R. Trask, San Diego: Harcourt Brace.

Fash, W. L., and Sharer, R. J. (1991) "Sociopolitical Developments and Methodological Issues at Copan, Honduras: A Conjunctive Perspective," *Latin American Antiquity* 2: 166–87.

Fedick, S. L. (ed.) (1996) *The Managed Mosaic: Ancient Maya Agriculture and Resource Use*, Salt Lake City: University of Utah Press.

Fisher, C. T., and Thurston, T. L. (eds.) (1999) "Special Section: Dynamic Landscapes and Socio-political Process: The Topography of Anthropogenic Environments in Global Perspective,"*Antiquity* 73: 630–88.

Freidel, D., Schele, L., and Parker, J. (1993) *Maya Cosmos: Three Thousand Years on the Shaman's Path*, New York: William Morrow.

Gillespie, S. D. (1991) "Ballgames and Boundaries," in V. L. Scarborough and D. R. Wilcox (eds.), *The Mesoamerican Ballgame*, pp. 317–45, Tucson: University of Arizona Press.

———(1993) "Power, Pathways, and Appropriations in Mesoamerican Art," in D. S. Whitten and N. E. Whitten (eds.), *Imagery and Creativity: Ethnoaesthetics and Art Worlds in the Americas*, pp. 67–107, Tucson: University of Arizona Press.

———(2000) "Maya 'Nested Houses': The Ritual Construction of Place," in R. A. Joyce and S. D. Gillespie (eds.), *Beyond Kinship: Social and Material Reproduction in House Societies*, pp. 135–60, Philadelphia: University of Pennsylvania Press.

Grove, D. C. (1999) "Public Monuments and Sacred Mountains: Observations on Three Formative Period Sacred Landscapes," in D. C. Grove and R. A. Joyce (eds.), *Social Patterns in Preclassic Mesoamerica*, pp. 255–95, Washington DC: Dumbarton Oaks.

Gunn, J. D., and Folan, W. J. (2000) "Three Rivers: Subregional Variations in Earth System Impacts in the Southwestern Maya Lowlands (Candelaria, Usumacinta, and Champotón watersheds)," in R. J. McIntosh, J. A. Tainter, and S. K. McIntosh (eds.), *The Way the Wind Blows: Climate, History, and Human Action*, pp. 223–70, New York: Columbia University Press.

Hanks, W. F. (1991) *Referential Practice: Language and Lived Space among the Maya*, Chicago: University of Chicago Press.

Hirsch, E., and O'Hanlon, M. (eds.) (1995) *The Anthropology of Landscape: Perspectives on Place and Space*, Oxford: Oxford University Press.

Ingold, T. (1993) "The Temporality of the Landscape," *World Archaeology* 25: 152–74.

Kappelman, J. G. (2001) "Sacred Geography at Izapa and the Performance of Rulership," in R. Koontz, K. Reese-Taylor, and A. Headrick (eds.), *Landscape and Power in Ancient Mesoamerica*, pp. 81–111, Boulder CO: Westview Press.

Kirch, P. V. (2000) *On the Road of the Winds: An Archaeological History of the Pacific Islands before European Contact*, Berkeley: University of California Press.

Knapp, A. B., and Ashmore, W. (1999) "Archaeological Landscapes: Constructed, Conceptualized, Ideational," in W. Ashmore and A. B. Knapp (eds.), *Archaeologies of Landscape: Contemporary Perspectives*, pp. 1–30, Oxford: Blackwell.

Koontz, R., Reese-Taylor, K., and Headrick, A. (eds.) (2001) *Landscape and Power in Ancient Mesoamerica*, Boulder CO: Westview Press.

Looper, M. G. (1995) *The Sculpture Programs of Butz'-Tiliw, an Eighth-century Maya King of Quiriguá, Guatemala*, unpublished Ph.D. dissertation, University of Texas at Austin.

Lucero, L. J. (1999) "Water Control and Maya Politics in the Southern Maya Lowlands," in E. A. Bacus and L. J. Lucero (eds.), *Complex Polities in the Ancient Tropical World*, pp. 35–49, Archeological paper of the AAA no. 9, Arlington, VA: American Anthropological Association.

Martin, S. (2001) "Court and Realm: Architectural Signatures in the Classic Maya Southern Lowlands," in T. Inomata and S. D. Houston (eds.), *Royal Courts of the Ancient Maya, Vol. 1: Theory, Comparison, and Synthesis*, pp. 168–94, Boulder CO: Westview Press.

McAnany, P., Storey, R., and Lockard, A. K. (1999) "Mortuary Ritual and Family Politics at Formative and Early Classic K'axob, Belize," *Ancient Mesoamerica* 10: 129–46.

McCafferty, G. G. (2001) "Mountain of Heaven, Mountain of Earth: The Great Pyramid of Cholula as Sacred Landscape," in R. Koontz, K. Reese-Taylor, and A. Headrick (eds.), *Landscape and Power in Ancient Mesoamerica*, pp. 279–316, Boulder CO: Westview Press.

Reese-Taylor, K. (2002) "Ritual Circuits as Key Elements in Maya Civic Center Design," in A. Stone (ed.), *Heart of Creation: The Mesoamerican World and the Legacy of Linda Schele*, pp. 143–65, Tuscaloosa: University of Alabama Press.

Reese-Taylor, K., and Koontz, R. (2001) "The Cultural Poetics of Power and Space in Ancient Mesoamerica," in R. Koontz, K. Reese-Taylor, and A. Headrick (eds.), *Landscape and Power in Ancient Mesoamerica*, pp. 1–27, Boulder CO: Westview Press.

Reilly III, F. K. (2002) "The Landscape of Creation: Architecture, Tomb, and Monument Placement at the Olmec Site of La Venta," in A. Stone (ed.), *Heart of Creation: The Mesoamerican World and the Legacy of Linda Schele*, pp. 34–65, Tuscaloosa: University of Alabama Press.

Rice, D. S. (1993) "Eighth-century Physical Geography, Environment, and Natural Resources in the Maya Lowlands," in J. A. Sabloff and J. S. Henderson (eds.), *Lowland Maya Civilization in the Eighth Century A.D.*, pp. 11–63, Washington DC: Dumbarton Oaks.

Richards, C. (1996) "Henges and Water: Toward an Elemental Understanding of Monumentality and Landscape in Late Neolithic Britain," *Journal of Material Culture* 1: 313–36.

Richards, J. E. (1999) "Conceptual Landscapes in the Egyptian Nile Valley," in W. Ashmore and A. B. Knapp (eds.), *Archaeologies of Landscape: Contemporary Perspectives*, pp. 83–100, Oxford: Blackwell.

Ringle, W. M. (1999) "Preclassic Cityscapes: Ritual Politics among the Early Lowland Maya," in D. C. Grove and R. A. Joyce (eds.), *Social Patterns in Preclassic Mesoamerica*, pp. 183–215, Washington DC: Dumbarton Oaks.

Sabloff, J. A. (1973) "Major Themes in the Past Hypotheses of the Maya Collapse," in T. P. Culbert (ed.), *The Classic Maya Collapse*, pp. 35–40, Albuquerque: University of New Mexico Press.

Sabloff, J. A., and Ashmore, W. (2001) "An Aspect of Archaeology's Recent Past and Its Relevance in the New Millennium," in G. M. Feinman and T. D. Price (eds.), *Archaeology at the Millennium: A Sourcebook*, pp. 11–32, New York: Kluwer Academic/Plenum.

Sanders, W. T. (1977) "Environmental Heterogeneity and the Evolution of Lowland Maya Civilization," in R. E. W. Adams (ed.), *The Origins of Maya Civilization*, pp. 287–97, Albuquerque: University of New Mexico Press.

Sauer, C. (1925) "The Morphology of Landscapes," *University of California Publications in Geography* 2: 19–54.

Scarborough, V. L. (1998) "Ecology and Ritual: Water Management and the Maya," *Latin American Antiquity* 9: 135–59.

Schama, S. (1995) *Landscape and Memory*, New York: Alfred A. Knopf.

Schele, L. (1977) "Palenque: The House of the Dying Sun," in A. F. Aveni (ed.), *Native American Astronomy*, pp. 42–56, Austin: University of Texas Press.

Schele, L., and Freidel, D. (1990) *A Forest of Kings*, New York: William Morrow.

Schele, L., and Kappelman, J. G. (2001) "What the Heck's Coatépec? The Formative Roots of an Enduring Mythology," in R. Koontz, K. Reese-Taylor, and A. Headrick (eds.), *Landscape and Power in Ancient Mesoamerica*, pp. 29–53, Boulder CO: Westview Press.

Schele, L., and Mathews, P. (1998) *The Code of Kings: The Language of Seven Sacred Maya Temples and Tombs*, New York: Scribners.

Sheets, P. (ed.) (2002) *Before the Volcano Erupted: The Ancient Cerén Village in Central America*, Austin: University of Texas Press.

Sofaer, A., Marshall, M. P., and Sinclair, R. M. (1989) "The Great North Road: A Cosmographic Expression of the Chaco Culture in New Mexico," in A. F. Aveni (ed.), *World Archaeoastronomy*, pp. 365–76, Cambridge, UK: Cambridge University Press.

Spirn, A. W. (1996) "Constructing Nature: The Legacy of Frederick Law Olmsted," in W. Cronon (ed.), *Uncommon Ground: Rethinking the Human Place in Nature*, pp. 91–113, New York: W. W. Norton.

Stephens, J. L. (1969 [1841]) *Incidents of Travel in Central America, Chiapas and Yucatán*, New York: Dover.

Stone, A. (1992) "From Ritual in the Landscape to Capture in the Urban Center: The Recreation of Ritual Environments in Mesoamerica," *Journal of Ritual Studies* 6: 109–32.

———(1995) *Images from the Underworld: Naj Tunich and the Tradition of Maya Cave Painting*, Austin: University of Texas Press.

———(ed.) (2002a) *Heart of Creation: The Mesoamerican World and the Legacy of Linda Schele*, Tuscaloosa: University of Alabama Press.

———(2002b) "Introduction," in A. Stone (ed.), *Heart of Creation: The Mesoamerican World and the Legacy of Linda Schele*, pp. 1–12, Tuscaloosa: University of Alabama Press.

Taçon, P. S. C. (1999) "Identifying Ancient Sacred Landscapes in Australia: From Physical to Social," in W. Ashmore and A. B. Knapp (eds.), *Archaeologies of Landscape: Contemporary Perspectives*, pp. 33–57, Oxford: Blackwell.

Tate, C. (1985) "Summer Solstice Ceremonies Performed by Bird Jaguar III of Yaxchilan, Chiapas, Mexico," *Estudios de Cultura Maya* 16: 85–112.

Taube, K. A. (1992) "The Iconography of Mirrors at Teotihuacan," in J. C. Berlo (ed.), *Art, Ideology, and the City of Teotihuacan*, pp. 169–204, Washington DC: Dumbarton Oaks.

———(1998) "The Jade Hearth: Centrality, Rulership, and the Classic Maya Temple," in S. D. Houston (ed.), *Function and Meaning in Classic Maya Architecture*, pp. 427–78, Washington DC: Dumbarton Oaks.

———(in press) "Ancient and Contemporary Maya Conceptions about Field and Forest," in A. Gomez-Pompa, M. F. Allen, S. Fedick, and J. J. Jimenez-Osornio (eds.), *Lowland Maya Area: Three Millennia at the Human-Wildland Interface*, Binghamton, NY: Haworth Press.

Thomas, J. (2001) "Archaeologies of Place and Landscape," in I. Hodder (ed.), *Archaeological Theory Today*, pp. 165–86, Cambridge, UK: Polity Press.

Tuan, Yi-Fu (1977) *Space and Place: The Perspective of Experience*, Minneapolis: University of Minnesota Press.

Van Dyke, R. M., and Alcock, S. E. (eds.) (2002) *Archaeologies of Memory*, Oxford: Blackwell.

Vogt, E. Z. (1992) "The Persistence of Maya Tradition in Zinacantan," in R. F. Townsend (ed.), *The Ancient Americas: Art from Ancient Landscapes*, pp. 60–9, Chicago and Munich: Art Institute of Chicago and Prestel-Verlag.

Webster, D. (2002) *The Fall of the Ancient Maya: Solving the Mystery of the Maya Collapse*, London: Thames and Hudson.

Wren, L., Spencer, K., and Hochstetler, K. (2001) "Political Rhetoric and the Unification of Natural Geography, Cosmic Space, and Gender Spheres," in R. Koontz, K. Reese-Taylor, and A. Headrick (eds.), *Landscape and Power in Ancient Mesoamerica*, pp. 257–77, Boulder CO: Westview Press.

PART 3
Textual and Material Analysis

7
Maya Epigraphy at the Millennium: Personal Notes

STEPHEN D. HOUSTON
ALFONSO LACADENA GARCÍA-GALLO

Staring into a crystal ball can lead to blurred vision: Are we looking at what will come to pass, or simply at a desired future? The great strides made over the last decade in Maya epigraphy—which we define broadly as the study of *all* Maya texts, whether inscribed or not—deepen our sense of future expectation and wonderment. As predicted from past events, further work will result in developments that few can imagine. In this chapter we glimpse into the crystal ball of Maya epigraphy, with the proviso that ten years out the picture becomes murky and unpredictable. A similar exercise appears in two other publications (Houston 2000; Houston et al. 2001), but here we address our remarks in a more personal, less veiled fashion. Nonetheless, the tone is meant to be allusive and olympian, not sharp and accusatory: The general lessons to be learned are more important than any attempt to laud or upbraid specific colleagues.

Being There: Sociology and Pedagogy

Both of the authors have been Maya epigraphers for some time: Stephen Houston began to look wistfully at Maya glyphs in the late 1970s, Alfonso Lacadena only a few years later, both on different continents, and trained in varying traditions—Houston as an anthropologist and archaeologist, Lacadena in philology, paleography, and history. At that time Maya epigraphy had not yet changed sociologically from an esoteric specialty, practiced by a handful of specialists, to the field it is today: namely, a discipline occupied by large numbers of graduate students and interested laypersons. In the late 1970s and early 1980s the act of contemplating a text was a fairly lonesome endeavor. The interlocutors were few, and, truth be told, ideas were only slowly dislodging from inherited doctrines. Texts consisted of isolated readings, some still valid, many not, and long stretches of what were euphemistically called "titles" or, seemingly, in the early to mid-1980s, "bloodletting" glyphs. Paraphrastic readings, transferred casually into English or, less frequently, into Spanish, held the day and gave the unwarranted impression of seamless decipherment. Journalists played along, declaring every so often that Maya glyphs had been deciphered. In fact, many lacunae, especially of logographs or word signs, remain to this day.

Within a decade, even more so within two, this scenario had shifted to one of frenetic (and sometimes off-putting) discussion, from solitary contemplation to the feeling of a competitive foxhunt. After all, a glyph is only deciphered once, and the glory that accrues can be giddy stuff. In every scholarly career, the mirror turns: Having once been over-eager graduate students, we now interact with the same, hoping to be helpful and encouraging, but, at the same time, occasionally wanting simply to be left alone. What had once been an open academic landscape is now a congested one. It may be harder and harder for younger scholars to make a mark that could have been taken for granted among the more ambitious and talented students even ten years ago. E-mail has now replaced the long, painfully typed single-spaced letters from the luminous likes of Floyd Lounsbury, with a communicative system in which replies are expected instantly. In such a milieu, developments happen quickly. But does progress? (. . .Which as scientific realists, we assert does exist.)

The problem of samizdat and xeroxed papers is that they do not ferment long enough nor do they benefit from editorial pruning. The other problem is that intellectual authorship becomes confused when ideas ricochet about quickly and heedlessly. The hidden underside of Maya epigraphy bubbles with grievances about misplaced credit, although some attempts to declare authoritatively the authorship of particular ideas founder when they prove inaccurate or misleading. We also understand that writing a history of Maya decipherment easily becomes a political act, highlighting valued colleagues, diminishing the role of others who are less esteemed.

Maya epigraphy has two other sociological idiosyncrasies, at least over the last decade. The persistent complaints that Maya epigraphy is built on "sand" or represents a "house of cards" (the self-delusionist critique), or that, with epigraphers, it is always one darned thing or the other (the unstable and unverifiable knowledge theory), seem to have receded because of their inherent banality. Anyone conversant with Maya epigraphy knows that, at its scholarly core, the discipline relies on austere and remorseless standards of proof (Houston et al. 2001). The latest theory of, say, gender or sexuality fluxes like a love affair through cycles of embrace and boredom. In contrast, a bad decipherment will fall out of use, just as a good one will stay and ripple out in many surprising directions.

But the other two characteristics are still here. The first is the amateur or, better put, "enthusiast" input that has led to the creation—or been partly created by—the weekend meetings first convened at the University of Texas, Austin, and then at a variety of other locations under varying supervision and sponsorship. Some excellent ideas have come out of this enlarged network of communication—it would be foolish to claim that epigraphic smarts only resides in the brains of specialists, who often spend years acquiring knowledge and, it must be said, wooden eyes and impenetrable blinders. That is why teaching is necessary. To skeptical students (is there any other kind?), it exposes flimsy ideas for what they are. But there have also been costs, ranging from impatience with the more technical or linguistic arguments that increasingly dominate "hard-core" epigraphy, to a need for high entertainment value that molds interpretation into ways that do not necessarily follow productive directions.

Both of us have experienced groans and complaints when giving public lectures on recondite matters of Maya grammar. Between sessions, one person hissed at us, "You're giving the wrong impression, that doing epigraphy requires specialist knowledge." Exactly! We intuitively dislike the apparent "spin" of these weekends, that anyone can learn glyphs in a matter of days and go on to make serious contributions to the field. This is not a level of "truth-in-advertising" that makes us comfortable. Our own mosquito bites, destroyed vision, and flogged brains tell us that claims for easy advances simply are not so, and that decipherment forms a landscape sprinkled with sweat and furrowed with disappointment.

Our suspicion is that, for better or worse, the wave of amateur interest is on a downhill slump. At one recent meeting, in a session containing many dozens of regulars from earlier years, the average age seemed to be close to retirement or beyond. The passing of Linda Schele, that peerless advocate of all things Maya, has surely reduced the degree of amateur involvement. The daunting, technical features of Maya epigraphy, the sheer memory load of information required of participants, have also played a souring and expulsive role. Younger audiences must be engaged, as seems to be the case in Europe, or the field, particularly in the United States, will head into a domain of restricted participants. The irony is that, despite general interest, high-level teaching of hieroglyphic writing is limited to only a few programs (perhaps to be remedied soon at certain key institutions). Europe has more robust traditions, especially in Germany, although not always of a generalizing sort that appeals to North American scholars. Lacadena has promoted epigraphic training in Mexico by yearly stints of teaching at the Universidad de Yucatán, and there are promising young scholars elsewhere in Mexico; for many years, Federico Fahsen made similar, noble efforts in Guatemala.

Regrettably, we cannot know how the Maya taught their image-making and writing, other than through, to judge from comparative evidence, tedious, rote learning and numerous smacked palms. Our charge is to teach the tools that are necessary to understand the Maya from all dimensions, and as they can be understood from present-day vantage points. Every generation of epigraphers will have, in a sense, a new script to study, remade and reshaped by their background and interests. The proviso will be to balance such visions against a certain squeamishness about modish theories that dictate predetermined conclusions. There are, for example, some recent works on burials or residences that use epigraphy as a pivotal source of data, yet in ways that no specialist would condone: The data are consistently mishandled, but not in a manner detectable to a general, nonepigraphic readership.

Thus, we need to engineer minimal standards or credentials for those who want to be "Maya epigraphers." Will those standards involve the ability to do field recording, skills in historical linguistics or iconography? History, cultural studies, and archaeology? Or can tour guides and river rats, in a fairly common bluster throughout the Maya region, call themselves Maya epigraphers at whim? We do not believe that professionalization and standards are a bad thing. Most of us would prefer to be cut by a board-rated surgeon, not by someone who has done some casual reading and attended, with slight comprehension, a medical conference or two.

Of course, all of us begin as amateurs and, in some respects, feverishly work to improve at every opportunity. What passed as cutting-edge scholarship even five years ago lies far behind the edge today, and the risk is that the indolent specialist will fall behind. However, this does not relieve professionals of the burden to be interesting or generally insightful. They must demonstrate to a mindful public that Maya glyphs take us to a world of marvel, splendor, and paradox, of the sort that can only excite human passion and abiding curiosity.

Aside from the "amateur" or enthusiast movement in Maya epigraphy, there is another that involves complicated issues of moral debt, namely, those owed to modern Maya. For good and honest reasons, some scholars feel strongly about this matter and advocate active involvement of these Maya in learning, teaching, and decipherment. Here we must name a critic, if only because of the acerbic and, in our view, unfair rhetoric: Professor Marvin Cohodas of the University of British Columbia lodges accusations against what he claims are unethical epigraphers and archaeologists (see <http://ethical.arts.ubc.ca>). Any discussion of the issue is little more than an emotional minefield. It is difficult to escape the reproach of being either too hard-hearted or too soft-headed. As much as we lament, ardently, the many crimes visited on the modern Maya, we do not feel the solution is to abridge scholarly freedom. Interpretation follows data and current methods of analysis, not self-censorship, political objectives, or commands that epigraphers seek approval from self-selected and often fractious activists. It strikes us as wrong-headed in any case to lavish so much blame on what are, after all, a fairly innocuous, well-intentioned group of academics. Is it the intrinsic nature of post-modernists, as Martha Nussbaum (2000) and Terry Eagleton (1999) suggest, to focus only on the blemishes and *bêtises* of other scholars, rather than on more pressing issues, such as practical remedies to gender inequality or, in a Maya context, problems of land rights, water quality, medical services, and education? Once the objective becomes the modern Maya, their struggles and identities, however constituted, then Maya epigraphy becomes about something *other than* the past. In all frankness, we did not sign up for this "presentist" assignment, and have no wish to lose our way in its inconstant movements or apparent deference to North American models of ethnicity and ethnic relations (Houston 2000). There would seem to be ethical commandments closer to home, of publishing well and in timely fashion, of being true to sources, of crediting properly and generously, and of advancing knowledge of antiquity.

Pain Is Progress, Progress Is Pain

Over the last five years several directions have taken shape in Maya epigraphy. All result from various sorts of dissatisfaction, with earlier databases, translations, linkages to language and iconography, historical synthesis, and even the state of decipherment. A Zen koan: Disgruntlement drives progress; progress engenders pain. At the most basic level, epigraphers need to have access to information and to reliable presentations of that evidence. A bad drawing or murky photograph is, in our judgment, a sin. In this there have been many positive attempts to present data. Some are massive efforts funded by grants from the U.S. government, but, unfortunately, these appear already to be outdated or rest on arguable classifications of glyphs. The fundamental problem is that, in contrast to these projects, scholars have now moved beyond sign-based catalogues to those that focus on deciphered lexemes or morphemes. Sign-based systems look back to the time of J. E. S. Thompson and his catalogue from 1962, an opus recently republished by the University of Oklahoma Press (Thompson 1962, reissued in 1991). But they do not look forward: It is transparently obvious that lexemic dictionaries, now being compiled informally by a number of specialists, will themselves drive further decipherment by compelling scholars to think more carefully about spelling rules, etymologies, derivational or grammatical particles, and sundry shades of meaning. These dictionaries should be sensitive to time and space, and to varying interpretation, yet remain flexible and open-ended, perhaps as periodic releases in hard-copy, web, and other digital formats. Such a project is now in the planning stages at the Peabody Museum, under the financial aegis of the Foundation for the Advancement of Mesoamerican Studies.

The matter of spellings is an important one, for it has become a proxy for points of tension in Maya epigraphy. In 1998 Houston, David Stuart, and John Robertson posited the presence of what they called "vowel complexity" in Maya writing, as cued by the use of disharmonic vowels (Houston et al. 1998). A few years earlier, a growing feeling had begun to strike Houston, Lacadena, Barbara MacLeod, Robertson, Robert Wald, and a few others that the grammatical formulations of the 1980s, as embodied principally in the pioneering work of Schele (1982), Victoria Bricker (1986), MacLeod (1984, 1987), and, among others, John Justeson (1989), needed to be furthered, rectified, and deepened. The discovery of vowel complexity was surprising because it ran counter to prevailing ideas about vowel patterns in the languages of the inscriptions. This feeling also accompanied an increasing realization that the grammatical patterns in the inscriptions, now becoming more comprehensible in their reading, were pointing to one particular branch of the Mayan family tree, that in line with colonial Ch'olti'an and modern Ch'orti' (e.g., Houston et al. 2000; Lacadena 1997a, 1997b, 2000). From this developed a suite of arguments, still under discussion and refinement, about the presence of diglossia and "high language" in the inscriptions, with various percolations from other Mayan languages. In short, many things once thought clear—from "split ergativity" (a technical term relating to patterns of pronominal prefixation in verbal and nominal constructions) to matters of "aspect" or "tense"—were in motion once again. Robertson put this most clearly in a personal comment to us: "This [the language of the inscriptions] has to be a coherent language, not a mish-mash of elements—we have to find its place in the family tree of Mayan languages."

The reaction to these proposals was, at times, intemperate, even disturbing. In a published comment, one linguist dismissed any such revisions wholesale. In so many words, he characterized some of us as members of the lunatic fringe, without, however, offering any substantive rebuttal. In a less public occasion, another scholar was seen literally to weep with rage after a presentation of new results. That same person then copublished a report on diglossia (the concurrent use of different languages or dialects, often as conditioned by prestige, status, or religion) in the inscriptions without once mentioning prior research on the topic. Another demanded an apology. Yet another person, we understand, is now preparing opaquely erudite counterproposals, some in press or in submission. We must be clear about our position: Vigorous discussion is all to the good, but not when it veers into calculated obscurantism. Positive data must be discarded before alternatives acquire force. To our knowledge, that standard is not being met by critics.

It is hard to know what to make of these reactions. We have seen nothing like them before. Now and then, our inclination has been to shift to another, less combustible topic and leave the battlefield behind, although Lacadena's experience has been somewhat softer than Houston's. Some of the rawness may derive from the fact that linguists with a decade's-long stake in certain languages are finding those tongues marginalized by the diglossia hypothesis. A key motivating force in Mayan linguistics over the past few decades has been its relevance to high-flying, high-profile decipherment. But these responses are groundless. The languages continue to be important for their own sake, and historical linguistics, now of paramount importance in decipherment, requires broad databases from all Mayan languages, not just those in one target branch. Another explanation may be that most linguists working with Mayan languages are trained in synchronic rather than diachronic approaches. Those who do undertake what is often first-rate work in historical patterns come from the North American structuralist tradition, which, to over-generalize, perhaps, focuses more on sound changes than grammatical shifts. The need to redefine oneself as a diachronist must be unsettling. It is telling to us that younger epigraphers are taking some of the new work as a given and going on to develop productive hypotheses on such a foundation. This leads us to believe that, with a few exceptions, a generational shift is taking place. The battlefield will become, like Verdun, a place of poppies and peace—or perhaps a setting for other conflicts that have not yet appeared on the horizon.

Another development is—thank heaven!—less barbed and unpleasant: This is the historical consensus, beautifully sewn together by Simon Martin and Nikolai Grube, of high-order hegemonies centered on the key dynasties of Tikal and, especially, Calakmul (Martin and Grube 2000). Ten years ago, it had begun to seem possible that such hegemonies existed, especially in what Houston and Stuart described as three-way interactions of a hegemonic sort between Dos Pilas, its rival Tikal, and its overlord Calakmul—these musings were prompted by the discovery of Dos Pilas Hieroglyphic Stairway 4 as part of the Vanderbilt University Petexbatun Project; although written up, these remarks were not, alas, ever published (Houston et al. n.d.). But, as with many thoughts, Houston could also retain what seemed to be contradictory inclinations, to see such hegemonies at the same time as "weak" or poorly extractive polities. To some extent, he has not yet abandoned that package of thoughts, although, under Martin's influence, he does perceive that the evidence for more intrusive control appears stronger and stronger at some sites.

The Crystal Ball Cracks

Finding out what will happen several years out takes us beyond the scope of present insight. In our view, it would not be a good thing if Maya epigraphy came to resemble a caricature of cuneiform or Egyptological research: technical and specialized to an exclusive and excluding extent, taught to greying graduate students in the nth year of their Ph.D. program, the epigraphers summoned occasionally to the field, figures respected but not envied. Despite their elite focus, Maya texts are central to understanding past world views and dispositions. In the hierarchy of understanding, we are hard put to equate them with, say, the study of flint-knapping or other specialities. This means that *all* Mayanists should understand something about hieroglyphs, their possibilities for study, their limitations, their linkages to other features of ancient life. To put it baldly: Their nonstudy is a nonoption. The issue of two general guides to Maya writing, one (Coe and Van Stone 2001) better than the other (Montgomery 2002), makes the material more accessible than it has ever been before.

A decisive way of crafting that future is to return to the problem of pedagogy. The best of two worlds needs to be combined: the rigorous argumentation of the European philological tradition—which, if unchecked, tends to move toward our caricature of the cuneiformist or Egyptologist—with the New World focus on anthropological conceptualization—which, if unrestrained, makes epigraphy subservient to the glibber elements of social and cultural theory. There should not be a choice between rigor and tedium on the one hand, intellectual scope and excessive novelty on the other: Scope belongs with rigor, rigor with scope. It may be too late for some of us, but younger generations—with whom we herewith promise to correspond regularly and encouragingly—will surely soar with Maya epigraphy into the next millennium.

References

Bricker, V. R. (1986) *A Grammar of Mayan Hieroglyphs*, Middle American Research Institute, Publication 56, Tulane University: New Orleans.

Coe, M. D., and Van Stone, M. (2001) *Reading the Maya Glyphs*, London: Thames and Hudson.

Eagleton, T. (1999) "In the Gaudy Supermarket," *London Review of Books* 21(10), available from <http://www.lrb.co.uk/v21/n10/eagl01_.html>.

Houston, S. D. (2000) "Into the Minds of Ancients: Advances in Maya Glyph Studies," *Journal of World Prehistory* 14(2): 121–201.

Houston, S. D., Chinchilla, O., and Stuart, D. (eds.) (2001) *Essays on Ancient Maya Writing: A Sourcebook*, Norman: University of Oklahoma Press.

Houston, S. D., Robertson, J., and Stuart, D. (2000) "The Language of Classic Maya Inscriptions," *Current Anthropology* 41(3): 321–56.

Houston, S. D., Stuart, D., and Robertson, J. (1998) "Disharmony in Maya Hieroglyphic Writing: Linguistic Change and Continuity in Classic Society," in A. Ciudad Ruiz, Y. Fernandez M., J. M. Garcia Campillo, M. J. Iglesias Ponce de Leon, A. Lacadena Garcia-Gallo, and L. T. Sanz Castro (eds.), *Anatomía de Una Civilización: Aproximaciones Interdisciplinarias a la Cultura Maya*, pp. 275–96, Madrid: Sociedad Española de Estudios Mayas.

Houston, S. D., Symonds, S., Stuart, D., and Demarest, A. A. (n.d.) *A Civil War of the Late Classic Period: Evidence from Hieroglyphic Stairway 4, Recent Findings at Dos Pilas Guatemala, III*, unpublished ms.

Justeson, J. S. (1989) "The Representational Conventions of Mayan Hieroglyphic Writing," in W. F. Hanks and D. S. Rice (eds.), *Word and Image in Maya Culture: Explorations in Language, Writing, and Representation*, pp. 25–38, Salt Lake City: University of Utah Press.

Lacadena, A. (1997a) "Bilingüismo en el Códice de Madrid," in *Los investigadores de la cultura Maya*, no. 5, pp. 184–204, Universidad Autónoma de Campeche y Secretaría de Educación Pública, campeche.

———(1997b) "On Classic -w Suffix Morphology," *Yumtzilob* 9(1): 45–51.

———(2000) "Antipassive Constructions in the Maya Glyphic Texts," *Written Language and Literacy* 3(1): 155–80.

MacLeod, B. (1984) "Cholan and Yucatecan Verb Morphology and Glyphic Verbal Affixes in the Inscriptions," in J. S. Justeson and L. Campbell (eds.), *Phoneticism in Mayan Hieroglyphic Writing*, pp. 77–106, Institute for Mesoamerican Studies, Publication 9, Albany: State University of New York.

———(1987) *An Epigrapher's Annotated Index to Cholan and Yucatecan Verb Morphology*, University of Missouri Monographs in Anthropology 9, Columbia: University of Missouri.

Martin, S., and Grube, N. (2000) *Chronicle of the Maya Kings and Queens: Deciphering the Dynasties of the Ancient Maya*, London: Thames and Hudson.

Montgomery, J. (2002) *How to Read Maya Hieroglyphs*, New York: Hippocrene Books.

Nussbaum, M. (2000) "The Professor of Parody," *The New Republic Online*, available from <http://www.tnr.com/archive/0299/022299/nussbaum022299.html>.

Schele, L. (1982) *Maya Glyphs: The Verbs*, Austin: University of Texas Press.

Thompson, J. E. S. (1962) *A Catalog of Maya Hieroglyphs*, 1991 edition, preface by C. Stuart, Norman: University of Oklahoma Press.

8

Noxious or Nurturing Nature? Maya Civilization in Environmental Context

NICHOLAS P. DUNNING
TIMOTHY BEACH

After a century of scientific thinking on the Maya lowlands environment, what we still do not know is daunting. That said, our knowledge about the environmental adaptations made by the Maya and the attendant environmental impacts associated with Maya civilization has grown and matured exponentially. Our lack of knowledge today, however, results from the vastness of this topic: We are only on the start of an exponential growth curve that started to rise in the 1960s. We can also view our changes in thinking in terms of paradigm shifts or changing orthodoxies (Turner 1993). Until the mid- to late 1960s, a view prevailed that ancient Maya civilization represented an anomaly in world history: a complex civilization supported by rotating, long-fallow (swidden) agriculture in a relatively homogeneous, environmentally limiting tropical forest setting. This view also saw ancient Maya population densities as necessarily low and dispersed, and Maya cities as largely vacant ceremonial centers. This early paradigm was clearly a product of the intellectual and cultural milieu of its day, as well as the site-center-focused nature of archaeology before the 1960s (Hammond 1978; Turner 1978a; Schele and Miller 1986).

It is also now clear that early scientific thinking about the Pre-Hispanic Maya was strongly influenced by the effects of centuries of colonial and post-colonial changes to the Maya world. Lastly, stereotypes in science also influenced the way scientists perceived the Maya environment. For example, such tropical stereotypes as low-quality soils and fragile forests are giving way to more complex understanding of the tropics as a whole (Lal and Sanchez 1992; Woods and Mann 2000) and the Maya world in particular (Beach 1998a; Dunning and Beach 2000).

Over the last three decades, archaeological investigations began to look more closely at areas beyond site centers, modern forest clearance exposed increasingly large areas of terrain, and aerial imagery improved and became more available. From these sources evidence mounted in the Maya lowlands for much more densely settled rural and urban populations as well as for intensive agricultural land use manifest in field walls, terraces, and visible wetland fields. Thus, a new view that emphasized the environmental heterogeneity, intensively cultivated landscapes, and diverse agricultural systems replaced the old, deterministic orthodoxy, derived from the available information of the period (Harrison and Turner 1978). What also fueled this revised view of the ancient Maya was a growing toolbox of techniques from paleoecology, chemistry, and geoscience that are increasingly parts of regional archaeological surveys (Rice 1990).

The "new orthodoxy" has also been challenged as too anthropocentric. For example, recent scholarship indicates that both relatively permanent elements within the lowland environment (e.g., groundwater hydrology) and factors of environmental change (e.g., environmental degradation or climate change) may have significantly constrained Maya environmental adaptations as well as influenced the course of Maya civilization. Such evidence is often being produced using integrated systems studies in which human–environment relationships form a central part of investigations and a battery of archaeological, geological, and paleoecological methods are brought to bear (Hodell et al. 1995).

If a new paradigm is emerging, it is one that recognizes the inherent instability and complexity of the biophysical environment and the dynamic flux that characterizes human–environment interactions. This view is rooted in modern geoscience and the "New Ecology," an approach that is attempting to move beyond the artificial limitations imposed by older equilibrium-based ecological models (Botkin 1990; Thorn and Welford 1994; Zimmerer 1994). In this perspective, we understand human–environment interactions to be oscillating between states of relative stability and instability with changes brought about by adjustments of both human and biophysical factors (Dunning and Beach 2000). In this sense, adaptation is seen as a constant and continual process, often leading to sustained reproductive success, but at times becoming catastrophically maladaptive.

We here review the development and decline of prevailing views on ancient Maya environmental interactions over the past one hundred years. This review is intended as an interpretive synthesis of our evolving understanding of Maya civilization in its environmental context and not as a comprehensive summary of all the related work that has been or is being done.

As with any brief history of a complex intellectual process to which there have been many, many contributors, it is impossible to include mention of all major and minor parties, contributions, and points of view. We have not left out any one or any ideas except for the sake of brevity. We will conclude with a discussion of the directions in which we see such research going, or where we think it should go in the future.

Early Views

The image of crumbling temples shrouded by the rain forest has traditionally lent an air of mystery to the relationship between ancient Maya civilization and the environment where it arose, flourished, and declined. In the first half of the twentieth century, scholars viewed the tropical environment of the Maya lowlands principally as a constraining force imposing significant limits on Maya civilization. This view emerged within the intellectual context of environmental determinism in which the biophysical world was seen as having a unidirectional influence on human cultures (Huntington 1917). In the study of the Maya, this view was reinforced by site-center-focused archaeology and a generally rudimentary consideration of environmental context, which never called into question the crystallizing model of Maya civilization. It is also apparent that this view of the Maya lowlands environment as largely noxious was also indirectly the product of Spanish colonialism.

When Spaniards first arrived on the shores of the Yucatán Peninsula in the early 1500s, they encountered a civilization already 2,500 years old and a landscape far removed from its pristine or pre-human past (Butzer 1993; Denevan 1992). Population was again growing and expanding in many regions in the centuries following the collapse of Classic Maya civilization between A.D. 800 and 1000. However, the introduction of Old World diseases during the course of the prolonged Spanish Conquest of the Maya lowlands sent population levels plummeting in the sixteenth century A.D., helping to solidify the Spaniards' view of the Yucatán as largely a wilderness: a view that would shape their activities and help mask the nature of the civilization that had preceded them.

Writing in 1568, Bishop Diego de Landa described agricultural land as being held in common and cultivated using a long-fallow swidden system (de Landa 1982). However, by this point the Maya agricultural system was already reeling from the impacts of severe population loss and centralization (*reducción*). Furthermore, Spanish views of fallow land were fundamentally different from those of the Maya. In the late sixteenth century, long- or forest-fallow agriculture had become the prevalent mode of Maya cultivation. The Maya term for fallow land was *k'ax*, a word that also indicates secondary forest. To the Spaniards, *k'ax* became simply "forest," unused wilderness needing to be put to good use (McAnany 1995), and largely disregarding or dismissing Maya land ownership traditions (Restall 1997). This misinterpretation conveniently fit the Spanish program of social and economic reorganization, which included population relocation and the appropriation of inherited or ancestral lands. Like most Europeans arriving in the New World in the sixteenth and seventeenth centuries, the Spaniards understood the Yucatán in strongly religious terms and attendant practices operated according to theologically informed politics and economics (Clendinnen 1987; Sanford 1969). This view not only justified the conversion and reorganization of native populations, but also included a view of the New World environment as a largely untamed wilderness, given by God for the use of man.

Ethnographic work among the lowland Maya in the first half of the twentieth century further codified swidden cultivation as the typical and traditional form of Maya agriculture. The Carnegie Institution of Washington's sustained Maya research between 1914 and 1955 was particularly influential (Redfield 1934, 1941; Steggerda 1941), as well as that of their Mexican colleagues (Hernández 1959; Pérez Toro 1942; Villa Rojas 1979). Carnegie-sponsored ethnohistorical research interpreted available records in terms of the swidden paradigm (Roys 1943). The Carnegie archaeologists who lived and worked among the Yucatec Maya, particularly during the many years at Chichén Itzá, clearly fell under the bucolic spell of the regional "folk culture." Sylvanus Morely, the leader of Carnegie's archaeological efforts, echoed this romance, and de Landa of three hundred years earlier, when he wrote:

> The modern Maya method of raising maize is the same as it has been for the past three thousand years or more—a simple process of felling the forest, burning the dried leaves and bush, of planting and changing the location of the cornfields every few years. This is practically the system of agriculture practiced in the American wet tropics even today, and indeed is the only method available to a primitive people living in a heavily wooded, rocky, shallow-soiled country like that of the northern Yucatán Peninsula. . . . (Morley 1946:141)

This model for the subsistence base of Maya civilization was predicated on the assumption that the environment of the Maya lowlands had remained largely stable over millennia and stressed a homogenous, resource-poor view of the biophysical lowland world.

Another leading Mayanist of the time, Eric Thompson, wrote: "The central core of the Petén and adjacent regions is singularly deficient in natural resources, and the soil is scant except in the valleys" (Thompson 1954:25). Further, he gave no consideration to the possibility that agriculture other than "traditional" swidden may have been in use (Thompson 1954:26, 234–40), despite having himself encountered evidence of ancient terracing in Belize (Thompson 1931). Thompson also used the largely vacant market towns of highland Guatemala as the model for the vacant ceremonial center, populated by a few "calendar priests," the theocratic rulers of a largely rural population (Becker 1979). This view also included the idea of the Maya as a fundamentally peaceful society, a view that was perhaps created in part as an intellectual refuge from the brutality of a contemporary world dominated by war (Schele and Miller 1986). Most Mayanists chose to ignore the fact that there was no significant archaeological evidence supporting the swidden model, and an ever-growing body of information that contradicted this view (Turner 1978a). Thus, ancient Maya civilization came to be seen as an exception to prevailing sociopolitical theories, namely an advanced society emerging in the humid tropics, supported by a dispersed population practicing swidden cultivation (Steward et al. 1955). In extreme forms, this "exceptionalist" view of the Maya continued even to hearken back to environmental deterministic arguments (Meggers 1954). The swidden model of Maya civilization was also highly Malthusian in nature, including the suggestion that agricultural exhaustion led to the abandonment of the "old empire" in the Southern Lowlands and the establishment of the "new empire" in the north (Morley 1946; Thompson 1954).

Emergence of a New Model

Even during its heyday, the swidden model of Maya civilization was sometimes called into question. The population estimates produced by the Carnegie's own project at Uaxactun in the central Petén indicated that it was a true urban place (Ricketson 1937), but were dismissed by others (Morley 1946). Investigations at Uaxactun also included the first paleoecological study in the Maya lowlands, a single, deep soil pit excavated into the margins of a *bajo* adjacent to the site. Interpretation of this pit, together with the settlement data, led to the creation of a theory attributing the collapse of Classic Maya civilization to intensifying agricultural production, increased soil erosion, and the sedimentation of former lakes (converting them into seasonal swamps or *bajos*) (Cooke 1931). This view may be connected to an earlier view by the American soil scientist Hugh Hammond Bennett that the Maya collapse was due to soil erosion (Bennett 1926). In any case, this theory overstepped the available data and was also widely rejected because it was out of step with the reigning paradigm.

Similarly, early reports of terracing, field walls, and other indicators of intensive agriculture were pointedly ignored (Lundell 1937; Schufeldt 1950). But with the introduction of settlement pattern research in Maya archaeology and the systematic collection of data indicating high population densities, the swidden model's demise was inevitable. However, even the pioneers of settlement archaeology let go of the paradigm begrudgingly (and a small minority still argue for parts of it). In 1965 Gordon R. Willey and William R. Bullard wrote: "Concerning land use there is no good evidence that the Maya ever placed primary reliance on anything but the *milpa* or 'slash-and-burn' system of farming... today intensive cultivation in the Petén is impossible without artificial fertilizers" (Willey and Bullard 1965:372–3). These "last gasp" claims were temporarily bolstered by exaggerated claims for the productivity of swidden systems (Cowgill 1962), and an active debate ensued between those arguing in favor of high swidden yields and lower population estimates (Haviland 1965; Sanders 1973; Thompson 1971) and those who believed that population densities clearly exceeded the carrying capacity of swidden cultivation (Andrews IV 1965; Coe 1965; Kurjack 1974; Willey and Shimkin 1973). This debate was further fueled by suggestions that alternative foods or more intensive forms of cultivation may have replaced or supplemented maize-based swidden (Bronson 1966; Lange 1971; Puleston 1968; Wilken 1971). Finally, in the early 1970s, the rapid revelation of widespread areas of ancient terracing and probable wetland fields sounded the death knell of the swidden model (Siemens 1983; Siemens and Puleston 1972; Turner 1974). Even as the "old othodoxy" was losing ground, however, some scholars cautioned not to throw out the baby with the bath water, noting that swidden, in varying degrees of intensity, was undoubtedly an important component of Maya agriculture, but varying tremendously in its practice across space and time (Hammond 1978; Turner 1978a).

A "new oxthodoxy" emerged with the demise of the swidden model. The new paradigm envisioned dense urban and rural populations supported by a varied and largely intensive agricultural system. Underpinning this model was an appreciation of the environmental heterogeneity and productivity of the Maya lowlands, which created the basis for much of the diversification of subsistence (Turner 1978b). In contrast to the Malthusian view inherent in the swidden model, the new orthodoxy had its theoretical basis in ideas most commonly associated with Ester Boserup, namely that population growth leads to agricultural intensification or technological innovation resulting in increased carrying capacity (Boserup 1965).

A major impetus for scientific thinking about Maya civilization came from studies using an integrated systems approach to human–environment interactions. Early efforts derived from Ursula Cowgill's soil and paleoecology work in the 1960s (Cowgill 1962; Cowgill and Hutchinson 1963), which led to the pioneering work started in 1972 by the Central Petén Historical Ecology Project directed by Edward Deevey. Deevey's team designed the project to study tropical forest genesis and change, viewing the Maya as agents of environmental transformation (Deevey 1969; Deevey et al. 1979). Although this research program focused on collecting paleoecological information from a large number of lake cores, it also closely integrated the environmental and archaeological survey of several lake watersheds (Rice 1978). In this manner, the researchers were able to model gradual, but accelerating environmental disturbance associated with Maya clearance of the forest and cultivation as population increased around the central Petén lakes and attendant soil erosion and sedimentation occurred (Binford et al. 1987; Rice 1996). This research made clear the advantages of an integrated systems approach to archaeological investigations of the ancient Maya by demanding the inclusion of environmental factors as a fundamental and integrated part of research design.

The rush to create a new model of the ancient civilization had its share of pitfalls. One of these was the innovative use of air-borne synthetic aperture radar (SAR) to survey large areas of forested terrain in the Southern Lowlands (Adams et al. 1981). For a time, it appeared that the radar survey had successfully detected patterning consistent with canals and wetland fields across wide areas (Adams 1980; Adams et al. 1990; Harrison 1990). But any remote sensing technique has potential errors and requires field-checking. In this case, system noise in the SAR data or bedrock fracturing produced large amounts of false patterning, including in areas that were not wetlands (Adams 1993:383; Dunning and Beach in press; Dunning et al. 1997; Pope and Dahlin 1989, 1993).

Ground-based investigations of wetland field systems have also been a source of controversy. Since Alfred Siemens first noticed possible wetland fields near Campeche in 1968, scholars have studied these features that might provide the answers to ancient intensive agriculture in the Maya lowlands (Siemens and Puleston 1972). Some have variously interpreted these field systems, or at least some phases in the development of these fields, as entirely anthropogenic, entirely the result of natural processes, or some combination of the two (Adams et al. 1990; Beach et al. in press; Culbert et al. 1990; Dahlin and Dahlin 1994; Dahlin et al. 1980; Dunning et al. 2002; Gliessman et al. 1983; Harrison 1990, 1996; Jacob 1995; Kunen et al. 2000; Pohl et al. 1990, 1996; Pope and Dahlin 1989, 1993; Pope et al. 1996, 2000; Rejmankova et al. 1995; Turner 1993; Turner and Harrison 1983). In this instance, more detailed environmental and archaeological research has produced more disagreement than consensus. Part of this controversy centers on several ideas that are fundamentally at odds with the new orthodoxy: (1) The natural variation in the hydrology of different wetlands significantly limited Maya exploitation of many wetlands, (2) natural environmental change in the form of sea-level rise curtailed the agricultural use of many wetlands at an early date, (3) some of the wetland patterns may be natural features formed by any of several processes, and (4) some wetland features may be more the product of unintentional environmental degradation than of purposeful human action.

Some studies have correlated the Classic Maya collapse with environmental changes. For example, studies such as those in the Copan Valley that posit environmental degradation as the root cause of the collapse of Classic Maya civilization call attention to significant constraints and risks associated with continued population growth in areas with limited land resources (Abrams and Rue 1988; Wingard 1996). However, such interpretations run the risk of overly discounting the ability of human societies to adapt to environmental change (Turner 1993). A similar risk is run by investigations focusing on the documentation of environmental (chiefly climate) change, with secondary cross-comparisons to the cultural historical record (Brenner et al. 2002; Curtis et al. 1996, 1998; Gill 2000; Gunn et al. 1983; Hodell et al. 1995, 2000, 2001). Although such studies may illuminate the numerous and complex environmental circumstances to which the Maya were forced to adapt, they face the problem of implying simple environmental causation for complex phenomena and downplaying human agency and adaptability (Webster 2002). That is not to say that the "*über* Maya" were somehow capable of adapting to and overcoming all environmental problems. These studies and those parallel studies elsewhere in the world (such as linking the Bronze Age Akkadian collapse with climatic change or bolide impacts) show a natural attempt toward scientific understanding through multiple working hypotheses. Natural science tends to be averse to catastrophic change and recognizes resiliency because of its grounding in uniformitarianism, but it has learned that low-frequency, high-magnitude events do occur within the natural parameters of ecosystems. It is equally oversimplified to think that large-scale change cannot at least act as the coup de grâce for civilizations, no matter how ingenious they are.

Building a Newer Model

What has become abundantly clear is that no single model of human–environment interactions can be applied ubiquitously across the Maya lowlands and throughout the time-span of Maya culture. Clearly, ancient Maya agriculture was highly varied in nature, adapting to a mosaic of environments (Dunning 1996; Dunning et al. 1998; Fedick 1996), and responding to shifting environmental conditions, as well as population, political and economic pressures (Pyburn 1996). It is equally clear that neither nature nor culture dictates the relationship between the two.

Particularly within the past decade, Maya archaeology has become an increasingly multidisciplinary endeavor. Complex problems demand complex methods. Our investigations can now draw on a large array of techniques producing data answering questions about human–environment interactions. These techniques include the analyses of paleoliminology and hydrology, speleothems, elemental analysis, chemical biomarkers, pollen, diatoms, phytoliths, macrobotanical remains, animal bones (including paleodietary analyses), human bones (including demographic indicators), health studies, DNA typing, and dietary information, soil studies, and geomorphology, to name a few (Beach 1998a; Carr 1996; Dahlin et al. 1998, in press; Danforth 1999; Dunning et al. 2002; Emery 1997; Frappier et al. 2002; Jones 1994; Lentz 1999; Leyden 2002; Luzzadder-Beach 2000; McKillop 1996; Shaw 1999; Turner et al. 1995; Whittington and Reed 1997; Woods and Mann 2000; Wright and White 1996). The data produced by such investigations are proving increasingly detailed and create a complex picture of the ancient Maya world and how it varied across space and time. Any new model or synthesis attempting to explain the nature of human–environment interactions in the Maya lowlands should draw on the myriad information now at hand, but recognizing that data may at times be contradictory and that no interpretation can hope to resolve all the issues raised by the evidence.

In 1978, Alan Covich hastened to point out that ecological research was increasingly indicating that tropical ecosystems are characterized by considerable inherent instability, and that numerous natural and human factors could have significant, cascading destabilizing effects (Covich 1978). Furthermore, when both human and natural variables are in play, the effects attributable to both may be impossible to separate. Despite the wealth of techniques being employed by scholars working in the Maya lowlands, this inseparability of human and natural causes and effects persists now and will continue for some time in the future.

If a new paradigm is emerging, it is one which recognizes that both instability and stability exist in ecosystems and that dynamic flux characterizes human–environment interactions. Environmental change and human adaptation are often not unidirectional, with population distributions and agricultural systems being adapted not only to environmental variability but also in response to changing political and economic circumstances. In the Petexbatun region, we found agricultural changes to be linked with population changes associated with natural growth, but even more strongly with political processes (Dunning and Beach in press, 1994; Dunning et al. 1997, 1998). In northern Belize, regional settlement patterns and the use of wetland fields appear to have been closely linked to changing hydrological conditions, soil erosion and sedimentation, local population dynamics, and the food production demands of larger-scale political-economic systems (Beach et al. 2002; Dunning et al. 2002; Harrison 1996; Jacob 1995; Pohl et al. 1996; Pyburn 1998). In such circumstances, human–environment interactions in the Maya lowlands can be seen as oscillating between states of relative stability and instability with changes brought about by adjustments of both human and biophysical factors, and with adaptation as a constant and continual process, often leading to sustained reproductive success, but at times becoming catastrophically maladaptive. For example, in the Puuc Hills the Maya adapted a system of rain capture and storage *chultunes* in order to exploit the good soils of this nearly water-less region (Dunning 1992). However, as regional population grew and became more susceptible to perturbation, the *chultun* system would have become potentially maladaptive if climatic conditions became less stable due to either natural processes or processes related to deforestation (Hodell et al. 2001; Leyden et al. 1998). In contrast, recent investigations indicate that Maya forest clearance and attendant accelerated soil erosion during the Late Preclassic period may have transformed many *bajos* in the Southern Maya Lowlands from perennial wetlands to seasonal swamps (Beach et al. 2002; Dunning et al. 1999; Hanson et al. 2000). Although this change seems to have been disastrous in the Mirador Basin, in other areas the Maya adapted highly productive *bajo*-margin cultivation systems and water-storage techniques (Dunning et al. 2002; Gunn et al. 2000).

One important component of cultural ecological systems models that has been missing from most considerations of the ancient Maya is environmental perception. Understanding how the Maya perceived the environment is, of course, a key element needed to more fully interpret the adaptive choices they made. Environmental perception studies based on our the limited information in glyphs and from modern ethnography clearly provide a productive means of integrating ecological, ethnographic, archaeological, epigraphic, and iconographic scholarship and shedding light on such fundamental human–environment issues as soil and water management (Atran 2003; Atran et al. 1996; Dunning 2000; Dunning et al. 1999; Freidel et al. 1993; Taube in press).

Another important aspect of both archaeological and environmental studies in the Maya lowlands is their increasingly political nature. Investigations of ancient Maya culture are now often scrutinized in terms of their implications for contemporary Maya cultural identity—which also can be a political identity (see Ivic de Monterroso in this volume; Pyburn in this volume). In this way, statements made by those investigating ancient Maya environmental interactions can also fuel political debate on such issues as what constitutes "traditional" or sustainable land use. Just as important, archaeological land use and paleoenvironmental records are a vital component needed to effectively evaluate and assess contemporary environmental changes occurring in conjunction with expanding human settlement in many parts of the Maya lowlands and to provide useful analogues for agricultural intensification (Beach and Dunning 1995; Klepeis and Turner 2001). At the end of the millennium, environmental science and archaeology are also being increasingly integrated in the development of parks and conservation areas that focus both on the natural world and ancient remains. These range from multinational biosphere corridors, national parks, and conservation areas, to local, community-based efforts.

Use of our early paradigms accrued sizable knowledge, but we have a long way to go up the exponential growth curve. To talk of the environment in any field of study includes the diversity of disciplines in the modern field of environmental studies, everything from physical science to social science and the humanities. We can only chart a course based on our own backgrounds in geoscience, cultural ecology, archaeology, and environmental management. We will continue to need interdisciplinary teams working together from all of these fields. With the vast new array of instruments, we need more studies of remote sensing and geographic information science (GIS), sediment cores, speleothems, soils, elemental and isotopic chemistry, organic chemistry, hydrological modeling, climate reconstruction of El Niño, the North Atlantic oscillation, and hurricanes, sea-level reconstruction, volcanism, and many others. But all of these studies benefit from research in teams with archaeologists, anthropologists, geographers, and other social scientists and humanists who have long records of interpreting human behavioral possibilities. It is all too easy to make correlations between the chimera of general trends in proxy evidence with general trends in history. As always with science, we will need multidisciplinary teams that can forge multiple lines of converging evidence, and a few lone wolves working in the creative margins.

References

Abrams, E. M., and Rue, D. J. (1988) "The Causes and Consequences of Deforestation among the Prehistoric Maya," *Human Ecology* 16: 377–95.

Adams, R. E. W. (1980) "Swamps, Canals, and the Location of Ancient Maya Cities," *Antiquity* 54: 206–14.

———(1993) "Rebuttal to Pope and Dahlin: 2," *Journal of Field Archaeology* 20: 383.

Adams, R. E. W., Brown Jr., W. E., and Culbert, T. P. (1981) "Radar Mapping, Archaeology, and Ancient Maya Land Use," *Science* 213: 1457–63.

Adams, R. E. W., Culbert, T. P., Brown Jr., W. E., Harrison, P. D., and Levi, L. J. (1990) "Rebuttal to Pope and Dahlin," *Journal of Field Archaeology* 17: 241–44.

Andrews IV, E. W. (1965) "Archaeology and Prehistory in the Northern Lowlands," in G. R. Willey (ed.), *Archaeology of Southern Mesoamerica, Part 1, Handbook of Middle American Indians*, Vol. 2, pp. 288–330, Austin: University of Texas Press.

Atran, S. (2003) "Anthropogenic Vegetation," in A. Gomez-Pompa, M. Allen, and S. Fedick (eds.), *Lowland Maya Area: Three Millennia at the Human-Wildland Interface*, Binghamton, NY: Haworth Press.

Atran, S., Medin, D., Ross, N., Lynch, E., Coley, J., Ucan Ek', E., and Vapnarsky, V. (1996) "Folkecology and Commons Management in the Maya Lowlands," *Proceeding of the National Academy of Science* 96: 7598–603.

Beach, T. (1998a) "Soil Catenas, Tropical Deforestation, and Ancient and Contemporary Soil Erosion in the Petén, Guatemala," *Physical Geography* 19: 378–405.

———(1998b) "Soil Constraints on Northwest Yucatán, Mexico: Pedoarchaeology and Maya Subsistence at Chunchucmil," *Geoarchaeology* 13: 759–91.

Beach, T., and Dunning, N. P. (1995) "Ancient Maya Terracing and Soil Conservation in the Petén Rainforest of Guatemala," *Journal of Soil and Water Conservation* 50: 138–45.

Beach, T., Luzzadder-Beach, S., Dunning, N., Hageman, J., and Lohse, J. (2002) "Upland Agriculture in the Maya Lowlands: Ancient Conservation in Northwestern Belize," *The Geographical Review* 92(3): 372–97.

Beach, T., Luzzadder-Beach, S., Dunning, N. P., and Scarborough, V. (in press) "Depression Soils in the Lowland Tropics of Northwestern Belize," in A. Gomez-Pompa, M. Allen, and S. Fedick (eds.), *Lowland Maya Area: Three Millennia at the Human-Wildland Interface*, Binghamton, NY: Haworth Press.

Becker, M. (1979) "Peasants, Priests, and Ceremonial Centers: The Intellectual History of a Model," in N. Hammond (ed.), *Maya Archaeology and Ethnohistory*, pp. 3–20, Austin: University of Texas Press.

Bennett, H. H. (1926) "Agriculture in Central America,"*Annals of the Association of American Geographers* 16: 63–84.

Binford, M. W., Brenner, M., Whitmore, T. J., Higuera-Gundy, A., Deevey, E. S., and Leyden, B. W. (1987) "Ecosystems, Paleoecology, and Human Disturbance in Subtropical and Tropical America," *Quaternary Science Reviews* 6: 115–28.

Boserup, E. (1965) *The Conditions of Agricultural Growth: The Economics of Agrarian Change under Population Pressure*, Chicago: Aldine Press.

Botkin, D. B. (1990) *Discordant Harmonies*, Oxford: Oxford University Press.

Brenner, M., Rosenmeier, M. F., Hodell, D., and Curtis, J. (2002) "Paleolimnology of the Maya Lowlands," *Ancient Mesoamerica* 13: 141–57.

Bronson, B. (1996) "Roots and the Subsistence of the Ancient Maya," *Southwestern Journal of Anthropology* 22: 251–79.

Butzer, K. W. (1993) "No Eden in the New World," *Nature* 362: 15–17.

———(1996) "Ecology in the Long View: Settlement Histories, Agrosystemic Strategies, and Ecological Performance," *Journal of Field Archaeology* 23: 141–50.

Carr, H. S. (1996) "Precolumbian Maya Exploitation and Management of Deer Populations," in S. Fedick (ed.), *The Managed Mosaic: Ancient Maya Agriculture and Resource Use*, pp. 251–61, Salt Lake City: University of Utah Press.

Clendinnen, I. (1987) *Ambivalent Conquests: Maya and Spaniard in Yucatán, 1517–1570*, Cambridge, UK: Cambridge University Press.

Coe, W. R. (1965) "Tikal: Ten Years of Study of a Mayan Ruin in the Lowlands of Guatemala," *Expedition* 7: 5–56.

Cooke, C. W. (1931) "Why the Mayan Cities of the Petén District, Guatemala, Were Abandoned," *Journal of the Washington Academy of Sciences* 21: 283–7.

Covich, A. P. (1978) "A Reassessment of Ecological Stability in the Maya Area: Evidence from Lake Studies of Early Agricultural Impacts on Biotic Communities," in P. D. Harrison and B. L. Turner (eds.), *Pre-Hispanic Maya Agriculture*, pp. 145–56, Albuquerque: University of New Mexico Press.

Cowgill, U. M. (1962) "An Agricultural Study of the Southern Maya Lowlands," *American Anthropologist* 64: 273–86.

Cowgill, U. M., and Hutchinson, G. E. (1963) "El Bajo de Santa Fe," *Transactions of the American Philosophical Society* 53(7): 3–44.

Culbert, T. P., Levi, L. J., and Cruz, L. (1990) "Lowland Maya Wetland Agriculture: The Rio Azul Agronomy Program," in F. S. Clancy and P. D. Harrison (eds.), *Vision and Revision in Maya Studies*, pp. 115–24, Albuquerque: University of New Mexico Press.

Curtis, J. H., Brenner, M., Hodell, D. A., Balser, R. A., Islebe, G. A., and Hooghiemstra, H. (1998)

"A Multi-Proxy Study of Holocene Environmental Change in the Maya Lowlands of Petén, Guatemala," *Journal of Paleolimnology* 19: 139–59.

Curtis, J. H., Hodell, D., and Brenner, M. (1996) "Climate Variability on the Yucatán Peninsula (Mexico) During the Past 3,500 Years, and Its Implications for Maya Cultural Evolution," *Quaternary Research* 46: 37–47.

Dahlin, B., Andrews, A., Beach, T., Bezanilla, C., Farrell, P., Luzzadder-Beach, S., and McCormick, V. (1998) "Punta Canbalam in Context: A Peripatetic Coastal Site in Northwest Campeche, Mexico," *Ancient Mesoamerica* 9: 1–15.

Dahlin, B., Beach, T., Luzzadder-Beach, S., and Pope, K. (in press) "Water, Soil, and Landscape in the Prehistoric Past: A Short Natural History of the Yucatec Maya," in L. E. Marin, W. Ward, and E. C. Perry (eds.), *The Hydrogeology of Yucatán*, Washington, DC: National Ground Water Association.

Dahlin, B. H., and Dahlin, A. (1994) "Platforms in the *Akalche* at El Mirador, Petén, Guatemala and Their Implications," *Geoarchaeology* 9: 203–37.

Dahlin, B. H., Foss, J. E., and Chambers, M. E. (1980) "Project Akalches: Reconstructing the Natural and Cultural History of a Seasonal Swamp: Preliminary Results," in R. T. Matheny (eds.), *El Mirador, El Petén, Guatemala: An Interim Report*, Papers of the New World Archaeological Foundation, no. 45, pp. 37–58, Provo, UT: Brigham Young University.

Danforth, M. E. (1999) "Coming Up Short: Stature and Nutrition among the Ancient Maya of the Southern Lowlands," in C. D. White (ed.), *Reconstructing Ancient Maya Diet*, pp. 103–18, Salt Lake City: University of Utah Press.

de Landa, Diego (1982) *Relación de las Cosas de Yucatán*, Mexico City: Editorial Porrua.

Deevey, E. S. (1969) "Coaxing History to Conduct Experiments," *Bioscience* 19: 40–3.

Deevey, E. S., Rice, D. S., Rice, P. M., Vaughan, H. H., Brenner, M., and Flannery, M. S. (1979) "Maya Urbanism: Impact on a Tropical Karst Environment," *Science* 206: 298–306.

Denevan, W. M. (1992) "The Pristine Myth: The Landscape of the Americas in 1492," *Annals of Association of American Geographers* 82: 369–85.

Dunning, N. P. (1992) *Lords of the Hills: Ancient Maya Settlement in the Puuc Region, Yucatán, Mexico*, Monographs in World Prehistory 15, Madison, WI: Prehistory Press.

———(1996) "A Reexamination of Regional Variability in the Prehistoric Agricultural Landscape," in S. Fedick (ed.), *The Managed Mosaic: Ancient Maya Agriculture and Resource Use*, pp. 53–68, Salt Lake City: University of Utah Press.

———(2000) "Birth and Death of Waters: Environmental Change, Adaptation, and Symbolism in the Southern Maya Lowlands," paper presented at the colloquium "Les Espaces Mayas: Représentations, Utilisations, Croyances," Dec. 6–8, 2000, University of Paris X-Nanterre.

Dunning, N. P., and Beach, T. (1994) "Soil Erosion, Slope Management, and Ancient Terracing in the Maya Lowlands," *Latin American Antiquity* 5: 51–69.

———(2000) "Stability and Instability in Prehispanic Maya Landscapes," in D. Lentz (ed.), *An Imperfect Balance: Precolumbian New World Ecosystems*, pp. 179–202, New York: Columbia University Press.

———(in press) *An Ancient Maya Tropical Lanscape: Environmental Archaeology and Ancient Settlement of the Petexbatun Region, Guatemala*, Nashville: Vanderbilt University Press.

Dunning, N. P., Beach, T., Farrell, P., and Luzzadder-Beach, S. (1998) "Prehispanic Agrosystems and Adaptive Regions in the Maya Lowlands," *Culture and Agriculture* 20: 87–100.

Dunning, N. P., Beach, T., and Rue, D. J. (1997) "The Paleoecology and Ancient Settlement of the Petexbatun Region, Guatemala," *Ancient Mesoamerica* 8: 185–97.

Dunning, N. P., Luzzadder-Beach, S., Beach, T., Jones, J. G., Scarborough, V., and Culbert, T. P. (2002) "Arising from the *Bajos*: The Evolution of a Neotropical Landscape and the Rise of Maya Civilization," *Annals of the Association of American Geographers* 92: 267–83.

Dunning, N. P., Rue, D. J., Beach, T., Covich, A., and Traverse, A. (1998) "Human-Environment Interactions in a Tropical Watershed: The Paleoecology of Laguna Tamarindito, El Petén, Guatemala," *Journal of Field Archaeology* 25: 139–51.

Dunning, N. P., Scarborough, V. L., Valdez Jr., F., Luzzadder-Beach, S., Beach, T., and Jones, J. G. (1999) "Temple Mountains, Sacred Lakes, and Fertile Fields: Ancient Maya Landscapes in Northwestern Belize," *Antiquity* 73: 650–60.

Emery, K. F. (1997) *The Maya Collapse: A Zooarchaeological Perspective*, unpublished Ph.D. dissertation, Ithaca, NY: Cornell University.

Fedick, S. L. (1996) "An Interpretive Kaleidoscope: Alternative Perspectives on Ancient Agricultural Landscapes in the Maya Lowlands" in S. Fedick (ed.), *The Managed Mosaic: Ancient Maya Agriculture and Resource Use*, pp. 107–31, Salt Lake City: University of Utah Press.

Frappier, A. D., González, L. A., and Carpenter, S. J. (2002) "El Niño Events Recorded by Stalagmite Carbon Isotopes," *Science* 298: 565.

Freidel, D., Schele, L., and Parker, J. (1993) *Maya Cosmos: Three Thousand Years on the Shaman's Path*, New York: William Morrow.

Gill, R. B. (2000) *The Great Maya Droughts: Water, Life, and Death*, Albuquerque: University of New Mexico Press.

Gliessman, S. R., Turner II, B. L., Rosado May, F. J., and Amador, M. F. (1983) "Ancient Raised Field Agriculture in the Maya Lowlands of Southeastern Mexico," in J. P. Darch (ed.), *Drained Field Agriculture in Central and South America*, pp. 91–110, British Archaeological Reports, International Series no. 189, Oxford: BAR.

Gunn, J. D., Folan, W. J., Eaton, J., and Patch, R. (1983) "Paleoclimatic Patterning in Southern Mesoamerica," *Journal of Field Archaeology* 10: 453–68.

Gunn, J. D., Foss, J. E., Folan, W. J., and del Rosario Dominguez Carrasco, M. (2000) "Environments of Elevated Cities in the Interior Yucatán Peninsula," paper presented at the 65th Annual Meeting of the Society for American Archaeology, April 5–9, 2000, Philadelphia, PA.

Hammond, N. (1978) "The Myth of the Milpa: Agricultural Expansion in the Maya Lowlands," in P. D. Harrison and B. L. Turner (eds.), *Pre-Hispanic Maya Agriculture*, pp. 23–34, Albuquerque: University of New Mexico Press.

Hanson, R. D., Bosarth, S., Byrne, R., Jacob, J., and Schreiner, T. (2000) "Climatic and Environmental Variability in the Rise of Maya Civilization: A Perspective from Northern Petén," paper presented at the 65th Annual Meeting of the Society for American Archaeology, April 5–9, 2000, Philadelphia, PA.

Harrison, P. D. (1990) "The Revolution in Ancient Maya Subsistence," in F. S. Clancy and P. D. Harrison (eds.), *Vision and Revision in Maya Studies*, pp. 99–113, Albuquerque: University of New Mexico Press.

———(1996) "Settlement and Land Use in the Pulltrouser Swamp Archaeological Zone," in S. L. Fedick (ed.), *The Managed Mosaic: Ancient Maya Agriculture and Resource Use*, pp. 177–90, Salt Lake City: University of Utah Press.

Harrison, P. D., and Turner II, B. L. (eds.) (1978) *Pre-Hispanic Maya Agriculture*, Albuquerque: University of New Mexico Press.

Haviland, W. A. (1965) "Prehistoric Settlement at Tikal, Guatemala" *Expedition* 7: 14–23.

Hernández, X. E. (1959) "La Agricultura," in *Los Recursos Naturales del Sureste y su Aprovechamiento*, Mexico City: Instituto Mexicano de Recursos Naturales Renovables.

Hodell, D. A., Brenner, M., and Curtis, J. H. (2000) "Climate Change in the Northern American Tropics and Subtropics since the Last Ice Age: Implications for Environment and Culture," in D. Lentz (ed.), *An Imperfect Balance: Precolumbian New World Ecosystems*, pp. 13–38, New York: Columbia University Press.

Hodell, D. A., Brenner, M., Curtis, J. H., and Guilderson, T. (2001) "Solar Forcing of Drought Frequency in the Maya Lowlands," *Science* 292: 1367–70.

Hodell, D. A., Curtis, J. H., and Brenner, M. (1995) "Possible Role of Climate in the Collapse of Classic Maya Civilization," *Nature* 375: 391–4.

Huntington, E. (1917) "Maya Civilization and Climatic Change," in *Proceedings of the 19th International Congress of Americanists*, pp. 150–64, Washington, DC.

Jacob, J. S. (1995) "Archaeological Pedology in the Maya Lowlands," in *Pedological Perspectives in Archaeological Research*, pp. 51–80, Special Publication no. 44, Madison, WI: Soil Science Society of America.

Jones, J. G. (1994) "Pollen Evidence for Early Settlement and Agriculture in Northern Belize," *Palynology* 18: 205–11.

Klepeis, P., and Turner II, B. L. (2001) "Integrated Land History and Global Change Science: The Example of the Southern Yucatán Peninsular Region Project," *Land Use Policy* 18: 239–72.

Kunen, J. L., Culbert, T. P., Fialko, V., McKee, B. R., and Grazioso, L. (2000) "*Bajo* Communities: A Case Study from the Central Petén," *Culture and Agriculture* 22: 15–31.

Kurjack, E. B. (1974) *Prehistoric Lowland Maya Community and Social Organization: A Case Study at Dzibilchaltun, Yucatán, Mexico*, Middle American Research Institute Publication 38, New Orleans: Tulane University.

Lal, R., and Sanchez, P. A. (1992) *Myths and Science of Soils in the Tropics*, Special Publication no. 29, Madison, WI: Soil Science Society of America.

Lange, F. W. (1971) "Marine Resources: A Viable Subsistence Alternative for the Prehistoric Lowland Maya," *American Anthropologist* 73: 619–39.

Lentz, D. L. (1999) "Plant Resources of the Ancient Maya: The Paleoethnobotanical Evidence," in C. D. White (ed.), *Reconstructing Ancient Maya Diet*, pp. 3–18, Salt Lake City: University of Utah Press.

Leyden, B. W. (2002) "Pollen Evidence for Climatic Variability and Cultural Disturbance in the Maya Lowlands," *Ancient Mesoamerica* 13: 85–101.

Leyden, B. W., Brenner, M., and Dahlin, B. (1998) "Cultural and Climatic History of a Lowland Maya City: Coba, Quintana Roo," *Quaternary Research* 49: 111–22.

Lundell, C. L. (1937) *The Vegetation of the Petén*, Publication 478, Washington, DC: Carnegie Institution of Washington.

Luzzadder-Beach, S. (2000) "Water Resources of the Chunchucmil Maya," *Geographical Review* 90: 493–510.

McAnany, P. A. (1995) *Living with the Ancestors: Kinship and Kingship in Ancient Maya Society*, Austin: University of Texas Press.

McKillop, H. (1996) "Prehistoric Maya Use of Native Palms: Archaeobotanical and Ethnobotanical Evidence," in S. Fedick (ed.), *The Managed Mosaic: Ancient Maya Agriculture and Resource Use*, pp. 278–95, Salt Lake City: University of Utah Press.

Meggers, B. J. (1954) "Environmental Limitation on the Development of Culture," *American Anthropologist* 56: 801–24.

Morley, S. G. (1946) *The Ancient Maya*, Stanford, CA: Stanford University Press.

Pérez Toro, A. (1942) *La Milpa*, Merida: Gobierno de Yucatán.

Pohl, M. D., Bloom, P. R., and Pope, K. O. (1990) "Interpretation of Wetland Farming in Northern Belize," in M. D. Pohl (ed.), *Ancient Maya Wetland Agriculture: Excavations on Albion Island, Northern Belize*, pp. 187–237, Boulder, CO: Westview Press.

Pohl, M. D., Pope, K. O., Jones, J. G., Jacob, J. S., Piperno, D. R., deFrance, S. D., Lentz, D. L., Gifford, J. A., Danforth, M. E., and Josserand, J. K. (1996) "Early Agriculture in the Maya Lowlands," *Latin American Antiquity* 7: 355–72.

Pope, K. O., and Dahlin, B. H. (1989) "Ancient Maya Wetland Agriculture: New Insights from Ecological and Remote Sensing Research," *Journal of Field Archaeology* 16: 87–106.

———(1993) "Radar Detection and Ecology of Ancient Maya Canal Systems: Reply to Adams et al.," *Journal of Field Archaeology* 20: 379–83.

Pope, K. O., Pohl, M. D., and Jacob, J. S. (1996) "Formation of Ancient Maya Wetland Fields: Natural and Anthropogenic Processes," in S. Fedick (ed.), *The Managed Mosaic: Ancient Maya Agriculture and Resource Use*, pp. 165–76, Salt Lake City: University of Utah Press.

Pope, K. O., Pohl, M. D., Jacob, J. S., Jones, J. G., and Rejmankova, E. (2000) "Ecosystem Dynamics: The Paleoecological Imperative in Archaeological Research," paper presented at the 65th Annual Meeting of the Society for American Archaeology, April 5–9, 2000, Philadelphia, PA.

Puleston, D. E. (1968) *Brosimum Alicastrum as a Subsistence Alternative for the Classic Maya of the Central Southern Lowlands*, unpublished M. A. thesis, Philadelphia: University of Pennsylvania.

Pyburn, K. A. (1996) "The Political Economy of Ancient Maya Land Use: The Road to Ruin," in S. Fedick (ed.), *The Managed Mosaic: Ancient Maya Agriculture and Resource Use*, pp. 236–50, Salt Lake City: University of Utah Press.

———(1998) "The Albion Island Settlement Pattern Project: Domination and Resistance in Early Classic Northern Belize," *Journal of Field Archaeology* 25: 37–62.

Redfield, R. C. (1934) *Chan Kom: A Maya village*, Publication no. 444, Washington, DC: Carnegie Institution of Washington.

———(1941) *The Folk Culture of Yucatán*, Chicago: University of Chicago Press.

Rejmankova, E., Pope, K. O., Pohl, M. D., and Rey-Benayas, J. M. (1995) "Freshwater Wetland Plant Competition in Northern Belize: Implications for Paleoecological Studies of Maya Wetland Agriculture," *Biotropica* 27: 28–36.

Restall, M. (1997) *The Maya World: Yucatec Culture and Society 1550–1850*, Stanford, CA: Standord University Press.

Rice, D. S. (1978) "Population Growth and Subsistence Alternatives in a Tropical Lacustrine Environment," in P. D. Harrison and B. L. Turner (ed.), *Pre-Hispanic Maya Agriculture*, pp. 35–62, Albuquerque: University of New Mexico Press.

———(1990) "Paradise Lost: Classic Maya Impact on a Lacustrine Environment," in M. D. Pohl (ed.), *Prehistoric Lowland Maya Environment and Subsistence Economy*, Papers of the Peabody Museum of Archaeology and Ethnology, Vol. 77, pp. 91–105, Cambridge, MA: Harvard University.

———(1996) "Paleolimnological Analysis in the Central Petén, Guatemala," in S. Fedick (ed.), *The Managed Mosaic: Ancient Maya Agriculture and Resource Use*, pp. 193–206, Salt Lake City: University of Utah Press.

Ricketson, O. G., Jr. (1937) *Uaxactun, Guatemala, Group E—1926–1931. Part 1: The Excavations*, Publication no. 477, Washington, DC: Carnegie Institution of Washington.

Roys, R. L. (1943) *The Indian Background of Colonial Yucatán*, Publication 548, Washington, DC: Carnegie Institution of Washington.

Sanders, W. T. (1973) "The Cultural Ecology of the Lowland Maya: A Reevaluation," in T. P. Culbert (ed.), *The Classic Maya Collapse*, pp. 325–65, Albuquerque: University of New Mexico Press.

Sanford, C. L. (1969) *The Quest for Paradise*, Urbana: University of Illinois Press.

Schele, L., and Miller, M. E. (1986) *The Blood of Kings: Dynasty and Ritual in Maya Art*, Fort Worth, TX: Kimball Art Museum.

Schufeldt, P. W. (1950) "Reminiscences of a Chiclero," in *Morleyana: A Collection of Writings in Memorium: Sylvanus Griswald Morley*, Santa Fe: School of American Research.

Shaw, L. C. (1999) "Social and Ecological Aspects of Preclassic Maya Meat Consumption at Colha, Belize," in C. D. White (ed.), *Reconstructing Ancient Maya Diet*, pp. 83–101, Salt Lake City: University of Utah Press.

Siemens, A. H. (1983) "Wetland Agriculture in Pre-Hispanic Mesoamerica," *Geographical Review* 73: 166–81.

Siemens, A. H., and Puleston, D. E. (1972) "Ridged Fields and Associated Features in Southern Campeche: New Perspectives on the Lowland Maya," *American Antiquity* 37: 228–39.

Steggerda, M. (1941) *Maya Indians of Yucatán*, Publication no. 531, Washington, DC: Carnegie Institution of Washington.

Steward, J. H., McAdams, R., Collier, M. D., Palerm, A., Wittfogel, K. A., and Beals, R. (1955) *Irrigation Civilizations: A Comparative Study*, Social Science Monograph no. 1, Washington, DC: Pan American Union.

Taube, K. (in press) "Ancient and Contemporary Maya Conceptions about Field and Forest.," in A. Gomez-Pompa, M. Allen, and S. Fedick (eds.), *Lowland Maya Area: Three Millennia at the Human-Wildland Interface*, Binghamton, NY: Haworth Press.

Thompson, J. E. S. (1931) *Archaeological Investigations in the Southern Cayo District, British Honduras*, Publication no. 301, Anthropological Series 17, 3, Chicago: Field Museum of Natural History.

———(1954) *The Rise and Fall of Maya Civilization*, Norman: University of Oklahoma Press.

———(1971) "Estimates of Maya Population: Deranging Factors," *American Antiquity* 36: 214–6.

Thorn, C. E., and Welford, M. R. (1994) "The Equilibrium Concept in Geomorphology," *Annals of the Association of American Geographers* 84: 666–96.

Turner, B. L., II. (1974) "Prehistoric Intensive Agriculture in the Mayan Lowlands," *Science* 185: 118–24.

———(1978a) "The Development and Demise of the Swidden Theory of Maya Agriculture," in P. D. Harrison and B. L. Turner (eds.), *Pre-Hispanic Maya Agriculture*, pp. 13–22, Albuquerque: University of New Mexico Press.

———(1978b) "Ancient Agricultural Land Use in the Central Lowlands," in P. D. Harrison and B. L. Turner (eds.), *Pre-Hispanic Maya Agriculture*, pp. 163–83, Albuquerque: University of New Mexico Press.

———(1983) *Once beneath the Forest: Prehistoric Terracing in the Rio Bec Region of the Maya Lowlands*, Boulder, CO: Westview Press.

———(1993) "Rethinking the 'New Orthodoxy': Interpreting Ancient Maya Agriculture and Environment," in K. W. Mathewson (ed.), *Culture, Form, and Place: Essays in Cultural and Historical Geography*, Geosciences and Man 32, pp. 57–88, Baton Rouge, LA: Geoscience Publications, Dept. of Geography and Anthropology, Louisiana State University.

Turner, B. L. II, Gómez Sal, A., González Bernáldez, F., and di Castri, F. (1995) *Global Land-Use Change: A Perspective from the Columbian Encounter*, Madrid: Consejo Superior de Investigaciones Científicas.

Turner, B. L. II, and Harrison, P. D. (1983) "Pulltrouser Swamp and Maya Raised Fields: A Summation," in B. L. Turner and P. D. Harrison (eds.), *Pulltrouser Swamp: Ancient Maya Habitat, Agriculture, and Settlement in Northern Belize*, pp. 246–69, Austin: University of Texas Press.

Turner, B. L. II, and Miksicek, C. H. (1985) "Economic Plant Species Associated with Prehistoric Agriculture in the Maya Lowlands," *Economic Botany* 38: 179–93.

Villa Rojas, A. (1979) *Los Elegidos de Diós: Etnografía de los Mayas de Quintana Roo*, Publicación Antropología Social no. 56, Mexico City: Instituto Nacional Indigenista.

Webster, D. L. (2002) *The Fall of the Ancient Maya: Solving the Mystery of the Maya Collapse*, London: Thames and Hudson.

Whittington, S. L., and Reed, D. L. (eds.) (1997) *Bones of the Maya: Studies of Ancient Skeletons*, Washington, DC: Smithsonian Institution Press.

Wilken, G. C. (1971) "Food-Producing Systems Available to the Ancient Maya," *American Antiquity* 36: 432–48.

Willey, G. R., and Bullard, W. R. (1965) "Prehistoric Settlement Patterns in the Maya Lowlands," in G. R. Willey (ed.), *Archaeology of Southern Mesoamerica, Part 1, Handbook of Middle American Indians*, Vol. 2, pp. 360–77, Austin: University of Texas Press.

Willey, G. R., and Shimkin, D. B. (1973) "The Maya Collapse: A Summary View," in T. P. Culbert (ed.), *The Classic Maya Collapse*, pp. 457–501, Albuquerque: University of New Mexico Press.

Wingard, J. D. (1996) "Interactions between Demographic Processes and Soil Resources in the Copan Valley, Honduras," in S. Fedick (ed.), *The Managed Mosaic: Ancient Maya Agriculture and Resource Use*, pp. 207–35, Salt Lake City: University of Utah Press.

Woods, W. I., and Mann, C. C. (2000) "Earthmovers of the Amazon." *Science* 287: 786–9.

Wright, L. E., and White, C. D. (1996) "Human Biology in the Classic Maya Collapse: Evidence from Paleopathology and Paleodiet," *Journal of World Prehistory* 10: 147–98.

Zimmerer, K. S. (1994) "Human Geography and the 'New Ecology': The Prospect and Promise of Integration," *Annals of the Association of American Geographers* 84: 108–25.

9
The Past and Future of Maya Ceramic Studies

ANTONIA E. FOIAS

As one of the founding stones of Maya archaeology, ceramic studies have a long and illustrious history. In this chapter, I will examine the roots of Maya ceramic analysis and its trajectory over the last century. However, the focus will be on the most recent studies, their approaches, and future directions of analysis. Maya pottery was first seen as the key to the reconstruction of the cultural history of this Mesoamerican civilization, so types, varieties, complexes, and phases became the parlance in the first half of the twentieth century. The polychrome vessels of the Classic period painted with elaborate scenes involving humans, animals, deities, and hieroglyphs had continuously attracted the eye of collectors, but also art historians who began deciphering their iconography and texts. Maya ceramic studies have flourished in the last decades as interdisciplinary research among art historians, archaeologists, ceramicists, chemists, geologists, and physicists has come to bear fruit. Pottery has been viewed not only as a chronological tool, but also as the masterpieces of individual scribes, as goods in a flourishing economic system, as political currency or control devices, and so on.

Origins: Taxonomic Approaches and Chronological Concerns

Maya ceramic studies originated early in the twentieth century, together with the birth of modern archaeology and stratigraphic excavations in the lowlands in the 1910s and 1920s (e.g., at Holmul, Merwin and Vaillant 1932;

at Uaxactun, A. L. Smith 1936; R. E. Smith 1936; at San Jose, Thompson 1939; at Chichén Itzá, Vaillant 1927, 1933). The most famous of these earliest works are Robert E. Smith's studies of the Uaxactun (1936) and Mayapan[1] (1955, 1971) pottery. These two seminal monographs mark the birth of systematic ceramic studies in the Maya lowlands. Characteristic of that time period in American archaeology (see Willey and Sabloff 1980:83), the primary goals of Smith's monographs and the other early Maya ceramic studies (Thompson 1939, 1940; Longyear 1952; Brainerd 1940–1942, 1958; Willey et al. 1965; Gifford 1960, 1976) were chronological and classificatory. These overarching concerns were imperative at the time as no dating method was available in Mesoamerica, and little or no systematic classification of the material culture had been undertaken. Thus, pottery was seen as the key to the reconstruction of Maya cultural history, and remains so up to the present.

With the development of ceramic classificatory frameworks in the southeast and southwest United States (Wheat et al. 1958), the early concerns of Maya ceramic studies were systematized into the dominant paradigm of Maya pottery research: the type-variety-mode system of classification (Smith, Willey, and Gifford 1960; Gifford 1960, 1976; Willey, Culbert, and Adams 1967; Sabloff and Smith 1969; Smith and Gifford 1966). The goal of the type-variety system was not only to provide an instrument of chronological calibration, but also to allow intersite and regional comparisons and to formalize the methodology of ceramic classification (Gifford 1976:2). Many, if not most, Maya ceramicists continue to use the type-variety system to classify and describe their pottery collections and to formulate site or regional chronologies. However, although the reconstruction of cultural histories was the goal of Maya ceramicists until the 1960s, now it is considered only a first step in pottery analysis .

This classificatory framework has not been exempt from strong critiques (Dunnell 1971; Hammond 1972; Smith 1979; Pendergast 1979; Chase 1994). As the type-variety system emphasizes surface treatment and decoration in the definition of types and varieties, morphological and paste characteristics have been devalued, and many ceramicists have argued quite rightly that these are crucial aspects of ancient pottery.[2] Thus, compromises have been attempted and successfully carried out. Maya ceramic type-variety reports routinely include detailed descriptions of form and paste classes for each type defined. Prudence Rice (1976a) has strongly advocated systematizing the use of the ware as a technological unit for pottery with identical attributes of paste composition, including temper.

Another shortcoming of the type-variety system in its original application (Smith and Gifford 1966) was that all the pottery of each phase received new type names, even if there were no differences between the assemblages (Forsyth 1982:4–11, 1989:5–6; Adams 1971:30). Donald Forsyth has made the most concerted effort to resolve this problem in the application of the type-variety system. Arlen Chase (1994:158–60) has rightly attacked the use of this classificatory system apart from archaeological stratigraphy and contextual data, championing together with David Pendergast (1979) a contextual approach that centers on the contexts and assemblages in which the different pottery types are found, not only on typological distinctions (Pendergast 1979; Chase 1994). In fact, as Chase affirms (1994:159), most ceramicists use such a contextual analysis in conjunction with type-variety. Joseph Ball's (1993) discussion of the sociocultural meaning of the most common units in the type-variety system, the ceramic group, paste variant, complex, sphere, and system for the Maya lowlands, is noteworthy and illustrates the usefulness of this classificatory framework in making broader cultural interpretations.

It might be an opportune time to ask if the type-variety system advanced or retarded Maya ceramic studies, although time and space limitations do not allow me to deal with this issue in detail. I would argue that it did both. Certainly, early on, it was a breakthrough in systematizing Maya ceramic classification. However, it has also retarded ceramic research because it has taken on the aura of being an analysis of the material rather than just a classification. Its exclusive focus on surface treatment makes the system useless for dealing with paste and morphological aspects of the pottery. Because it takes an extended period of time to carry out, it has impeded ceramicists from further studies or from formulating other classifications. Its creators defended it so staunchly that it has become entrenched in Maya ceramic studies. Let us imagine, for a second, what Maya studies would be like today if morphological or paste attributes had formed the basis for the definition of classificatory units. We would probably know a great deal more about Maya pottery economies. However, without the existence of a broadly applied classification system, we would not be able to make comparisons between sites and regions.

As type-variety-mode "analyses" and chronological studies fall out of favor with Maya archaeologists, we should not lose sight of the chronological issues that remain to be resolved. Several phases are still problematic and need further intensive research. For example, the scarcity of Early Classic Tzakol-sphere pottery beyond central Petén (e.g., Tikal, Uaxactun, Holmul) has led many archaeologists to suggest a demographic decline in the Maya lowlands from the Late Preclassic highs. However, Charles E. Lincoln (1985) and more recently Juan Pedro Laporte (1995) have proposed that this is not the case, but rather an effect of the type-variety system as originally developed from a Central Petén perspective: They suggest that at most sites, Preclassic waxy wares continue to be used, while the Tzakol glossy wares were employed restrictively by the few elites. Associated with this issue is the definition and significance of the Protoclassic period, originally interpreted as a ceramic component intrusive from the southern highlands during the first two centuries A.D. In their recent review, James Brady et al. (1998) advocate the redefinition of the Protoclassic as extending until the fifth century A.D. and thus contemporaneous with the Tzakol glossy wares.

A third chronological problem centers on the contemporaneity or overlap of the Cehpech and Sotuta ceramic spheres in the Northern Maya Lowlands (Andrews and Robles 1985; Lincoln 1986; Robles and Andrews 1986; Bey et al. 1992, 1998). These were originally defined as chronologically distinct spheres, with Cehpech (pertaining to the Terminal Classic) preceding Sotuta[3] (pertaining to the Early Postclassic). However, more recently, the degree of contemporaneity and the cultural meaning of these two ceramic spheres have been under debate (Lincoln 1986; Robles and Andrews 1986; Robles 1987, 1988; Bey et al. 1992, 1998; Anderson 1998; Kepecs 1998; Ringle et al. 1998; Suhler et al. 1998). Michael P. Smyth (1998) has even suggested that types characteristic of the Cehpech phase appear as early as the Early Classic in the Puuc region, at sites such as Chac II. Of course, the result of this Cehpech/Sotuta overlap is that the Early Postclassic of northern Yucatán becomes undefined ceramically (Stanton and Gallareta Negron 2001) unless the Tases/Hocaba ceramic sphere, now defined for the Middle and Late Postclassic, is extended back into time, or if the Cehpech/Sotuta era extends later into the Early Postclassic (Bey et al. 1998; Kepecs 1998).

New Archaeology and New Ceramic Studies

After the 1960s, paralleling the rise of Processual and then Post-Processual Archaeology, an overwhelming reaction ensued against the emphasis on pottery as a chronological marker only, disregarding to a large degree the people who made and used it in social, economic, political, and ritual contexts. However, during the 1960s and 1970s, the first applications of the type-variety system were carried out at Tikal (Culbert 1979, 1993), Altar de Sacrificios (Adams 1971), Seibal (Sabloff 1975), Becan (Ball 1977), Aguacatal (Matheny 1970), Chalchuapa (Sharer 1978), and Bilbao (Parsons 1967/1969), all of which are considered "classics" in Maya pottery studies. Since then, Maya ceramic research has flourished, ranging widely from technological studies to iconographic and stylistic analysis of polychrome pottery to ethnoarchaeology. In this chapter, I can only highlight the recent trends and give some examples to illustrate these different approaches.

Technological Studies of Maya Pottery: Not So New!

One of the most important trends in Maya pottery studies has been a strong concern with technological aspects. These technological studies have approached questions of production and sourcing, production, and exchange, and on a general level they have aimed to reconstruct the economic structures of the ancient Maya. This concern with ceramic technology is not a recent development, though, but has much older roots in the precocious work of Anna Shepard (1936, 1939, 1946a, 1946b, 1948, 1956, 1964; cf. Bishop and Lange 1991). Her tradition has a strong following among Maya ceramicists who now actively collaborate with geologists, chemists, and physicists and apply methods such as neutron activation (INAA), x-ray fluorescence, inductively coupled plasma spectroscopy, and so on, to reconstruct pottery manufacture and distribution (Sayre 1958; Harbottle and Sayre 1977; Bishop 1975, 1980; Bishop et al. 1982; Bishop and Neff 1989; Iceland and Goldberg 1999; Varela and Leclaire 1999; Chung et al. 1995; Hammond et al. 1976). Surprisingly, Shepard herself did not believe that chemical analyses would be of much use in Maya ceramic studies and argued instead for the employment of mineralogical approaches to the study of ceramic technology (Beaudry 1991:226).

Within this tradition, Prudence Rice (1982, 1985, 1987a, 1987b, 1987c) has published at length, elucidating many aspects of Maya pottery technology. Also following in Shepard's footsteps are the pan-regional INAA pottery survey projects of Ronald Bishop and his colleagues (Rands et al. 1982; Bishop 1994, in press; Rands and Bishop n.d.; Reents-Budet et al. 1993, 1994a). Bishop's team has sampled fine paste and polychrome pottery extensively from all parts of the Maya lowlands over the last thirty years. The broad perspective of these INAA surveys and the incorporation of Reents-Budet's art historical approach have led to a deeper understanding of the developmental history and regional variations of these two Maya ceramic traditions. The Maya Fine Paste Ceramics Project has been able to show that, although originally considered foreign commodities brought by Putun invaders, fine paste wares have long developmental histories in the western lowlands along the Usumacinta and in the greater Palenque zone; furthermore, they were manufactured in many different locales within the Usumacinta-Pasion drainage (Rands et al. 1982; Bishop 1994, in press; Rands and Bishop n.d.). The Maya Polychrome Ceramics Project intertwines archaeological, chemical, and art historical methods to define polychrome styles, their distribution, and their production context and location within the Maya lowlands (Reents-Budet et al. 1993, 1994b, 2000; Bishop 1994).

Sourcing studies based on mineralogical and chemical data[4] from Copan and the southeastern Maya periphery, Palenque, and the western Maya periphery, and from Tikal and central Petén have shown localized, dispersed, nonurban production and flourishing regional trade in pottery (Bishop 1980, 1994; Rands and Bishop 1980; Beaudry 1984; Fry 1979, 1980, 1981; Fry and Cox 1974; Culbert and Schwalbe 1987). Studies of pottery manufacture have multiplied, focusing on the end products, the vessels themselves, as few workshops have been identified in the Maya lowlands. Thus, pottery manufacture has been explored through indirect methods such as standardization, diversity, and labor investment measures as indices or estimates of the scale of production or level of specialization (Rice 1981, 1989, 1991; Beaudry 1984; Foias 1996; Le Count 1996; Bill 1997). However, limitations to these indirect approaches have also received attention (Rice 1991; Arnold 1991; Costin 1991; Arnold and Nieves 1992).

Epigraphy, Iconography, and Polychromes

Art historians and epigraphers have also joined the recent boom in Maya ceramic studies and have applied their different perspectives and approaches specifically to the Classic Maya polychromes painted with elaborate scenes of royal courts and palaces, rituals, dances, processions, battles, and glyphic texts.[5] Decipherments of the glyphic texts on these vessels (denominated primary standard sequences or PSS[6]) have revealed a wealth of information about Classic Maya society. The PSS includes the Classic Maya terms for several polychrome vessel forms, such as *lak* for shallow dishes and *uch'ab* for drinking vases (Houston et al. 1989; Stuart 1989). The PSS even tells us specifically what was eaten or drunk in these vessels (Stuart 1989; MacLeod and Reents-Budet 1994; Reents-Budet et al. 1994).

Furthermore, the inclusion of the names of the scribes and/or patron-owners in the PSS texts have allowed detailed studies of scribal styles and of the distribution of these intricate polychrome styles across the Maya lowlands (cf. Reents-Budet et al. 1994). Reents-Budet and her colleagues (1993, 1994b, 1998, 2000) have been able to identify a number of polychrome styles and their production area generally associated with one Maya site but often imitated within the local region. Among these styles, the most famous are the Holmul style centered in eastern Petén and adjacent Belize (with its typical dancers surrounded by elaborate death, underworld, and creation imagery); the Tikal dancer plate style (produced at Tikal and Uaxactun); the Codex style (produced at Nakbe and Calakmul); the Ik site style produced northwest of Lake Petén Itzá and presumably in the environs of Motul de San Jose (characterized by historical texts and scenes of palace activities); the Chama style with its processions of humans with animal masks, musicians, or warriors framed by bands of black-and-white chevron motifs (manufactured in the Chama Valley in the southern Guatemalan highlands); the turkey vulture plates produced in northern Campeche and southwestern Yucatán; the Altun Ha style, produced in the region of the Belizean site by the same name, (that typically depicting birds, supernatural symbols, or mythological scenes on a black background color) (Reents-Budet et al. 1994b, 1998, 2000; Danien 1998; Bishop 1994; Hansen et al. 1991).

The conjunctive approach used by the Maya Polychrome Ceramics Project has been extremely successful in illuminating distinctions between individual polychrome painting styles and their possible production loci at the intra- and interregional scales. For example, using stylistic, epigraphic, and chemical data, Dorie Reents-Budet et al. (2000) have been able to identify the production of Chinos black-on-cream and Cabrito cream-polychrome at Buenavista separately from their production at Naranjo and Holmul in adjacent eastern Petén. The neutron activation analyses were able to separate five groups or paste-temper recipes among the polychrome manufactured in the Buenavista palace school/workshop(s), which correlated with style, form, and ceramic type, illustrating a high degree of specialization. Furthermore, Reents-Budet et al. have distinguished a range in the quality of the painted pottery produced in the Buenavista palace school workshop, from the finest, well-formed, glyphic-bearing vessels, to less elaborate, technically less well made vessels, bearing pseudoglyphs and simple scenes. This gamut in polychrome quality was associated with distinct consumer audiences: the most elaborate destined for the highest elite echelons and the simplest for all socioeconomic levels of Maya society (as implied by their restricted vs. broad distributions in archaeological contexts) (Reents-Budet 1985; Reents-Budet et al. 1994b, 2000; Ball 1993; Ball and Taschek 1991).

Maya polychrome pottery is also a rich source of insights into Classic period courtly life and courtiers, all of which are generally invisible in the public monumental art carved in stone. Palace scenes depicting not only the paramount rulers but also secondary elites, captives, musicians, servants, dwarves, and so on, are common, and provide a window into the lives of the Maya rich and famous. Polychrome vessels record a variety of court events, including visits among the elites of different polities; presentations of tribute, gifts, or captives; marriage negotiations; a myriad of rituals (including bloodletting, divination using mirrors, dances); court feasts or receptions; and finally artistic undertaking, such as the carving of masks or painting (Reents-Budet 2001:213). Central to these scenes is, of course, the figure of the paramount ruler (*k'uhul ajaw*), surrounded by secondary elites, courtiers, and so on. The second most commonly depicted individual is the scribe *ah ts'ib*, who had multiple functions within the Classic Maya court, probably including recordkeeper, tribute collector, savant, diviner, and master of ceremonies (Coe and Kerr 1997; Reents-Budet et al. 1994b; Reents-Budet 2001:214). Another common individual on these vessels carries the so-called God C title (Houston 1993), provisionally translated as *ah k'uhun*, "keeper of the sacred books" or "royal scribe" (Grube in Coe and Kerr 1997). However, Sarah Jackson and David Stuart (2001) posit a broader interpretation of this title as referring to secondary nobles who "kept" tribute (or sacred/special objects?) or "venerated/worshipped" for specific rulers. The frequency of this title in the pottery and monumental corpus also suggests that this was an important figure in Classic Maya courts.

Maya painted pottery is also famous for its beautiful mythological scenes that parallel the Postclassic Quiche Maya "bible" *Popol Vuh.* Michael Coe (1973) was the first to link the supernatural imagery on Classic Maya pots with the Postclassic recounting of the creation and origins of the Quiche Maya presented in the *Popol Vuh* (Tedlock 1985). Thus, these vessels provide a window into Classic Maya ideology and religion.[7] The description and interpretation of these mythological scenes continue to be a strong locus of research in Maya ceramic studies (Coe 1975, 1978, 1982, 1989; Robicsesk and Hales 1981, 1982; Hammond 1985; Houston and Stuart 1989; Grube and Nahm 1994; Reents-Budet 1994, 1998; Taube 1985, 1992), facilitated by Justin Kerr's continuous publication of the corpus in his multivolume *The Maya Vase Book* (1989–2000). An especially critical discovery in the decipherment of supernaturals painted on Maya pottery has been the existence of coessences or *wayob,* highlighting the importance of shamanism[8] in prehispanic Maya ideology (Houston and Stuart 1989; Grube and Nahm 1994; Calvin 1997).

Maya Pottery and Sociopolitical Reconstructions of the Classic Maya

Today, pottery is seen as crucial in debates concerning Classic Maya sociopolitical structures and relations. This is not a new invention by any means. Archaeologists have used the distribution of specific pottery types to show diffusion, conquest, migration, and so on, for a long time. For example, the discovery of Teotihuacanlike pottery (as well as the talud-tablero architecture typical of Teotihuacan) at Kaminaljuyu and Tikal was the basis for suggesting the conquest of the former and the imposition of a foreign king at the latter Maya city (Kidder et al. 1946; Santley 1983; Coggins 1975, 1979). Others have rejected this interpretation and proposed instead that elite interaction between these two major cultures was the mechanism for the dispersal of the Teotihuacan pottery styles (e.g., Ball 1983; Demarest and Foias 1993). The debate on the nature of Teotihuacan influence in the Maya region is far from over, as new decipherments of Tikal Early Classic stelae suggest the arrival of new groups at the time when Teotihuacan influence appears in the material culture at the site (Stuart 2000).

However, the equation of pottery style with conquest or political control is highly problematic as numerous studies have shown (Conkey and Hastorf 1990; Carr 1995; Wobst 1999). It is surprising, then, that such interpretations are still made in the Maya region. In their reassessment of the extent of the

Itzá polity in ancient Yucatán, Travis Stanton and Tomás Gallareta Negrón (2001) critique the simplistic equivalencies made by a number of scholars between the presence of Sotuta-sphere pottery (in contrast to Cehpech sphere) and Itzá control. They advocate a much more nuanced analysis of the specific contexts in which these types are found, and provenance studies of these presumed-foreign ceramics to determine their origins. When such a contextual analysis is performed, the evidence for the Itzá conquest of Yaxuna and Uxmal is weak or completely disappears.

However, the hottest recent focus in Maya ceramic studies has been in highlighting and elucidating the role of Maya serving vessels (in particular, elaborate polychrome) in elite alliance and exchange networks, and feasting associated with many elite rituals (McAnany 1995; Reents-Budet et al. 1994b; Reents-Budet 1998, 2000; Le Count 1999, 2001; Foias 2002; Stanton and Gallareta Negrón 2001). The restricted but long-distance distribution of elaborate polychrome styles and their archaeological contexts have been highly suggestive that this painted pottery functioned as social or political currency, tightly controlled by the elite (Reents-Budet 1994, 1998; Reents-Budet et al. 1994b). They were created by elite scribal artists within the Classic Maya royal courts, and were gifted among elites of the same or different polities to establish networks of alliances,[9] to maintain power relationships, and to compete for and increase one's prestige, status, and power (see detailed discussions in Reents-Budet 1994:72–105 and Reents-Budet 1998).

Reents-Budet (1998) emphasizes the multifaceted features of these fancy polychromes that imbued them with high prestige, transforming them from crafted objects into sociopolitical currency: their high "technical and aesthetic sophistication, the rendering of historical and mythological events tied to the esoterica of Maya intellectualism, distinctive painting styles connected to specific places and individuals, and the hieroglyphic (and sometimes pictorial) recording on the vessels of the patrons and artists" (1998:85). More important, though, the crafting of these vessels was not seen as secular production, but rather as an act of creation or bringing to life of such ceramics, as the gods created and brought to life humans at the beginning of time: "Maya artistic endeavors were metaphors for the original act of cosmic Creation, and the Classic Maya linked artistic creativity to the gods of Creation." (Reents-Budet 1998:77). The PSS itself starts with the glyphs *ay-a hoy-i/huy-i*, "it came into being/it was blessed" (MacLeod and Reents-Budet 1994:109–11; Reents-Budet 1998:76), intimating that the creation of these masterpieces was not a secular endeavor, but a sacred act. The titles of the scribes, *miyats* ("sage"), and *chehen* ("maker, creator, doer") also imply that the artists were seen as having special powers akin to those of the gods (MacLeod and Reents-Budet 1994:121; Reents-Budet 1998:76). Finally, the moment of creation itself is frequently depicted on polychrome vessels. Even more important, the symbolism on a number of plates transforms the vessel into a cosmogram, so that the scribe who painted it becomes the Creator of the universe (Reents-Budet 1998:77–85).

The role of elaborately decorated pottery as political currency is highlighted in the recent ceramic research at the Late and Terminal Classic center of Xunantunich, Belize (Le Count 1999). Lisa Le Count's study contends that polychrome pottery was used by the local elites in their shifting political strategies for maintaining and increasing their power. During the Late Classic, the elaborate pottery was restricted to elite households in the civic center due to rival elite displays of prestige goods, (Le Count 1999). In contrast by the Terminal Classic, with the disintegrating political power of the Xunantunich rulers, the elites attempted to consolidate popular support "by gifting luxury items down through the social hierarchy" reflected in the much broader distribution of fine pottery among all social strata (Le Count 1999).

Feasting is at the core of many social, political, economic, and religious events among modern Mayas as well as Postclassic Yucatecos (Monaghan 1990; Vogt 1990, 1992; de Landa 1941), and it must have been just as central among the Classic city-states. Patricia McAnany (1995), Reents-Budet (1994, 1998, 2000; Reents-Budet et al. 1994b), and Le Count (2001) have stressed the importance of feasting in Classic elite-sponsored ritual and secular events. Polychrome vessels as well as simpler pottery would have been used to serve food and drink at these elite banquets.

In support of this hypothesis, Reents-Budet (2000) considers the common depictions of feasts on Classic Maya painted pots, and pottery-rich middens such as one found behind one of the main palaces in Altun Ha Group A. Le Count (2001) uses particular vessel form categories (vases and platters) favored in Maya feasting to show the importance of banquets for royal, elite, and non-elite segments of Classic Maya society at Xunantunich; she presents the distribution of vases (known from the PSS to have been used for drinking, most commonly of cacao) and platters (known from the PSS to have served solid foods, such as tamales) across civic and household contexts to show that only vases are highly restricted to the civic and royal elite contexts (and found at extremely low frequencies in other elite and non-elite contexts), suggesting that "drinking was a highly charged political ritual among the late Classic Maya, a critical act that consolidated political allegiance and cemented civic agreements between individuals, both elite and common" (Le Count 2001:947).[10]

Extending this hypothesis, I have pointed at the intersection between elite alliance networks and feasting, arguing that the gifting of polychrome vessels was part of the elite receptions and banquets that followed political events, as it was in contact period Yucatán. Diego de Landa (1941:92) describes such repasts in the following passage:

> The first [type of feast], which is that of the nobles and of the principal people, obliges each one of the invited guests to give another similar feast. And to each guest they give a roasted fowl, bread and drink of cacao in abundance; and at the end of the repast, they were accustomed to give a manta to each to wear, and a little stand and vessel, as beautiful as possible.

Furthermore, gifting and feasting were also part of non-elite rituals (Le Count 2001; Landa 1941; Redfield and Villa Rojas 1934; Vogt 1992; Monaghan 1990). If the elite controlled the manufacture of the items required to be exchanged during these feasts and rituals (such as the polychrome vases and platters used for serving) and the production of cacao (drunk in these feasts and rituals), they would have had a powerful source of social and political power (Foias 2002).

The political relationships represented and fossilized in these polychrome vases are highly complex. For example, a vase held by Dumbarton Oaks (B-564; figure 9.1) is finely painted in a style related to the Ik school (Reents-Budet et al. 1994b: 178, Figures 4.44 and 5.12). Although its style is closely linked to one of the best scribes of the Ik school (Reents-Budet, personal communication 2000), its paste-heavily charged with calcite-advocates the possibility that an Ik-trained scribe painted this vessel at another site; in other words, it appears that a scribe from the Ik school was invited to create this vessel by the elite or royal family of another site.

However, the mystery deepens as the PSS names its owner/patron as *Chuk-hi Ti Chan Its'at* ("artist") *Pits* ("adorned"), the son of Sak Muan, holy lord of the Ik polity (MacLeod and Reents-Budet 1994:150, Figure 4.44). The court scene includes a secondary text that records a dance or the accession of the ruler of La Florida, a site located to the west of Motul de San Jose (Mark Zender, personal communication 2000). The scene intimates feasting through the incorporation of food seen on a platter positioned below the throne, on a small plate being handed to the main individual by a secondary elite kneeling to the right of the bench, and in the two lidded cylindrical vases on the bench (Reents-Budet et al. 1994b). Behind the ruler, the bench is covered by a black bundle or box, an animal mask, a ballgame yoke, and a tall cylindrical vase (possibly a gift just received from the two nobles seated in front of the bench?). So, the vessel's style and PSS connect it to the Motul de San Jose polity, but it was produced at another site where presumably the scribe was invited by the son of the Motul de San Jose ruler, where he may have resided or visited for a particular occasion. Since the secondary text centers on the La Florida ruler, it is possible that this is the site in question where the vessel was painted to commemorate the visit by

Fig. 9.1 Elaborate polychrome vase (Dumbarton Oaks B564), painted with a palace scene, and hieroglyphic texts that mention the sites of Motul de San Jose and La Florida (Dumbarton Oaks, Pre-Columbian Collection, Washington, D.C.).

the son of Sak Muan, possibly to attend the enthronment of the La Florida ruler.

Stanton and Gallareta Negrón (2001:232) also emphasize the importance of Terminal Classic Yucatán serving vessels as political currency used in alliance building and then consumed:

> in feasting rituals designed to cement personal relationships, in feasting associated with veneration rituals, in cacheing rituals designed to imbue places or things with supernatural power, . . . in mortuary rituals . . . [and in] feasting during desecratory termination rituals designed to "kill" places or objects associated with defeated enemies.

However, Stanton and Gallareta Negrón do not explain which types of serving ware fulfilled this role, nor do they give evidence that this model applies to the simply decorated Yucatecan pottery such as the ubiquitous slatewares. They contend that feasting was an important part of desecratory rituals, and that sourcing the pottery found in such contexts will indicate the origin of the conquerors of the site desecrated. But, it is difficult to understand why these warriors would bring pottery from their home site rather than use that from nearby.

Another application of pottery analysis to sociopolitical issues is provided by Ball (1993) who considers the cultural correlates of the utilitarian ceramic production-distribution patterns shown by a number of studies, including Robert Fry's work at Tikal, and Bishop and Robert Rands' research at Palenque (see below). Ball concludes that the role of the major Maya cities as consumers rather than producers or redistributors of pottery places Classic Maya sociopolitical organization under the rubric of regal-ritual centers and segmentary states, rather than centralized bureaucratic states or mercantile city-states, as defined by Richard Fox (1977). Ball's conclusion has gained further support from ceramic studies in the Petexbatun region (Foias 1996, 2002; Foias and Bishop 1997, in press) and at Copan (Bill 1997).

Ethnoarchaeology among Modern Maya Potters

A third more minor trend, although important, has been ethnoarchaeology and ethnography among modern Maya potters. Starting with Raymond Thompson's research on modern Yucatecan potters (1958), this line of inquiry has continued, under the rubric of ceramic ecology, principally by Dean Arnold (1971, 1978a, 1978b, 1985; Arnold et al. 1991). Thompson (1958), J. Howry (1978), Robert Reina and Robert Hill (1978), Rice (1977), and M. Deal (1998) detail the full repertoire of potting techniques and manufacturing processes of individual Maya potters from the first stage of raw material exploitation to paste preparation, and vessel forming to firing. The equipment involved, from the small scrapers to the large kilns, is described in enough detail to help archaeologists identify them in the ancient remains of the prehispanic periods. These studies have also examined the material correlates of potting activities, including the maximum area of raw material exploitation for clays, tempers, fuel, water, and even the climatic conditions needed for pottery manufacture (Arnold 1985).

The functions of the pottery forms still produced in the Maya highlands and Yucatán as described by Reina and Hill (1978) and Thompson (1958) have allowed archaeologists to propose hypotheses concerning the functions of similar forms in ancient ceramic complexes (cf. Deal 1982; Feldman 1982; Henrickson and MacDonald 1983). Arnold's study of the Maya potters of Ticul, Yucatán (1971), and Howry's work with Chamula potters in the Chiapas highlands (1978) highlight the consistent selection and mixture of clays and tempers by individual potters to produce their wares, which suggests that chemical profiles of the products of individual communities or potters can be identified through paste compositional analysis. In the same vein, Thompson's careful inventory of a number of Maya potting communities in Yucatán (1958) identified a suite of features in paste recipes, vessel forms, and decoration that distinguish the production of each community. This is again directly relevant to paste chemical analysis as it implies that chemical sourcing, stylistic and modal analyses can identify and differentiate between the products of different producing communities or even individual potting groups (cf. Reents-Budet 1994; Reents-Budet et al. 2000).

Deal (1998) has focused on small scale production of either domestic or part-time specialist potters among the Tzeltal communities of Chanal and Aguacatenango in the central Maya highlands of Chiapas. He described the potting and nonpotting households as production, consumption, and depositional units, tailoring his research to be directly applicable to archaeological questions, such as the material visibility of potting, emic pottery classifications versus the archaeological type-variety system,[11] and so on. Arnold (1980, 1981) together with Hector Neff and Bishop (1991, 1999) have considered the intersection between the assumptions of chemical sourcing analyses such as INAA and the raw material resource selection and pottery technology of modern traditional potters in order to refine the theory and methods of paste compositional analysis.

The need to incorporate ceramic ecology and ethnoarchaeology into studies of ancient Maya pottery cannot be overemphasized. To illustrate the importance of such collaborative research, I include an example from my own research at Motul de San Jose. As the project aims to reconstruct pottery production and exchange at this Late Classic center (Foias 2000a, Foias and Bishop forthcoming), we wanted to undertake a survey of clay sources. However, most clay deposits in this area are buried and frankly we thought that we had an impossible task at hand. However, one of my graduate students, Matt Moriarty, began a modern soil survey with an Itzá informant from the nearby village of San Jose and, not surprisingly, our informant knew exactly that clay sources such as these are associated with low depressions in the hilly topography surrounding the site (Moriarty 2001). Cassandra Bill's research (1997) on the Classic pottery of Copan is an excellent example of the importance of pottery ethnoarchaeology to understand ancient craft production: She employs data from modern Maya potting communities to illuminate the archaeological correlates of distinct ceramic-producing communities or units, and to discern the conditions under which production changes or intensifies.

Putting It All Together: What We Know and What We Do Not Know about Maya Pottery Production and Exchange

The most recent syntheses of Classic Maya pottery economy reconstruct a pluralistic pre-capitalist system consisting of two layers: the "prestige or political economy" and the "general or household economy" (Taschek and Ball 1992; McAnany 1993a; Potter and King 1995). The *prestige economy* refers specifically and restrictively to the production, exchange, and consumption of wealth[12] pottery used to affirm elite status or to form and maintain alliances between elites (Ball and Taschek 1992:17). The *general economy* is defined as the economic activities pertaining to the production, exchange, and consumption of *subsistence* goods such as utilitarian pottery (including lower-grade polychromes) (Ball and Taschek 1992; McAnany 1989, 1993a). Each of these two economic spheres may have had different and possibly separate systems of production and distribution.

Within the pottery prestige economy, the elite patronage of artisans may have been the normal pattern of manufacture of elaborate polychromes and ritual pottery (Rands 1967; Rands and Bishop 1980; Becker 1973; Hammond 1975; Rice 1987a). The scribes who painted the most elaborate of these polychrome masterpieces often signed them with their names and titles, including the title *ajaw*, highly suggestive that they were of the elite and even royal status, such as the royal artists from Naranjo, Ah-Maxam[13] (Reents-Budet et al. 1993, 1994b; Reents-Budet 1994, 1998; Stuart 1987; MacLeod and Reents-Budet 1994; Coe and Kerr 1997). Archaeological excavations have also brought to light several scribal palaces or palace workshops where these fine polychromes were produced. One such example, the Buenavista "palace school," represents the sociopolitical context of production in the pottery prestige economy and of the implied tight elite control over this institution (Reents-Budet et al. 2000; Ball 1993; Taschek and Ball 1992).

Takeshi Inomata has also identified a scribe's residence and workshop in the epicenter of Aguateca, where shell jewelry manufacture and painting also took place (1995, 1997). A third example of palace schools may be the House of the Bacabs at Copan (Stuart 1992; Webster 1989). Coggins (1975:429–30, 513–14) and Becker (1973, 1983) argue that the Group 4H-1 on the eastern edge of central Tikal may have been an elite pottery workshop. Finally, a possible polychrome workshop dump was discovered behind the royal palace complex at Motul de San Jose (Foias 2000a, 2000b). However, the scarcity of archaeological examples of such scribal schools has severely limited our knowledge of the nature and organization of these polychrome ateliers.

The nature of the processes involved in the distribution of wealth items remains under debate. Fry (1980) and Georgia West (2002) propose a market exchange model, whereas others believe that they may have been distributed through gift exchange between the elites of different Maya polities (Tourtellot and Sabloff 1972; Sabloff 1975; Rice 1987a; Ball 1993; Adams 1971). It is more likely that these elaborate polychrome vessels were gifted among nobility, as they were found in restricted elite contexts[14] and because they functioned as "political currency" (as discussed above) (Le Count 1999; Ball 1993; Bishop 1994; Reents-Budet et al. 1994b; Rice 1987b; Sabloff 1975; Tourtellot and Sabloff 1972).

Within the general economy, utilitarian pottery (unslipped, monochrome, and simple polychromes) was probably produced by part-time non-elite specialists in independent small-scale family workshops, generally beyond the major centers (Ball 1993; Beaudry 1984; Fry 1980; Potter and King 1995; Rands and Bishop 1980; Reents-Budet et al. 1994b; Rice 1987a; Iceland and Goldberg 1999). Reconstructions of pottery manufacture have been based on indirect studies rather than direct excavations of workshops or production loci since none had been discovered in the Southern and Northern Maya Lowlands until recently.[15] The absence of identified workshops has suggested to some scholars that production was small-scale, but it also may be the result of sampling bias as excavations have focused on the major centers (Rice 1985).

We have conflicting evidence about the gender identity of the potters. Overwhelming ethnographic data show that pottery manufacture is the domain of females in modern Maya potting households in the Guatemalan highlands, with the clear implication that the same pattern applied to the earlier Classic Maya civilization (Reina and Hill 1978:21). Yet, two other lines of evidence suggest the opposite. Titles associated with scribes or artisans who painted the beautiful polychromes vessels of the Late Classic carry the male glyphic identifier (MacLeod and Reents-Budet 1994; Reents-Budet et al. 1994b; Stuart 1989). Furthermore, ethnohistorical accounts as well as the Vienna and Motul dictionaries from Post-Conquest Yucatán show that potting was a male craft, and weaving was the female metier (Clark and Houston 1998; Roys 1943). In contrast, Carolyn Tate (2000) contends that based on Maya gender roles and the dual-gendered nature of the sacred in Maya cosmovision, females probably made the pottery and the men painted their surfaces. Archaeological identification and excavations of actual Classic workshops could clarify this issue.

Technological studies of Classic pottery have also allowed us to understand specific aspects of the organization of pottery production. Classic Maya pottery was made by hand without the use of a potter's wheel as no evidence of rapid turning action has been found in Maya ceramics (Rice 1985). Ancient potters may have used a slow turning device called a *kabal* that is common among modern Yucatán potters (Thompson 1958). The *kabal* is a low disk of wood on which the vessel is formed and that is rotated slowly with the feet. Unfortunately, such devices would not be preserved in the archaeological record.

Coiling is the forming technique used today in the Maya area (Reina and Hill 1978), and technological analysis of the breakage pattern of Classic pottery supports that it was also used in the past. The weakest points in the vessel are along the joints between the coils, and the vessel tends to break along them, displaying a horizontal or slightly spiraling breakage pattern (Rice 1985:128). In the Petexbatun region, the horizontal breakage pattern of large red slipped jars is characteristic of coiling (Foias 1996; Foias and Bishop in press). Furthermore, the breakage pattern shows that these vessels were made in parts following a standard sequence: The concave base was made separately and probably first, possibly using a simple mold; the body of the jar was then formed through coiling and attached to the base; finally the jar neck made separately was added (Foias and Bishop in press). This standard sequence of vessel forming in the jars suggests a degree of specialization among Classic Maya potters.

Decoration of Classic Maya pottery varied from the striation of unslipped jars, to slips (but no glazes) to incision, fluting, grooving, carving, gouging, plano-relief, punctuation, dentate stamping, and so on. Classic slips of cream, orange, red, black, brown, and gray tend to be thin and highly glossy or lustrous, whereas Preclassic slips had a waxy quality seen again in the slatewares of northern Yucatán. These slips consist of very fine montmorillonite clay particles and minerals mixed in water (Rice 1985:123–5). Plant and/or mineral extracts may have been added to the slips or used to coat the pottery after firing to increase the surface luster (Rice 1985:125; Shepard 1942; Reents-Budet 1994).

Firing formed the final stage in pottery manufacture. Until recently, no kilns had been found in the Southern Maya Lowlands (Rice 1985, 1987a,

1987b). Yet, Late Classic kilns are known from accidental bulldozer excavations on the Pacific coast of Guatemala and through archaeological excavations in the Naco and Ulua Valleys in Honduras and Belize (Bishop, personal communication 1992; Stone and Turnbull 1940; Urban et al. 1997; Wells 1999; Lopez et al. 2001, 2002). The preferred method of firing in the Southern Maya Lowlands appears to have been open pit firing (cf. Reina and Hill 1978). Such firing is hard to control, creating a very uneven atmosphere and reaching only medium-low temperatures (under 950°C) (Rice 1985). It is possible that the ancient Maya potters preferred open firing because glossy slips lose their color with high firing temperatures (Rice 1985). Furthermore, a large percentage of Classic pottery is tempered with calcium carbonate found widely in this limestone karstic region. Calcium carbonate disintegrates when fired above 750°C (Rye 1981:32–3), and so provides the upper firing limit under which calcite-tempered pottery was fired.

The common fireclouding of monochrome and unslipped pottery in the Petexbatun region suggests the uneven atmosphere characteristic of open pit firing (Foias and Bishop in press). This stands in marked contrast to the Petexbatun polychromes that rarely have fireclouding (Foias and Bishop in press). Thus, there is a significant difference in firing technology between these groups of Classic pottery. Rice suggests that the polychromes were placed in saggars or inside another vessel to provide them with a more even firing atmosphere (1985:118). It also appears that the polychromes were fired at somewhat lower temperatures than the monochromes or unslipped types (between 600 and 700°C) (Cowgill and Hutchinson 1969; Shepard 1939).

Chemical and petrographic sourcing analyses at Palenque (Rands and Bishop 1980; Bishop et al. 1982; Bishop 1994) and Tikal (Culbert and Schwalbe 1987; Fry 1979, 1980) have shown that utilitarian pottery production was dispersed beyond the ceremonial core of Maya cities. In both these studies of intraregional production, the center imported pottery from surrounding areas, rather than producing it. Ball (1993), McAnany (1993b), and Rands and Bishop (1980) have contended that small communities outside the major centers may have specialized in the manufacture of particular items. The ethnographic study of modern Maya potters in Guatemala has supported this conclusion (Reina and Hill 1978). Several scholars (Arnold 1985; Ford 1991, 1992; Rice 1981) have also argued that there is a positive correlation between the location of pottery craft production and poor soils, suggesting that where foodstuffs were locally unavailable, these were acquired intraregionally in exchange for utilitarian craft goods, especially pottery.

This view of small-scale, dispersed pottery manufacture in "suburban" areas is contrary to discoveries at Sayil and Quirigua. Intensive survey and surface collection at Sayil in the Puuc area have uncovered a large-scale utilitarian ceramic production zone within the southwest elite group in the site core (Smyth et al. 1995:331). Spatial analysis of manufacturing activities at Quirigua revealed that both obsidian and pottery production took place in the site core and periphery, sometimes within elaborate or elite architectural groups (Ashmore 1988). Thus, although the general pattern for pottery manufacture is of a small-scale suburban craft, both the implied degree of elite control and scale of production vary between different Maya centers.

Indirect methods have been employed to understand pottery production in the absence of excavated pottery locales. Standardization[16] was one such means, used to reconstruct changes in pottery craft specialization in the Petexbatun region (Foias 1996; Foias and Bishop 1997, in press). The high coefficients of variation suggesting low standardization of the Late and Terminal Classic polychrome and monochrome pottery of the Petexbatun centers are in accordance with the view of localized small-scale dispersed manufacture by many potters. The variability in ancient Maya pottery economies is shown by the large-scale and standardized production of salt-making vessels along the Belizean coast (McKillop 1994, 1996; Andrews and Mock 2002). Bill's (1997) study of the Classic period pottery economy at Copan employed diversity measures to understand changes in production. She defines assemblage or product diversity as the number of different ceramic products (identified by specific combinations of paste, surface treatment, and general vessel forms) and considers it an important measure of the number of different production units during a given time period. A second measure, intraproduct diversity, is the number of morphological variants of a particular type or ceramic product (such as necked vessels), and relates to the number of potters involved in the production of that particular item.

Although there is no general consensus, the exchange of subsistence goods may have varied from simple barter to a complex market system, possibly associated with fairs at the major centers or embedded in the social organization (Freidel 1981; Fry 1979, 1980, 1981; Rands and Bishop 1980; Rice 1987a; Stanton and Gallareta Negrón 2001:232, footnote 7; West 2002). Studies of distribution have been used to understand the nature and scale of exchange, as well as the degree of elite control over distribution. The most extensive investigations of intraregional exchange have been based on chemical and petrological sourcing analyses again at Palenque, Tikal, and Copan (Bishop 1994; Culbert and Schwalbe 1987; Fry 1979, 1980, 1981; Rands and Bishop 1980; Beaudry 1984). This research has suggested that the largest utilitarian pottery types (unslipped storage jars) were most likely distributed through localized barter or supply zone exchange, whereas the slipped utilitarian pottery was distributed through many small markets and/or other mechanisms embedded in social or kinship networks (Freidel 1981; Fry 1979, 1980; Rice 1987a).

I suspect that generally, the elite had little control over the distribution of these subsistence goods and utilitarian wares if they involved many noncentralized markets and/or nonmarket exchange relationships (Fry 1980, 1981; Rice 1987a; Rands and Bishop 1980; McAnany 1993a; Potter and King 1995:28; Ball 1993:247). Elites could more easily control exchange if it took place in a central location either through redistribution or market exchange. However, markets have been difficult to detect archaeologically (Hirth 1998), although the large central plazas common in Maya centers are often seen as functioning in such a role (Freidel 1981; Jones 1996; Marcus 1993; Rice 1987b). Unfortunately, no features or artifact accumulations suggestive of markets have been found in these central plazas, so this hypothesis remains unconfirmed (Potter and King 1995:24). More recently, a possible market has been discovered at Sayil within one of the large central architectural complexes (the Mirador Complex): Linear stone features are suggestive of market stalls, and a high density of utilitarian ceramic wares hints at marketing or storage activities (Smyth et al. 1995; Tourtellot et al. 1992). In counterpoint, West (2002) puts together a strong case in favor of the existence of markets in Classic Maya centers, and elite control over these through a monopoly over exotic or specialized goods manufactured in the city itself.

Although space limitations do not allow an in-depth treatment, it is important to consider if there were any differences in pottery economics between the Southern and Northern Maya Lowlands. Studies of pottery production and exchange in the Northern Lowlands are few in number, possibly because chronological concerns in this region are still foremost (see Bey et al. 1997, 1998; Kepecs 1998; Smyth 1998; Anderson 1998; Suhler et al. 1998). One difference between the two zones has been the dominance of high-gloss polychromes in the Southern Lowlands and of slatewares in the Northern Lowlands during the Classic period, with the Rio Bec region forming the frontier between the two. Although Yucatecan polychromes are not absent (Ball 1975, 1978), they become more and more rare toward the north, and are generally nonfigural and nonglyphic. The sociocultural correlates of this significant ceramic distinction remain to be investigated (Ball 1993:257).

However, it seems clear that "the need to visually distinguish multiple individual centers through the production of distinctive local fineware traditions [such as the different polychrome styles of the Southern Lowlands] does not seem to have been so strongly developed" in the Northern Lowlands (Ball 1993:263). This suggests that political competition may have been less fierce in the north than in the south. But, as Ball (1993:263–4) states, we have to await more studies of Northern Lowland pottery before we can understand and explain these distinctions between north and south. West's detailed review of the evidence on Classic and Postclassic ceramic exchange highlights the long-term continuity of Maya pottery economies of generally dispersed rural production and market exchange at both regional and local centers (2002). Nevertheless, evidence from Terminal Classic Sayil for large-scale slateware production and marketing, and the seemingly significant homogeneity or standardization of Sotuta slates (Kepecs 1998; West 2002) may indicate an economic shift to state-controlled large-scale ceramic production at that time. A formal study of the degree of uniformity in Sotuta slates is needed to support this final assertion.

Conclusion: The Future of Maya Ceramic Studies

I have tried to show in this chapter that Maya ceramic studies do not form a sterile search for chronology. Rather it is a vibrant, rich field of inquiry geared to answer questions about the social, political, economic, and even ideological spheres of Maya society. I would like to conclude with a few caveats for the future of Maya ceramic research. First, it is crucial that we do not lose sight of ceramic chronology. We still have some problematic periods that need to be studied in further detail, especially in the Northern Lowlands. A second caveat for Maya ceramicists is really an entreaty that we must collaborate even further with geologists, chemists, soil specialists, art historians, epigraphers, ethnoarchaeologists, and modern Maya potters. As Ron Bishop tells me often, archaeologists need to be better educated about the chemical and physical methods used in pottery analysis, and that can only be achieved through collaboration between these fields. Finally, my third caveat is that we need to begin to incorporate post-processual models of social agency into our analyses of Maya pottery. Most Maya ceramic studies lack a focus on the individual, but culture is created continuously by the human agent through the production, use, and consumption of pottery.

To take ceramic studies into the new millenium, Maya ceramicists must extend beyond considerations of process from the societal perspective, to seeing process from the perspective of the human individual involved. We must consider the act of production as an individual's act of creating culture. This may be the most difficult of steps, but the door has already been opened by such publications as Helms (1993) and Costin and Wright (1998) who examine how social or political identity is created through crafting cross-culturally, or Inomata (2001) who considers the power and ideology of artistic creation among Classic Maya craft specialists.

Notes

1. Both the Uaxactun and Mayapan ceramic complex terminology serve as the names of broad ceramic spheres as established at the 1965 Maya Ceramic Conference (Willey et al. 1967), such as Mamom, Chicanel, Tzakol, Tepeu, Cehpech, Sotuta, Hocaba, and Tases.

2. This is not to say that Gifford and the first generation of Maya ceramicists did not think that pottery technology should be studied, but rather that "technology had only minimal relevance to the pottery *type* as such" (Gifford 1976:19).
3. A similar pattern applies to the Middle Postclassic Hocaba and Late Postclassic Tases complexes originally identified by Smith (1971) as sequential. Later studies suggest that these are contemporary, with Hocaba evolving out of the Sotuta traditions, and Tases out of the Cehpech traditions (Andrews V 1981:337; Kepecs 1998; Bey et al. 1998:117).
4. Other paste compositional investigations are Rice's analysis of Valley of Guatemala whiteware (1976b, 1977, 1978), Hammond et al.'s study of pottery and clays from Lubaantun Belize (Hammond et al. 1976; Hammond 1975), Bishop et al.'s Miraflores ceramic sphere project (1989), Neff's long-term work on Plumbate (Neff 1984, 1988a, 1988b, 1991; Neff and Bishop 1988; Neff and Bishop 1988). Also see Beaudry (1991) for a review of New World paste compositional investigations. Less common, petrographic studies have explored a myriad of questions, such as clay utilization at the Formative site of K'axob (Bartlett et al. 2000), production and distribution of Yucatecan slatewares (Chung et al. 1995; Barba and Varela 1992), trends in Maya pottery tempering (Jones 1986, 1991), inter- and intrasite technological variability in the ceramic production of late Classic pottery in Belize (Iceland and Goldberg 1999).
5. See Mary Miller's (1989) excellent overview of the development of Maya vase painting studies.
6. Michael Coe's *The Maya Scribe and His World* (1973) was the major breakthrough in research on Maya vase painting (see Miller 1989:137–8). Coe (1973) was the first to name the repetitive pottery texts as the primary standard sequence (PSS). His original interpretation of the function of the texts and vessels as wholly mortuary or ritual has been overturned by the "decipherment revolution" of the 1980s and 1990s that has elucidated the complex name tagging represented by PSS, and the very important political and social functions of the elaborate Maya polychrome vessels (see Reents-Budet 1994; Reents-Budet et al. 1994b).
7. Prudence Rice (1999) has also delved into the depths of Classic Maya ritual and religion by examining a nonpolychrome pottery category, unslipped censers.
8. Also of note is the recent and critical reassessment of the role of shamanism in Maya art by Klein et al. (2002). Although I would argue that their case is overstated, they bring to our attention a number of weaknesses in Mesoamerican shamanism studies.
9. Spheres of alliances among the many Classic period polities can then be reconstructed by monitoring the distribution of specific polychrome styles. For example, I used the distribution of Ik-style polychromes, produced in the Motul de San Jose region north of Lake Petén Itzá, to reconstruct its political alliances (Foias n.d.). Although Motul de San Jose was under Tikal's sphere of influence for at least part of the Late Classic, Ik-style pottery concentrates in the Petexbatun centers, such as Dos Pilas and Aguateca, known to have been Tikal's enemies and the allies of Calakmul. Furthermore, Ik-style pottery is lacking at Tikal. This uneven distribution suggests that Tikal's control over Motul de San Jose was weak or indirect (Foias n.d.). Unfortunately, a more detailed study of the distribution of the Ik style is not possible because most Ik vessels lack archaeological context.
10. It is of note that in the Petexbatun region, the majority of the polychrome vases are imported from the Motul de San Jose-Tikal or Tikal-Uaxactun zones in central Petén, whereas most of the polychrome tripod platters are locally made (Foias and Bishop n.d.). This clear distinction also accords polychrome vases a special status, probably because ritual drinking was such a central element in political competitive feasting and alliance building.
11. Perhaps not surprisingly, ethnoarchaeological studies of Maya potters have found that emic classifications were based on formal-functional attributes, rather than decorative style characteristics (Deal 1998:53; Culbert 1959 quoted in Deal 1998; Howry 1978:252; Thompson 1958:29).
12. I use the typology established by Brumfiel and Earle (1987:4) who distinguish between two classes of goods (subsistence and wealth): Subsistence items fulfill basic needs in all households of all individuals, whereas wealth items are used to display, reinforce, and increase status.
13. This does not preclude the possibility that there were also non-elite scribes or assistants in the elite workshops.
14. However, West (2002) points out that fine Codex style polychromes are found broadly at Nakbe (Hansen et al. 1991). This may be due to the fact that Nakbe was producing this style.

15. Pottery manufacturing loci have been identified in the peripheral areas, including Belize and Honduras (Urban et al. 1997; Wells 1999; Lopez Varela et al. 2001, 2002; Lopiparo et al. in press).
16. I want to stress here that standardization indices must be seen as very generalized guides to the nature of craft specialization as discussed by Costin (1991), Arnold (1991), Blackman et al. (1993), and Kvamme et al. (1996).

References

Adams, R. E. W. (1971) *Ceramics of Altar de Sacrificios, Guatemala*, Peabody Museum Papers 63, Cambridge: Harvard University Press.

Anderson, P. K. (1998) "Yula, Yucatán, Mexico: Terminal Classic Maya Ceramic Chronology for the Chichén Itzá Area," *Ancient Mesoamerica* 9: 151–65.

Andrews V. E. W. (1981) "Dzibilchaltun," in V. R. Bricker (ed.), *Supplement to the Handbook of Middle American Indians, Vol. 1: Archaeology*, Austin: University of Texas Press.

Andrews, A. P., and Mock, S. B. (2002) "New Perspectives on the Prehispanic Maya Salt Trade," in M. Masson and D. Freidel (eds.), *Ancient Maya Political Economies*, pp.307–34, Oxford: Altamira Press.

Andrews, A. P., and Robles, F. (1985) "Chichén Itzá and Cobá: An Itza Maya Standoff in Early Postclassic Yucatán," in A. Chase and P. Rice (eds.), *Lowland Maya Postclassic*, pp. 62–72, Austin: University of Texas Press.

Arnold, D. (1971) "Ethnomineralogy of Ticul: Yucatán Potters," *American Antiquity* 36: 20–40.

———(1978a) "Ceramic Variability, Environment, and Culture History among the Pokom in the Valley of Guatemala," in I. Hodder (ed.), *Spatial Organization of Culture*, pp. 39–60, Pittsburgh: University of Pittsburgh Press.

———(1978b) "Ethnography of Pottery Making in the Valley of Guatemala," in R. K. Wetherington (ed.), *The Ceramics of Kaminaljuyu*, pp. 327–400, University Park: Pennsylvania State University Press.

———(1980) "Localized Exchange: An Ethnoarchaeological Perspective," in R. Fry (ed.) *Models and Methods in Regional Exchange*, pp. 147–50, Paper no. 1, Washington, DC: Society for American Archaeology.

———(1981) "A Model for the Identification of Non-local Ceramic Distribution. View from the Present," in H. Howard and E. Morris (eds.), *Production and Distribution: A Ceramic Viewpoint*, pp. 31–44, BAR International Series 120, Oxford: Archaeopress.

———(1985) *Ceramic Theory and Cultural Process*, New York: Cambridge University Press.

Arnold, D., and Nieves, A. L. (1992) "Factors Affecting Ceramic Standardization," in G. Bey and C. Pool (eds.), *Ceramic Production and Distribution: An Integrated Approach*, pp. 93–113, Boulder, CO: Westview Press.

Arnold, D., Neff, H., and Bishop, R. L. (1991) "Compositional Analysis and 'Sources' of Pottery: An Ethnoarchaeological Approach," *American Anthropologist* 93: 70–90.

———(1999) "Testing Interpretative Assumptions of Neutron Activation Analysis: Contemporary Pottery in Yucatán, 1964–1994," in E. S. Chilton (ed.), *Material Meanings, Critical Approaches to the Interpretation of Material Culture*, pp. 61–84, Salt Lake City: University of Utah Press.

Arnold III, P. J. (1991) "Dimensional Standardization and Production Scale in Mesoamerican Ceramics,"*Latin American Antiquity* 2: 363–70.

Ashmore, W. (1988) "Household and Community at Classic Quirigua," in R. Wilk and W. Ashmore (eds.), *Household and Community in the Mesoamerican Past*, pp. 153–170, Albuquerque: University of New Mexico Press.

Ball, J. W. (1975) "The Polychrome Pottery of Dzibilchaltun, Yucatán, Mexico: Typology," in E. W. Andrews (ed.), *Archaeological Investigations on the Yucatan Peninsula*, Middle American Research Institute Publication 31, pp. 231–3, New Orleans: Tulane University.

———(1977) *The Archaeological Ceramics of Becan, Campeche, Mexico*, Middle American Research Institute Publication 43, New Orleans: Tulane University.

———(1978) "Archaeological Pottery of the Yucatán-Campeche Coast," in *Studies in the Archaeology of Coastal Yucatán and Campeche, Mexico*, pp. 71–146, Middle American Research Institute Publication 46, New Orleans: Tulane University.

———(1983) "Teotihuacan, the Maya, and Ceramic Interchange: A Contextual Perspective," in A. G. Miller (ed.), *Highland-Lowland Interaction in Mesoamerica*, pp. 125–46, Washington: Dumbarton Oaks.

———(1993) "Pottery, Potters, Palaces and Polities: Some Socioeconomic and Political Implications of Late Classic Maya Ceramic Industries," in J. A. Sabloff and J. S. Henderson (eds.), *Lowland Maya Civilization in the Eighth Century A.D.: A Symposium at Dumbarton Oaks, 7th and 8th October 1989*, pp. 243–72, Washington, DC: Dumbarton Oaks.

Ball, J. W., and Taschek, J. T. (1991) "Late Classic Lowland Maya Political Organization and Central-Place Analysis: New Insights from the Upper Belize Valley," *Ancient Mesoamerica* 2: 149–65.

Ball, J. W., and Taschek, J. T. (1992) "Economics and Economics in the Late Classic Maya Lowlands: A Trial Examination of Some Apparent Patterns and Their Implications," Paper presented at the Symposium "The Segmentary State and the Classic Lowland Maya," Cleveland State University April.

Barba, L. A., and Varela Torrecilla, C. (1992) "Las propiedades físicas de las cerámicas de Oxkintok: on estudio analítico," in M. R. Dorado (ed.), *Misión Arqucológico de España en Mexico*, pp. 147–59, Madrid: Ministerio de Cultura.

Bartlett, M. L., Neff, H., and McAnany, P. A. (2000) "Differentiation of Clay Resources on a Limestone Plain: The Analysis of Clay Utilization during the Maya Formative at K'axob Belize," *Geoarchaeology* 15(2): 95–133.

Beaudry, M. (1984) *Ceramic Production and Distribution in the Southeast Maya Periphery: Late Classic Painted Serving Vessels*, BAR International Series 203, Oxford: Archaeopress.

———(1991) "New World Paste Compositional Investigations," in R. L. Bishop and F. W. Lange (eds.), *The Ceramic Legacy of Anna O. Shepard*, pp. 224–56, Niwot: University of Colorado Press.

Becker, M. J. (1973) "Archaeological Evidence for Occupational Specialization among the Classic Period Maya at Tikal, Guatemala," *American Antiquity* 38: 396–406.

———(1983) "Indications of Social Class Differences Based on the Archaeological Evidence for Occupational Specialization among the Classic Maya at Tikal, Guatemala," *Revista Espanola de Antropologia Americana* 13: 29–46.

Bey III, G. J., Hanson, C. A., and Ringle, W. M. (1997) "Classic to Postclassic at Ek Balam: Architectural and Ceramic Evidence for Defining the Transition," *Latin American Antiquity* 8: 237–54.

Bey III, G. J., Peraza L. C., and Ringle, W. M. (1992) "Comparative Analysis of Late Classic Period Ceramic Complexes of the Northern Maya Lowlands," *Ceramica de Cultura Maya* 16: 11–7.

Bey III, G. J., et al. (1998) "The Ceramic Chronology of Ek Balam, Yucatán, Mexico," *Ancient Mesoamerica* (91): 101–20.

Bill, C. R. (1997) *Patterns of Variation and Change in Dynastic Period Ceramics and Ceramic Production at Copan, Honduras*, unpublished Ph.D. dissertation, Tulane University.

Bishop, R. L. (1975) *Western Lowland Maya Ceramic Trade: An Archaeological Application of Nuclear Chemical and Geological Data Analysis*, unpublished Ph.D. dissertation, Southern Illinois University, Carbondale.

———(1980) "Aspects of Ceramic Compositional Modeling," in R. Fry (ed.), *Models and Methods in Regional Exchange*, pp. 47–65, SAA Paper no. 1, Washington, DC: Society for American Archaeology.

———(1994) "Pre-Columbian Pottery: Research in the Maya Region," in D. A. Scott and P. Meyers (eds.), *Archaeometry of Pre-Columbian Sites and Artifacts*, pp. 15–65, Los Angeles: The Getty Conservation Institute.

———(in press) "Five Decades of Maya Fine Orange Ceramic Investigation by INAA," in L. van Zelst (ed.), *Patterns and Process: A Two-day Symposium in Honor of Dr. Edward V. Sayre*, Washington, DC: Smithsonian Institution Press.

Bishop, R. L., and Lange, F. W. (1991) *The Ceramic Legacy of Anna O. Shepard*, Niwot: University of Colorado Press.

Bishop, R. L., and Neff, H. (1989) "Compositional Data Analysis in Archaeology," in R. O. Allen (ed.), *Archaeological Chemistry IV*, pp. 57–86, Advances in Chemistry Series 220, Washington, DC: American Chemical Society.

Bishop, R. L., Demarest, A. A., and Sharer, R. J. (1989) "Chemical Analysis and the Interpretation of the Late Preclassic Intersite Ceramic Patterns in the Southeast Highlands of Mesoamerica," in F. Bove and L. Heller (eds.), *New Frontiers in the Archaeology of the Pacific Coast of Southern*

Mesoamerica, pp. 135–45, Anthropological Research Paper 39, Temple: Arizona State University.

Bishop, R. L., Rands, R. L., and Holley, G. R. (1982) "Ceramic Compositional Analysis in Archaeological Perspective," in M. B. Schiffer (ed.), *Advances in Archaeological Method and Theory*, Vol. 5, pp. 275–330, New York: Academic Press.

Blackman, M. J., Stein, G. J., and Vandiver, P. B. (1993) "The Standardization Hypothesis and Ceramic Mass Production: Technological, Compositional, and Metric Indexes of Craft Specialization at Tell Leilan, Syria," *American Antiquity* 58: 60–80.

Brady, J. E., Ball, J. W., Bishop, R. L., Pring, D. C., Hammond, N., and Housley, R. A. (1998) "The Lowland Maya "Protoclassic": A Reconsideration of its Nature and Significance," *Ancient Mesoamerica* 9(1): 17–38.

Brainerd, G. W. (1940–1942) "Yucatán Pottery," in *Carnegie Institution of Washington Yearbook*, no.'s 39–41, Washington, DC: Carnegie Institution of Washington.

———(1941) "Fine Orange Pottery in Yucatán," *Revista Mexicana de Estudios Antropologicos* 5: 163–83.

———(1958) *The Archaeological Ceramics of Yucatán*, Anthropological Records, no. 19, Berkeley and Los Angeles: University of California.

Brumfiel, E. M., and Earle, T. K. (1987) "Specialization, Exchange, and Complex Society: An Introduction," in E. Brumfiel and T. Earle (eds.), *Specialization, Exchange, and Complex Society*, pp. 1–9, Cambridge, UK: Cambridge University Press.

Calvin, I. (1997) "Where the *Wayob* Live: A Further Examination of Classic Maya Supernaturals," in J. Kerr (ed.), *The Maya Vase Book*, Vol. 5, pp. 868–83. New York: Kerr Associates.

Carr, C. (1995) "Building a Unified Middle-range Theory of Artifact Design," in C. Carr and J. E. Neitzel (eds.), *Style, Society, and Person: Archaeological and Ethnological Approaches*, pp. 151–258, New York: Plenum Press.

Chase, A. F. (1994) "A Contextual Approach to the Ceramics of Caracol, Belize," in D. Z. Chase and A. F. Chase (eds.), *Studies in the Archaeology of Caracol, Belize*, pp. 157–182, San Francisco: Pre-Columbian Art Research Institute.

Chung, H., Barba, L., and Varela, C. (1995) "Inferencias sobre distintivos sociales en Chichén Itzá a través del estudio de la cerámica pizarra chichén (Chichén Slate Ware)," in *Religión y Sociedad en el Area Maya*, pp. 177–95, Publicaciones de la Sociedad Española de Estudios Mayas no. 3, Madrid: Sociedad Española de Estudios Mayas.

Clark, J. E. and Houston, S. D. (1998) "Craft Specialization, Gender, and Personhood among the Postconquest Maya of Yucatán," in C. Costin and R. Wright (eds.), *Craft and Social Identity*, pp. 31–46, Papers of the American Anthropolgical Association, no. 8, Washington: American Anthropological Association.

Coe, M. D. (1973) *The Maya Scribe and His World*, New York: Grolier Club.

———(1975) *Classic Maya Pottery at Dumbarton Oaks*, Washington, DC: Dumbarton Oaks, Harvard University.

———(1978) *Lords of the Underworld: Masterpieces of Classic Maya Ceramics*, Princeton: Princeton University Art Museum, Princeton University Press.

———(1982) *Old Gods and Young Heroes: The Pearlman Collection of Maya Ceramics*, Jerusalem, The Israel Museum.

———(1989) "The Hero Twins: Myth and Image," in J. Kerr (ed.), *The Maya Vase Book*, Vol. 1, pp. 161–84, New York: Kerr Associates.

Coe, M. D., and Kerr, J. (1997) *The Art of the Maya Scribe*, New York: Harry N. Abrams.

Coggins, C. (1975) *Painting and Drawing Styles at Tikal: A Historical and Iconographic Reconstruction*, unpublished Ph.D. dissertation, Harvard University.

———(1979) "A New Order and the Role of the Calendar: Some Characteristics of the Middle Classic Period at Tikal," in N. Hammond and G. R. Willey (eds.), *Maya Archaeology and Ethnohistory*, pp. 38–50, Austin: University of Texas Press.

Conkey, M. W., and Hastorf, C. A. (eds.) (1990) *The Uses of Style in Archaeology*, Cambridge, UK: Cambridge University Press.

Costin, C. L. (1991) "Craft Specialization: Issues in Defining, Documenting, and Explaining the Organization of Production," in M. B. Schiffer (ed.), *Archaeological Method and Theory*, Vol. 3, pp. 1–56, Tucson: University of Arizona Press.

Costin, C. L., and Wright, R. P. (eds.) (1998) *Craft and Social Identity*, Archaeological Paper no. 8, Washington, DC: American Anthropological Association.

Cowgill, U. M., and Hutchinson, G. E. (1969) "A Chemical and Mineralogical Examination of the Ceramic Sequence from Tikal, El Petén, Guatemala," *American Journal of Science* 267: 465–77.
Culbert, T. P. (1959) "Modern and Prehistoric Pottery Making in Chiapas, Mexico," paper presented at the 5th Annual Meeting of the American Anthropological Association, Mexico.
———(1979) *Ceramics of Tikal: Eb, Tzec, Chuen and Manik Complexes*, manuscript, Department of Anthropology, University of Arizona, Tucson.
———(1993) *The Ceramics of Tikal: Vessels from the Burials, Caches and Problematical Deposits*, Tikal Reports 25, Part A, Philadelphia: University Museum, University of Pennsylvania.
Culbert, T. P., and Schwalbe, L. A. (1987) "X-Ray Fluorescence Survey of Tikal Ceramics," *Journal of Archaeological Science* 14: 635–57.
Danien, E. C. (1998) *The Chama Polychrome Ceramic Cylinders (Maya, Guatemala, Museum Collections, University of Pennsylvania Museum of Archaeology and Anthropology)*, unpublished Ph.D. dissertation, University of Pennsylvania.
de Landa, D. (1941) *Landa's Relación de las Cosas de Yucatán*, translation by A. M. Tozzer, Peabody Museum Papers, Vol. 18, Cambridge: Harvard University.
Deal, M. (1982) "Functional Variation of Maya Spiked Vessels: A Practical Guide," *American Antiquity* 47: 614–33.
———(1998) *Pottery Ethnoarchaeology in the Central Maya Highlands*, Salt Lake City: University of Utah Press.
Demarest, A. A., and Foias, A. E. (1993) "Mesoamerican Horizons and the Cultural Transformations of Maya Civilization," in D. Rice (ed.), *Latin American Horizons: Symposium at Dumbarton Oaks, 11th and 12th October 1986*, pp.147–92, Washington, DC: Dumbarton Oaks, Harvard University.
Dunnell, R. C. (1971) "Sabloff and Smith's 'The Importance of Both Analytic and Taxonomic Classification in the Type-Variety System,'" *American Antiquity* 36: 115–8.
Feldman, L. H. (1982) "Paper Pots," *Journal de la Societe des Americanistes* 68: 41–7.
Foias, A. E. (n.d.) "History, Politics and Economics at Motul de San Jose," paper presented at the 2000 Maya Hieroglyphic Meeting, March 9–10, 2000, Austin, TX: University of Texas.
———(1996) *Changing Ceramic Production and Exchange Systems and the Classic Maya Collapse in the Petexbatun Region*, unpublished Ph.D. dissertation, Vanderbilt University.
———(2000a) "Entre la Politica y Economia: Resultados Preliminares de las Primeras Dos Temporadas del Proyecto Arqueologico Motul de San José," in J. P. Laporte et al. (eds.), *XIII Simposio de Investigaciones Arqueologicas en Guatemala*, pp. 945–73, Guatemala City: Ministerio de Cultura y Deportes, IDAEH, Asociacion Tikal, Guatemala.
———(2000b) "Entre Politica y Economia: Cual era la Naturaleza de la Economia Maya Clasica?" in W. Folan (ed.), *Los Investigadores de la Cultura Maya 8*, Vol. II, pp. 298–311, Campeche, Mexico: Universidad Autonoma de Campeche, SECUD.
———(2002) "At the Crossroads: The Economic Basis of Political Power in the Petexbatun Region," in M. Masson and D. Freidel (eds.), *Ancient Maya Political Economies*, pp. 223–48, Oxford: Altamira Press.
Foias, A. E., and Bishop, R. L. (1997) "Changing Ceramic Production and Exchange in the Petexbatun Region, Guatemala: Reconsidering the Classic Maya Collapse," *Ancient Mesoamerica* 8: 275–91.
———(forthcoming) "Pots, Sherds and Glyphs: Pottery Production and Exchange at the Twin Capitals of the Petexbatun Polity, Petén, Guatemala," in C. Poole and G. Bey (eds.), *Pottery Economies in Mesoamerica: Integrated Approaches*, Tucson: University of Arizona Press.
———(in press) *Ceramics, Production and Exchange in the Petexbatun Region: The Economic Parameters of the Classic Maya Collapse*, VIMA Petexbatun Monograph Series, Nashville: Vanderbilt University.
Ford, A. (1991) "Economic Variation of Ancient Maya Residential Settlement in the Upper Belize River Area," *Ancient Mesoamerica* 2: 35–46.
———(1992) "The Ancient Maya Domestic Economy: An Examination of Settlement in the Upper Belize River Area," in *Memorias del Primer Congreso Internacional de Mayistas: Mesas Redondas, Arqueologia, Epigrafia*, pp. 143–56, Mexico City: UNAM, Instituto de Investigaciones Filologicas.
Forsyth, D. W. (1982) "The Ceramic Sequence at El Mirador, Petén, Guatemala and the Smith

and Gifford Type-Variety Classification of Maya Ceramics," paper presented at the 44th International Congress of Americanists, Manchester, England.

———(1989) *The Ceramics of El Mirador, Petén, Guatemala, El Mirador Series, Part 4*, Papers of the New World Archaeological Foundation no. 63, Provo: Brigham Young University.

Fox, R. G. (1977) *Urban Anthropology: Cities in Their Cultural Settings*, Englewood Cliffs, NJ: Prentice-Hall.

Freidel, D. A. (1981) "Political Economics of Residential Dispersion among the Lowland Maya," in W. Ashmore (ed.), *Lowland Maya Settlement Patterns*, pp. 371–84, Albuquerque: University of New Mexico Press.

Fry, R. E. (1979) "The Economics of Pottery at Tikal, Guatemala: Models of Exchange for Serving Vessels," *American Antiquity* 44: 494–512.

———(1980) "Models for Exchange for Major Shape Classes of Lowland Maya Pottery," in R. Fry (ed.), *Models and Methods in Regional Exchange*, pp. 3–18, SAA Paper no. 1, Washington, DC: Society for American Archaeology.

———(1981) "Pottery Production-Distribution Systems in the Southern Maya Lowlands," in H. Howard and E. Morris (eds.), *Production and Distribution: A Ceramic Viewpoint*, pp. 145–67, BAR International Series 120, Oxford: Archaeopress.

Fry, R. E., and Cox, S. E. (1974) "The Structure of Ceramic Exchange at Tikal, Guatemala." *World Archaeology* 6: 209–25.

Gifford, J. (1960) "The Type-Variety Method of Ceramic Classification as an Indicator of Cultural Phenomena," *American Antiquity* 25: 341–7.

———(1976) *Prehistoric Pottery Analysis and the Ceramics of Barton Ramie in the Belize Valley*, Memoirs of the Peabody Museum of Archaeology and Ethnology, Vol. 18, Cambridge: Harvard University.

Grube, N., and Nahm, W. (1994) "A Census of Xibalba: A Complete Inventory of *Way* Characters on Maya Ceramics," in J. Kerr (ed.), *The Maya Vase Book*, Vol. 4, pp. 686–715, New York: Kerr Associates.

Hammond, N. (1972) "A Minor Criticism of the Type-Variety System of Ceramic Analysis," *American Antiquity* 37: 450–2.

———(1975) *Lubaantun: A Late Classic Maya Realm*, Monographs of the Peabody Museum of Archaeology and Ethnology, no. 2, Cambridge: Harvard University.

———(1985) "The Sun Is Hid: Classic Depictions of a Maya Myth," in E. P. Benson (ed.), *Fourth Palenque Roundtable, 1980*, San Francisco, Pre-Columbian Art Research Institute.

Hammond, N., Harbottle, G., and Gazard, T. (1976) "Neutron Activation and Statistical Analysis of Maya Ceramics and Clays from Lubaantun, Belize," *Archaeometry* 18: 147–68.

Hansen, R. D., Bishop, R. L., and Fahsen, F. (1991) "Notes on Maya Codex-style Ceramics from Nakbe, Petén, Guatemala," *Ancient Mesoamerica* 2: 225–43.

Harbottle , G., and Sayre, E. V. (1977) "Nuetron Activation Analyses: Teotihuacan Trade Ceramics," Sociedad Mexicana de Antropología, *Mesa Redonda* 15(2): 313–16.

Helms, M. W. (1993) *Craft and the Kingly Ideal: Art, Trade, and Power*, Austin: University of Texas Press.

Henrickson, E. F., and McDonald, M. M. A. (1983) "Ceramic Form and Function: An Ethnographic Search and an Archaeological Application," *American Anthropologist* 85: 630–43.

Houston, S. D. (1993) *Hieroglyphs and History at Dos Pilas: Dynastic Politics of the Classic Maya*, Austin: University of Texas Press.

———(1997) "A King Worth a Hill of Beans," *Archaeology* 50: 40.

Houston, S. D., and Stuart, D. (1989) "The *Way* Glyph: Evidence for 'Co-essences' among the Classic Maya," in *Research Reports on Ancient Maya Writing* 30, Washington, DC: Center for Maya Research.

Houston, S. D., Stuart, D., Taube, K. A. (1989) "Folk Classification of Classic Maya Pottery," *American Anthropologist* 9(3): 720–36.

Howry, J. (1978) "Ethnographic Realities of Mayan Prehistory," in D. Browman (ed.), *Cultural Continuity in Mesoamerica*, pp. 239–57, Chicago: Aldine.

Iceland, H. B., and Goldberg, P. (1999) "Late-terminal Classic Maya Pottery in Northern Belize: A Petrographic Analysis of Sherd Samples from Colha and Kichpanha," *Journal of Archaeological Science* 26(8): 951–66.

Inomata, T. (1995) *Archaeological Investigation at the Fortified Center of Aguateca, El Petén,*

Guatemala: Implications for the Study of the Classic Maya Collapse, unpublished Ph.D. dissertation, Vanderbilt University.

———(1997) "The Last Day of a Fortified Classic Maya Center: Archaeological Investigations at Aguateca, Guatemala," *Ancient Mesoamerica* 8: 337–51.

———(2001) "The Power and Ideology of Artistic Creation: Elite Craft Specialists in Classic Maya Society," *Current Anthropology* 42(3): 321–49.

Jackson, S., and Stuart, D. (2001) "The *Aj K'uhun* Title: Deciphering a Classic Maya Term of Rank," *Ancient Mesoamerica* 12: 217–28.

Jones, C. (1996) *Excavations in the East Plaza of Tikal*, Tikal Report no. 16. Philadelphia: University Museum Publications.

Jones, L. D. (1986) *Lowland Maya Pottery: The Place of Petrological Analysis*, BAR International Series no. 288, London: Archaeopress.

———(1991) "Tempering Trends in Lowland Mayan Ceramics," in A. Middleton and I. Freestone (eds.), *Recent Developments in Ceramic Petrology*, pp. 165–84, British Museum Occasional Paper no. 81, London: British Museum.

Kepecs, S. (1998) "Diachronic Ceramic Evidence and Its Social Implications in the Chikinchel Region, Northeastern Yucatán, Mexico," *Ancient Mesoamerica* 9: 121–35.

Kerr, J. (1989, 1990, 1992, 1994, 1997, 2000) *The Maya Vase Book*, Vols. 1–6, New York: Kerr Associates.

Kidder, A. V., Jennings, J. D., and Shook, E. M. (1946) *Excavations at Kaminaljuyu, Guatemala*, Publication 561, Washington, DC: Carnegie Institution of Washington.

Klein, C., et al. (2002) "The Role of Shamanism in Mesoamerican Art," *Current Anthropology* 43(3): 383–419.

Kvamme, K. L., Stark, M. T., and Longacre, W. A. (1996) "Alternative Procedures for Assessing Standardization in Ceramic Assemblages," *Amercan Antiquity* 61: 116–26.

La Porte, J. P. (1995) "Despoblamiento o problema analítico?: el clásico temprano en el sureste de Petén," in J. P. Laporte (ed.), *VIII Simposio de Investigaciones Arqueológicas en Guatemala*, pp. 729–61, Guatemala City: Museo Nacional de Antropología e Historia.

Le Count, L. (1996) *Pottery and Power: Feasting, Gifting, and Displaying Wealth among the Late and Terminal Classic Lowland Maya*, unpublished Ph.D. dissertation, University of California, Los Angeles.

———(1999) "Polychrome Pottery and Political Strategies in Late and Terminal Classic Maya Society," *Latin American Antiquity* 10: 239–58.

———(2001) "Like Water for Chocolate: Feasting and Political Ritual among Late Classic Maya at Xunantunich, Belize," *American Anthropologist* 103: 935–53.

Lincoln, C. E. (1985) "Ceramics and Ceramic Chronology," in G. R. Willey and P. Mathews (eds.), *A Consideration of the Early Classic Period in the Maya Lowlands*, pp. 55–94, Mesoamerican Studies Publication 10, Albany: SUNY.

———(1986) "The Chronology of Chichén Itzá: A Review of the Literature," in J. A. Sabloff and E. W. Andrews V (eds.), *Late Lowland Maya Civilization*, pp. 141–96, Albuquerque: School of American Research, University of New Mexico Press.

Longyear III, J. M. (1952) *Copan Ceramics: A Study of Southeastern Maya Pottery*, Publication 597, Washington, DC: Carnegie Institution of Washington.

Lopez V., S. L., van Gijn, A., and Jacobs, L. (2002) "De-mystifying Pottery Production in the Maya Lowlands: Detection of Traces of Use-Wear on Pottery Sherds through Microscopic Analysis and Experimental Replication," *Journal of Archaeological Science* 29: 1133–47.

Lopez V., S., et al. (2001) "Identifying Late Classic Maya Pottery Kilns and Ceramic Production Activities at K'axob, Belize," *Journal of Field Archaeology* 27(1/2): 177–192.

Lopiparo, J., Joyce, R. A., and Hendon, J. A. (in press) "Pottery Production in the Terminal Classic Ulua Valley," in S. Lopez V. and A. Foias (eds.), *Terminal Classic Socioeconomic Processes in the Maya Lowlands through a Ceramic Lens*, British Archaeological Reports (BAR), Oxford: Archaeopress.

MacLeod, B., and Reents-Budet, D. (1994) "The Art of Calligraphy: Image and Meaning," in D. Reents-Budet (ed.), *Painting the Maya Universe: Royal Ceramics of the Classic Period*, pp. 106–63, Durham, NC: Duke University Press.

Marcus, J. (1993) "Ancient Maya Political Organization," in J. Sabloff and J. Henderson (eds.), *Lowland Maya Civilization in the Eighth Century A. D.*, pp. 111–84, Washington: Dumbarton Oaks.

Matheny, R. T. (1970) *The Ceramics of Aguacatal, Campeche, Mexico*, Paper 27, Provo: New World Archaeological Foundation.

McAnany, P. A. (1989) "Introduction," in P. McAnany and B. Isaac (eds.), *Prehistoric Maya Economies of Belize*, pp. 1–16, Research in Economic Anthropology, Vol. 4, Greenwich, CT: JAI Press.

———(1993a) "The Economics of Social Power and Wealth among Eighth-Century Maya Households," in J. A. Sabloff and J. S. Henderson (eds.), *Lowland Maya Civilization in the Eighth Century A.D.: A Symposium at Dumbarton Oaks, 7th and 8th October 1989*, pp. 65–89, Washington, DC: Dumbarton Oaks.

———(1993b) "Resources, Specialization and Exchange in the Maya Lowlands," in J. E. Ericson and T. G. Baugh (eds.), *The American Southwest and Mesoamerica*, pp. 213–45, New York: Plenum Press.

———(1995) *Living with the Ancestors: Kinship and Kingship in Ancient Maya Society*, Austin: University of Texas Press.

McKillop, H. (1994) "Traders of the Maya Coast: Five Field Seasons in the Swamps of Southern Belize, 1988–1993," *Mexicon* 16(6): 115–9.

———(1996) "Ancient Maya Trading Ports and the Integration of Long-Distance and Regional Economies: Wild Cane Cay in South-Coastal Belize," *Ancient Mesoamerica* 7: 49–62.

Merwin, R. E., and Vaillant, G. C. (1932) *The Ruins of Holmul, Guatemala*, Memoirs of the Peabody Museum of Archaeology and Ethnology, Vol. 3, no. 2, Cambridge: Harvard University Press.

Miller, M. E. (1989) "The History of the Study of Maya Vase Painting," in J. Kerr (ed.), *The Maya Vase Book: A Corpus of Rollout Photographs of Maya Vases*, Vol. 1, pp. 128–45, New York: Kerr Associates.

Monaghan, J. (1990) "Reciprocity, Redistribution and the Transaction of Value in the Mesoamerican Fiesta," *American Ethnologist* 17: 758–74.

Moriarty, M. D. (2001) "Notas Preliminares sobre la Clasificación Indígena de Suelos en San José, Petén, Guatemala," in A. Foias (ed.), *Proyecto Arqueologico Motul de San José: Informe Preliminar # 4 de la Cuarta Temporada 2001*, pp.131–5, report presented to the Guatemalan Institute of Anthropology and History, Williamstown MA: Williams College.

Neff, H. (1984) *Developmental History of the Plumbate Pottery Industry in the Eastern Soconusco Region, A.D.. 600 through A.D.. 1250*, unpublished Ph.D. dissertation, University of California, Santa Barbara.

———(1988a) "Origins of Plumbate Pottery Production," in B. Voorhies (ed.), *Ancient Trade and Tribute: Economies of the Soconusco Region of Mesoamerica*, pp. 175–93, Salt Lake City: University of Utah Press.

———(1988b) "The Effect of Interregional Distribution on Plumbate Pottery Production," in B. Voorhies (ed.), *Ancient Trade and Tribute: Economies of the Soconusco Region of Mesoamerica*, pp. 249–67, Salt Lake City: University of Utah Press.

———(1991) "The Theoretical and Methodological Lessons of Shepard's Research on Plumbate Ware," in R. L. Bishop and F. W. Lange (eds.), *The Ceramic Legacy of Anna O. Shepard*, pp. 177–204, Niwot: University of Colorado Press.

Neff, H., and Bishop, R. L. (1988) "Plumbate Origins and Development," *American Antiquity* 53: 505–22.

Neff, H., Bishop, R. L., and Bove, F. J. (1989) "Compositional Patterning in Ceramics from Pacific Coastal and Highland Guatemala," *Archaeomaterials* 3: 97–109.

Parsons, L. A. (1967/1969) *Bilbao, Guatemala: An Archaeological Study of the Pacific Coast Cotzumalhuapa Region*, Publications in Anthropology 11 and 12, Milwaukee: Milwaukee Public Museum.

Pendergast, D. (1979) *Excavations at Altun Ha, Belize, 1964–1970*, Toronto: Royal Ontario Museum.

Potter, D. R., and King, E. M. (1995) "A Heterarchical Approach to Lowland Maya Socioeconomics," in R. Ehrenreich, C. Crumley, and J. Levy (eds.), *Heterarchy and the Analysis of Complex Societies*, pp. 17–32, Archaeological Papers of the American Anthropological Association no. 6, Washington: American Anthropological Association.

Rands, R. L. (1967) "Ceramic Technology and Trade in the Palenque Region, Mexico," in C. Riley and W. Taylor (eds.), *American Historical Anthropology*, pp. 127–51, Carbondale: Southern Illinois University Press.

Rands, R. L., and Bishop, R. L. (1980) "Resource Procurement Zones and Patterns of Ceramic Exchange in the Palenque Region, Mexico," in R. Fry (ed.), *Models and Methods in Regional Exchange*, pp. 19–46, SAA Paper no. 1, Washington, DC: Society for American Archaeology.

———(n.d.) *From Black to Gray to Orange: New Perspectives on the Lowland Maya Fine Paste Tradition*, manuscript on file at CAL, Smithsonian Institution, Washington, DC.
Rands, R. L., Bishop, R. L., and Sabloff, J. A. (1982) "Maya Fine Paste Ceramics: An Archaeological Perspective," in J. A. Sabloff (ed.), *Analyses of Fine Paste Ceramics*, Memoirs of the Peabody Museum of Archaeology and Ethnology, Vol. 15, no. 2, Cambridge: Harvard University Press.
Redfield, R., and Villa Rojas, A. (1934) *Chan Kom: A Maya Village*, Publication no. 448, Washington, DC: Carnegie Institution of Washington.
Reents-Budet, D. J. (1985) *The Late Classic Maya Holmul Style Polychrome Pottery*, unpublished Ph.D. dissertation, University of Texas at Austin.
———(1994) *Painting the Maya Universe: Royal Ceramics of the Classic Period*, Durham, NC: Duke University Press, Duke University Museum.
———(1998) "Elite Maya Pottery and Artisans as Social Indicators," in C. L. Costin and R. P. Wright (eds.), *Craft and Social Identity*, pp. 71–89, Archeological Paper no. 8, Washington, DC: American Anthropological Association.
———(2000) "Feasting among the Classic Maya: Evidence from the Pictorial Ceramics," in J. Kerr (ed.), *The Maya Vase Book*, Vol. 6, pp. 1022–37, New York: Kerr Associates.
———(2001) "Classic Maya Concepts of the Royal Court: An Analysis of Renderings on Pictorial Ceramics," in T. Inomata and S. D. Houston (eds.), *Royal Courts of the Ancient Maya, Vol. 1: Theory, Comparison and Synthesis*, pp. 195–233, Boulder, CO: Westview Press.
Reents-Budet, D. J., Bishop, R. L., and Fahsen, F. (1994a) "Una ceramica Maya negro-sobre-crema del periodo Clasico Tardio de la region oriental de Petén y Belice," in J. P. Laporte et al. (ed.), *VII Simposio de Investigaciones Arqueologicas en Guatemala, 1993*, pp. 49–67, Guatemala City: Ministerio de Cultura y Deportes, IDAEH, Asociacion Tikal.
Reents-Budet, D. J., Bishop, R. L., and MacLeod, B. (1993) "Acercamiento Integrado a la Ceramica Pintada Clasica Maya," in J. P. Laporte et al. (eds.), *VI Simposio de Investigaciones Arqueologicas en Guatemala, 1992*, pp. 71–113, Guatemala City: Ministerio de Cultura y Deportes, IDAEH, Asociacion Tikal.
———(1994b) "Painting Styles, Workshop Locations and Pottery Production," in D. J. Reents-Budet (ed.), *Painting the Maya Universe: Royal Ceramics of the Classic Period*, pp. 164–233, Durham, NC: Duke University Press, Duke University Museum.
Reents-Budet, D. J., et al. (1998) "Codex-Style Pottery: Recovering Context, Narrative and Meaning," manuscript.
Reents-Budet, D. J., et al. (2000) "Out of the Palace Dumps: Ceramic Production and Use at Buenavista del Cayo," *Ancient Mesoamerica* 11: 99–121.
Reina, R. E., and Hill II, R. M. (1978) *The Traditional Pottery of Guatemala*, Austin: University of Texas Press.
Rice, P. (1976a) "Rethinking the Ware Concept," *American Antiquity* 41: 538–43.
———(1976b) *Continuity and Change in the Valley of Guatemala: A Study of Whiteware Pottery Production*, unpublished Ph.D. dissertation, Pennsylvania State University.
———(1977) "Whiteware Pottery Production in the Valley of Guatemala: Specialization and Resource Utilization," *Journal of Field Archaeology* 4(2): 221–33.
———(1981) "Evolution of Specialized Pottery Production: A Trial Model," *Current Anthropology* 22: 219–40.
———(1982) "Pottery Production, Pottery Classification, and the Role of Physicochemical Analyses," in J. S. Olin and A. D. Franklin (eds.), *Archaeological Ceramics*, pp. 47–55, Washington, DC: Smithsonian Institution.
———(1983) "Serpents and Style in Petén Postclassic Pottery," *American Anthropologist* 85: 866–80.
———(1985) "Maya Pottery Techniques and Technology," in W. D. Kingery (ed.), *Ancient Technology to Modern Science*, pp. 113–32, Vol. 1, Ceramics and Civilization, Columbus, OH: American Ceramic Society.
———(1987a) "Lowland Maya Pottery in the Late Classic Period," in P. Rice and R. J. Sharer (eds.), *Maya Ceramics: Papers from the 1985 Maya Ceramic Conference*, pp. 525–43, BAR International Series 345 (ii), Oxford: Archaeopress.
———(1987b) "Economic Change in the Lowland Maya Late Classic Period," in E. M. Brumfiel and T. K. Earle (eds.), *Specialization, Exchange, and Complex Societies*, pp. 76–85, Cambridge, UK: Cambridge University Press.
———(1987c) *Pottery Analysis: A Sourcebook*, Chicago: University of Chicago Press.

———(1989) "Ceramic Diversity, Production and Use," in R. D. Leonard and G. T. Jones (eds.), *Quantifying Diversity in Archaeology*, pp. 109–17, New York: Cambridge University Press.
———(1991) "Specialization, Standardization, and Diversity: A Retrospective," in R. L. Bishop and F. W. Lange (eds.), *The Ceramic Legacy of Anna O. Shepard*, pp. 257–79, Niwot: University of Colorado Press.
———(1999) "Rethinking Classic Lowland Maya Pottery Censers," *Ancient Mesoamerica* 10: 25–50.
Ringle, W. A., et al. (1998) "The Return of Quetzalcoatl: Evidence for the Spread of a World Religion during the Epiclassic Period," *Anciente Mesoamerica* 9: 183–232.
Robles C., F. (1987) "La Secuencia Ceramica Preliminar de Isla Cerritos, Costa Centro-Norte de Yucatán," in P. Rice and R. J. Sharer (eds.), *Maya Ceramics: Papers from the 1985 Maya Ceramic Conference*, pp. 99–109, BAR International Series 345 (i), Oxford: Archaeopress.
———(1988) "Ceramic Units from Isla Cerritos, North Coast of Yucatán," *Ceramica de la Cultura Maya* 15: 65–71.
Robles C., F., and Andrews, A. P. (1986) "A Review and Synthesis of Recent Postclassic Archaeology in Northern Yucatán," in J. A. Sabloff and E. W. Andrews (eds.), *Late Lowland Maya Civilization*, pp. 53–98, Albuquerque: University of New Mexico Press.
Robicsek, F., and Hales, D. (1981) *The Maya Book of the Dead: The Ceramic Codex*, Charlottesville: University of Virginia Art Museum.
———(1982) *Maya Ceramic Vases from the Late Classic Period: The November Collection of Maya Ceramics*, Charlottesville: University of Virginia Bayly Memorial Museum of Art.
Roys, R. (1943) *Indian Background of Colonial Yucatán*, Washington: Carnegie Institution of Washington.
Rye, O. S. (1981) *Pottery Technology: Principles and Reconstruction*, Washington, DC: Taraxacum.
Sabloff, J. A. (1975) *Excavations at Seibal: Ceramics*, Memoirs of the Peabody Museum of Archaeology and Ethnology, no. 13(2), Cambridge, MA: Harvard University Press.
Sabloff, J. A., and Smith, R. E. (1969) "Importance of Both Analytic and Taxonomic Classification in the Type-Variety System," *American Antiquity* 34(3): 278–85.
Santley, R. S. (1983) "Obsidian Trade and Teotihuacan Influence in Mesoamerica," in A. G. Miller (ed.), *Highland-Lowland Interaction in Mesoamerica: Interdisciplinary Approaches*, pp. 69–124, Washington, DC: Dumbarton Oaks, Harvard University.
Sayre, E. V. (1958) "Studies of Ancient Ceramic Objects by Means of Neutron Bombardment and Emission Spectroscopy," in *Application of Science in the Examination of Works of Art, Proceedings of the Boston Museum of Fine Arts Seminar*, pp. 153–80, Boston: Museum of Fine Arts.
Sharer, R. J. (1978) *The Prehistory of Chalchuapa, El Salvador, Vol. 3: Pottery and Conclusions*, Philadelphia: University of Pennsylvania Press.
Shepard, A. O. (1936) "Review of Petrographic Analyses" by A. Williams Postel in *Piedras Negras Pottery*, by Mary Butler, The University Museum, Philadelphia, 1935," *Maya Research* 3: 113–6.
———(1939) "Technological Notes on the Pottery of San Jose," in J. E. S. Thompson (ed.), *Excavations at San Jose, British Honduras*, pp. 251–77, Publication 506, Washington, DC: Carnegie Institution of Washington.
———(1942) Ceramic Technology. Carnegie Institution of Washington Yearbook 41: 271–2.
———(1946a) "Technological Notes," in A. V. Kidder, J. D. Jennings, and E. M. Shook (eds.), *Excavations at Kaminaljuyu, Guatemala*, pp. 261–77, Publication 561, Washington, DC: Carnegie Institution of Washington.
———(1946b) "Technological Features of Thin Orange Ware," in A. V. Kidder, J. D. Jennings, and E. M. Shook (eds.), *Excavations at Kaminaljuyu, Guatemala*, pp. 198–201, Publication 561, Washington, DC: Carnegie Institution of Washington.
———(1948) *Plumbate: A Mesoamerican Tradeware*, Publication 473, Washington, DC: Carnegie Institution of Washington.
———(1956) *Ceramics for the Archaeologist*, Publication 609, Washington, DC: Carnegie Institution of Washington.
———(1964) "Ceramic Development of the Lowland and Highland Maya," in *Actas y Memorias del XXXV Congreso Internacional de Americanistas* (Mexico City, 1962), Vol. 1, pp. 249–62, Mexico City: Instituto Nacional de Antropologia e Historia.

Smith, A. L. (1936) "Uaxactun,". *Carnegie Institution of Washington Yearbook* 35: 115–17, Washington: Carnegie Institution of Washington.
Smith, M. E. (1979) "A Further Criticism of the Type-Variety System: The Data Can't Be Used," *American Antiquity* 44: 822–26.
Smith, R. E. (1955) *Early Ceramic Horizons at Mayapan and Santa Cruz,* Current Reports no. 26, Washington, DC: Carnegie Institution of Washington.
Smith, R. E. (1936) *Ceramics of Uaxactun: A Preliminary Analysis of Decorative Techniques and Design,* Washington: Carnegie Institution of Washington.
Smith, R. E., Willey, G. R., and Gifford, J. (1960) "The Type-Variety Concept as a basis for the analysis of Maya Pottery" *American Antiquity* 24(2): 330–40.
Smith, R. E., and Gifford, J. G. (1966) "Maya Ceramic Varieties, Types, and Wares at Uaxactun: Supplement to the Ceramic Sequence at Uaxactun, Guatemala," in *Middle American Research Records,* Vol. 3, pp. 125–74, New Orleans: Middle American Research institute.
Smith, R. E. (1971) *Pottery of Mayapan, including studies of Ceramic Material from Uxmal, Kabah, and Chichén Itzá,* Papers of the Peaboby Museum of Archaeology & Ethnology, no. 66, Cambridge, MA: Harvard University Press.
Smyth, M. P. (1998) "Before the Florescence: Chronological Reconstructions at Chac II, Yucatán, Mexico," *Ancient Mesoamerica* 9: 137–50.
Smyth, M. P., et al. (1995) "The Origin of Puuc Slate Ware: New Data from Sayil, Yucatán, Mexico," *Ancient Mesoamerica* 6: 119–34.
Stanton, T. W., and Gallareta N., T. (2001) "Warfare, Ceramic Economy, and the Itza: A Reconsideration of the Itza Polity in Ancient Yucatán," *Ancient Mesoamerica* 12: 229–45.
Stone, D., and Turnbull, C. (1940) "A Sula-Ulua Pottery Kiln," *American Antiquity* 7: 39–47.
Stuart, D. (1987) *Ten Phonetic Syllables,* Research Reports on Ancient Maya Writing no. 14, Washington, DC: Center for Maya Research.
———(1989) "Hieroglyphs on Maya Vessels," in J. Kerr (ed.), *The Maya Vase Book: A Corpus of Rollout Photographs of Maya Vases,* Vol. 1, pp. 149–60, New York: Kerr Associates.
———(1992) "Hieroglyphs and Archaeology at Copan," *Ancient Mesoamerica* 3: 169–84.
———(2000) "The Arrival of Strangers: Teotihuacan and Tollan in Classic Maya History," in D. Carrasco et al. (eds.), *Mesoamerica's Classic Heritage: From Teotihuacan to the Aztecs,* pp. 465–513, Niwot: University of Colorado Press.
Suhler, C. K., Arden, T., and Johnstone, D. (1998) "The Chronology of Yaxuna: Evidence from Excavation and Ceramics," *Ancient Mesoamerica* 9: 167–82.
Taschek, J. T., and Ball, J. W. (1992) "Lord Smoke-Squirrel's Cacao Cup: The Archaeological Context and Sociohistorical Significance of the Buena Vista "Jauncy" Vase," in J. Kerr (ed.), *Maya Vase Book, Vol. 3,* pp. 490–97, New York: Kerr Associates.
Tate, C. (2000) "Writing on the Face of the Moon: Women as Potters, Men as Painters in Classic Maya Civilization," in J. Kerr (ed.), *The Maya Vase Book,* Vol. 6, pp. 1056–71, New York: Kerr Associates.
Taube, K. (1985) "The Classic Maya Maize God: A Reappraisal," in V. Fields (ed.), *Fifth Palenque Round Table, 1983,* pp. 171–82, San Francisco: Pre-Columbian Research Institute.
———(1992) *The Major Gods of Ancient Yucatán,* Studies in Pre-Columbian Art and Archaeology 32, Washington, DC: Dumbarton Oaks, Harvard University.
Tedlock, D. (trans.) (1985) *Popol Vuh: The Definitive Edition of the Mayan Book of the Dawn of Life and the Glories of Gods and Kings,* New York: Touchstone, Simon & Schuster.
Thompson, J. E. S. (1939) *Excavations at San Jose, British Honduras,* Publication 506, Washington, DC: Carnegie Institution of Washington.
———(1940) *Late Ceramic Horizons at Benque Viejo, British Honduras,* Contributions to American Anthropology and History no. 35, Washington, DC: Carnegie Institution of Washington.
Thompson, R. H. (1958) *Modern Yucatec Pottery Making,* Memoirs of the Society for American Archaeology no. 15, Salt Lake City: Society for American Archaeology.
Tourtellot, G, and Sabloff, J. A. (1972) "Exchange Systems among the Ancient Maya," *American Antiquity* 37(1): 126–135.
Tourtellot, G., Sabloff, J. A., and Carmean, K. (1992) "Will the Real Elites Please Stand Up?: An Archaeological Assessment of Maya Elite Behavior in the Terminal Classic period," in D. Chase and A. Chase (ed.), *Mesoamerican Elites: An Archaeological Assessment,* pp. 80–98, Norman: University of Oklahoma Press.

Urban, P., Wells, E. C., and Ausec, M. T. (1997) "The Fires without and the Fires within: Evidence for Ceramic Production Facilities at the Late Classic Site of La Sierra, Naco Valley, Northwestern Honduras, and In Its Environs," in P. Rice (ed.), *The Prehistory & History of Ceramic Kilns*, pp. 173–94, Westerville, OH: American Ceramic Society.
Vaillant, G. (1927) *The Chronological Significance of Maya Ceramics*, unpublished Ph.D. dissertation, Harvard University.
———(1933) "Hidden History," *Natural History* 33: 618–28.
Varela T., C., and Leclaire, A. (1999) "Enigmas cerámicos: Análisis petrográfico de la cerámica pizarra de Oxkintok, Yucatán, Mexico," *Revista Española de Antropología Americana* 29: 101–29.
Vogt, E. (1990) *The Zinacantecos of Mexico: A Modern Maya Way of Life*, 2nd edition, Fort Worth: Holt, Rinehart and Winston.
———(1992) *Tortillas for the Gods: A Symbolic Analysis of Zincanteco Rituals*, Norman: University of Oklahoma Press.
Webster, David (ed.) (1989) *The House of the Bacabs, Copan, Honduras*, Washington, DC: Dumbarton Oaks.
Wells, E. C. (1999) "La organizacion de la produccion de ceramica en La Sierra y sus implicaciones para la administracion local," *Yaxkin* XVII: 37–59, Tegucigalpa: Instituto Hondureno de Antropologia e Historia.
West, G. (2002) "Ceramic Exchange in the Late Classic and Postclassic Maya Lowlands: A Diachronic Approach," in M. Masson and D. Freidel (eds.), *Ancient Maya Political Economies*, pp. 140–96, Oxford: Altamira Press.
Wheat, J. B., Gifford, J. C., and Wasley, W. W. (1958) "Ceramic Variety, Type Cluster, and Ceramic System in Southwestern Pottery Analysis," *American Antiquity* 24: 34–47.
Willey, G. R. and Sabloff, J. A. (1980) *A History of American Archaeology*, San Francisco: Freeman.
Willey, G. R., Bullard, W. R., Grass, J., and Gifford, J. (1965) *Prehistoric Maya Settlements in the Belize Valley*, Papers of the Peabody Museum, Vol. 54, Cambridge: Harvard University Press.
Willey, G. R., Culbert, T. P., and Adams, R. E. W. (eds.) (1967) "Maya Lowlands Ceramics: A Report from the 1965 Guatemala City Conference," *American Antiquity* 32: 289–315.
Wobst, H. M. (1999) "Style in Archaeology or Archaeologists in Style," in E. S. Chilton (ed.), *Material Meanings: Critical Approaches to the Interpretation of Material Culture*, pp. 118–32, Salt Lake City: University of Utah Press.

10
Lithic Analysis in the Maya Area

GEOFFREY E. BRASWELL

Ancient Mesoamerican chipped-stone tools made of chert and obsidian, as well as the quarries and outcrops from which raw material was extracted, have long been subjects of archaeological study (e.g., Breton 1902; Holmes 1900; Washington 1921). Culture historians of the early and middle decades of the twentieth century were drawn to Maya stone tools for three principal reasons. First, lithic artifacts are well represented in most archaeological assemblages. Second, they preserve well in nearly all depositional contexts, including the rainforest environments of the Pacific piedmont and the Maya lowlands. Third, archaeological investigations in North America and the Old World had demonstrated that lithic artifacts—like other objects of material culture—are subject to gradual change in technology and morphology. Thus, early Maya scholars hoped to use lithic artifacts as temporal and cultural markers, allowing diachronic comparison within and between sites and regions.

Nevertheless, lithic analysis played only a minor role in Maya archaeology until the mid-1970s. There are many reasons why stone tools were regarded as less important than architecture, ceramics, iconography, and hieroglyphs. Excavation methods practiced until at least the 1960s were—and still are, in many cases—insufficient for recovering small lithic tools and debitage (by-products). Quite simply, we did not know what the full range of lithic assemblages looked like because only bifacial tools and the largest blades were recovered. Incomplete, biased, and otherwise unrepresentative samples, I believe, are still the greatest obstacles to the Maya lithicist. In addition, temporal and spatial variation in the morphological and technological characteristics of stone tools was thought to be quite limited. No less a scholar than Alfred V. Kidder dismissed the culture-historical value of Maya lithic artifacts.[1] Compared to ceramics, architecture, and sculpture, the common Maya prismatic blade and even the less-frequent biface seemed to be remarkably homogeneous and unchanging. Thus, it was believed that stone artifacts were of less value to understanding space-time dynamics than other classes of material culture subject to a greater degree of formal variation. By the 1930s, then, ceramic classification and seriation became important temporal and spatial tools for archaeologists working in the Maya highlands and Southern Lowlands, architectural analysis played a similar preëminent role in the Northern Lowlands, and lithic studies were given far less attention. Notable exceptions are the excellent typological—if not analytical—descriptions presented by Oliver and Edith Ricketson (1937), Kidder (1947), Gordon Willey (1972; Willey et al. 1965), William Coe (1959), Richard B. Woodbury and Aubrey Trik (1953), and Tatiana Proskouriakoff (1962).[2] Another important study of this period is the descriptive catalogue of obsidian and chert eccentrics compiled by the British archaeologist Thomas A. Joyce (1932). It is still a critical resource for Mayanists interested in the symbolic and noneconomic importance of lithic artifacts.

A third reason why Maya stone tools and debitage were seldom studied in detail until the late twentieth century is that the kinds of questions for which lithic analysis is most appropriate—questions related to production, technology, use, and exchange—are fundamentally economic in character. Despite the widely acknowledged importance of ancient trade, the nature of Maya economic systems was rarely subject to systematic study before 1970. The proponents of the early and late empire model and the supporters of the empty ceremonial center paradigm—two views of ancient Maya political and urban organization that dominated our discipline from the 1920s through the 1960s—had little interest in economic questions. To these scholars, economy was truly epiphenomenal and was determined by the politico-religious structures of either highly centralized empires or completely decentralized polities. Moreover, the tenor of debates within the field of economic anthropology was so strident that it may have seemed prudent to some scholars to avoid studies of ancient economy. It is no surprise, therefore, that Maya economy and lithic artifacts were not the subjects of deep and sustained inquiry until after the death of J. Eric S. Thompson and a cease-fire of sorts had emerged in the substantivist-formalist debate.

Characteristics of Lithic Artifacts Relevant to the Study of Ancient Economy

As archaeologists, including Maya scholars, turned to economic questions in the late twentieth century, several important characteristics of chipped-stone tools and debitage became apparent. First, because stone-tool manufacturing is a subtractive process, each artifact carries the marks of human behavior; flake scars, ground platforms, and bulbs of percussion all represent production activities. Second, subtractive by-products reveal important technological information, and replicative experiments can test hypotheses concerning how artifacts were produced (e.g., Ahler 1986; Baumler and Downum 1989; Crabtree 1968; Clark 1982, 1984, 1985; Odell 1989; Patterson 1990; Shott 1994; Towner and Warburton 1990). Third, knapping errors—recorded as scars, poor terminations, and the like—on finished artifacts and debitage provide key information regarding the skill and efficiency of lithic producers. This, in turn, may be related to labor specialization and the organization of production. Fourth, despite the inherent hardness of stone, characteristic wear patterns develop on lithic tools. Through replicative experiments and microscopic (both high- and low-magnification) comparisons of wear patterns, analyses of function, and therefore of material-cultural adaptations, are often possible (e.g., Aoyama 1989, 1993, 1999; Keeley 1977, 1980; Lewenstein 1981, 1987; Semenov 1964; Shea 1992; Tringham et al. 1974). Fifth, social, ideological, and "stylistic" information is sometimes encoded in lithic tools (e.g., Jones 1990; Sackett 1985; Taçon 1991; Weissner 1983, 1985; Whittaker 1987; Young and Bonnichsen 1984). Sixth, lithic materials are often either visually or chemically distinctive, and their ultimate sources can sometimes be determined, allowing trade routes and exchange patterns to be studied (e.g., Dixon et al. 1968; Gramly 1980; Renfrew et al. 1966, 1968; Shafer and Hester 1983, 1985).

Obsidian, or volcanic glass, has several additional properties useful to archaeologists. Unlike cherts, which are commonly encountered in secondary deposits wherever limestone is found, obsidian is relatively scarce. At many sites, the presence of obsidian artifacts necessarily implies interregional or even long-distance exchange (*sensu* Marcus 1983:477–9). Since obsidian outcrops are uncommon, it is usually easy to determine the source of a particular artifact because the compositional "fingerprints" of only a few geological sources need be known, and because obsidian from a particular outcrop or source area is usually homogeneous in composition (cf. Braswell and Glascock 1998; Glascock et al. 1998). In comparison, cherts may be quite heterogeneous (Luedtke 1992), often making source attribution by chemical means a difficult or impossible task. This is particularly true in the Northern Maya Lowlands, where cherts are derived from sedimentary strata deposited on the ocean floor over millions of years. Finally, and related to the compositional homogeneity (particularly the intrinsic water content) of volcanic glass from a particular source area, obsidian hydrates at rates that may ultimately prove to be determinable. For this reason, measurements of hydration-rind thicknesses may provide relative or even absolute chronological data. In practice, however, the determination of hydration rates is often subject to great error (e.g., Braswell 1992, 1997; Ridings 1991). New research confirms that water-glass diffusion should not be modeled in the simple manner that has been used in the Maya region,[3] and that the optical phenomenon measured in the laboratory does not represent a boundary between hydrated and nonhydrated obsidian (Anovitz et al. 1999). Given that the model employed to date is demonstrably flawed and that the observed phenomenon has been misinterpreted, absolute dates generated for the Maya area should not be given much credence. Statistical naiveté and what I consider to be an irrational enthusiasm for the method have led, unfortunately, to unrealistic claims of accuracy and unsupportable revisionist interpretations of chronology (for a discussion of the statistical misinterpretation of large hydration data sets, see Cowgill and Kintigh 1997).

The Lithic Revolution in Maya Studies

Although there are numerous early studies of Maya stone tools worthy of admiration, lithic analysis began to play a prominent role in the study of ancient Maya society only in the 1970s, when Maya archaeologists began to focus in earnest on economic questions. In the mid-1970s a revolution—comparable in several respects to the epigraphic revolution yet distinctly different in outcome—was brought about by several young scholars. Much of the new work was conducted in areas long considered peripheral to the Petén heartland, particularly the southeastern periphery, northern Belize, highland Chiapas, and the Northern Lowlands. The beginnings of this lithic revolution can be dated rather confidently to 1974 through 1976. In the course of these years, several important dissertations were written. These include Payson Sheets's (1974) analysis of the artifacts of Chalchuapa, a followup to earlier work that introduced the notion of the behavioral typology to Maya lithic studies (Sheets 1972, 1975a); Irwin Rovner's (1975; Rovner and Lewenstein 1997) pivotal diachronic study of stone tools from the Northern Maya Lowlands, a pioneering technological and culture-historical analysis; and Jay Johnson's (1976) study of the stone tools of the western Maya periphery.

The year 1976 also saw the first of two Maya lithic conferences. Held in Orange Walk Town, Belize, it had the dual goals of examining the status of lithic research in the Maya region and of introducing archaeologists to the vast chert workshops at Colhá. The papers presented at that conference

(Hester and Hammond 1976), and also those from a second meeting held in San Antonio in 1982 (Hester and Shafer 1991), are valuable not only to the Maya lithicist, but also to the historian of lithic studies. Both conference volumes contain chapters that explicitly discuss the status of Maya lithic studies and describe programs of investigation for later research (Fowler 1991; Sheets 1976; see also Coe 1965, Sheets 1977, and Woodbury 1965 for summary discussions of lithic studies in the Maya lowlands, southeast periphery, and Maya highlands).

In the early 1980s a second generation of lithic scholars began to consider ancient Maya economy. Many of these, such as Patricia McAnany (1986, 1988, 1989, 1991), Suzanne Lewenstein (1981, 1987, 1991), and Beverly Mitchum (1981, 1989, 1991), worked at sites in northern Belize, including Colhá and Cerros. Research at or near Colhá directed by Thomas Hester and Harry Shafer during the 1970s and 1980s not only provided training for several lithicists, but also stands as the lone example of a supply-zone study of lithic production in the Maya lowlands (e.g., Hester 1976; Hester and Shafer 1983, 1991; Hester et al. 1980, 1982, 1991; Potter 1991; Roemer 1991; Shafer 1976, 1991; Shafer and Hester 1979, 1983, 1985; Wilk 1976). In 1979 John Clark wrote his crucially important M.A. thesis, a technological study of the obsidian of La Libertad, Chiapas (published nine years later as Clark 1988a). Since then, Clark has both figuratively and literally towered over lithic studies in Mexico and northern Central America. Another very important dissertation of the late 1970s, Conran Hay's (1978) study of craft production, is the single most important work generated by the Pennsylvania State University Kaminaljuyu Project. It is a great shame that it was never published as a monograph.

In 1981 two Mexican conferences contributed greatly to our understanding of Mesoamerican lithics. The first, held in Pachuca, Hidalgo, and organized by Margarita Gaxiola González and Clark, focused on obsidian studies in Mesoamerica. An important result is the first volume of collected papers devoted to that subject (Clark and Gaxiola 1989). The second, held in concert with the obsidian symposium, was more broadly dedicated to Mesoamerican lithic studies (Soto de Arechavaleta 1990). The two volumes resulting from these conferences are source books of great importance to the student of Mesoamerican lithics.

Five scholars—Frank Asaro, Fred Stross, Fred Nelson, Michael Glascock, and Garman Harbottle—and the large teams employed in their laboratories have conducted critically important chemical studies of obsidian. Although Henry S. Washington (1921) pioneered the chemical sourcing of Maya obsidian in the early twentieth century, these scientists are largely responsible for developing, modifying, and applying X-ray fluorescence, neutron activation analysis, and a host of other techniques used to identify the geological sources of Maya obsidian. Their work in the laboratory has been complemented and made possible by surveys of Maya obsidian outcrops (e.g., Aoyama 1994; Braswell 1996; Braswell and Glascock 1992, 1998; Clark 1981; Cobean et al. 1971; Mejía and Suyuc 2000; Sheets et al. 1990; Sidrys et al. 1976; Williams 1960; Williams et al. 1964).

Many more archaeologists who are not explicitly discussed above made lasting contributions to Maya lithic studies during the 1970s, 1980s, and beyond: Hattula Moholy-Nagy (1975, 1976, 1989, 1990, 1991, 1994, 1997, 1999; Moholy-Nagy et al. 1984; Moholy-Nagy and Nelson 1991), James B. Stoltman (1978), Kazuo Aoyama (1988, 1989, 1993, 1994, 1995, 1996, 1999), Norman Hammond (1972, 1976; Hammond et al. 1984), Brian Hayden (1979, 1987), Heather McKillop (1995, 1996), Rebecca McSwain (1991), Prudence Rice (1984; Rice et al. 1985), and many others come immediately to mind. Mexican and Guatemalan scholars have contributed equally to the understanding of Maya stone tools. These include María Elena Ruiz Aguilar (1981, 1982, 1985, 1986, 1987, 1989, 1996), Carlos Brokmann (2000), Pura Cervera (1996; Andrews et al. 1989), Edgar Carpio Rezzio (1993a, 1993b, 1994, 2000), Rómulo Sánchez (1991), and Héctor Mejía Amaya and Edgar Suyuc Ley (1997, 2000).

Recent Studies of Maya Lithics

The life of a stone artifact can be divided crudely into five stages. These are material procurement and initial production, exchange, secondary production, use, and discard. Exchange, of course, can take place at nearly any point in this sequence, as can additional phases of production and use. This simplified life cycle provides a crude way to organize recent studies of lithic tools and debitage according to different sorts of analytical questions.

Resource-Zone Studies: Material Extraction, Production, and Regional Exchange

To be blunt, there are few adequate studies of raw material procurement and initial production—what may be considered resource-zone studies—for either chert or obsidian in the Maya region. Such studies, of course, are crucial; the only place within a distribution network through which all material of a specific sort flows is its origin. We desperately need to know more about the organization of production in and around both chert- and obsidian-bearing zones.

Colhá remains *the* great example of a resource-zone study of Maya lithics. Craft production and specialization on a large scale at Colhá are particularly well documented. Shafer's (1982) study identified a high degree of craft specialization by quantifying error rates, material-use efficiency, time-input efficiency, standardization, and other factors. His work demonstrates the power of an approach firmly rooted in technological analysis. McAnany's (1986, 1989) groundbreaking research at nearby sites where Colhá chert was consumed provides a dynamic picture of a regional economic system.

Clark (1981), Sheets (1975b), Sidrys et al. (1976), John Graham and Robert Heizer (1968), Michael Coe and Kent Flannery (1964), and Joseph Michels (1975) wrote fascinating short articles on the obsidian sources of the Guatemalan highlands. These reports, for the most part, are derived from single-day visits, but they do contain much useful information. A similar piece by Sheets et al. (1990) provides the only description of two source areas in Honduras, and is relevant more to the study of lower Central American lithics than to the analysis of Maya stone tools.

More recently, small-scale projects have tackled two of the three most important Maya obsidian sources: El Chayal and San Martín Jilotepeque. In 1996 Héctor Mejía and Edgar Suyuc, then students at the Universidad de San Carlos de Guatemala, began a systematic settlement survey and workshop study of the vast and complex El Chayal source region (Mejía and Suyuc 1997, 2000). Their work indicates some level of specialization in the resource zone, but does not support many earlier claims that Kaminaljuyu somehow controlled El Chayal. Although there is significant settlement in the region, it is not dense. Nor are there any signs of garrisons, large state-controlled workshops, or symbols of power and hierarchy. Together, these suggest to Mejía and Suyuc that the source area was not controlled by any large polity. Instead, they posit that access to the *technology* of prismatic blade and bifacial tool production may have been limited.

My own work in San Martín Jilotepeque (SMJ) focused on the relationship between resources, settlement patterns, and economic organization (Braswell 1996, 1998, 2002; Braswell and Glascock 1998). Like Mejía and Suyuc, I concluded that the region was not the center of any large polity, and indeed seemed in many ways to be interstitial, particularly during the Preclassic and Postclassic periods. I could find no evidence of a large Chimaltenango chiefdom, for which some have argued, dating to the Middle and Late Preclassic when SMJ obsidian was widespread throughout the Maya lowlands. Indeed, the region was abandoned during the Late Preclassic, implying that no polity controlled the source at that time. Moreover, there is no evidence for the development of a social hierarchy until the onset of the Classic period. Although I cannot comment on exchange mechanisms near distant consumer nodes such as La Venta and Komchen, finished tools and cores of SMJ obsidian most likely left the region through limited acts of down-the-line dyadic exchange.

In contrast, during the Classic and Postclassic periods there is ample evidence for the development of some level of specialized production of polyhedral cores, prismatic blades, and especially bifacially worked projectile points. Evidence of off-quarry workshops specializing in biface production was found at intermediate-ranked sites located comparatively short distances from exploited quarries. But there is no evidence of the high degree of specialization, skill, and efficiency exhibited by the chert workshops of Colhá. Even the specialized biface workshops of SMJ produced rather crude, error-filled, and highly unstandardized projectile points and handheld bifaces. Most striking, there is no artifactual evidence in SMJ for exchange with communities more distant than about 50 km away. Thus, despite the presence of massive beds of debitage, often more than 1 m deep, there is no reason to suspect that SMJ was ever the center of a large-scale, state- or chiefdom-controlled industry. As an aside, I believe the same to be true for the Ixtepeque source. There currently is no clear evidence that this source region was ever politically, economically, or militarily dominated by a powerful polity such as Copan or Chalchuapa, or that production at the source was standardized, efficient, or otherwise describable in terms that suggest a high level of craft specialization. Still, Maya obsidian source-areas have received considerably less archaeological attention than several of their counterparts in central and west Mexico (e.g., Cruz Antillón 1994; Darras 1999; Healan 1997; Pastrana 1990, 1998). It may be that further study will reveal evidence of more complexly organized forms of production.

Exchange beyond Procurement Zones

Joyce Marcus (1983) has characterized exchange in terms of three levels of scale: intraregional, interregional, and long-distance. With the exception of northern Belize, where McAnany (1986, 1989) brilliantly described the exchange of Colhá chert tools as part of an interdependent regional system, we know nothing at all about the intraregional exchange of chert. For example, I have observed great variety in the cherts, chalcedonies, jaspers, and other similar materials used at Chichén Itzá and in the Puuc region. But I have little idea where these materials came from, except in the negative: They do not seem to come from the chert-bearing zone of northern Belize. Someone needs to go to the vicinity of Xkichmook, in the southern Puuc, where good-quality chert is readily available, and begin a study modeled after Hester's, Shafer's, and McAnany's research. At Copan the vast majority of the chert is local, probably pulled right out of the river and flaked by nonspecialists. The exceptions—material used to make fine bifaces, including the exquisite eccentrics from the Rosalila offerings—come from unknown sources.

Intraregional Obsidian Exchange. We know a bit more about the intraregional exchange of obsidian, particularly in Soconusco and western Honduras (Aoyama 1999, 2001; Clark et al. 1989; Clark and Salcedo

1989), two areas on or beyond the fringes of the Maya area. Aoyama has studied the relationship between politics and exchange in the Copan and La Entrada Valleys. During the fifth through ninth centuries (Acbi through Coner phases), the dynastic center of Copan was a regional hub for the distribution of obsidian from the Ixtepeque, Guatemala, source area. Aoyama's study demonstrates important distinctions between obsidian consumption patterns in elite portions of the city and in non-elite sites in the surrounding Copan pocket. In particular, he concludes that prepared obsidian cores were redistributed rather than subject to market exchange. He notes that redistribution of a utilitarian good may have been important as a means of reinforcing status differences as well as creating and maintaining political power (Aoyama 1999:177). Moreover, although there is ample evidence of part-time lithic production, no data from either Copan or the La Entrada region suggest the existence of full-time specialists engaging in either workshop- or factory-level production. His study, therefore, paints a picture of what might be termed an intermediate economy: one where low-intensity production and traditional ties between individuals and groups have not been replaced by market forces governing production and exchange.

I have studied the intraregional exchange of obsidian in the Northern Maya Lowlands, particularly within the Itzá state and *between* Chichén Itzá and the Puuc region (Braswell and Glascock 2003). My conclusion is that a bounded administered market system focused on Chichén Itzá became part of a more integrated market economy after about A.D. 900. Thus, the intermediate-level economy described by Aoyama for Late Classic Copan was replaced by more complex forms during the Terminal Classic. New levels of economic integration undoubtedly contributed to the vibrant florescence of the Northern Lowlands during the Terminal Classic and Postclassic periods. Still, we desperately need more intraregional research like Aoyama's work in the Copan and La Entrada regions, McAnany's study of northern Belize, and Clark's investigations in Soconusco if we are to develop a diachronic and areawide understanding of the structure of ancient Maya economies.

Interregional Obsidian Exchange. Both interregional and long-distance exchange research has concentrated on the identification of the source of artifacts, usually accomplished through X-ray fluorescence, neutron activation analysis, or other chemical and physical techniques. This aspect of modern Maya lithic studies truly began the decade before the revolution of the 1970s. After initial success with X-ray fluorescence and neutron activation analysis in the 1960s (e.g., Jack and Heizer 1968; Stross et al. 1968; Weaver and Stross 1965), Hammond (1972, 1976) made critical contributions to the subject of interregional obsidian exchange, and Rice (1984; Rice et al. 1985) provided the first diachronic look at shifting obsidian procurement patterns for a single region. More recently, Marie Charlotte Arnauld (1990) has reexamined the movement of obsidian from the Maya highlands to the lowlands. The single most important contribution on interregional and long-distance obsidian exchange, however, is Fred Nelson's (1985) article in *Scanning Electron Microscopy.* In this work, Nelson provides a period-by-period summary of all that was known in the early 1980s about obsidian procurement patterns in the Maya region. Today, we have multiplied the number of sites for which we have obsidian procurement data by at least thirty, and our total sample size is on the order of hundreds of thousands of pieces, most of which come from Copan, Soconusco, and the central Guatemalan highlands (see Braswell 2003). It is high time for large collections from other regions, particularly the central Petén, the western highlands, and the Gulf Coast to be analyzed in a systematic fashion. More to the point, it is time that we begin to discuss what, precisely, procurement data tell us about the structure of ancient economies, and how interregional exchange within the Maya area changed over time. To do this, we need to develop more meaningful ways of quantifying and comparing our data.

Long-distance Obsidian Exchange. Studies of long-distance or transisthmian obsidian exchange have often focused on the trickle of green obsidian from Pachuca, Hidalgo, that reached the Maya region during the Early Classic. In contrast, far less information has been presented regarding long-distance interaction during other periods (Andrews et al. 1989; Braswell 2003; Moholy-Nagy 1999; Nelson 1985; Spence 1996). Moreover, little attention has been given to the trade of Maya-source obsidian beyond the Maya area.

I would like to emphasize three observations. First, far greater quantities of central and west Mexican obsidian entered the Maya region during the ninth through eleventh centuries than during any other period. Second, exotic Mexican obsidian brought to the Maya area before the Terminal Classic period was traded as *finished* artifacts. In contrast, beginning in A.D. 800, most highland Mexican obsidian entered the Maya region in the form of small, refurbished cores from which blades were locally produced. These cores were recycled in much the same fashion as described for Xochicalco by Kenneth Hirth (2002). Third, exotic obsidian in the Maya area that dates to before the Terminal Classic tends to be limited to elite tombs, caches, middens, or other contexts in the epicenters of large sites (Spence 1996). In contrast, there is little or no evidence for status-based access to highland Mexico obsidian after A.D. 800. This tells us something very important about the nature of transisthmian trade before and after this date. Before the Terminal Classic, long-distance obsidian exchange was conducted between elites and for elites. By A.D. 800, obsidian had become a commodity in the

Maya lowlands, and almost certainly was subject to some sort of market exchange. I strongly suspect that the commodification of obsidian and the commercialization of its exchange began earlier on the northwestern side of the Isthmus of Tehuantepec (see Santley 1994), but this is an important subject that needs further study.

Production and Use at Consumption Nodes

Although chert is a resource distributed widely throughout the central and Northern Lowlands, most archaeological projects in the Maya area have been conducted at sites that are more accurately described as concentrations of dwellings and special function structures than as lithic procurement areas. Thus, even though naturally occurring chert can be found at ancient cities such as Calakmul and Copan, they are more usefully thought of as places of secondary production (i.e., production from cores or blanks transported to the site) and consumption than as quarries where initial production activities were the focus of activity.

Secondary Production. Descriptive studies of chipped-stone tool collections from large Maya sites are common; many of the principal studies are cited above. But detailed technological studies of secondary production are largely lacking in the Maya area. There are, in fact, many ways to make a blade from an imported core or to knap a biface from an imported blank, and the details of alternative technological pathways need to be described. Such studies may tell us something about the organization of production at consumer nodes, and also may be relevant to the more basic chores of space-time systematics. A recent symposium on alternative core-blade reduction sequences in Mesoamerica yielded an interesting volume (Hirth and Andrews 2002), but I was disappointed to see that only one Maya lithicist contributed to it. In her chapter, Rissa M. Trachman (2002) discussed provisioning and production constraints at Dos Hombres, northern Belize, and described in detail a newly observed technique of core rejuvenation based on pecking and scoring. The importance of her study is that it broadens our understanding of the complexity of obsidian production technology, and emphasizes the ancient need to carefully curate and reduce imported cores. Clark (1988a, 1997; Clark and Bryant 1997) is among the few other Maya lithicists who pursue the fine details of alternative reduction strategies. It is a subject, no doubt, that will continue to bear fruit.

As discussed above, Aoyama's work at Copan and at other sites in western Honduras has provided us with an important picture of the organization of production and distribution in an important Maya kingdom. What we do not yet fully understand is the physical and social context of secondary production. Signs of lithic production and resharpening—in the form of exhausted polyhedral cores, thinning flakes, and the chunks and shatter resulting from casual percussion industries—can be found in many contexts at nearly all habitation sites. Relatively small concentrations of debitage are routinely recovered from construction fill, slump, middens, floor contexts, and even burials. In most cases, debitage is thoroughly mixed with a wide variety of material remains resulting from the full range of quotidian activities. Does this indicate that nearly all habitation groups were loci of lithic production, if only on a modest household scale? If so, did nearly all households have at least one unspecialized lithic producer or even a part-time specialist? Alternatively, did lithic producers—practicing their craft at whatever level of specialization—routinely travel throughout and between habitation sites not only to exchange, but also to produce lithic tools? Finally, to what degree does the presence of lithic debitage at most habitation groups indicate scavenging of materials from other locations for potential reuse? What seems clear is that at most Maya sites, places of secondary lithic production were not far removed from the house lot.

Use-wear Studies. Functional analyses of Maya stone tools began with Kidder's (1947) monograph on the artifacts of Uaxactun. Nevertheless, Americanist archaeologists did not become fully aware of the promise of use-wear studies until Sergej Aristarchovich Semenov's (1964) book *Prehistoric Technology* became available in English (e.g., Wilk 1978). Early applications of his technique in the Maya region addressed issues such as the manioc grater hypothesis (Lewenstein and Walker 1984; Walker and Wilk 1989), and many studies focused on collections from Belize. The most outstanding and important of these is Suzanne Lewenstein's (1987, 1989, 1991) analysis of the stone tools of Cerros. Several Maya lithicists have used low-powered microscopy techniques for use-wear studies (e.g., Doonan 1996; Dreiss 1988; Menzies 2003; Nance and Kirk 1991; Valdez 1994), but high-powered techniques have also been used (e.g., Aldenderfer et al. 1989), occasionally in conjunction with microscopic analyses of residues (Shafer and Holloway 1979; Sievert 1990, 1992; see also Triadan and Inomata in this volume). Aoyama (1989, 1993, 1995, 1999) is one of the preeminent Maya lithicists using the high-powered technique today, and his work is especially worthy of note. Nonetheless, it is uncommon for lithic analysts in the Maya region to encounter tools and contexts that beg to be analyzed in this way. As others have noted, use-wear analysis is a powerful method waiting for a question.

Discard: Lithic Concentrations as Disposal Sites and Identifying Workshop Loci

Although old tools and debitage were often scavenged from middens and surface contexts for further use or reduction, in most cases disposal, loss, or discard was the final stage in the life of a stone tool. The interpretation of concentrations of lithic materials, including debitage, has been a focus of archaeological and ethnoarchaeological work in the Maya area and throughout Mesoamerica, mirroring the New Archaeology's interest in site formation processes. James Nations (1989) and Clark (1989a) have analyzed the production of stone-tipped arrows by modern Lacandon Maya. An important part of Clark's research is the discard of lithic debris (Clark 1991a, 1991b). His study reveals a variety of disposal patterns, often beginning with the temporary storage of debitage in a gourd kept in the house. Final deposition of debitage is usually in a small, specialized dump 100 to 200 m from the household workshop. Because debitage is sharp, dumps are placed where people are unlikely to tread or engage in milpa farming (e.g., inside an old tree stump, at the base of a rocky slope, and even on the talus of a prehistoric mound). Such patterns of disposal of dangerous material are in accord with Brian Hayden and Aubrey Cannon's (1983) ethnoarchaeological observations and with Robert Santley and Ronald Kneebone's (1993) expectations for ancient disposal patterns.

An important implication is that the archaeological identification of lithic production loci is often indirect. Ancient households, like most of their Lacandon counterparts, were generally swept clean. Because most excavations are conducted in and around structures, rather than in empty terrain between habitation groups, Maya archaeologists have often missed the specialized dumps described by Clark.[4] If we wish to identify places of lithic production and to recover dense concentrations of debitage for study, we will need to excavate interstitial spaces between mound groups (e.g., Healan et al. 1983).

Related to ethnoarchaeological studies of lithic disposal is the question of the identification of lithic workshop spaces (e.g., Clark 1986, 1988b, 1989b; Moholy-Nagy 1990). Although the discussion has occasionally been contentious, it is generally agreed that dense deposits of lithic material do not in themselves indicate the presence of a lithic reduction site. This is particularly true if the stone artifacts are finished tools exhibiting use wear. In most cases, such deposits are either dumps associated with "workshops" where other materials (such as wood) were worked, or are specialized offerings or caches. Examples of the former include some of the obsidian workshops identified at Teotihuacan (Clark 1986), whereas the latter includes the beds of lithic material often found above or below burials in the eastern Petén and western Belize. A few discussions of workshops have, unfortunately, focused on the question of recognizing lithic reduction sites at the expense of identifying a *workshop scale* of production. Questions of production scale, organization, specialization, and intensity—fundamentally economic issues—are of greater interest and importance than the identification of actual workshop spaces. The identification of a workshop industry is not, in fact, dependent on locating and excavating a workshop space.

The Future of Maya Lithic Studies

The lithic revolution of the mid-1970s was markedly different from the epigraphic revolution that began to affect Maya studies during the same decade. Despite a promising beginning, lithic studies have not engendered a new way of thinking about ancient Maya civilization comparable to that afforded by advances in hieroglyph interpretation, even in that area where stone-tool analysis potentially can have its greatest impact: ancient economy. The fundamental reason for this is that we all too often have become enchanted either with our trace-element data or with the minutiae of technological analyses (the latter is far less common). Trace-element data are not particularly important unless we use them to formulate and test models of exchange, which, in turn, can tell us something about the structure of economic systems. Technological details are not especially interesting unless they tell us something about the structure of production, which, again, can tell us something about economy. In particular, we need to move beyond the site as the unit of archaeological analysis, and begin to understand the regional system as the unit of economic integration. As McAnany, Aoyama, and Clark have empirically demonstrated, it is at the regional level of scale that Maya economic structure is most evident. Regional studies of lithics, therefore, should be the focus of our efforts.

Because of its embeddedness in even broader cultural realms, economy is a subject of interest to all Mayanists. The ability to move from the particular to the general has been the strength of the epigraphic revolution; for example, several models of Maya political structure are rooted in hieroglyph interpretation. Maya lithics have much to tell us about the nature of production and exchange, and hence, about the structure of power, about wealth, and even about the nature of political systems. The subject of our volume is the last century of Maya archaeology, but, like most readers, I am much more interested in the next hundred years. I hope that in the coming century we will turn more to these issues, which are relevant not only to our fellow lithicists but also to all Maya archaeologists.

Notes

1. On several occasions, Edwin M. Shook emphasized to me that only exceptional obsidian and chert artifacts (chiefly bifacially worked tools and eccentrics) were routinely recovered during most Carnegie excavations. According to him, A. V. Kidder was particularly dismayed by the apparent lack of regional and temporal variation in the ubiquitous Maya prismatic blade. T. R. Kidder (personal communication, 1995) provided corroborative evidence of Shook's recollection.
2. I have been fortunate to supervise Bárbara Escamilla Ojeda, a *licenciatura* student at the Universidad Autónoma de Yucatán, in her lithic analysis of materials excavated recently by the Proyecto Mayapán, directed by Carlos Peraza Lope. While examining the obsidian collection with Escamilla, my appreciation for Proskouriakoff's (1962) important work at Mayapán deepened. It should be of no surprise that Proskouriakoff brought to lithic

studies the same observational skills, keen intellect, and deductive powers that infuse her better-known research on Maya iconography and architecture.

3. Simple, in this case, is not a pejorative. It means that hydration rates have not been modeled as dependent on concentration. Simple diffusion models (such as those applied until now in the Maya region) are generally more applicable to liquid–liquid diffusion, whereas concentration-dependent diffusion models are more appropriate for liquid–solid diffusion. As liquids diffuse into solids, they often open pathways, increasing the rate of diffusion. Thus, as water concentrations increase in a solid, the diffusion rate may also increase.
4. I have studied materials recovered from a specialized biface dump excavated by the Proyecto Dzibilchaltún, directed by Rubén Maldenado. In this case, thinning flakes were found within, outside, and on top of a small structure. The pattern of deposition suggests that an already abandoned structure was used as a disposal site, analogous to Clark's observation of Lacandon use of an ancient mound.

References

Ahler, S. A. (1986) *The Knife River Flint Quarries: Excavations at Site 32DU508*, Bismarck: State Historical Society of North Dakota.

Aldenderfer, M. S., et al. (1989) "A Microwear Analysis in the Maya Lowlands: The Use of Functional Data in a Complex Society Setting," *Journal of Field Archaeology* 12: 47–60.

Andrews, A. P., et al. (1989) "The Obsidian Trade at Isla Cerritos, Yucatán, Mexico," *Journal of Field Archaeology* 16: 355–63.

Anovitz, L. M., et al. (1999) "The Failure of Obsidian Hydration Dating: Sources, Implications, and New Directions," *Journal of Archaeological Sciences* 26: 735–52.

Aoyama, K. (1988) "Some Socio-economic Observations on Obsidian and Chert Artifacts in the La Venta Valley, Honduras," paper presented at the 53rd Annual Meeting of the Society for American Archaeology, Phoenix, AZ.

———(1989) "Estudio experimental de las huellas de uso sobre material lítico de obsidiana y sílex," *Mesoamérica* 17: 185–214.

———(1993) "Experimental Microwear Analysis on Maya Obsidian Tools: Case Study of the La Entrada Region, Honduras," in *Traces et Fonction: Les gestes retrouvés*, pp. 423–32, Colloque International de Liège, Vol. 50, Liège: Éditions ERAUL.

———(1994) "Socioeconomic Implications of Chipped Stone from the La Entrada Region, Western Honduras," *Journal of Field Archaeology* 21: 133–45.

———(1995) "Microwear Analysis in the Southeast Maya Lowlands: Two Case Studies at Copan, Honduras," *Latin American Antiquity* 6:129–44.

———(1996) *Exchange, Craft Specialization, and Ancient Maya State Formation: A Study of Chipped Stone Artifacts from the Southeast Maya Lowlands*, unpublished PhD Dissertation, Department of Anthropology, University of Pittsburgh.

———(1999) *Ancient Maya State, Urbanism, Exchange, and Craft Specialization: Chipped Stone Evidence of the Copan Valley and the La Entrada Region, Honduras*, Memoirs in Latin American Archaeology, no. 12, Pittsburgh: University of Pittsburgh.

———(2001) "Classic Maya State, Urbanism, and Exchange: Chipped Stone Evidence of the Copan Valley and Its Hinterland," *American Anthropologist* 103: 346–60.

Arnauld, M. C. (1990) "El comercio clásico de obsidiana: Rutas entre tierras altas y tierras bajas en el área maya," *Latin American Antiquity* 1: 347–67.

Baumler, M. F., and Downum, C. E. (1989) "Between Micro and Macro: A Study in the Interpretation of Small-sized Lithic Debitage," in D. S. Amick and R. P. Maudlin (eds.), *Experiments in Lithic Technology*, pp. 101–16, BAR International Series 528, Oxford: British Archaeological Reports.

Braswell, G. E. (1992) "Obsidian-hydration Dating, the Coner Phase, and Revisionist Chronology at Copan, Honduras," *Latin American Antiquity* 3: 130–47.

———(1996) *A Maya Obsidian Source: The Geoarchaeology, Settlement History, and Prehistoric Economy of San Martín Jilotepeque, Guatemala*, unpublished Ph.D. dissertation, Department of Anthropology, Tulane University.

———(1997) "La cronología y la estructura del colapso en Copan, Honduras," in *Los Investigadores de la Cultura Maya 5*, pp. 262–73, Campeche: Universidad Autónoma de Campeche.

———(1998) "La arqueología de San Martín Jilotepeque, Guatemala," *Mesoamérica* 35: 117–54.

———(2002) "Praise the Gods and Pass the Obsidian?: The Organization of Ancient Economy in San Martín Jilotepeque, Guatemala," in M. Masson and D. Freidel (eds.), *Ancient Maya Political Economies*, pp. 285–306, Walnut Creek CA: Altamira Press.

———(2003) "Obsidian Exchange Spheres of Postclassic Mesoamerica," in M. E. Smith and F. Berdan (eds.), *The Postclassic Mesoamerican World*, pp. 131–58, Salt Lake City: University of Utah Press.

Braswell, G. E., and Glascock, M. D. (1992) "A New Obsidian Source in the Highlands of Guatemala," *Ancient Mesoamerica* 3:47–9.

———(1998) "Interpreting Intrasource Variation in the Composition of Obsidian: The Geoarchaeology of San Martín Jilotepeque, Guatemala," *Latin American Antiquity* 9: 353–69.

———(2003) "The Emergence of Market Economies in the Ancient Maya World: Obsidian Exchange in Terminal Classic Yucatán, Mexico," in M. D. Glascock (ed.),*Geochemical Evidence for Long Distance Exchange*, pp. 33–52, Westport: Bergin and Garvey.

Breton, A. (1902) "Some Obsidian Workings in Mexico," *Proceedings of the International Congress of Americanists* 13: 265–68.

Brokmann, C. (2000) *Tipología y análisis de la obsidiana de Yaxchilán, Chiapas*, Colección Científica no. 422, Mexico City: Instituto Nacional de Antropología e Historia.

Carpio Rezzio, E. H. (1993a) "Algunos apuntes acerca de los utensilios de piedra en las sociedades originales de Guatemala," in *Estudios* 1: 57–68, Guatemala City: Instituto de Investigaciones Históricas, Antropológicas y Arqueológicas.

———(1993b) "Obsidian at Balberta," in F. J. Bove, S. Medrano B., B. Lou, and B. Arroyo (eds.), *The Balberta Project: The Terminal Formative—Early Classic Transition on the Pacific Coast of Guatemala*, pp. 83–106, Memoirs in Latin American Archaeology, no. 6, Pittsburgh: University of Pittsburgh.

———(1994) "Obsidiana de La Colonia, Sansare: Utilización de recursos locales," in J. P. Laporte and H. Escobedo (eds.), *VII Simposio de Investigaciones Arqueológicas en Guatemala, 1993*, pp. 147–53, Guatemala City: Museo Nacional de Antropología.

———(2000) "Uso y comercio de la obsidiana, en el área de Tecojate, Escuintla, Guatemala," *Estudios de Cultura Maya* 21: 25–32.

Cervera, M. P. (1996) *Los Artifactos Líticos de Isla Cerritos*, unpublished licenciatura thesis, Facultad de Ciencias Antropológicas, Universidad Autónoma de Yucatán, Mérida, Mexico.

Clark, J. E. (1981) "Guatemalan Obsidian Sources and Quarries: Additional Notes," *Journal of New World Archaeology* 4: 1–15.

———(1982) "Manufacture of Mesoamerican Prismatic Blades: An Alternative Technique," *American Antiquity* 47: 355–76.

———(1984) "Counterflaking and the Manufacture of Mesoamerican Prismatic Blades," *Lithic Technology* 13: 52–61.

———(1985) "Platforms, Bits, Punches and Vises: A Potpourri of Mesoamerican Blade Technology," *Lithic Technology* 14: 1–15.

———(1986) "From Mountains to Molehills: A Critical Review of Teotihuacan's Obsidian Industry," in B. L. Isaac (ed.), *Economic Aspects of Prehispanic Highland Mexico*, pp. 23–74, Research in Economic Anthropology, Supplement no. 2, Greenwich, Connecticut: JAI Press.

———(1988a) *The Lithic Artifacts of La Libertad, Chiapas, Mexico*, Paper no. 52, Provo: New World Archaeological Foundation, Brigham Young University.

———(1988b) "Fifteen Fallacies in Lithic Workshop Interpretation: An Experimental and Ethnoarchaeological Perspective," paper presented at the Pedro Bosch-Gimpera Symposium on Ethnoarchaeology, Mexico City.

———(1989a) "La técnica de talla de los lacandones de Chiapas," in J. E. Clark and M. Gaxiola G. (eds.), *La obsidiana en mesoamérica*, pp. 443–8, Colección Científica no. 176, Mexico City: Instituto Nacional de Antropología e Historia.

———(1989b) "Hacia una definición de talleres," in J. E. Clark and M. Gaxiola G. (eds.), *La obsidiana en mesoamérica*, pp. 213–7, Colección Científica no. 176, Mexico City: Instituto Nacional de Antropología e Historia.

———(1991a) "Flintknapping and Debitage Disposal among the Lacandon Maya of Chiapas, Mexico," in E. Staski and L. D. Sutro (eds.), *The Ethnoarchaeology of Refuse Disposal*, pp. 63–88, Anthropological Research Paper no. 42, Tempe: Arizona State University.

———(1991b) "Modern Lacandon Lithic Technology and Blade Workshops.," in T. R. Hester and

H. J. Shafer (eds.), *Maya Stone Tools: Selected Papers from the Second Maya Lithic Conference*, pp. 251–65, Monographs in World Archaeology, no. 1, Madison: Prehistory Press.

———(1997) "Prismatic Blade Making, Craftsmanship, and Production: An Analysis of Obsidian Refuse from Ojo de Agua, Chiapas, Mexico," *Ancient Mesoamerica* 8: 137–59.

Clark, J. E., and Bryant, D. (1997) "A Technological Typology of Prismatic Blades and Debitage from Ojo de Agua, Chiapas, Mexico," *Ancient Mesoamerica* 8: 111–36.

Clark, J. E., and Gaxiola González, M. (eds.) (1989) *La obsidiana en mesoamérica*, Colección Científica no. 176, Mexico City: Instituto Nacional de Antropología e Historia.

Clark, J. E., and Salcedo Romero, T. (1989) "Ocós Obsidian Distribution in Chiapas, Mexico," in F. J. Bove and L. Heller (eds.), *New Frontiers in the Archaeology of the Pacific Coast of Southern Mesoamerica*, pp. 15–24, Anthropological Research Paper no. 39, Tempe: Arizona State University.

Clark, J. E., et al. (1989) "The Distribution of Obsidian," in B. Voorhies (ed.), *Ancient Trade and Tribute, Economies of the Soconusco Region of Mesoamerica*, pp. 268–84, Salt Lake City: University of Utah Press.

Cobean, R. H., et al. (1971) "Obsidian Trade at San Lorenzo Tenochtitlan, Mexico," *Science* 174: 666–71.

Coe, M. D., and Flannery, K. V. (1964) "The Precolumbian Obsidian Industry of El Chayal, Guatemala," *American Antiquity* 30: 43–9.

Coe, W. R. (1959) *Piedras Negras Archaeology: Artifacts, Caches, and Burials*, Philadelphia: The University Museum, University of Pennsylvania.

———(1965) "Artifacts of the Maya Lowlands" in G. R. Willey (ed.), *Archaeology of Southern Mesoamerica*, Part 2, pp. 594–602, Handbook of Middle American Indians, Vol. 3, Austin: University of Texas Press.

Cowgill, G. L., and Kintigh, K. W. (1997) "How Random Errors in Dates Increase Apparent Lengths of Intervals," paper presented at the 62nd Annual Meeting of the Society for American Archaeology, Nashville, TN.

Crabtree, D. E. (1968) "Mesoamerican Polyhedral Cores and Prismatic Blades," *American Antiquity* 33: 446–78.

Cruz Antillón, R. (1994) *Análisis arqueológico del yacimiento de obsidiana de Sierra de Las Navajas, Hidalgo*, Coleción Científica, Vol. 281, Mexico City: Instituto Nacional de Antropología e Historia.

Darras, V. (1999) *Tecnologías prehispánicas de la obsidiana: Los centros de producción de la región de Zináparo-Prieto, Michoacán*, Cuadernos de Estudios Michoacanos, Vol. 9, Mexico City: Centre d'Études Mexicanes et Centroaméricanes.

Dixon, J. E., Cann, J. R., and Renfrew, C. (1968) "Obsidian and the Origins of Trade," *Scientific American* 218: 38–46.

Doonan, W. (1996) *The Artifacts of Group 10L-2, Copan, Honduras: Variation in Material Culture and Behavior in a Royal Residential Compound*, unpublished Ph.D. dissertation, Department of Anthropology, Tulane University.

Dreiss, M. L. (1988) "Obsidian at Colha, Belize: A Technological Analysis and Distributional Study Based on Trace Element Data," *Papers of the Colha Project*, Vol. 4, San Antonio: Texas Archaeological Research Laboratory, University of Texas.

Fowler, W. R., Jr. (1991) "Lithic Analysis as a Means of Processual Inference in Southern Mesoamerica: A Review of Recent Research," in T. R. Hester and H. J. Shafer (eds.), *Maya Stone Tools: Selected Papers from the Second Maya Lithic Conference*, pp. 1–19, Monographs in World Archaeology, no. 1, Madison: Prehistory Press.

Glascock, M. D., et al. (1998) "A Systematic Approach to Obsidian Source Characterization," in M. S. Shackley (ed.), *Method and Theory in Archaeological Volcanic Glass Studies*, pp. 15–65, New York: Plenum Press.

Graham, J. A., and Heizer, R. F. (1968) "Notes on the Papalhuapa Site, Guatemala," *Contributions of the University of California Archaeological Research Facility* 5: 101–25.

Gramly, R. M. (1980) "Raw Materials Source Areas and Curated Tool Assemblages," *American Antiquity* 45: 823–33.

Hammond, N. (1972) "Obsidian Trade Routes in the Maya Area." *Science* 178: 1092–93.

———(1976) "Maya Obsidian Trade in Southern Belize," in T. R. Hester and N. Hammond (eds.), *Maya Lithic Studies: Papers from the 1976 Belize Field Symposium*, pp. 71–81, Special Report no. 4, San Antonio: Center for Archaeological Research, University of Texas at San Antonio.

Hammond, N., et al. (1984) "Trace Element Analysis of Obsidian Artifacts from a Classic Maya Residential Group at Nohmul, Belize," *American Antiquity* 49: 815–20.

Hay, C. A. (1978) *Kaminaljuyu Obsidian: Lithic Analysis and Economic Organization of a Prehistoric Mayan Chiefdom*, unpublished Ph.D. dissertation, Department of Anthropology, Pennsylvania State University.

Hayden, B. (ed.) (1979) *Lithic Usewear Analysis*, New York: Academic Press.

———(ed.) (1987) *Lithic Studies among the Contemporary Highland Maya*, Tucson: University of Arizona Press.

Hayden, B., and Cannon, A. (1983) "Where the Garbage Goes: Refuse Disposal in the Maya Highlands," *Journal of Anthropological Archaeology* 1: 132–58.

Healan, D. M. (1997) "Pre-Hispanic Quarrying in the Ucareo-Zinapecuaro Obsdian Source Area," *Ancient Mesoamerica* 8: 77–100.

Healan, D. M., et al. (1983) "Excavation and Preliminary Analysis of an Obsidian Workshop in Tula, Hidalgo, Mexico," *Journal of Field Archaeology* 10: 127–45.

Hester, T. R. (1976) "Belize Lithics: Forms and Functions," in T. R. Hester and N. Hammond (eds.), *Maya Lithic Studies: Papers from the 1976 Belize Field Symposium*, pp. 11–19, Special Report no. 4, San Antonio: Center for Archaeological Research, University of Texas at San Antonio.

Hester, T. R., and Hammond, N. (eds.) (1976) *Maya Lithic Studies: Papers from the 1976 Belize Field Symposium*, Special Report no. 4, San Antonio: Center for Archaeological Research, University of Texas at San Antonio.

Hester, T. R., and Shafer, H. J. (1983) "On Obsidian Supply at Colha, Belize," *Current Anthropology* 21: 810–11.

———(1991) "Lithics of the Early Postclassic at Colha, Belize," in T. R. Hester and H. J. Shafer (eds.), *Maya Stone Tools: Selected Papers from the Second Maya Lithic Conference*, pp. 155–61, Monographs in World Archaeology, no. 1, Madison: Prehistory Press.

Hester, T. R., et al. (eds.) (1980) *The Colha Project Second Season, 1980 Interim Report*, San Antonio and Venice: Center for Archaeological Research, University of Texas at San Antonio and Centro Studi Ricerche Ligabue.

———(eds.) (1982) *Archaeology at Colha, Belize: The 1981 Interim Report*, San Antonio and Venice: Center for Archaeological Research, University of Texas at San Antonio and Centro Studi Ricerche Ligabue.

———(1991) "Technological and Comparative Analyses of the Chipped Stone Artifacts from El Pozito, Belize," in T. R. Hester and H. J. Shafer (eds.), *Maya Stone Tools: Selected Papers from the Second Maya Lithic Conference*, pp. 67–83, Monographs in World Archaeology, no. 1, Madison: Prehistory Press.

Hirth, K. (2002) "Provisioning Constraints and the Production of Obsidian Prismatic Blades at Xochicalco, Mexico," in *Pathways to Prismatic Blades: A Study in Mesoamerican Obsidian Core-blade Technology*, pp. 81–90, Monograph 45, Los Angeles: The Cotsen Institute of Archaeology, University of California, Los Angeles.

Hirth, K., and Andrews, B. (eds.) (2002) *Pathways to Prismatic Blades: A Study in Mesoamerican Obsidian Core-blade Technology*, Monograph 45, Los Angeles: The Cotsen Institute of Archaeology, University of California, Los Angeles.

Holmes, W. H. (1900) "The Obsidian Mines of Hidalgo, Mexico," *American Anthropologist* 2: 405–41.

Jack, R. N., and Heizer, R. F. (1968) "'Finger-Printing' of Some Mesoamerican Obsidian Artifacts," *Contributions of the University of California Archaeological Research Facility* 5: 81–100.

Johnson, J. K. (1976) *Chipped Stone Artifacts from the Western Maya Periphery*, unpublished Ph.D. dissertation, Department of Anthropology and Sociology, Southern Illinois University, Carbondale.

Jones, R. (1990) "Hunters of the Dreaming: Some Ideational, Economic and Ecological Parameters of the Australian Aboriginal Productive System," in D. Yen and J. Mummery (eds.), *Pacific Production Systems: Approaches to Economic Prehistory*, pp. 25–52, Canberra: Australian National University.

Joyce, T. A. (1932) "The Eccentric Flints of Central America," *Journal of the Royal Anthropological Institute* 62: xvii–xxvi.

Keeley, L. H. (1977) "The Functions of Paleolithic Flint Tools," *Scientific American* 237: 108–26.

———(1980) *Experimental Determinations of Stone Tool Uses: A Microwear Analysis*, Chicago: University of Chicago Press.

Kidder, A. V. (1947) *The Artifacts of Uaxactun, Guatemala*, Publication 576, Washington, DC: Carnegie Institute of Washington.

Lewenstein, S. M. (1981) "Mesoamerican Obsidian Blades: An Experimental Approach to Function," *Journal of Field Archaeology* 8: 175–88.

———(1987) *Stone Tool Use at Cerros*, Austin: University of Texas Press.

———(1989) "Usos utilitarios de la obsidiana de Cerros, un sitio preclásico en la costa septentrional de Belice," in J. E. Clark and M. Gaxiola G. (eds.), *La obsidiana en mesoamérica*, pp. 177–89, Colección Científica no. 176, Mexico City: Instituto Nacional de Antropología e Historia.

———(1991) "Edge Angles and Tool Function among the Maya: A Meaningful Relationship?" in T. R. Hester and H. J. Shafer (eds.), *Maya Stone Tools: Selected Papers from the Second Maya Lithic Conference*, pp. 207–17, Monographs in World Archaeology, no. 1, Madison: Prehistory Press.

Lewenstein, S. M., and Walker, J. (1984) "The Obsidian Chip/Manioc Grating Hypothesis and the Mesoamerican Preclassic," *Journal of New World Archaeology* 6: 25–38.

Luedtke, B. (1992) *An Archaeologist's Guide to Chert and Flint*, Archaeological Research Tools 7, Los Angeles: The Cotsen Institute of Archaeology, University of California, Los Angeles.

Marcus, J. (1983) "Lowland Maya Archaeology at the Crossroads," *American Antiquity* 48: 454–88.

McAnany, P. A. (1986) *Lithic Technology and Exchange among Wetland Farmers of the Eastern Maya Lowlands*, unpublished Ph.D. dissertation, Department of Anthropology, University of Arizona.

———(1988) "Effects of Lithic Procurement Strategies on Tool Curation and Recycling," *Lithic Technology* 17: 3–11.

———(1989) "Stone-tool Production and Exchange in the Eastern Maya Lowlands: The Consumer Perspective from Pulltrouser Swamp, Belize," *American Antiquity* 54: 332–46.

———(1991) "Structure and Dynamics of Intercommunity Exchange," in T. R. Hester and H. J. Shafer (eds.), *Maya Stone Tools: Selected Papers from the Second Maya Lithic Conference*, pp. 271–93, Monographs in World Archaeology, no. 1, Madison: Prehistory Press.

McKillop, H. I. (1995) "The Role of Northern Ambergris Caye in Maya Obsidian Trade: Evidence from Visual Sourcing and Blade Technology," in T. H. Guderjan and J. F. Garber (eds.), *Maya Maritime Trade, Settlement, and Population on Ambergris Caye, Belize*, pp. 163–74, Lancaster, CA: Maya Research Program and Labyrinthos.

———(1996) "Ancient Maya Trading Ports and the Integration of Long-distance and Regional Economies: Wild Cane Caye in South-coastal Belize," *Ancient Mesoamerica* 7: 49–62.

McSwain, R. (1991) "A Comparative Evaluation of the Produce-consumer Model for Lithic Exchange in Northern Belize, Central America," *Latin American Antiquity* 2: 337–51.

Mejía Amaya, H. E., and Suyuc Ley, E. O. (1997) "Nuevos afloramientos en El Chayal," in J. P. Laporte and H. Escobedo (eds.), *X Simposio de Investigaciones Arqueológicas en Guatemala, 1996*, Vol. 1, pp. 47–59, Guatemala City: Museo Nacional de Antropología.

———(2000) *Ri chay abaj: Proyecto geológico-arqueológico El Chayal*, Utz'ib Serie Reportes, Vol. 1, no. 1, Guatemala City: Asociación Tikal.

Menzies, A. C. J. (2003) *A Technological and Functional Analysis of the Obsidian Assemblage from Minanhá, Cayo Distric, Belize*, unpublished M. A. thesis, Department of Anthropology, Trent University, Peterborough, Ontario.

Michels, J. W. (1975) "El Chayal, Guatemala: A Chronological and Behavioral Reassessment," *American Antiquity* 40: 103–6.

Mitchum, B. A. (1981) "Lithic Artifacts from Cerros, Belize: Production, Consumption and Trade," *Revista mexicana de estudios antropológicos* 27(2): 139–56.

———(1989) "Obsidian as a Non-essential Resource," in J. E. Clark and M. Gaxiola G. (eds.), *La obsidiana en mesoamérica*, pp. 375–8, Colección Científica no. 176, Mexico City: Instituto Nacional de Antropología e Historia.

———(1991) "Lithic Artifacts from Cerros, Belize: Production, Consumption, and Trade," in T. R. Hester and H. J. Shafer (eds.), *Maya Stone Tools: Selected Papers from the Second Maya Lithic Conference*, pp. 45–53, Monographs in World Archaeology, no. 1, Madison: Prehistory Press.

Moholy-Nagy, H. (1975) "Obsidian at Tikal, Guatemala," *Actas del XLI Congreso Internacional de Americanistas*, no. 1, pp. 511–8, Mexico City: Instituto Nacional de Arqueología e Historia.

———(1976) "Spatial Distribution of Flint and Obsidian Artifacts at Tikal, Guatemala," in T. R. Hester and N. Hammond (eds.), *Maya Lithic Studies: Papers from the 1976 Belize Field Symposium*, pp. 91–108, Special Report no. 4, San Antonio: Center for Archaeological Research, University of Texas at San Antonio.
———(1989) "Who Used Obsidian at Tikal?" in J. E. Clark and M. Gaxiola G (eds.), *La obsidiana en mesoamérica*, pp. 379–89, Colección Científica no. 176, Mexico City: Instituto Nacional de Antropología e Historia.
———(1990) "The Misidentification of Mesoamerican Lithic Workshops," *Latin American Antiquity* 1: 268–79.
———(1991) "The Flaked Chert Industry of Tikal, Guatemala," in T. R. Hester and H. J. Shafer (eds.), *Maya Stone Tools: Selected Papers from the Second Maya Lithic Conference*, pp. 189–202, Monographs in World Archaeology, no. 1, Madison: Prehistory Press.
———(1994) *Tikal Material Culture: Artifacts and Social Structure at a Classic Lowland Maya City*, unpublished Ph.D. dissertation, Department of Anthropology, University of Michigan.
———(1997) "Middens, Construction Fill, and Offerings: Evidence for the Organization of Classic Period Craft Production at Tikal, Guatemala," *Journal of Field Archaeology* 24: 293–313.
———(1999) "Mexican Obsidian at Tikal, Guatemala," *Latin American Antiquity* 10: 300–13.
Moholy-Nagy, H., and Nelson, F. W. (1991) "New Data on Sources of Obsidian Artifacts from Tikal, Guatemala," *Ancient Mesoamerica* 1: 71–80.
Moholy-Nagy, H., et al. (1984) "Tikal Obsidian: Sources and Typology," *American Antiquity* 49: 104–17.
Nance, C. R., and Kirk, K. A. (1991) "Obsidian Blades from La Blanca: A Changing Lithic Industry on the South Coast of Guatemala," *Latin American Antiquity* 2: 371–84.
Nations, J. D. (1989) "The Lacandon Bow and Arrow: An Ethnoarchaeological Example of Postclassic Lowland Maya Weapon Manufacture," in J. E. Clark and M. Gaxiola G. (eds.), *La obsidiana en mesoamérica*, pp. 449–57, Colección Científica no. 176, Mexico City: Instituto Nacional de Antropología e Historia.
Nelson, F. W. (1985) "Summary of the Results of Analysis of Obsidian Artifacts from the Maya Lowlands," *Scanning Electron Microscopy* II: 631–49.
Odell, G. H. (1989) "Experiments in Lithic Reduction," in D. S. Amick and R. P. Maudlin (eds.), *Experiments in Lithic Technology*, pp. 163–97, BAR International Series 528, Oxford: British Archaeological Reports.
Pastrana, A. (1990) "Proyecto yacimientos de obsidiana," *Boletín del Consejo de Arqueología*: 190–5.
———(1998) *La explotación azteca de la obsidiana en la Sierra de las Navajas*, Colección Científica no. 383, Mexico City: Instituto Nacional de Antropología e Historia.
Patterson, L. W. (1990) "Characteristics of Bifacial-reduction Flake-size Distribution," *American Antiquity* 55: 550–8.
Potter, D. R. (1991) "A Descriptive Taxonomy of Middle Preclassic Chert Tools at Colha, Belize," in T. R. Hester and H. J. Shafer (eds.), *Maya Stone Tools: Selected Papers from the Second Maya Lithic Conference*, pp. 21–9, Monographs in World Archaeology, no. 1, Madison: Prehistory Press.
Proskouriakoff, T. (1962) "The Artifacts of Mayapán," in H. E. D. Pollock, R. L. Roys, T. Proskouriakoff, and A. L. Smith, (eds.), *Mayapán, Yucatán, Mexico*, pp. 87–169, Publication 619, Washington, DC: Carnegie Institute of Washington.
Renfrew, C., et al. (1966) "Obsidian and Early Cultural Contact in the Near East," *Proceedings of the Prehistoric Society* 32: 30–72.
———(1968) "Further Analysis of Near Eastern Obsidians," *Proceedings of the Prehistoric Society* 34: 319–31.
Rice, P. M. (1984) "Obsidian Procurement in the Central Petén Lakes Region," *Journal of Field Archaeology* 11: 181–94.
Rice, P. M., et al. (1985) "Provenience Analysis of Obsidians from the Central Petén Lakes Region, Guatemala," *American Antiquity* 50: 591–604.
Ricketson, O. G., Jr., and Ricketson, E. B. (1937) *Uaxactun, Guatemala, Group E, 1926–1931*, Publication 477, Washington, DC: Carnegie Institute of Washington.
Ridings, R. (1991) "Obsidian Hydration Dating: The Effects of Mean Exponential Ground Temperature and Depth of Artifact Recovery," *Journal of Field Archaeology* 18: 77–85.
Roemer, E. (1991) "A Late Classic Workshop at Colha, Belize," in T. R. Hester and H. J. Shafer

(eds.), *Maya Stone Tools: Selected Papers from the Second Maya Lithic Conference*, pp. 55–66, Monographs in World Archaeology, no. 1, Madison: Prehistory Press.

Rovner, I. (1975) *Lithic Sequences of the Maya Lowlands*, unpublished Ph.D. dissertation, Department of Anthropology, University of Wisconsin.

Rovner, I., and Lewenstein, S. M. (1997) *Maya Stone Tools of Dzibilchaltún, Yucatán, and Becán and Chicanná, Campeche*, Publication 65, New Orleans: Middle American Research Institute, Tulane University.

Ruíz Aguilar, M. E. (1981) "Estudio preliminar de la lítica de Aquiles Serdán, Chiapas," *Revista Mexicana de Estudios Antropológicos* 27(2): 13–26.

———(1982) "Tecnología lítica," *Anales de Antropología* 19: 151–63.

———(1985) "Observaciones sobre canteras en Petén, Guatemala," *Mesoamérica* 10: 421–49.

———(1986) "Análisis preliminar de la lítica de Mundo Perdido, Tikal," *Mesoamérica* 11: 113–33.

———(1987) "Análisis preliminar de la lítica de Mundo Perdido, Tikal," in *Memorias del Primer Coloquio Internacional de Mayistas*, pp. 331–59, Mexico City: Universidad Autónoma Nacional de Mexico.

———(1989) "Instrumentos líticos procedentes de un basurero, Tikal, Petén," in *Memorias del II° Coloquio Internacional de Mayistas*, pp. 569–601, Mexico City: Universidad Autónoma Nacional de Mexico.

———(1996) "Tecnología prehispánica: Los artefactos de piedra y el manejo de la obsidiana, el pedernal y el jade," in *Piezas maestras mayas: Patrimonio del Museo Nacional de Arqueología y Etnología de Guatemala, Galerías Guatemala III*, pp. 34–43, Guatemala City: Fundación G&T.

Sackett, J. R. (1985) "Style and Ethnicity in the Kalahari: A Reply to Weissner," *American Antiquity* 50: 154–9.

Sánchez, R. (1991) *Las navajas prismáticas de Kaminaljuyu/San Jorge: Un análisis tecnológico funcional*, unpublished *licenciatura* thesis, área de arqueología, Escuela de Historia, Universidad de San Carlos de Guatemala, Guatemala City.

Santley, R. S. (1994) "The Economy of Ancient Matacapan." *Ancient Mesoamerica* 5: 243–66.

Santley, R. S., and Kneebone, R. R. (1993) "Craft Specialization, Refuse Disposal, and the Creation of Spatial Archaeological Records in Prehispanic America," in R. S. Santley and K. G. Hirth (eds.), *Prehispanic Domestic Units in Western Mesoamerica: Studies of the Household, Compound, and Residence*, pp. 37–63, Boca Raton: CRC Press.

Semenov, S. A. (1964) *Prehistoric Technology*, London: Cory, Adams, Mackay.

Shafer, H. J. (1976) "Belize Lithics: 'Orange Peel' Flakes and Adze Manufacture," in T. R. Hester and N. Hammond (eds.), *Maya Lithic Studies: Papers from the 1976 Belize Field Symposium*, pp. 21–34, Special Report no. 4, San Antonio: Center for Archaeological Research, University of Texas at San Antonio.

———(1982) "Maya Lithic Craft Specialization in Northern Belize," in T. R. Hester et al., *Archaeology at Colha, Belize: The 1981 Interim Report*, pp. 31–8, San Antonio and Venice: Center for Archaeological Research, University of Texas at San Antonio and Centro Studi Ricerche Ligabue.

———(1991) "Late Preclassic Formal Stone Tool Production at Colha, Belize," in T. R. Hester and H. J. Shafer (eds.), *Maya Stone Tools: Selected Papers from the Second Maya Lithic Conference*, pp. 31–44, Monographs in World Archaeology, no. 1, Madison: Prehistory Press.

Shafer, H. J., and Hester, T. R. (1979) "Lithic Research at Colha: An Overview," in T. R. Hester (ed.), *The Colha Project, 1979: A Collection of Interim Papers*, pp. 18–27, San Antonio: Center for Archaeological Research, University of Texas at San Antonio.

———(1983) "Ancient Maya Chert Workshops in Northern Belize, Central America," *American Antiquity* 48: 519–43.

———(1985) "A Technological Study of Two Maya Lithic Workshops at Colha, Belize," in M. G. Plew, J. C. Woods, and M. G. Pavesic (eds.), *Stone Tool Analysis: Essays in Honor of Don E. Crabtree*, pp. 277–315, Albuquerque: University of New Mexico Press.

Shafer, H. J., and Holloway, R. G. (1979) "Organic Residue Analysis in Determining Stone Tool Function," in B. Hayden (eds.), *Lithic Usewear Analysis*, pp. 385–99, New York: Academic Press.

Shea, J. J. (1992) "Lithic Microwear Analysis in Archaeology," *Evolutionary Anthropology* 1: 143–50.

Sheets, P. D. (1972) "A Model of Mesoamerican Obsidian Technology Based on Preclassic Workshop Debris in El Salvador," *Ceramica de Cultura Maya* 8: 17–33.

———(1974) *Differential Change among the Precolumbian Artifacts of Chalchuapa, El Salvador*, unpublished Ph.D. dissertation, University of Pennsylvania.

———(1975a) "Behavioral Analysis and the Structure of a Prehistoric Industry," *Current Anthropology* 16: 369–91.

———(1975b) "A Reassessment of the Precolumbian Obsidian Industry of El Chayal, Guatemala," *American Antiquity* 40: 98–103.

———(1976) "Islands of Lithic Knowledge amid Seas of Ignorance in the Maya Area," in T. R. Hester and N. Hammond (eds.), *Maya Lithic Studies: Papers from the 1976 Belize Field Symposium*, pp. 1–9, Special Report no. 4, San Antonio: Center for Archaeological Research, University of Texas at San Antonio.

———(1977) "The Analysis of Chipped Stone Artifacts in Southern Mesoamerica: An Assessment," *Latin American Research Review* 12: 139–58.

Sheets, P. D., et al. (1990) "Obsidian Sources and Elemental Analysis of Artifacts in Southern Mesoamerica and the Northern Intermediate Area," *American Antiquity* 55: 144–58.

Shott, M. J. (1994) "Size and Form in the Analysis of Flake Debris: Review and Recent Approaches," *Journal of Archaeological Method and Theory* 1: 69–110.

Sidrys, R. V., et al. (1976) "Obsidian Sources in the Maya Area," *Journal of New World Archaeology* 1: 1–13.

Sievert, A. K. (1990) "Postclassic Maya Ritual Behavior: Microwear Analysis of Stone Tools from Ceremonial Contexts," in B. Gräslund, H. Knutsson, K. Knutsson, and J. Taffinder (eds.), *The Interpretative Possibilities of Microwear Studies: Proceedings of the International Conference on Use-wear Studies*, pp. 147–57, Uppsala: Societas Archaeologica Upsaliensis and Department of Archaeology, Uppsala Universitet.

———(1992) *Maya Ceremonial Specialization: Lithic Tools from the Sacred Cenote at Chichén Itzá, Yucatán*, Monographs in World Prehistory no. 12, Madison: Prehistory Press.

Soto de Arechavaleta, M. (ed.) (1990) *Nuevos enfoques en el estudio de la lítica*, Mexico City: Universidad Nacional Autónoma de Mexico.

Spence, M. W. (1996) "Commodity or Gift: Teotihuacan Obsidian in the Maya Region," *Latin American Antiquity* 7: 21–39.

Stoltman, J. B. (1978) *Lithic Artifacts from a Complex Society: The Chipped Stone Tools of Becan, Campeche, Mexico*, Occasional Paper 2, New Orleans: Middle American Research Institute, Tulane University.

Stross, F. H., et al. (1968) "Analysis of American Obsidians by X-ray Fluorescence and Neutron Activation Analysis," *Contributions of the University of California Archaeological Research Facility* 5: 59–79.

Taçon, P. S. C. (1991) "The Power of Stone: Symbolic Aspects of Stone Use and Tool Development in Western Arnhem Land, Australia," *Antiquity* 65: 192–207.

Towner, R. H., and Warburton, M. (1990) "Projectile Point Rejuvenation: A Technological Analysis," *Journal of Field Archaeology* 17: 311–21.

Trachman, R. M. (2002) "Early Classic Obsidian Core-blade Production: An Example from the Site of Dos Hombres, Belize," in K. G. Hirth and B. Andrews (ed.), *Pathways to Prismatic Blades: A Study in Mesoamerican Obsidian Core-blade Technology*, pp. 105–19, Monograph 45, Los Angeles: The Cotsen Institute of Archaeology, University of California, Los Angeles.

Tringham, R., et al. (1974) "Experimentation in the Formation of Edge Damage: A New Approach to Lithic Analysis," *Journal of Field Archaeology* 1: 171–96.

Valdez, F. (1994) "Chipped Stone (Obsidian)," in G. R. Willey, R. M. Leventhal, A. A. Demarest, and W. Fash (eds.), *Ceramics and Artifacts from Excavations in the Copan Residential Zone*, pp. 273–90, Papers of the Peabody Museum of Archaeology and Ethnology, Vol. 80, Cambridge, MA: Peabody Museum of Archaeology and Ethnology, Harvard University.

Walker, J., and Wilk, R. (1989) "The Manufacture and Use-wear Characteristics of Ethnographic, Replicated, and Archaeological Maioc [sic] Grater Board Teeth," in J. E. Clark and M. Gaxiola G. (eds.), *La obsidiana en mesoamérica*, pp. 459–63, Colección Científica no. 176, Mexico City: Instituto Nacional de Antropología e Historia.

Washington, H. S. (1921) "Obsidian from Copan and Chichén Itzá," *Journal of the Washington Academy of Sciences* 11: 481–7.

Weaver, J. R., and Stross, F. H. (1965) "Analysis by X-ray Fluorescence of Some American Obsidians," *Contributions of the University of California Archaeological Research Facility* 1: 89–93.

Weissner, P. (1983) "Style and Social Information in Kalahari San Projectile Points," *American Antiquity* 48: 253–76.
———(1985) "Style or Isochrestic Variation? A Reply to Sackett," *American Antiquity* 50: 160–6.
Whittaker, J. C. (1987) "Individual Variation as an Approach to Economic Organization: Projectile Points at Grasshopper Pueblo, Arizona," *Journal of Field Archaeology* 14: 465–80.
Wilk, R. (1976) "Work in Progress at Colha, Belize, 1976," in T. R. Hester and N. Hammond (eds.), *Maya Lithic Studies: Papers from the 1976 Belize Field Symposium*, pp. 35–40, Special Report no. 4, San Antonio: Center for Archaeological Research, University of Texas at San Antonio.
———(1978) "Microscopic Analysis of Chipped Flint and Obsidian," in G. R. Willey (eds.), *Excavations at Seibal*, pp. 139–45, Memoirs of the Peabody Museum of Archaeology and Ethnology, Vol. 14, no. 1, Cambridge, MA: Peabody Museum of Archaeology and Ethnology, Harvard University.
Willey, G. R. (1972) *The Artifacts of Altar de Sacrificios*, Papers of the Peabody Museum of Archaeology and Ethnology, Vol. 64, no. 1, Cambridge, MA: Peabody Museum of Archaeology and Ethnology, Harvard University.
Willey, G. R., et al. (1965) *Prehistoric Maya Settlements in the Belize Valley*, Papers of the Peabody Museum of Archaeology and Ethnology, Vol. 54, Cambridge, MA: Peabody Museum of Archaeology and Ethnology, Harvard University.
Williams, H. (1960) "Volcanic History of the Guatemalan Highlands," in *University of California Publication in Geological Sciences*, Vol. 38, no. 1, pp. 1–86, Berkeley and Los Angeles: University of California Press.
Williams, H., et al. (1964) "Geologic Reconnaissance of Southeastern Guatemala," In *University of California Publication in Geological Sciences*, Vol. 50, no. 1, pp. 1–54, Berkeley and Los Angeles: University of California Press.
Woodbury, R. B. (1965) "Artifacts of the Guatemalan Highlands," in G. R. Willey (ed.), *Archaeology of Southern Mesoamerica*, Part 1, pp. 163–79, Handbook of Middle American Indians, Vol. 2, Austin: University of Texas Press.
Woodbury, R. B., and Trik, A. S. (1953) *The Ruins of Zaculeu, Guatemala*, 2 vols., Richmond, VA: William Byrd Press.
Young, D. E., and Bonnichsen, R. (1984) *Understanding Stone Tools: A Cognitive Approach*, Orono: University of Maine.

11
Osteological Investigations of Ancient Maya Lives

LORI E. WRIGHT

Interest in ancient Maya skeletons has grown dramatically since the landmark studies by William Haviland (1967) at Tikal and Frank Saul (1972) at Altar de Sacrificios. Indeed, Maya bioarchaeology has blossomed in the last fifteen years to a very active field, with a large number of new scholars. Many of these new scholars have focused their work in Belize; however, research at Guatemalan, Mexican, and Honduran sites is also on the rise, both by both local and foreign scholars. Many of the issues addressed in the early works of Maya osteology (Haviland 1967; Saul 1972) remain key areas of active research for bioarchaeologists, especially questions about the health costs of population density in a rainforest setting and the biological correlates of social status. Yet the scope of Maya bioarchaeology has broadened considerably to incorporate new tools for hypothesis testing, such as stable isotopic studies of ancient diet and migration, biodistance studies of dental traits, as well as ancient DNA.

In this chapter, I review recent work in Maya bioarchaeology, with an emphasis on developments and directions that have emerged since the reviews by Jane Buikstra (1997) and Lori Wright and Christine White (1996). I focus on several interrelated themes that I expect will be important areas for future work. The first is the growing interest in social heterogeneity and its implications for diet and health. Together with traditional paleopathology, advances in paleodiet research permit the detailed reconstruction of life histories that parallel Saul's (1972) early interest in "osteobiography." Skeletal biodistance studies, coupled with new isotopic approaches to track migration, will further understanding of ancient Maya social organization in the near future. Finally, I explore the role that forensic anthropology may play in the future of our field.

Paleonutrition and Social Inequality

The Maya area has seen one of the most intensive applications of stable isotopes to reconstruct past diets. Bone collagen data are now available for at least twenty-six lowland and two highland Maya sites. Recent stable isotope studies include the sites of Altun Ha (White et al. 2001), Yaxuna, Chunchucmil (Mansell et al. 2002), La Milpa (Tykot 2002), Caracol (Chase, Chase, and White 2001), Topoxte (Wright, Schwarcz, and Acevedo 2000), Cahal Pech (Powis et al. 1999), K'axob (Henderson 1998), Kaminaljuyu (Wright and Schwarcz 1998, 1999), and Iximche (Nance, Whittington, and Borg 2003). As first described by Gerry and Krueger (1997), maize consumption—as measured by stable carbon isotopes ($\delta^{13}C$) in bone collagen—was lowest in Belize, and higher in central Petén, at Copan, and especially at Protohistoric Iximche. Preliminary data from Chunchucmil suggest that maize was less important in Yucatec diets than in the Classic period Petén (Mansell et al. 2002). Nitrogen isotope ($\delta^{15}N$) variation highlights greater consumption of marine fish at coastal sites, and freshwater fish consumption at some riverine sites, such as Seibal. Unfortunately, most diachronic studies suffer from small sample sizes and confounding social heterogeneity. However, it is clear that diets varied in concert with environmental factors and local population density over time (Wright 1997a; Wright and White 1996).

Social heterogeneity provides one of the greatest challenges to bioarchaeological research on a complex society like that of the Maya, but is perhaps the most interesting if elusive of research questions for Maya bioarchaeology to address. That all members of ancient Maya society did not have access to the same resources is clear from the archaeological record, but the extent to which this inequality determined diet, health, and survivorship is much more difficult to document. Skeletal series that are large enough to subdivide by social status, sex, age at death, and chronological time period are extremely rare, so these potentially confounding factors complicate the interpretation of data at virtually all sites. Moreover, determining the social position of individual skeletons is a much more complicated undertaking (Gillespie 2001) than Mayanists typically assume. Although several researchers have carried out sophisticated statistical analyses of mortuary patterning, most have explored different archaeological dimensions that might reflect status, and have reported only select dietary differences they encountered. Indeed, virtually every study has used a different archaeological measure of social rank, such as aspects of architectural group morphology, location within the site, grave form, skeletal position, and grave goods (Wright 2003). Additional factors that hinder consistent interpretation of dietary inequality include excavation sampling error, small sample size, as well as the confounding issue of sex differences in diet.

Isotopic evidence for social inequality in Maya diets is not straightforward. Very clear differences in isotope ratios between groups of burials can be seen at some sites, but at others the distinctions are subtle or absent. Differences in $\delta^{13}C$ ratios, and thus maize consumption, have been reported more commonly than distinctions in $\delta^{15}N$. At most sites, these results suggest that maize provided more protein to elites than non-elites; animal protein appears to have been a benefit of status at few sites.

Although this trend holds for most Classic period sites where differences have been reported, it is critical to note that many sites show quite subtle patterning. For instance, David Reed (1998) reports significant differences in the aggregate values for males by site type at Copan; however, skeletons buried in diverse site types show considerable dietary overlap. Much clearer patterning is found at Caracol, where Arlen Chase and colleagues (Chase and Chase 2001; Chase, Chase, and White 2001) describe a "palace diet" for skeletons buried in the site center and in palaces at causeway termini; these skeletons show heavier $\delta^{13}C$ and $\delta^{15}N$ ratios than those buried in peripheral locations. At Tikal, $\delta^{13}C$ ratios vary among skeletons buried in domestic groups of diverse size, and among artifact clusters, whereas $\delta^{15}N$ varies with skeletal position, and interment with cylinder vases and plates (Wright 2003).

Maize may have been a socially valued food at many Classic period sites, as White (1997) suggests for Terminal Classic Pacbitun; however, it would be unwise to generalize this tendency to a pan-Maya preference. Figure 11.1 shows that elite Topoxte skeletons buried around the main plaza of this Post classic Petén site consumed less maize than skeletons buried in domestic contexts on the peripheries of the island, a trend evidenced by both collagen and third molar enamel carbonate $\delta^{13}C$ values (Wright, Schwarcz, and Acevedo 2000). Despite ethnohistoric observations that nobles consumed more meat, the nitrogen isotopes indicate equivalent levels of carnivory among these Topoxte social groups. It seems likely that the social value of foods was conditioned by local factors of supply and demand.

The health implications of such social variation in diet have barely been explored; very few studies have shown social differences in skeletal indicators of health status, despite the widespread perception that social inequality had significant implications for disparity in health and survivorship among the Maya. This view comes from Haviland's (1967) landmark study of stature at Tikal. Although Haviland described a discrepancy in the stature of male

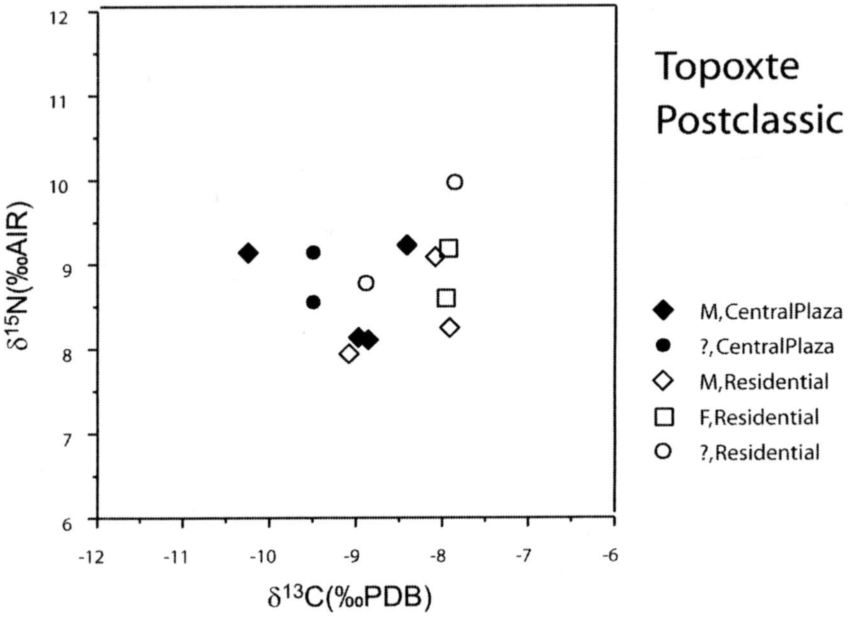

Fig. 11.1 Stable isotopic composition of bone collagen of adult skeletons from Postclassic Topoxté, Petén. (Modified after Fig. 6 of Acevedo et al. 1997:598).

skeletons buried in tombs and that of non-tomb interments, the differences he reported are not statistically meaningful unless all time periods are lumped together (Reed 1998:65). However, work underway at Tikal does indicate a difference in female stature among skeletons buried in domestic groups of differing architectural complexity (Vásquez Gómez 2003). Elsewhere, the only statistically significant differences in stature among status groups within a site that have been reported are from Copan (Storey 1999), among males from 9N-8 versus rural sites. Rebecca Storey (1999) reports fewer healed anemic lesions in females buried in 9N-8 than in rural Copan house groups, but differences among status groups in infectious disease or dental growth disruption are not statistically significant (Storey 1999; Whittington 1992). Thus, a clear-cut discrepancy in health status among social groups has not been widely confirmed at this time. Such analyses are compromised by the small numbers of skeletons available from different status groups at each site, together with the poor skeletal preservation at Maya sites. Documenting such differences will require extremely precise scoring of lesions by specific subsections of each skeletal element to control for the vagaries of preservation.

Few studies have yet attempted to examine the relationship between individual dietary signals and the expression of bony pathology. At Copan, Stephen Whittington and David Reed (1997) found no difference between the isotope values for adult skeletons with and without porotic hyperostosis. As they note, this may be because adult diets recorded in bone collagen differ from those of childhood when the anemic lesions developed. If social differences in diet did affect health status, it is most likely to have played out in childrens' health, due to the greater nutritional demands for growth and development as well as the maturing immune systems of children. Indeed, children's health has been a focus of paleopathological work on the Maya, principally through the abundance and patterning of growth defects in tooth enamel. These studies have demonstrated subtle patterning in childhood health status among sites and time periods (Danforth 1997; Storey 1992; Wright 1997b; Whittington 1992), but have not yet been linked directly to dietary intake for the prehistoric Maya, although the role of nutritional adequacy in the formation of such lesions is well documented in Mesoamerica (May, Goodman, and Meindl 1993).

Through isotopic sampling of diverse tissues in both child and adult skeletons, new work attempts to track dietary changes from early childhood through the lifespan. Together with the study of skeletal indicators of health stress, these life history approaches may soon permit a more direct evaluation of the biological consequences of ancient Maya foodways. For instance, breastfeeding is a cultural behavior shaped by economic circumstance and perceptions of child welfare, with well-documented implications for both morbidity and mortality. Nursing and weaning practices may vary dramatically within and between cultures (Dettwyler and Fishman 1992); it is here that social inequality may have the greatest impact on health.

At Kaminaljuyu, we collected tooth enamel isotope data to look at dietary change with age during childhood (Wright and Schwarcz 1998, 1999). We found that premolars and third molars showed higher $\delta^{13}C$ ratios than first molars from the same adult skeletons. Since teeth mineralize during childhood, this indicates that children began to consume solids by at least the age of two years, and that this weanling diet was largely a maize-based one. Oxygen isotopes in enamel and bone reflect the $\delta^{18}O$ ratios of the water that we drink. Because we breathe out proportionately more of the isotopically light water ($H_2{}^{16}O$), body fluids such as breastmilk contain relatively more $H_2{}^{18}O$ molecules than local drinking water. At Kaminaljuyu, we found that both first molar and premolar enamel carbonate has higher $\delta^{18}O$ ratios than third molar enamel carbonate. This indicates that breastmilk continued to provide a significant proportion of the water that children drank up to five years of age (through the period of premolar mineralization) on average (Wright and Schwarcz 1998).

To study variability within ancient Maya children in greater detail, we are now drilling small samples of enamel from sections of teeth to reconstruct childhood dietary change with greater precision (Wright in review). Studies that integrate enamel carbonate data with dentine collagen data have the potential to examine breastfeeding also through stable nitrogen isotope ratios of collagen and the offset between dentine collagen and enamel carbonate (Richards, Mays, and Fuller 2002; Wright and Schwarcz 1999).

At Tikal, our preliminary data show that children's diets changed dramatically as they grew up, and were often quite different from the diets that those same individuals consumed during later adulthood (Wright, unpublished data). Marie Danforth is studying microscopic defects of enamel growth in these same teeth. We hope to correlate these episodes of growth faltering with isotopic data on breastfeeding duration and the composition of children's diets. Such approaches should allow a more nuanced reconstruction of life history than has been possible from the disparate studies of adult diets and pathology that have characterized Maya bioarchaeology in the past. Considered together with skeletal pathology (Buikstra et al. in press), and the biomechanical analysis of activity patterns (Tiesler Blos 2001), these new inferences will shed new light on the nature of ancient Maya lives at various positions in the social hierarchy.

Biodistance and Migration

Social inequality in diet and health at Maya sites may also be complicated by genetic differences in susceptibility to illness, at the hand of both social and geographic patterns of interaction, and migration. Biological distance studies have traditionally provided the means to test archaeological models of biological population distance and relationships, but are only recently finding a home in the Maya area. Saul's (1972) monograph on Altar de Sacrificios contained the first use of Maya biodistance data to test an archaeological hypothesis. In an appendix to Saul's volume, Donald Austin (1972) used dental traits to evaluate the hypothesized Putun invasion of Altar in the Terminal Classic (Sabloff and Willey 1967), finding considerable biological continuity. Surprisingly, dental morphological studies of Maya remains have been rare until recently despite the fact that teeth are well preserved at most Maya sites, and show little attrition.

Beginning with studies of colonial mission cemeteries (Lang 1990; Jacobi 2000), a new generation of scholars is beginning to address biodistance questions at both the regional and intrasite level. Currently four dissertations that employ dental morphological data are underway. Elsewhere, skeletal and dental morphological research has made great strides in recent years by incorporating sophisticated population genetic modeling into the statistical analysis of biological distance (e.g., Powell and Neves 1999; Stojanowski

2001). The challenge to these new Mayanists will be to integrate such models into their work, and to account for fluctuations in population size and migration.

Research on ancient DNA (aDNA) has been underway using Maya remains for several years (Merriwether et al. 1997), but has not shown much promise to date. Although human DNA has been recovered at both Copan (Merriwether et al. 1997; Matheson et al. 2001) and Tikal (Iglesias Ponce de León et al. 2002), it has not yet contributed to a better understanding of ancient Maya history, or social organization. The recovery and sequencing of both mitochondrial and chromosomal aDNA in the Maya area are challenged by poor preservation and contamination (Merriwether et al. 1997), as has been reported elsewhere in humid tropical environments (Kumar et al. 2000). Poor curation conditions, considerable post-excavation handling, and the preservatives that have been applied to many Maya skeletons further limit the success of molecular techniques.

The multiethnic nature of ancient Mesoamerican states is becoming increasingly apparent, as are the extent and intensity of interaction between distant cities. City cycles of growth and decline imply some movement of population, perhaps in part caused by increasing militarism through the Classic period. Thus, regional and intrasite patterning in genetic features will provide important windows into understanding this interaction. Migration between ancient cities may also be a significant factor that contributes to multidimensional variation in diet and health among individuals buried at a given site, and could obscure social patterning in diet and health, especially if migrants differ from local populations in nutritional status and frailty (ability to withstand disease). However, new isotopic techniques may help to identify the remains of first generation migrants in archaeological sites.

In the last few years, we have begun to identify migrants both within and beyond the Maya area through oxygen and strontium isotopic analysis of tooth enamel. The oxygen isotopic composition of rainfall—and thus drinking water—varies with latitude and climate, whereas strontium isotope ratios in foods are dependant on the age and geological origin of soils. Clouds that form over tropical seas gradually lose the heavier $H_2{}^{18}O$ through rainfall as they move over land masses and toward higher latitudes, retaining disproportionately the lighter $H_2{}^{16}O$ to fall in later showers. Thus, the $\delta^{18}O$ of drinking water declines with increasing latitude, distance from the coast (or source of evaporated water), and elevation (Luz and Kolodny 1989; Schwarcz, Gibbs, and Knyf 1991; Longinelli 1984). The stable isotopes of strontium—specifically the $^{87}Sr/^{86}Sr$ ratio—instead reflect the geological origin of soils on which foods are grown. Very old bedrock, such as sedimentary limestones, and rocks containing high levels of rubidium have high $^{87}Sr/^{86}Sr$ ratios, whereas young volcanic rocks have lower $^{87}Sr/^{86}Sr$ (Faure 1986; Faure and Powell 1972). Thus, the oxygen isotope values of teeth and bones broadly reflect the local rain water values, whereas the strontium isotope ratios reflect the geology of local soils.

Thus, the teeth of individuals who spent their childhood far from the site where they were interred may show different oxygen and strontium isotope ratios than those of local children, if their site of origin had significantly different local values than the site to which they migrated. By comparing bone and tooth values, or by comparing teeth that formed in infancy among skeletons recovered from a given site, we can infer which may have migrated to their place of death, and who did not migrate. Given the geological and climatological diversity of the Maya area, these techniques have considerable potential for tracking migration.

Doug Price, Jim Burton, Jane Buikstra, and I have been working on oxygen and strontium isotopes to study migration at Tikal, Kaminaljuyu (Wright et al. 2002), and Copan (Buikstra et al. in press). David Hodell and colleagues are also working on strontium isotope applications to migration in the Maya area (Hodell et al. in press). At Teotihuacan, both oxygen and strontium isotopes have shed light on the geographic origin of migrants to the Tlailotlacan barrio, and among the sacrificial victims of the Temple of the Feathered Serpent (White et al. 1998, 2002; Price, Manzanilla, and Middleton 2000).

Although our oxygen and strontium data for the Maya area are still sparce, considerable patterning in site signatures is evident. Figure 11.2 shows

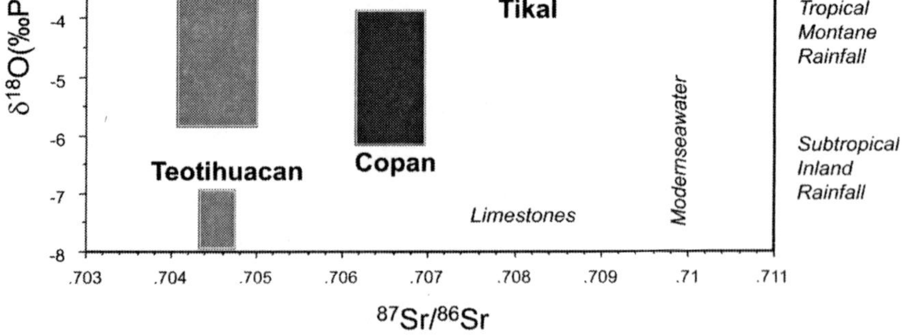

Fig. 11.2 Stable oxygen and strontium isotope composition of human tooth enamel from Tikal, Kaminaljuyu, Copan, and Teotihuacan. (Based on data from Price, Manzanilla, and Middleton 2000; Buikstra et al. 2003; and unpublished data).

preliminary local strontium and oxygen isotope ratios of human bone from Tikal, Kaminaljuyu, Copan, and Teotihuacan. The $^{87}Sr/^{86}Sr$ of those skeletons who consumed foods grown on recent volcanic soils lie toward the left on the horizontal scale, whereas skeletons recovered from sites situated on older sedimentary deposits are toward the right. The $\delta^{18}O$ of bones and teeth distinguishing sites in tropical lowlands that receive the first "isotopically heavy" rains from maritime clouds from. Montane regions, rainshadow areas, and higher latitudes that are lighter in $\delta^{18}O$. Our ability to identify the point of origin of skeletons that show "nonlocal" isotope values at a given site will thus depend on accurate mapping of both oxygen and strontium isotope ratios across Mesoamerica.

At Copan, isotopic analyses demonstrate that several elite burials from the Acropolis show non-local signatures. For instance, the Early Classic skeleton thought to be that of the dynastic founder, Yax K'uk'Mo', shows an isotopic composition that is consistent with data from the central Petén (Buikstra et al. in press). At Kaminaljuyu, we have identified several nonlocal skeletons among the Early Classic tombs, both through oxygen and strontium isotope ratios (Valdés and Wright in press; White et al. 2000), and preliminary data from Tikal demonstrate the presence of several nonlocal skeletons in both elite and non-elite domestic contexts (Wright et al. 2002). Additional analyses, especially of non-elite skeletons, will allow us to evaluate the extent to which migration contributed to the growth of the city, and to consider its implications for heterogeneity in diet and health as determined from skeletal remains.

Paleopathology and Forensic Osteology

Through paleopathology, we attempt to evaluate the implications of Maya subsistence choices and population density on health and survival. We are now moving away from simplistic assessments of bony lesion frequencies to a more sensitive exploration of the meaning of pathology in terms of individual differences in frailty, and thus illness (Storey 1997). Skeletal lesions have long been used to support arguments that overpopulation, environmental deterioration, and poor health were causal factors in the collapse, without any real evidence for changes in lesion abundance over time. Purposeful consideration of the meaning of bone pathology for past health is leading us to reëvaluate these simplistic inferences.

Early pathological studies of Maya remains were interpreted in a comparative vacuum, without reference to the expectations for lesion frequencies in populations of known disease loads and mortality profiles. Viewed today in a global perspective (Wright and White 1996), Maya health does not appear to have been so exceptionally compromised as it seemed when Saul (1972) first studied the Altar de Saciaficios skeletons. We are fortunate that intensive research on the diets and health status of the living Maya give us an exceptionally detailed frame of reference. Many intensive studies of growth and development, stature, diet, nutrition, anemia, and infection have been carried out over the last sixty years by scholars at the Institute of Nutrition of Central America and Panama (INCAP) in Guatemala City, and others (see, e.g., May, Goodman, and Meindl 1993; Martorell 1992, 1995; Bogin and MacVean 1983; Rivera and Ruel 1997). Although key nutritional and lifestyle factors have changed since Pre-Hispanic times, the modern rural Maya show a more significant continuity with their past than do decendant populations in most parts of the world where bioarchaeological work is carried out.

Unfortunately, we also now have a window into the abundance of bony pathology on modern skeletons, through forensic exhumations of clandestine cemeteries from Guatemala's civil war. Several forensic anthropology teams have been formed in recent years, and have been rapidly providing the hard documentation of Guatemalan wartime atrocities (Equipo de Antropología Forense de Guatemala 1997; Arzobispado de Guatemala 1998). These projects are fundamentally Guatemalan in initiative and implementation, but forensic osteologists who work on human rights projects in other world areas have shared their expertise and advice. However, very few Mayanist bioarchaeologists have sought them out. Physical anthroplogy now has a unique opportunity to begin dialogue with the Mayan people in Guatemala as allies in the reconstruction of a peaceful democratic society.

This forensic work is of interest to bioarchaeologists both in terms of the interpretation of paleopathological indicators of health, and the development of osteological methods. Moreover, it provides a new source of data on Maya health and adaptation during the twentieth century (Bogin and Rios in press). In a forensic series of rural Achi from Baja Verapaz, I found that cranial lesions caused by iron deficiency anemia were much less common than they are in archaeological skeletons. In view of the abundant anemia among modern children of this region and their high mortality, I believe this discrepancy should lead us to consider the possibility that ancient Maya children may have been somewhat better off than their modern descendants (Wright and Chew 1998). If so, the anemic scars indicate survival through childhood illness instead of the state of extreme frailty that we have assumed since Earnest Hooton (1940) first described the lesions in skeletons from the Cenote at Chichén Itzá. Together with detailed information on modern demographic processes, diet, and health, such forensic data provide a unique window into the implications of pathological lesions on prehistoric health status for the Maya.

Maya bioarchaeology and forensics are equally challenged by the population specificity of many of the standards we use in our work (Pérez,

Valdizón, and Herrera 1999; Wrobel, Danforth, and Armstrong 2002), so this is one area where collaboration can be especially fruitful. For instance, skeletal stature has figured largely in reconstructions of ancient Maya health (Danforth 1994), modern Maya health (Bogin and Rios 2003; Bogin and MacVean 1983), and is a key forensic attribute. Early in the development of Guatemalan forensic anthropology, Stefan Schmitt (1993) compared the accuracy of stature estimation formulae against statures reported on Guatemalan *cédulas* (identification papers) for a number of positively identified skeletons. Although the accuracy of the *cédula* data is perhaps also suspect, he finds that the standards of Santiago Genovés (1967) are most accurate for forensic Mayan remains.

Likewise, using forensic skeletons, Mario Vásquez and I have developed Maya regression standards for the estimation of bone length from the distance between bony landmarks on limb bones (Wright and Vásquez 2003). The standards will enhance stature estimation possibilities for forensic remains as well as archaeological collections. At Tikal, we have used these new forensic standards to estimate stature for fragmentary skeletons (Vásquez Gómez 2003). Such collaborations are critical both to the growth of a national physical anthropology in Guatemala, and to forging a productive dialogue with Mayan peoples who are finally achieving the political voice that they deserve.

Conclusions

Maya bioarchaeology may have a bright future. We are just beginning to have the tools to really delve into the nature of ancient biocultural adaptation. We will soon move beyond the search for class differences in diet to explore the very different expectations of life that members of a complex society may enjoy as a result of differential access to resources, genetic differences among migrants, and child-rearing practices. These "life history" approaches have begun to combine chemical and pathological data into a sensitive reconstruction of individual health and illness.

However, these advances are dependent on the availability of large and representative skeletal series that are carefully documented on excavation and subsequently well curated. Since many projects recover small numbers of skeletons, it is tempting to make much broader inferences about health status and the social implications of biological features than warranted from such samples. New life history approaches to skeletal analysis provide a more nuanced reconstruction of health that at first glance seem amenable to application on small skeletal series. Although these studies will provide a detailed glimpse at select lives among the ancient Maya, relationships between past behavior and biology can only be truly understood through a populational approach. The challenge to future osteologists is to integrate such individual life histories into a populational approach to ancient Maya biological history.

References

Acevedo, R., Wright, L. E., Hermes, B., and Schwarcz, H. P. (1997) "La Dieta Maya Después del Colapso: un Estudio Isotópico del Sitio Topoxté," In J. P. Laporte and H. L. Escobedo (eds.), *X Simposio de Investigaciones Arqueologicas en Guatemala, 1996*, pp. 587–600. Vol. 2. Guatemala City: Ministerio de Cultura y Deportes, Instituto de Antropología e Historia, Asociación Tikal.

Arzobispado de Guatemala, Oficina de Derechos Humanos (1998) *Guatemala: Nunca Más, Informe Proyecto Interdiocesano de Recuperación de la Memoria Historica*, Guatemala: ODHAG.

Austin, D. M. (1972) "Appendix: Morphology and Dimensions of the Altar de Sacrificios Teeth," in F. P. Saul (ed.), *The Human Skeletal Remains of Altar de Sacrificios: An Osteobiographic Analysis*, pp. 79–81, Cambridge, MA: Harvard University Press.

Bogin, B., and MacVean, R. B. (1983) "The Relationship of Socioeconomic Status and Sex to Body Size, Skeletal Maturation, and Cognitive Status of Guatemala City Schoolchildren," *Child Development* 54: 115–28.

Bogin, B., and Rios, L. (in press) "Rapid morphological change in living humans: implications for modern human origins," *Comparative Biochemistry and Physiology Part A.*

Buikstra, J. E. (1997) "Studying Maya Bioarchaeology," in S. Whittington and D. Reed (eds.), *Bones of the Maya: Studies of Ancient Skeletons*, pp. 221–8, Washington, DC: Smithsonian Institution Press.

Buikstra, J. E., Price, T. D., Wright, L. E., and Burton, J. H. (in press) "Tombs from the Copan Acropolis: A Life History Approach," in E. Bell, M. Canuto, and R. Sharer (eds.), *Understanding Early Classic Copan*, Philadelphia: University of Pennsylvania Museum.

Chase, A. F., and Chase, D. Z. (2001) "The Royal Court of Caracol, Belize: Its Palaces and People," in T. Inomata and S. D. Houston (eds.), *Royal Courts of the Ancienct Maya, Volume 2, Data and Case Studies*, pp. 102–137, Boulder: Westview.

Chase, A. F., Chase, D. Z., and White, C. D. (2001) "El paisaje urbano Maya: La integración de los espacios construidos y la estructura social en Caracol, Belice," in A. Ciudad-Ruiz, M. J. Iglesias Ponce de Leon, and M. D. C. Martinez (eds.), *Reconstruyendo la Ciudad Maya: El Urbanismo en las Sociedades Antiguas*, pp. 95–122, Madrid: Sociedad Española de Estudios Mayas.

Danforth, M. E. (1994) "Stature Change in Prehistoric Maya of the Southern Lowlands," *Latin American Antiquity* 5(3): 206–11.

———(1997) "Late Classic Maya Health Patterns: Evidence from Enamel Microdefects," in S. Whittington and D. Reed (eds.), *Bones of the Maya: Studies of Ancient Skeletons*, pp. 127–37, Washington, DC: Smithsonian Institution Press.

Dettwyler, K. A., and Fishman, C. (1992) "Infant Feeding Practices and Growth," *Annual Review of Anthropology* 21: 171–204.

Equipo de Antropología Forense de Guatemala (EAFG) (1997) *Las Masacres en Rabinal: Estudio Histórico Antropológico de las Masacres de Plan de Sánchez, Chichupac y Río Negro*, 2nd ed., Guatemala City: Editorial Serviprensa.

Faure, G. (1986) *Principles of Isotope Geology*, New York: John Wiley.

Faure, G., and Powell, T. (1972) *Strontium Isotope Geology*, New York: Springer-Verlag.

Genovés, S. (1967) "Proportionality of the Long Bones and Their Relation to Stature among Mesoamericans," *American Journal of Physical Anthropology* 26: 67–78.

Gerry, J. P., and Krueger, H. (1997) "Regional Diversity in Classic Maya Diets," in S. Whittington and D. Reed (eds.), *Bones of the Maya: Studies of Ancient Skeletons*, pp. 196–207, Washington, DC: Smithsonian Institution Press.

Gillespie, S. D. (2001) "Personhood, Agency, and Mortuary Ritual: A Case Study from the Ancient Maya," *Journal of Anthropological Archaeology* 20: 73–112.

Haviland, W. A. (1967) "Stature at Tikal, Guatemala: Implications for Classic Maya Demography and Social Organization," *American Antiquity* 32: 316–25.

Henderson, H. H. (1998) *The Organization of Staple Crop Production in Middle Formative, Late Formative, and Classic Period Farming Households at K'axob, Belize*, unpublished Ph.D. dissertation, Anthropology Department, University of Pittsburgh, Pittsburgh.

Hodell, D. A., Brenner, M., Kamenov, G., Quinn, R., and Anton, S. C. (in press) "Spatial Variation of Strontium Isotopes ($^{87}Sr/^{86}Sr$) in the Maya Region: A Tool for Tracking Human Migration," *Journal of Archaeological Science*.

Hooton, E. A. (1940) "Skeletons from the Cenote of Sacrifice at Chichén Itzá," in C. L. Hay et al. (eds.), *The Maya and Their Neighbors*, pp. 272–80, New York: D. Appleton-Century.

Iglesias Ponce de León, M. J., Alvarez López de Rodas, S., Fernández Domínguez, E., Arroyo-Pardo, E., Ciudad Ruiz, A., and Adánez Pavón, J. (2002) "Estudio de secuencias de DNA mitocondrial en una muestra maya de la ciudad de Tikal (Guatemala)," in J. P. Laporte (ed.), *XVI Simposio de Investigaciones Arqueológicas en Guatemala, July 20–24, 2002*, Guatemala City.

Jacobi, K. P. (2000) *Last Rites for the Tipu Maya: Genetic Structuring in a Colonial Cemetery*, Tuscaloosa: University of Alabama Press.

Kumar, S. S., Nasidze, I., Walimbe, S. R., and Stoneking, M. (2000) "Discouraging Prospects for Ancient DNA in India," *American Journal of Physical Anthropology* 113(1): 129–34.

Lang, C. A. (1990) "The Dental Morphology of the Maya from Lamanai and Tipu," unpublished master's thesis, Anthropology Department, Trent University, Peterborough, Ontario.

Longinelli, A. (1984) "Oxygen Isotopes in Mammal Bone Phosphate: A New Tool for Paleohydrological and Paleoclimatological Research?" *Geochimica et Cosmochimica Acta* 48: 385–90.

Luz, B., and Kolodny, Y. (1989) "Oxygen Isotope Variation in Bone Phosphate," *Applied Geochemistry* 4: 317–23.

Mansell, E. B., Tykot, R. H., Freidel, D., Ardren, T., and Dahlin, B. (2002) "Ancient Maya Diet in the Northern and Southern Lowlands: A Stable Isotope Study of Diet from Yucatán, Mexico and La Milpa, Belize," paper presented at 67th Annual Meeting of the Society for American Archaeology, April, Denver, CO.

Martorell, R. (1992) "Overview of Long-term Nutrition Intervention Studies in Guatemala, 1968–1989," *Food and Nutrition Bulletin* 14: 270–77.

———(1995) "Results and Implications of the INCAP Follow-up Study," *Journal of Nutrition* 125:1127S–1138S.

Matheson, C., Hall, J., Loy, T., and Viel, R. (2001) "The People of Copan," paper presented at 66th Annual Meeting of the Society for American Archaeology, New Orleans, LA, April 18–22, 2001.

May, R. L., Goodman, A. H., and Meindl, R. S. (1993) "Response of Bone and Enamel Formation to Nutritional Supplementation and Morbidity among Malnourished Guatemalan Children," *American Journal of Physical Anthropology* 92(1): 37–51.

Merriwether, D. A., Reed, D. M., and Ferrell, R. E. (1997) "Ancient and Contemporary Mitochondrial DNA Variation in the Maya," in S. Whittington and D. Reed (eds.), *Bones of the Maya: Studies of Ancient Skeletons*, pp. 208–18, Washington, DC: Smithsonian Institution Press.

Nance C. R., Whittington, S. L., and Borg, B. E. (2003) *Archaeology and Ethnohistory of Iximche*, Gainsville, FL: University Press of Florida.

Pérez, J. C., Valdizon, M., Herrera, J. P. (1999) "Determinación de sexo en una muestra ósea de poblaciones Ixil, Q'eqchi', K'iche', Poqomchí y Kaqchikel, utilizando mediciones de cabezas de huesos largos y clavícula," in J. P. Laporte, H. L. Escobedo, and A. C. Monzón de Suasnávar (eds.), *XII Simposio de Investigaciones Arqueológicas en Guatemala, 1998*. pp. 965–73. Guatemala City: Ministerio de Cultura y Deportes, Instituto de Antropología e Historia, Asociación Tikal.

Powell, J. F., and Neves, W. A. (1999) "Craniofacial Morphology of the First Americans: Pattern and Process in the Peopling of the New World," *Yearbook of Physical Anthropology* 42: 153–88.

Powis, T. G., Stanchly, N., White, C. D., Healy, P. F., Awe, J. J., and Longstaffe, F. (1999) "A Reconstruction of Middle Preclassic Maya Subsistence Economy at Cahal Pech, Belize," *Antiquity* 73: 364–76.

Price, T. D., Manzanilla, L., and Middleton, W. D. (2000) "Immigration and the Ancient City of Teotihuacan in Mexico: A Study Using Strontium Isotope Ratios in Human Bones and Teeth," *Journal of Archaeological Science* 27: 903–13.

Reed, D. M. (1998) *Ancient Maya Diet at Copan, Honduras*, unpublished Ph.D. dissertation, Anthropology Department, Pennsylvania State University, University Park.

Richards, M. P., Mays, S., and Fuller, B. T. (2002) "Stable Carbon and Nitrogen Isotope Values of Bone and Teeth Reflect Weaning Age at the Medieval Wharram Percy Site, Yorkshire, UK," *American Journal of Physical Anthropology* 119(3): 205–10.

Rivera, J., and Ruel, M. T. (1997) "Growth Retardation Starts in the First Three Months of Life, Among Rural Guatemalan Children," *European Journal of Clinical Nutrition* 51(2): 92–6.

Sabloff, J. A., and Willey, G. R. (1967) "The Collapse of Maya Civilization in the Southern Lowlands: A Consideration of History and Process," *Southwestern Journal of Anthropology* 23: 311–36.

Saul, F. P. (1972) *The Human Skeletal Remains of Altar de Sacrificios: An Osteobiographic Analysis*, Vol. 63, no. 2, Peabody Museum of Archaeology and Ethnology Papers, Cambridge, MA: Harvard University Press.

Schmitt, S. (1994) "La problemática en la determinación de edad y estatura a partir de restos óseos de poblaciones Mayas," in J. P. Laporte and H. L. Escobedo (eds.), *VII Simposio de Investigaciones Arqueológicas en Guatemala, 1993*, pp. 29–40. Guatemala City: Ministerio de Cultura y Deportes, Instituto de Antropología e Historia, Asociación Tikal.

Schwarcz, H. P., Gibbs, L., and Knyf, M. (1991) "Oxygen Isotope Analysis as an Indicator of Place of Origin," in S. Pfeiffer and R. F. Williamson (eds.), *Snake Hill: An Investigation of a Military Cemetery from the War of 1812*, pp. 263–8, Toronto: Dundurn Press.

Stojanowski, C. M. (2001) *Cemetery Structure, Population Aggregation and Biological Variability in the Mission Centers of La Florida*, unpublished Ph.D. dissertation, Anthropology Department, University of New Mexico, Albuquerque.

Storey, R. (1992) "Patterns of Susceptibility to Dental Defects in the Deciduous Dentition of a Precolumbian Skeletal Population," in A. L. Goodman and L. L. Capasso (eds.), *Recent Contributions to the Study of Enamel Developmental Defects*, pp. 171–183, Chieti, Italy: Edigrafital Teramo.

———(1997) "Individual Frailty, Children of Privilege, and Stress in Late Classic Copan," in S. Whittington and D. Reed (eds.), *Bones of the Maya: Studies of Ancient Skeletons*, pp. 116–26, Washington, DC: Smithsonian Institution Press.

———(1999) "Late Classic Nutrition and Skeletal Indicators at Copan, Honduras," in C. D. White (ed.), *Reconstructing Ancient Maya Diet*, pp. 169–79, Salt Lake City: University of Utah Press.

Tiesler Blos, V. (2001) "Patrones ocupacionales y subsistencia en la sociedad maya de la costa peninsular, Consideraciones bioculturales," *Mayab* 14: 30–41.

Tykot, R. H. (2002) "Contribution of Stable Isotope Analysis to Understanding Dietary Variation among the Maya," in K. Jakes (ed.), *Archaeological Chemistry. Materials, Methods, and Meaning*, Washington, DC: American Chemical Society.

Valdés, J. A., and Wright, L. E. (in press) "The Early Classic and Its Antecedents at Kaminaljuyu: A Complex Society, with Complex Problems," in E. Bell, M. Canuto, and R. Sharer (eds.), *Understanding Early Classic Copan*, Philadelphia: University of Pennsylvania Museum.

Vásquez Gómez, M. A. (2003) *Elaboración de Formularios de Medición de Huesos Largos en Contexto Forense para Estimar Estatura y su Aplicación en Restos Óseos Prehispanicos: El Caso de Tikal*, Licenciatura thesis, Area de Arqueología, Escuela de Historia, Universidad de San Carlos de Guatemala, Guatemala City.

White, C. D. (1997) "Ancient Diet at Lamanai and Pacbitun: Implications for the Ecological Model of Collapse," in S. Whittington and D. Reed (eds.), *Bones of the Maya: Studies of Ancient Skeletons*, pp. 171–80, Washington, DC: Smithsonian Institution Press.

White, C. D., Pendergast, D. M., Longstaffe, F. J., and Law, K. R. (2001) "Social Complexity and Food Systems at Altun Ha, Belize: The Isotopic Evidence," *Latin American Antiquity* 12(4): 371–93.

White, C. D., Spence, M. W., Longstaffe, F. J., and Law, K. R. (2000) "Testing the Nature of Teotihuacán Imperialism at Kaminaljuyu Using Phosphate Oxygen-isotope Ratios," *Journal of Anthropological Research* 56: 535–58.

White, C. D., Spence, M. W., Longstaffe, F. J., Stuart-Williams, H., and Law, K. R. (2002) "Geographic Identities of the Sacrificial Victims from the Feathered Serpent Pyramid, Teotihuacan: Implications for the Nature of State Power," *Latin American Antiquity* 13(2): 217–36.

White, C. D., Spence, M. W., Stuart-Williams, H., and Schwarcz, H. P. (1998) "Oxygen Isotopes and the Identification of Geographical Origins: The Valley of Oaxaca versus the Valley of Mexico," *Journal of Archaeological Science* 25(7): 643–55.

Whittington, S. (1992) "Enamel Hypoplasia in the Low Status Maya Population of Prehispanic Copan, Honduras," in A. L. Goodman and L. L. Capasso (eds.), *Recent Contributions to the Study of Enamel Developmental Defects*, pp. 185–205, Chieti, Italy: Edigrafital Teramo.

Whittington, S., and Reed, D. (1997) "Commoner Diet at Copan: Insights from Stable Isotopes and Porotic Hyperostosis," in S. Whittington and D. Reed (eds.), *Bones of the Maya: Studies of Ancient Skeletons*. pp. 151–70, Washington, DC: Smithsonian Institution Press.

Wright, L. E. (1997a) "Biological Perspectives on the Collapse of the Pasión Maya," *Ancient Mesoamerica* 8(2): 267–73.

———(1997b) "Intertooth Patterns of Hypoplasia Expression: Implications for Childhood Health in the Classic Maya Collapse," *American Journal of Physical Anthropology* 102(2): 233–47.

———(2003) "La muerte y estatus económico: investigando el simbolismo mortuorio y el acceso a los recursos alimenticios entre los mayas," In A. Ciudad, Ruiz, M. H. Ruz Soza, and M. J. Iglesias Ponce de León (eds.), *Antropología de la Eternidad: La Muerte en la Cultura Maya*, pp. 175–93, Madrid: Sociedad Española de Estudios Mayas.

———(in review) "Examining Childhood Diets at Kaminaljuyu, Guatemala, through Stable Isotopic Analysis of Enamel Microsamples," in C. D. White and A. Zeller (eds.), *Growth and Development of Physical Anthropology in Canada: Essays in Honour of Hermann Helmuth*, Toronto: Canadian Scholar's Press.

Wright, L. E., Burton, J., Price, T. D., and Rank, P. (2002) "Teotihuacanos at Tikal and Kaminaljuyu?" paper presented at 67th Annual Meeting of the Society for American Archaeology, March, Denver, CO.

Wright, L. E., and Chew, F. (1998) "Porotic Hyperostosis and Paleoepidemiology: A Forensic Perspective on Anemia among the Ancient Maya," *American Anthropologist* 100(4): 924–39.

Wright, L. E., and Schwarcz, H. P. (1998) "Stable Carbon and Oxygen Isotopes in Human Tooth Enamel: Identifying Breastfeeding and Weaning in Prehistory," *American Journal of Physical Anthropology* 106(1): 1–18.

———(1999) "Correspondence between Stable Carbon, Oxygen and Nitrogen Isotopes in Human Tooth Enamel and Dentine: Infant Diets and Weaning at Kaminaljuyu," *Journal of Archaeological Science* 26: 1159–70.

Wright, L. E., Schwarcz, H. P., and Acevedo, R. (2000) "La dieta de los habitantes de Topoxté, una reconstrucción isotópica," in W. Wurster (ed.), *El Sitio Maya de Topoxté: Investigaciones en una isla del lago Yaxhá, Petén, Guatemala*, pp. 158–63, Mainz: Verlag Philipp von Zabern.

Wright, L. E., and Vásquez, M. A. (2003) "Estimating Long Bone Length from Fragmentary Remains. Forensic Standards from Guatemala," *American Journal of Physical Anthropology* 120(3): 233–51.

Wright, L. E., and White, C. D. (1996). "Human Biology in the Classic Maya Collapse: Evidence from Paleopathology and Paleodiet," *Journal of World Prehistory* 10(2): 147–98.

Wrobel, G. D., Danforth, M. E., and Armstrong, C. (2002) "Estimating sex of Maya skeletons by discriminant function analysis of long bone measurements from the Protohistoric Maya site of Tipu, Belize," *Ancient Mesoamerica* 13: 255–63.

12
Maya Zooarchaeology: In Pursuit of Social Variability and Environmental Heterogeneity

KITTY F. EMERY

Zooarchaeology lies at the intersection of the biological and cultural sciences, and its practitioners respond to the development of new trends and paradigms in both fields. As culture historians, Maya zooarchaeologists provided species lists of animals used by the ancient Maya. As processualists, they attempted to define a Maya diet and patterns of Maya animal use. Today, zooarchaeologists in other parts of the world are examining ritual, economics, and politics within the context of a new "social zooarchaeology," describing local effects of environmental and anthropogenic change on the human–animal relationship and applying lessons learned from these studies to modern global sustainable development initiatives. Maya zooarchaeology is following suit and has made excellent progress in the study of social zooarchaeology. However, it remains hindered by a lack of either the detailed coverage or comparable samples from Maya archaeological sites that would be sufficient to fully describe patterns of ancient animal distribution and use across the region, or completely understand variability among households, community groups, or sites.

This review of the past, present, and possible future of Maya zooarchaeology will present a definition of the science as it would be recognized by a global audience, and a brief history of its development in Maya archaeology.

This background acts as a foundation to discuss the current needs and directions of the science in view of current trajectories in environmental archaeology and particularly Mesoamerican environmental archaeology. I will suggest that the field of Maya zooarchaeology, as many of the other environmental archaeology sciences, is simultaneously being asked to provide substantive models to be used in modern sustainable environmental management, while it remains marginalized as an integral part of archaeological research design, implementation, and publication. The result of these factors is a lack of regionally comparable reports on animal remains from a wide range of sites, and this has weakened zooarchaeology's ability to respond to a global need for the historical perspective on environmental change and management that is available in the zooarchaeological record. These problems can be remedied by an increase in the number of practicing zooarchaeologists particularly within the countries that make up the ancient Maya world, and an increasing collaboration between archaeologists and zooarchaeologists from the first stages of research design and throughout the process of excavation and data recovery. Together, these will serve to increase the quantity of zooarchaeological data and the quality of its recovery and interpretation, thereby creating a substantial database for modeling ancient and sustainable future human–environment interrelations.

Defining the Science of Zooarchaeology

Zooarchaeology is traditionally defined as the study of the ancient relationship between humans and animals, or the study of animal remains from archaeological sites (Reitz and Wing 1999:1). However, Maya zooarchaeology is a far broader science than is typically recognized, just as the relationship between environment, animal, and human is far more complex than we often realize. Zooarchaeology includes studies of both ancient (in archaeozoology) and modern (in studies of paleoethnozoology) animal–human interactions, as well as the biological (emphasizing the zoology) and archaeological (emphasizing the cultural) aspects of this enduring relationship. Faunal remains provide a proxy for the reconstruction of ancient environments, allowing us to describe natural resources as well as anthropogenic and natural environmental changes. Faunal remains are more directly used to trace the complex relationship between the ancient Maya and the animals around them by detailing dietary and other subsistence patterns (e.g., Carr 1991; Emery 1999), the economics of animal resource control and trade (e.g., Hamblin 1985; Pohl 1995), and the complex politico-religious meanings ascribed to different animals and represented by their use in ritual (e.g., Emery in press-c; Pohl 1994).

Zooarchaeological remains recovered from Maya archaeological sites are diverse, ranging from macro- to microscopic, but the most commonly recognized are the hard remains of both vertebrates and invertebrates. These include the bone, teeth, antler/horn, and shell, that are most likely to preserve in archaeological deposits. However, also included in the zooarchaeological arsenal are less well-recognized remains, including eggshell from birds and reptiles (e.g., Sidell 1993), and insect and crustacean remains (exoskeletons) (Robinson 2001), as well as various microscopic and molecular remains, including those of ostracods (microscopic calcareous-shelled crustaceans) (Griffiths and Holmes 2000), foraminifera (marine protist tests) (Wilson et al. 2000), parasites (eggs and cysts found in feces) (Jones 1982; Reinhard 1992), and various biomolecules (DNA, isotope and elemental signatures, and chemical residues) (Coyston 2002; Emery et al. 2000; Evershed and Bethell 1996; Hyland et al. 1990; White et al. 2001). Many of these remains have not been systematically recovered or included in Maya zooarchaeology, and some have not yet (to my knowledge) been used as a source of data in our region despite the fact that they may be recoverable in Maya archaeological deposits.

History of Maya Zooarchaeology[1]

Just as Maya zooarchaeology (and zooarchaeology in general) has not always fully exploited the wide range of physical remains that encompass a zooarchaeological assemblage, neither has it fully explored the theoretical or methodological arsenal that make up the science itself. A review of the history of Maya zooarchaeology can trace the gradual expansion of this science.

Early Traditions

As early as 1840 in Europe, Jens Jacob Worsaae (1849) argued that archaeological finds had to be studied in relationship with their paleoenvironmental settings, and certainly, as fascinated as the earliest explorers to the Central American jungles were by the ancient peoples, they were equally fascinated by the ability of those peoples to live in the tropical rainforests. However, despite a long history of European zooarchaeology (reviewed in Evans and O'Connor 1999; Trigger 1989), this tradition is relatively recent in the New World, dating only from the early 1930s in Mesoamerica.

In the 1920s and 1930s, the age of biological classification was in full bloom, and new taxonomic listings of lowland Mesoamerican tropical fauna, flora, and soils (Bartlett 1935; Cooke 1931; Goodrich and van der Schalie 1937; Hubbs 1935; Lundell 1937; Murie 1935; Stuart 1935; van Tyne 1935) were of immediate interest to archaeologists working in the area. Revolutionary excavations at the site of Uaxactun (Ricketson and Ricketson 1937) and smaller projects at the Southern Lowland sites of Piedras Negras (Coe 1959) and Holmul (Merwin and Vaillant 1932), the Northern Lowland sites of Chichén Itzá (Coggins 1992) and Jaina (Moedano-Koer 1946; Pina-Chan 1968), and highland sites like Kaminaljuyu (Kidder et al. 1946; Shook and Kidder 1952) and Zaculeu (Woodbury and Trik 1954), were the first to peripherally recognize the importance of animal populations to the early inhabitants of Mesoamerica. These early analyses of animal remains were traditionally made by zoologists and appended to site reports as incidental species lists (Kidder 1947; Pollock and Ray 1957; Ricketson 1937; Woodbury and Trik 1954). Analyses were restricted to faunal remains found in special deposits such as burials and caches, or to those that were artifactually modified. Despite these limitations, these early practitioners were instrumental in the first interdisciplinary research efforts toward elucidating the environmental and ecological history of the region.

New Archaeology and Processual Zooarchaeology

The "New Archaeology" movement of the 1960s followed models of cultural ecology and cultural evolution of the 1950s (Steward 1955) in advocating an ecologically based, systemic model for the quantification of behavioral patterning (Binford 1962, 1965; Caldwell 1959). Systems models proposed for both New and Old World agriculture and domestication incorporated earlier economic archaeology studies to define human processes of resource acquisition as active and adaptive strategies (Butzer 1982; Flannery 1968).

In the Maya lowlands, Gordon Willey included analyses of plant and animal remains in his Belize River Valley project (Willey et al. 1965), and later the Pasión Valley project in Guatemala (Willey 1973, 1990). Large settlement projects at Tikal and Dzibilchaltun specifically integrated environmental variables into research strategies and data collection (Jones et al. 1981; Kurjack 1974; Olson 1969; Puleston 1974, 1983; Rick 1968; Smithe and Paynter 1963; Stuart 1958). In Chiapas, the importance of animal resources in the development of Preclassic subsistence systems was recognised (Chavez-O 1969; Flannery 1969; Follett 1966; Green and Lowe 1967).

In this milieu, zooarchaeologists became accepted members of environmental and archaeological teams for the first time [at Altar de Sacrificios (Olsen 1972); Seibal (Olsen 1978); Tikal (Pohl 1976); and Eduardo Quiroz and other Belizean caves (Luther 1974; Pendergast 1971; Savage in Pendergastand Savage 1971, 1978)]. However, during the 1960s and 70s, despite a rapid rise in interest in Old World zooarchaeology, few Maya zooarchaeology studies moved beyond the limitations of the taxonomic list of subsistence species. In contrast, environmental archaeology developed quickly. Spurred by movements in ecology and environmental protection (Carson 1962), the first paleolimnological studies appeared in association with a burgeoning interest in the cause of the end of Classic Maya civilization in the ninth century A.D. (Cowgill 1961, 1962; Cowgill et al. 1966; Isukada and Deevey 1967). With these studies came the first use of molluscs as environmental indicators (Covich 1983; Covich and Stuiver 1974; Emery 1986; Feldman 1974; Willey et al. 1965). These complemented simultaneous studies of microfaunal variability and cultural origins in northern Mexico (e.g., Flannery 1986) to suggest a broader utility for zooarchaeological materials.

As a result of this wave of interest in the role of the tropical environment in Maya social transitions, Maya zooarchaeology finally reached its stride during the 1980s [Cozumel (Hamblin 1984); Cerros (Carr 1985, 1986); Colha (Scott 1979, 1982); Dzibilchaltun (Wing and Steadman 1980); Lubaantun (Wing 1975); Cancun (Wing 1974); and Salinas La Blanca (Coe and Flannery 1967; Follett 1966)]. In Mexico, zooarchaeological analyses were included in investigations in Chiapas (Agrinier 1975; Voorhies 1976) and the Yucatán (Alvarez 1976; Barrera-Rubio 1977; Miller 1977), and the Maya frontier at Yarumela (Colby 1988).

Methods of Maya faunal analysis also became more sophisticated, further increasing the scope of the science. Recovery of fish bones and mollusc remains through fine-screening generated interest in the use of lacustrine and riverine fauna (Dahlin 1979; Lange 1971; Moholy-Nagy 1978; Thompson 1974), and an enduring fascination with marine resources (Andrews 1969; Cobos 1989; Emery and Graham 2003; Hamblin 1985; McKillop 1984, 1985; Moholy-Nagy 1963; Vail 1988). Maya zooarchaeologists were among the first to investigate the potential of such measures as biomass and bone weight, and the value of osteometrics for both identification and analysis of dietary contribution (Hamblin 1984; Wing 1976, 1977). Renewed study of the process of domestication in the Old World (e.g., Brothwell 1975) in combination with animal population statistics generated through age and sex analyses (Pohl 1976) spurred an interest in animal domestication in the Maya world (Clutton-Brock 1981; Pohl and Feldman 1982; Wing 1978) that continues today (Clutton-Brock and Hammond 1994; Dillon 1988; White et al. 2001, in press).

As well, the first works discussing fauna from a wider perspective appeared, indicating a burgeoning recognition of regional and comparative patterns of faunal resource use (Benson 1977; Stark and Voorhies 1978; Wing 1981). Elizabeth Wing's early work (1981) on the definition of a Maya "menu," using statistical analyses of dietary patterns, remains unsurpassed in today's literature. With this new understanding of the versatility of zooarchaeology and its utility for the analysis of various social systems,

Maya faunal analysts also began to reflect on broader questions of social change (Carr 1985, 1989; Hamblin 1985; Wiseman 1983), as well as patterns in subsistence and environment use (Bradley 1983; McKillop 1984, 1985).

The Last Decade of Maya Zooarchaeology

Investigations of diet remain pivotal in modern Maya zooarchaeology. Building on Wing's early work, some recent studies have attempted to trace chronological change in diets across the Maya landscape (Carr 1996; Cliff and Crane 1989; Pohl 1994; Polaco and Guzman 1997; Wing and Scudder 1991). At Cozumel, Nancy L. Hamblin (1985) introduced faunal assemblages as indicators of patterns of trade, not only of artifactually modified marine molluscs, but also of animal resources for subsistence purposes. Others followed with investigations into the transport and exchange of animal products (Carr 1989, 1996; Emery 1999; Mock 1994). As well, some regional studies of specific species are appearing in the literature as zooarchaeologists begin to search for distribution across the Maya region (Baker 1992; Carr 1996; Polaco and Guzman 1997). Unfortunately, zooarchaeological studies are still nascent and not enough information has yet been gathered or identified to allow analysis of either variability or generalities of animal use in the Maya world.

In association with a growing interest in "social zooarchaeology" around the world, analyses pertinent to ancient Maya social organization are now also common. Animal remains are recognized for their use as potential markers of both status (Chase et al. 1998; Emery 2002a; Pyburn 1989; Shaw 1999) and ethnicity (Emery 1999), and considerable research is directed at differential access to resources between social groups (Emery 2002a; Moholy-Nagy 1994; Pohl 1994, 1995; Teeter 2001). The role of animals in Maya ceremonial life is not a new theme (Borhegyi 1961; Pohl 1983). However, specific ritual behavior (Ballinger and Stomper 2000; Benson 1988a, 1988b; Saunders 1994), including that associated with feasting or repetitive ceremony, is a topic for which Maya zooarchaeological data are well qualified (Emery n.d.b; Masson 1999; Shaw 1995b; Wharton 1998).

Again though, we must question whether these interpretations of social, political, or economic organization are based on strong enough foundations to justify our conclusions in any of these arenas. In the newest trends in biology, archaeology, and zooarchaeology in other parts of the world, there is a growing recognition of our need for robust and comparable datasets to describe both social and environmental patterning. These are not yet available in the Maya area, and our understanding of ancient Maya animal use requires more and better data.

Modern Maya Zooarchaeology: Facing a Lack of Data

The real question for this critical review of Maya zooarchaeology at the millenium is whether our science has continued its forward growth or is lagging behind the developing traditions of its parent disciplines zoology and archaeology, or even of zooarchaeology itself as it is reflected in global research trends. In fact, zooarchaeology around the world has been faced with a series of difficult challenges and its practitioners have rallied with varying degrees of success to create a stronger and more viable science. Maya zooarchaeology has joined the ranks of environmental archaeologies in search of a new foundation in response to calls from post-processualism and biosystematic taxonomy that emphasize environmental and cultural heterogeneity, and from society in general hoping for applicable models for modern sustainable environmental management.

Trends in Biology and Anthropology: Reflections in Zooarchaeology

As a direct challenge to the neo-evolutionary concepts of uniformity and global processes that characterized processualism, the many branches of Post-Processual Archaeology now argue that reductionist approaches in anthropology mask the true internal diversity of a society as represented by its individuals. Discussions of cultural diversity and individual choice, along with an on-going interest in the particularism of political and economic history, have returned as areas of interest for the archaeological community. A similar trend is apparent in the biological sciences, where taxonomy and biosystematics have become central foci in the drive to fully describe and understand the biological diversity of the world (Alberch 1993; Feldman and Manning 1992; Minelli 1993; Wheeler 1995). Although studies of process dominated the biological sciences during the middle decades of this century (Hull 1988; Vernon 1993), a recognition of the fundamental requirement for a better understanding of species diversity and environmental heterogeneity is reflected in the recent development of global projects in systematic research (Blackmore 1996; NSF 2002). This trend is reflected in a recent emphasis on the variability and heterogeneity of both ancient ecology and human responses to the environment in studies of ancient Maya landscapes (e.g., Fedick 1996).

While continuing to emphasize social zooarchaeology and the basic questions of process and change, the science of zooarchaeology has also shifted the focus of its investigation (figure 12.1). The newest trends result from an important theoretical movement derived from new global and broad regional perspectives that are driven by the need for a better understanding of the diversity of species and heterogeneity of environments in both ancient and modern biological data. Often termed "historical ecology" but more frequently subsumed as "applied" zooarchaeology, this new directive

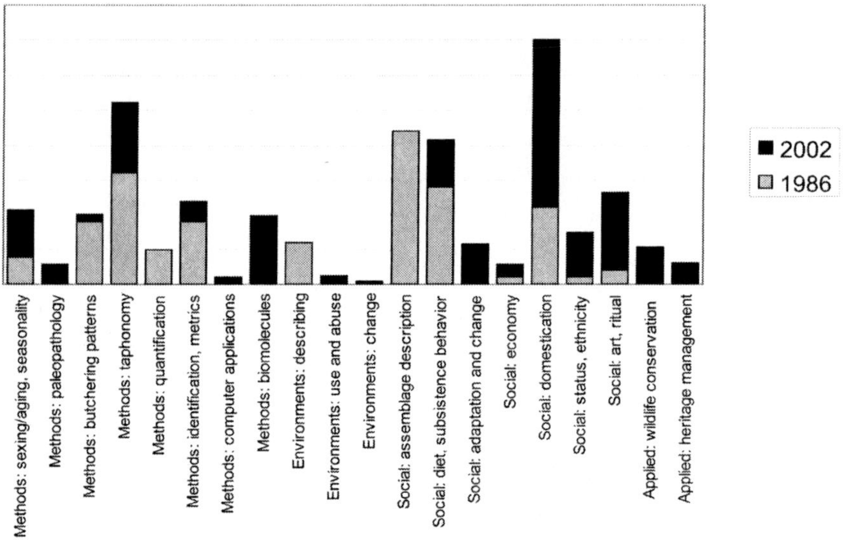

Fig. 12.1 Changing themes in Zooarchaeology as reflected in paper topics at the International Council of Zooarchaeology meetings (as proportion of papers dealing with themes).

recognizes the value of historical depth in the archaeological record as a heuristic device for deriving sustainable modern environmental management practices (Balee 1998; Barker 2001; Crumley 1994; Lyman 1996). Global biological projects are beginning to rely on zooarchaeological data to advise on wildlife management practices (Grayson 1991), to track extinctions (Steadman 1996) and local extirpations (Lyman 1991), and to predict the effects of current harvest practices (Jackson 1979; McGovern 1995) or the effects of global climate change (Amorosi 1992). Zooarchaeologists are therefore taking on a new moral obligation for detailed and accurate reconstructions of ancient animal distributions and habitats. These recent ideals are driving a renewed interest in methodological precision although questions have shifted from basic issues of recovery method to the incorporation of new biomolecular and computerized systems into research methods.

The combination of these archaeological and biological trends in theory and practice has encouraged zooarchaeologists and environmental archaeologists to reëvaluate their science. All have concluded that a real understanding of cultural or environmental variability requires appropriate coverage, sufficiently large assemblages, and comparable samples. These needs are spurring an increase in zooarchaeology education, a refinement of methods and techniques used by zooarchaeologists, and a determined effort to realizing effective collaboration with archaeologists studying more traditional materials. In the Maya world, the problem is the same, and the reality is that Maya zooarchaeologists need more and better samples from more sites before approaching this next phase of investigation. Achieving these goals will require (1) a greater attention to Maya zooarchaeological education, and (2) the implementation of standardized and appropriate methods for data recovery in Maya archaeology, a need that is itself predicated on the requirement for greater collaboration between Maya archaeologists and zooarchaeologists.

A Paucity of Practitioners

A real understanding of ancient biodiversity and environmental heterogeneity (or the distribution of taxa through varying habitats) must be based on broad regional studies with excellent data and thorough coverage. Without these, the results of Maya zooarchaeology cannot pretend to answer either the questions of social process or the needs of modern sustainability applications. The reality is that we do not have enough data or sufficient coverage, and that is because there are simply not enough Maya zooarchaeologists and not enough archaeology projects include zooarchaeology as one of their intrinsic research elements.

Although many archaeological investigations in the Maya region now include zooarchaeological investigations (Alvarez 1976; Andrews 1986; Blanco-Padilla 1987; Carr 1986; Coggins 1992; Hopkins 1992; Hudson et al. 1989; Marrinan 1986; Martinez-Muriel 1989; Morton 1987; Powis et al. 1999; Shaw 1991, 1995a; Stanchly 1995; Teeter 2001; Wing and Pohl 1990; Wing and Scudder 1991), zooarchaeologists are still not regularly included as part of the research team (to my knowledge, only 25% of all recent and current excavations in Guatemala, and 75% of excavations conducted by U.S. researchers in Guatemala include zooarchaeologists). And when zooarchaeologists are involved in archaeological projects, they are still often only contracted at the end of excavations, and their analyses are sometimes still relegated to "intriguing appendices."

It is self-evident that a lack of practicing zooarchaeologists is a problem. There are currently only three zooarchaeologists working in Guatemala, and none that are Guatemalan. In other countries of Central America, only Mexico has a fairly large number of researchers who have done zooarchaeological research (six researchers listed on the *Red Iberoamericana de Arqueolozoología* compiled by Juan Rofes and Arturo Morales). However, the real problem for the future is the lack of opportunity for widening the pool through education. There are currently no courses in zooarchaeology available in Guatemala or Honduras, and very few in Mexico. Even in the United States and Canada, opportunities for study in Maya zooarchaeology are slim

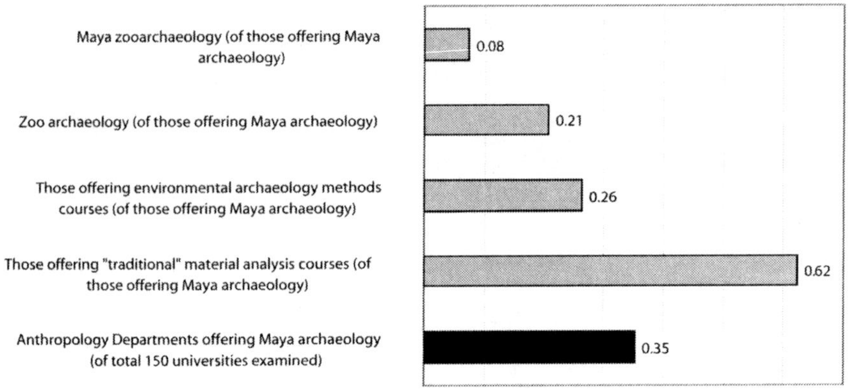

Fig. 12.2 Opportunities for overlapping courses in Maya Archaeology and Zooarchaeology at American and Canadian universities (data derived from AAA 2001/2002).

(figure 12.2). A brief review of 150 randomly selected anthropology departments in the latest AAA guide indicates that approximately one-third of these offer courses in Maya or Mesoamerican archaeology. Although 62 percent of these universities offering Maya archaeology also offer some other type of specialized material analysis (ceramic analysis, lithic analysis, GIS), only 20 percent offer courses in zooarchaeology (only 26 percent offer courses specific to any environmental archaeology study). Very few of those institutions offer directed study in Maya zooarchaeology. Clearly then, the first onus lies on zooarchaeologists to expand the cadre of courses and practical experience to students in both the United States and the countries of study.

It should be stressed that these problems are not specific to Maya zooarchaeology. Albarella (2001:7) complains that in Italy, environmental archaeology is rarely taught together with other archaeology topics. Ian Hodder and others have often complained that in many Old World countries, the need to integrate fieldwork and specialist environmental research continues to be ignored (Hodder 1997; Hughes and Hammon 2001) and zooarchaeological reports in these areas of the world continue to be "appendicized" (Albarella 2001:3; Barker 2001:310)

Regional Studies, Comparability, and Methodological Standards

During recent years in other parts of the world, zooarchaeological methods have become more complex and exacting—rapidly becoming more diverse and technologically sophisticated. Maya zooarchaeology has successfully incorporated many of the newest advances in techniques of investigation. Many Maya zooarchaeologists continue to access the valuable paleoenvironmental and subsistence data provided by molluscan and microfaunal studies (Dunning et al. 1997; Healy et al. 1990; McKillop and Winemiller in press; Miksicek 1991). And biomolecular studies integrating bone chemistry (Emery et al. 2000) or residue analysis (Emery 2002b) are becoming more common in Maya zooarchaeology, although these analyses are usually done by specialists from other disciplines (Coyston 1999; Tykot et al. 1996; van der Merwe et al. 2000; White et al. 2001). Zoological techniques emphasizing population statistics such as harvest rates and mortality curves (Carr 1996; Emery 1986; Pohl 1990), and ecological community statistics (Emery in press a) are also sometimes used, although not to the extent that they have been in neighboring regions (e.g., Broughton and Grayson 1993; Wing 2001).

However, to what extent have we been successful in integrating the latest discussions on the methods that are most basic to our science: recovery methods, taphonomic analysis, and quantification? Here we have been much less successful, and these are the areas that are most pivotal to the success of our interpretations. Accuracy in zooarchaeological data is dependent on appropriate methods of material recovery and analysis, as well as a detailed understanding of potential bias in the sample as a result of differential depositional and preservational factors (taphonomy). Before we can begin to compare our datasets to create regional analyses of either human or animal variation, we need samples that are directly comparable, and again, that goal is predicated on the use of standardized recovery and analysis methods and recognition of the conditions of archaeological context. A complete discussion of methods required for standardized and comparable data is beyond the scope of this paper (Emery in press b). However, two issues are particularly pertinent and worthy of discussion here: the effects of differential preservation in archaeological deposits, and the effects of different recovery methods on zooarchaeological assemblages.

Recovery Methods

It has become abundantly clear that the method of recovery used dramatically affects the composition of faunal assemblages because quantitative analyses depend on the equal opportunity for recovery of each and every specimen at a site (Shaffer and Sanchez 1994). Current acceptable practice dictates that zooarchaeological remains be recovered by sieving the archaeological matrix (Cannon 1999; Davis 1987; James 1997; Shaffer and Sanchez 1994). In the Maya world, although the majority of special deposits receive special attention, and many archaeologists now consistently screen and/or float occupational and midden debris, most deposits are still not screened.

Table 12.1 Effects of Recovery Method on Representation of Species and Taxa in Zooarchaeological Assemblages (example from Piedras Negras).

	% OF NISP SCREENED/ FLOATED		% OF NISP UNSCREENED/ UNFLOATED	
NISP	186		184	
N taxa	22	11.83	19	10.33
NISP microfauna	21	11.29	1	0.54
N microfauna taxa	9	4.84	1	0.54
No. identified to family and better	86	46.24	101	54.89
No. identified to class and below	84	45.16	83	45.11
No. unidentified to class level	16	8.60	0	0.00

As an example of the relevance of this argument in Maya zooarchaeology, I briefly compared samples that had been collected using traditional methods of collection by hand and those collected using screening or flotation from deposits at one structure at the site of Piedras Negras (Emery n.d.a). Although the number of specimens recovered is approximately equal between the two sets of assemblages (table 12.1), species richness (number of taxa) is higher in the screened/floated assemblages. Furthermore, the number of small taxa recovered is much greater in screened/floated samples. Samples collected using traditional methods and refined methods do not represent the same assemblage diversity or structure.

However, an increase in the recovery rate is only as useful as the remains are identifiable, and many sampling methods can be destructive of animal remains. One test of this effect is a comparison of the rate of identifiability between the screened/floated and traditionally collected assemblages. In this analysis, recovery method did not significantly reduce the identifiability of the remains recovered (table 12.1). Although a larger proportion of the remains were only identifiable above the level of class (e.g., Mammalia) in the screened/floated assemblage, this is a result of the increased recovery of long bone shaft fragments. The proportion identifiable at the class level and better is very similar between the two sets of assemblages, meaning that otherwise identifiable small remains were not affected by screening or flotation.

Zooarchaeologists are in agreement that at least a one-quarter-inch screen is required for the collection of representative samples. Research in many areas of the world has indicated that for optimal recovery the most effective method is flotation (Reitz and Wing 1999:120; Wing and Quitmyer 1992), although the time consumed in this process prohibits its use in all situations. The use of a one-eighth-inch screen has been shown to be more effective than a one-quarter-inch screen (Cannon et al. 1999; Shaffer 1992; Shaffer and Sanchez 1994; Wing and Brown 1979), but a real fear is that with clayey lowland soils, this mesh size can increase fragmentation unless wet screening procedures are used. Although correction factors have been derived to increase the compatibility between samples screened at one-eighth of an inch and those screened at one-quarter-inch (James 1997), these have been hotly debated (Cannon et al. 1999; Shaffer and Baker 1999). Brian Shaffer and Julia Sanchez (1994) argue that recovery methods must be standardized for accuracy, but in reality, these biases can be overcome without undue effort. Consistent tests of the validity of sample recovery methods in each situation (using, e.g., nested sieves to determine actual differential rates of recovery in different deposit types), and a clear discussion of sample recovery variability would go far to ameliorate the problem.

Differential Preservation

The single greatest source of bias in the archaeological and zooarchaeological record is the post-depositional history or taphonomy as a result of variation in conditions of preservation in archaeological deposits (Stanchly in press). The effects of disturbances at the point of initial deposition (biostratinomic processes) combine with the effects of preservational variability in the different depositional environments (diagenetic conditions) to produce considerable flux in the proportionate representation of any one individual animal in the deposited faunal assemblage (Reitz and Wing 1999:114). In the Maya world, the variability in long-term preservational conditions such as natural geomorphological processes like erosion, or the effects of soil acidity and water movement, can be quite high, not only between deposits but also between sites and even residential units within sites.

These taphonomic variables are the source of most worldwide zooarchaeological discussion at this point (e.g., Coard 1999; Higgins 1999; Nicholson 1993) and several of the arguments are of particular importance to Maya zooarchaeology. These include, for example, recent work by Joanne L. Bennett (1999), suggesting that subsurface faunal remains (to a depth of between 10 and 20 cm) can be morphologically altered by recent surface burning events, and observations by Martha Tappen (1994) regarding the effects of bone-weathering patterns in the humid tropics.

To illustrate these effects on a zooarchaeological assemblage, I have again included a simple test, this time done on the faunal remains from the site of Dos Pilas (more details on the Dos Pilas fauna can be found in Emery 1997). Here, the number of bone fragments recovered in the various deposits from a single operation does not correlate with excavation unit size

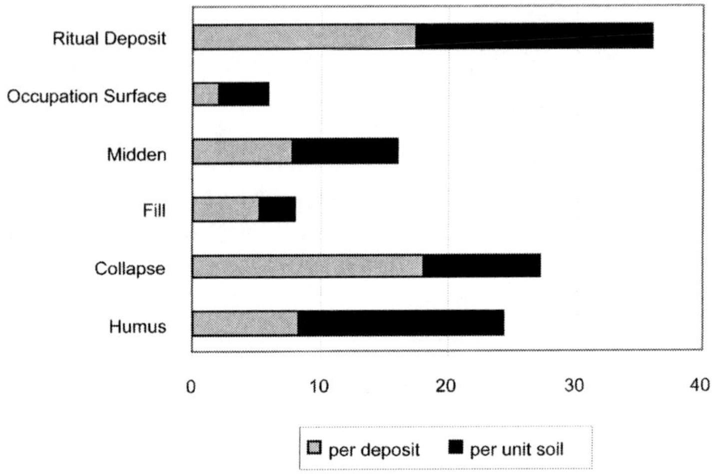

Fig. 12.3 Recovery of faunal remains in different deposit types at Dos Pilas. Unit sizes are measured as meter cubed based on provenience information provided by the excavators.

(figures 12.3 and 12.4), indicating that bone preservation is not standard and cannot be predicted as a quantity per unit of soil excavated. A comparison of remain frequencies recovered from different deposits indicates a high variability in return rate from different deposit types. The highest proportion of remains was recovered from ritual deposits (this may be an

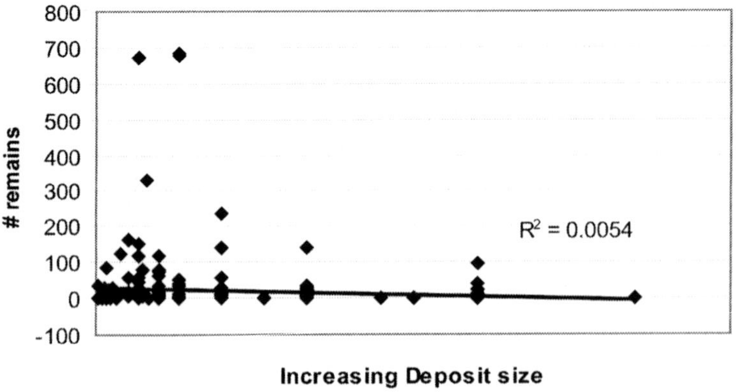

Fig. 12.4 Recovery of faunal remains as a function of unit size at Dos Pilas. Unit sizes are measured as meter cubed based on provenience information provided by the excavators.

effect either of differential deposition rates, differential preservation as a result of the protected nature of these deposits in caches or crypts, or of differential recovery since special deposits are often excavated with greater attention to detail). Collapse deposits, characterized by high limestone content, also provide very high frequencies of remains, and likely have better preservational conditions. Occupation surfaces and middens, on the other hand, return relatively few remains per excavation unit, and although occupation surfaces are not expected to retain large numbers of remains on their surfaces, middens are expected to have higher rates of return. In fact, the more acidic nature of midden deposits (because they are generally not associated with limestone building materials) and the high nutrient cycling in organic deposits, in combination with the exposure to transformational agents such as dogs and weathering, means that preservation is in fact lower in these important locations. So, bone frequency (as a measure of variation in either depositional and preservational rate) is highly variable through the deposits, and it is also not predictable between deposit types.

The reasons for this may be complex and are likely to include cultural factors, but surely have much to do first with the fact that midden and occupational deposits are open to disturbance by destructive agents for long periods of time, and second with the improvement in preservational conditions in deposits with high limestone content (decreasing the acidity of the matrix). The lesson then is that interdeposit comparisons must be made with specific attention to variations caused by taphonomic conditions. The route to sample comparability lies in the description and quantification of the post-depositional effects of animal alterations and weathering for each subassemblage of either chronological period or site. Clearly, we cannot overcome the effects of these biases, but without access to information about contextual condition, a zooarchaeologist may mistakenly ascribe patterns to behavioral and depositional activities that were in fact the result of taphonomic variability.

Discussion

The last millennium has seen a full cycle of scientific study in both the fields of archaeology and zoology—descriptive taxonomies and cultural histories grew out of early Renaissance style quests for knowledge of our world and its many inhabitants. These were challenged fairly recently in both fields by researchers demanding a broader picture and greater focus on the derivation of generalized laws and patterns. Ecology and animal behavior studies in zoology coincided with the New Archaeology and processualism in archaeology to ask the "whys and wherefores" characterizing our scientific data. Why have species evolved, why do cultures change? Most recently though, these broader studies were challenged by the growing evidence that we simply do not yet know enough to answer the questions we have raised. Without knowing the real variation in species or even how many species exist, how can we ask about evolutionary processes? Without a clear understanding of the forces of decision making in cultural trajectories and the details of push/pull cultural modifiers, how can we generalize about global culture change? Systematic taxonomy is one of the driving forces of zoological studies today, and post-processualism has encouraged a return to the study of particularism and individual behaviors in archaeology. In both sciences we have come to realize that environments and the animal and human populations that inhabit them are almost infinitely variable, and that to explain this variability, we simply need more and more detailed data.

Zooarchaeology, the study of the ancient relationship between humans and the animals of their environs through the analysis of animal remains from archaeological sites, straddles the two worlds of zoology and archaeology. Although the divide is sometimes almost insurmountable, this science has also followed the trajectories of the parent fields. Our earliest research was generally taxonomic and descriptive, a role call of animal remains. Challenged later by a call for broader questions to reveal general patterns through such formats as cultural evolution and cultural ecology (later derived into the specific methods and processual questions of the New Archaeology), zooarchaeologists responded with investigations spanning the vital environmental and cultural changes of the past: the origins of agriculture, the development of hunting versus scavenging techniques, human origins, and the development of complex society. However, like all other scientific disciplines, we have come to recognize that we do not have sufficient datasets to properly answer the questions at hand. As a result, our interests have returned in force to reexamine our methods of data recovery and interpretation, to collect basic but well-referenced data from a wider range of sources, and to reinterpret our processual questions with reference to both environmental heterogeneity and the extreme variability of individual human activities.

As this chapter has suggested, there are a variety of solutions to the current need for more detailed data and better coverage. Primary among these is an increase in the number of practitioners. Zooarchaeologists working in the Maya area should encourage students in both home institutions and the countries of practice. Another solution, and one that can be realized more quickly, is a higher level of collaboration between archaeologists and zooarchaeologists, beginning at the early stages of archaeological research design. The institution of sampling and recovery methods appropriate to both environmental and cultural questions will go far toward creating a substantial database and effective coverage. Again, the onus lies on the zooarchaeologist to ensure that the methods used to recover materials are appropriate to the area under investigation since soil types, microclimate variations, and disturbance factors are unique to each situation, and the variability of field and laboratory activities will require flexibility in the use of standardized zooarchaeological techniques.

Note

1. A more detailed discussion of the early history of Maya zooarchaeology can be found in Emery (in press b).

References

Agrinier, P. (1975) *Mound 1A, Chiapa de Corzo, Chiapas, Mexico: A Late Preclassic Architectural Complex*, New World Archaeological Foundation Paper 39, Provo: Brigham Young University.

Albarella, U. (2001) "Exploring the Real Nature of Environmental Archaeology: An Introduction," in U. Albarella (ed.), *Environmental Archaeology: Meaning and Purpose*, pp. 3–16, London: Kluwer.

Alberch, P. (1993) "Museums, Collections, and Biodiversity Inventories," *Trends in Ecology and Evolution* 8: 272–5.

Alvarez, T. (1976) "Restos Oseos Rescatados del Cenote Sagrado de Chichén Itzá, Yucatán," *Cuadernos de Trabajo, Mexico, INAH* 15: 19–39.

Amorosi, T. (1992) "Climate Impact and Human Response in Northeast Iceland: Archaeological Investigations at Svalbard, 1986–1988," in C. Morris and D. J. Rackham (eds.), *Norse and Later Settlement and Subsistence in the North Atlantic*, pp. 101–27, Archetype Publications, Glasgow: University of Glasgow.

Andrews, A. P. (1986) "La Fauna Arqueologica de El Meco," in A. P. Andrews and F. Robles-Castellanos (eds.), *Excavaciones Arqueologicas en El Meco, Quintana Roo, 1977*, pp. 1–162, Vol. 158, Mexico City: Instituto Nacional de Antropología e Historia (Cientifica).

Andrews, E. W. I. (1969) *The Archaeological Use and Distribution of Mollusca in the Maya Lowlands*, Publication 34, Middle American Research Institute, New Orleans: Tulane University.

Baker, M. (1992) "Capuchin Monkeys (Cebus capucinus) and the Ancient Maya," *Ancient Mesoamerica* 3: 219–28.

Balee, W. (ed.) (1998) *Advances in Historical Ecology*, New York: Columbia University Press.

Ballinger, D. A., and Stomper, J. (2000) "The Jaguars of Altar Q, Copan, Honduras: Faunal Analysis, Archaeology, and Ecology," *Journal of Ethnobiology* 20(2): 223–36.

Barker, G. (2001) "Agendas for Environmental Archaeology," in U. Albarella (ed.), *Environmental Archaeology: Meaning and Purpose*, pp. 305–14, London: Kluwer.

Barrera-Rubio, A. (1977) "Exploraciones Arqueologicas en Tulum, Quintana Roo," *Boletin de la Escuela de Ciencias Antropologicas de la Universidad de Yucatán* 24: 23–63.

Bartlett, H. H. (1935) *A Method of Procedure for Field Work in Tropical American Phytogeography Based upon a Botanical Reconnaissance in Parts of British Honduras and the Petén Forest of Guatemala*, Botany of the Maya Area, Miscellaneous Paper 1, Washington, DC: Carnegie Institution of Washington.

Bennett, J. L. (1999) "Thermal Alteration of Buried Bone," *Journal of Archaeological Science* 26: 1–8.

Benson, E. P. (ed.) (1977) *The Sea in the Pre-Columbian World*, Washington, DC: Dumbarton Oaks.

———(1988a) "A Knife in the Water: The Stingray in Mesoamerican Ritual Life," *Journal of Latin American Lore* 14(2): 173–91.

———(1988b) "The Maya and the Bat," *Latin American Indian Literatures Journal* 4(2): 99–124.

Binford, L. R. (1962) "Archaeology as Anthropology," *American Antiquity* 28: 217–25.

———(1965) "Archaeological Systematics and the Study of Culture Process," *American Antiquity* 31: 1–12.

Blackmore, S. (1996) "Knowing the Earth's Biodiversity: Challenges for the Infrastructure of Systematic Biology," *Science* 274: 63–64.

Blanco-Padilla, A. (1987). "Restos Oseos, Malacologicos, y de Celenterados del Proyecto Coba 1980," in L. Manzanilla (ed.), *Coba, Quintana Roo. Analisis de Dos Unidades Habitacionales Mayas del Horizonte Casico*, pp. 1–438, Arqueología, Serie Antropológica, Vol. 32, Instituto de Investigaciones Antropológicas, Mexico City: Universidad Nacional Autónoma de Mexico.

Borhegyi, S. F., de (1961) "Shark Teeth, Stingray Spines, and Shark Fishing in Ancient Mexico and Central America," *Southwestern Journal of Anthropology* 17(3): 273–96.

Bradley, R. (1983) "The Pre-Columbian Exploitation of the Manatee in Mesoamerica," *University of Oklahoma Papers in Anthropology* 24(1): 9–58.

Brothwell, D. R. (1975) "Salvaging the Term 'Domestication' for Certain Types of Man-Animal Relationships: The Possible Value of an Eight-Point Scoring System," *Journal of Archaeological Science* 2: 397–400.

Broughton, J. M., and Grayson, D. K. (1993) "Diet Breadth, Adaptive Change, and the White Mountains Faunas," *Journal of Archaeological Science* 20: 331–6.

Butzer, K. W. (1982) *Archaeology as Human Ecology: Methods and Theory for a Contextual Approach*, New York: Cambridge University Press.

Caldwell, J. R. (1959) "The New American Archaeology," *Science* 129: 303–7.

Cannon, A., Schwarcz, H. P., and Knyf, M. (1999) "Marine-based Subsistence Trends and the Stable Isotope Analysis of Dog Bones from Namu, British Columbia," *Journal of Archaeological Science* 26: 399–407.

Cannon, M. D. (1999) "A Mathematical Model of the Effects of Screen Size on Zooarchaeological Relative Abundance Measures," *Journal of Archaeological Science* 26: 205–14.

Carr, H. S. (1985) "Subsistence and Ceremony: Faunal Utilization in a Late Preclassic Community at Cerros, Belize," in M. D. Pohl (ed.), *Prehistoric Lowland Maya Environment and Subsistence Economy*, pp. 115–32, Papers of the Peabody Museum of Archaeology and Ethnology, Vol. 77, Cambridge, MA: Harvard University Press.

———(1986) *Faunal Utilization in a Late Preclassic Maya Community at Cerros, Belize*, unpublished Ph.D. dissertation, Department of Anthropology, New Orleans: Tulane University.

———(1989) "Patterns of Exploitation and Exchange of Subsistence Goods in the Late Classic—Early Postclassic Yucatán: A Zooarchaeological Perspective," paper presented at the Annual Meetings of the Society for American Archaeology. April, Atlanta.

———(1996) "Precolumbian Maya Exploitation and Management of Deer Populations," in S. L. Fedick (ed.), *The Managed Mosaic: Ancient Maya Agriculture and Resource Use*, pp. 251–61, Salt Lake City: University of Utah Press.

Carr, S. H. (1991) "The Maya Medicinal Turtle, Xkokak, and a Suggested Alternate Reading of Two Yucatec Ethnomedical Texts," *Journal of Ethnobiology* 11(2): 187–92.

Carson, R. (1962) *Silent Spring*, Boston: Houghton Mifflin.

Chase, D. Z., Chase, A. F., White, C. D., and Teeter, W. G. (1998) "Human Skeletal Remains in Archaeological Context: Status, Diet and Household at Caracol, Belize," July 26–August 1 paper presented at the International Congress of Anthropological and Ethnological Sciences, Williamsburg, VA.

Chavez-O, E. A. (1969) "Artifactual and Non-artifactual Material of the Phyla Mollusca, Arthropoda, and Chordata from Chiapa de Corzo, Chiapas," in T. A. Lee (ed.), *The Artifacts of Chiapa de Corzo, Chiapas, Mexico*, pp. 219–20, Papers of the New World Archaeological Foundation 26, Provo: Brigham Young University.

Cliff, M. B., and Crane, C. J. (1989) "Changing Subsistence Economy at a Late Preclassic Maya Community," in P. A. McAnany and B. L. Isaac (eds.), *Prehistoric Maya Economies of Belize*, pp. 295–324, London: JAI Press.

Clutton-Brock, J. (1981) *Domesticated Animals from Early Times*, Austin: University of Texas Press.

Clutton-Brock, J., and Hammond, N. (1994) "Hot Dogs: Comestible Canids in Preclassic Maya Culture at Cuello, Belize," *Journal of Archaeological Sciences* 21: 819–26.

Coard, R. (1999) "One Bone, Two Bones, Wet Bones, Dry Bones: Transport Potentials under Experimental Conditions," *Journal of Archaeological Science* 26: 1369–75.

Cobos, R. (1989) "Shelling In: Marine Mollusca at Chichén Itzá," in H. McKillop and P. F. Healy (eds.), *Coastal Maya Trade*, pp. 49–58, Occasional Paper in Anthropology no. 8, Peterborough, Ontario: Trent University.

Coe, M. D., and Flannery, K. V. (1967) *Early Cultures and Human Ecology in South Coastal Guatemala*, Contributions to Anthropology no. 3, Washington, DC: Smithsonian Institution.

Coe, W. R. (1959) *Piedras Negras Archaeology: Artifacts, Caches, and Burial*, Museum Monographs, Philadelphia: University Museum, University of Pennsylvania.

Coggins, C. C. (ed.) (1992) *Artifacts from the Cenote of Sacrifice: Chichén Itzá, Yucatán*, Cambridge, MA: Harvard University Press.

Colby, S. M. (1988) "An Analysis of Faunal Remains from Yarumela, Honduras," *Journal of New World Archaeology* 7(2/3): 71–94.

Cooke, C. W. (1931) "Why the Mayan Cities of the Petén District, Guatemala, Were Abandoned," *Journal of the Washington Academy of Sciences* 21(13): 283–7.

Covich, A. (1983) "Mollusca: A Contrast in Species Diversity from Aquatic and Terrestrial Habitats," in B. L. Turner and P. D. Harrison (eds.), *Pulltrouser Swamp: Ancient Maya Habitat, Agriculture, and Settlement in Northern Belize*, pp. 120–39, Austin: University of Texas Press.

Covich, A., and Stuiver, M. (1974) "Changes in Oxygen 18 as a Measure of Long-Term Fluctuations in Tropical Lake Levels and Molluscan Populations," *Limnology and Oceanography* 19: 682–91.

Cowgill, U. M. (1961) "Soil Fertility and the Ancient Maya," *Transactions of the Connecticut Academy of Arts and Sciences* 42: 1–56.

———(1962) "An Agricultural Study of the Southern Maya Lowlands," *American Anthropologist* 64: 273–86.

Cowgill, U. M., Hutchinson, G. E., Racek, A. A., Goulden, C. A., Patrick, R., and Tsukada, M. (1966) "The History of Laguna de Petenxil: A Small Lake in Northern Guatemala," *Connecticut Academy of Arts and Science Memoirs* 5–17: 1–126.

Coyston, S. (1999) "Dietary Carbonate Analysis of Bone and Enamel for Two Sites in Belize," in C. D. White (ed.), *Reconstructing Ancient Maya Diet*, pp. 221–44, Salt Lake City: University of Utah Press.

———(2002) *Noble Chemists and Archaeologists: Chemical Analyses of Food Residues from Ancient Maya Vessels*, unpublished Ph.D. dissertation, McMaster University, Hamilton, Ontario.

Crumley, C. L. (ed.) (1994) *Historical Ecology: Cultural Knowledge and Changing Landscapes*, Sante Fe: School of American Research Press.

Dahlin, B. H. (1979) "Cropping Cash in the Protoclassic: A Cultural Impact Statement," in N. Hammond and G. R. Willey (eds.), *Maya Archaeology and Ethnology*, pp. 21–37, Austin: University of Texas Press.

Davis, S. J. (1987) *The Archaeology of Animals*, New Haven: Yale University Press.

Dillon, B. D. (1988) "Meatless Maya? Ethnoarchaeological Implications for Ancient Subsistence," *Journal of New World Archaeology* 7(2/3): 59–70.

Dunning, N. P., Beach, T., and Rue, D. J. (1997) "The Paleoecology and Ancient Settlement of the Petexbatun Region, Guatemala," *Ancient Mesoamerica* 8(2): 255–66.

Emery, K. F. (1986) *Variation in a Tropical Gastropod Population: Implications for Ancient Maya Subsistence Patterns*, B.S. thesis, Peterborough, Ontario. Trent University.

———(1997) *The Maya Collapse: A Zooarchaeological Inquiry*, unpublished Ph.D. dissertation, Ithaca, NY: Cornell University.

———(1999) "Continuity and Variability in Postclassic and Colonial Animal Use at Lamanai and Tipu, Belize," in C. D. White (ed.), *Reconstructing Ancient Maya Diet*, pp. 61–82, Salt Lake City: University of Utah Press.

———(2002a) "The Noble Beast: Status and Differential Access to Animals in the Maya World," *World Archaeology* 34(3): 498–515.

———(2002b) *The Economics of Natural Resource Use at Ancient Motul de San Jose, Guatemala*, paper presented at the SAA Annual Meeting, April, Denver, CO.

———(in press a) "Environments of the Maya Collapse: A Zooarchaeological Perspective from the Petexbatun, Guatemala," in K. F. Emery (ed.), *Maya Zooarchaeology: New Directions in Method and Theory*, Los Angeles: Institute of Archaeology, UCLA Press.

———(in press b) "In Search of Assemblage Comparability: Methods in Maya Zooarchaeology," in K. F. Emery (ed.), *Maya Zooarchaeology: New Directions in Method and Theory*, Los Angeles: Institute of Archaeology, UCLA Press.

———(in press-c) "Animals from the Maya Underworld: Reconstructing Elite Maya Ritual at the Cueva de los Quetzales," in S. J. O'Day, W. van Neer, and A. Ervynck (eds.), *Behavior behind Bones: The Zooarchaeology of Religion, Ritual, Status, and Identity*, London: Oxbow Books.

———(n.d.a) "Animal Use at Piedras Negras: Diet, Ritual, and Crafting in a Classic Maya Community," in S. D. Houston and H. Escobedo (eds.), *In the Land of the Turtle Lords: Urban Archaeology at the Classic Maya City of Piedras Negras, Guatemala*, Norman: University of Oklahoma Press.

Emery, K. F., and Graham, E. (2003) "A Marine Resource Survey at Marco Gonzalez, Belize," in K. Stewart (ed.), *Transitions in Zooarchaeology: New Methods and New Results*, pp. 68–102, Ottawa: Canadian Museum of Nature.

Emery, K. F., Wright, L. E., and Schwarcz, H. P. (2000) "Isotopic Analysis of Ancient Deer Bone: Isotopic Stability in Collapse Period Maya Land-Use," *Journal of Archaeological Science* 27: 537–50.

Evans, J. G., and O'Connor, T. P. (1999) *Environmental Archaeology: Principles and Methods*, Gloucestershire: Sutton Publishing.

Evershed, R. P., and Bethell, P. H. (1996) "Application of Multimolecular Biomarker Techniques for the Identification of Fecal Material in Archaeological Soils and Sediments," in M. V. Orna (ed.), *Archaeological Chemistry: Organic, Inorganic, and Biochemical Analysis*, pp. 157–72, Washington, DC: American Chemical Society.

Fedick, S. L. (ed.) (1996) *The Managed Mosaic: Ancient Maya Agriculture and Resource Use*, Salt Lake City: University of Utah Press.

Feldman, L. H. (1974) "Ethnomalacology and Archaeomolluscan Studies in North Mexico, Mesoamerica, and Central America," *The Veliger* 16(3): 336–7.

Feldman, R. M., and Manning, R. B. (1992) "Crisis in Systematic Biology in the 'Age of Biodiversity,'" *Journal of Paleontology* 66: 157–8.

Flannery, K. V. (1968) "Archaeological Systems Theory and Early Mesoamerica," in B. Meggers (ed.), *Anthropological Archaeology in the Americas*, pp. 67–87, Washington, DC: Anthropological Society of Washington.

———(1969) "An Analysis of Animal Bones from Chiapa de Corzo, Chiapas," in T. A. Lee (ed.), *The Artifacts of Chiapa de Corzo, Chiapas, Mexico*, pp. 209–18, Papers of the New World Archaeological Foundation 26, Provo: Brigham Young University.

———(1986) *Guila Naquitz: Archaic Foraging and Early Agriculture in Oaxaca, Mexico*, Orlando: Academic Press.

Follett, W. I. (1966) "Fish Remains from Salinas la Blanca, an Archaeological Site on the Pacific Coast of Guatemala," *Smithsonian Contributions to Anthropology* 3: 129–34.

Goodrich, C., and van der Schalie, H. (1937) "Mollusca of Petén and North Alta Vera Paz, Guatemala," *University of Michigan Museum of Zoology*, Miscellaneous Publications 34: 7–50.

Grayson, D. K. (1991) "The Biogeographic History of Small Mammals in the Great Basin: Observations on the Last 20,000 Years," *Journal of Mammalogy* 68: 359–75.

Green, D. F., and Lowe, G. W. (1967) *Altamira and Padre Piedra, Early Preclassic Sites in Chiapas Mexico*, Papers of the New World Archaeological Foundation, Provo: Brigham Young University.

Griffiths, H. I., and Holmes, J. A. (2000) "Non-marine Ostracods and Quaternary Paleoenvironments," *Technical Guide* 8, London: Quaternary Research Association.

Hamblin, N. L. (1984) *Animal Use by the Cozumel Maya*, Tucson: University of Arizona Press.

———(1985) "The Role of Marine Resources in the Maya Economy: A Case Study from Cozumel, Mexico," in M. D. Pohl (ed.), *Prehistoric Lowland Maya Environment and Subsistence Economy*, pp. 159–74, Papers of the Peabody Museum of Archaeology and Ethnology, Vol. 77, Cambridge, MA: Harvard University.

Healy, P. F., Emery, K. F., and Wright, L. E. (1990) "Ancient and Modern Exploitation of the Jute Snail (Pachychilus)," *Latin American Antiquity* 1(2): 170–83.

Higgins, J. (1999) "Tunel: A Case Study of Avian Zooarchaeology and Taphonomy," *Journal of Archaeological Science* 26: 1449–57.

Hodder, I. (1997) "Always Momentary, Fluid, and Flexible: Toward a Reflexive Excavation Methodology," *Antiquity* 71: 691–700.

Hopkins, M. R. (1992) "Mammalian Remains," in C. C. Coggins (ed.), *Artifacts from the Cenote of Sacrifice, Chichén Itzá, Yucatán*, pp. 369–85, Cambridge, MA: Harvard University Press.

Hubbs, C. L. (1935) *Fresh-water Fishes Collected in British Honduras and Guatemala*, Miscellaneous Publication 28, University of Michigan, Museum of Zoology, Ann Arbor.

Hudson, J., Walker, P. L., and Voorhies, B. (1989) "Changing Patterns of Faunal Exploitation," in B. Voorhies (ed.), *Ancient Trade and Tribute: Economies of the Soconusco Region of Mesoamerica*, pp. 133–53, Salt Lake City: University of Utah Press.

Hughes, G., and Hammon, A. (2001) "Commercialising the Palaeoenvironment. Developer Funding and Environmental Archaeology," in U. Albarella (ed.), *Environmental Archaeology: Meaning and Purpose*, pp. 75–88, London: Kluwer.

Hull, D. L. (1988) *Science as a Process*, Chicago: University of Chicago Press.

Hyland, D. C., Tersak, J. M., Adovasio, J. M., and Siegal, M. (1990) "Identifications of Species of Origin of Residual Blood on Lithic Material," *American Antiquity* 55: 104–12.

Jackson, J. B. C. (1979) "Overgrowth Competition between Encrusting Cheilostome Ectoprocts in a Jamaican Cryptic Reef Environment," *Journal of Animal Ecology* 48: 805–23.

James, S. R. (1997) "Methodological Issues Concerning Screen Size Recovery Rates and Their Effects on Archaeofaunal Interpretations," *Journal of Archaeological Science* 24: 385–97.

Jones, A. K. G. (1982) "Human Parasite Remains: Prospects for a Quantitative Approach," in A. R. Hall and H. K. Kenward (eds.), *Environmental Archaeology in the Urban Context*, pp. 66–70, CBA Research Report 43, London: Prometheus Books.

Jones, C., Coe, W. R., and Haviland, W. A. (1981) "Tikal: An Outline of Its Field Study (1956–1970) and a Project Bibliography, " in V. Bricker and J. A. Sabloff (eds.), *Supplement to the Handbook of Middle American Indians*, pp. 296–312, Vol. 1, Austin: University of Texas Press.

Kidder, A. V. (1947) *The Artifacts of Uaxactun, Guatemala*, Publication 576, Washington, DC: Carnegie Institution of Washington.

Kidder, A. V., Jennings, J. D., and Shook, E. M. (1946) *Excavations at Kaminaljuyu, Guatemala*, Publication 576, Washington, DC: Carnegie Institution of Washington.

Kurjack, E. B. (1974) *Prehistoric Lowland Maya Community and Social Organization: A Case Study at Dzibilchaltun, Yucatán, Mexico*, Middle American Research Institute Publication 38, New Orleans: Tulane University.

Lange, F. W. (1971) "Marine Resources: A Viable Subsistence Alternative for the Prehistoric Lowland Maya," *American Anthropologist* 73(3): 619–39.

Lundell, C. L. (1937) *The Vegetation of the Petén*, Publication 478, Washington, DC: Carnegie Institution of Washington.

Luther, E. (1974) "Analysis of Faunal Material," in D. M. Pendergast (ed.), *Excavations at Actun Polbilche, Belize*, Archaeology Monograph 1, Toronto: Royal Ontario Museum.

Lyman, R. L. (1991) "Late Quaternary Biogeography of the Pygmy Rabbit (*Brachylagus idahoensis*) in Eastern Washington," *Journal of Mammalogy* 72: 110–7.

———(1996) "Applied Zooarchaeology: The Relevance of Faunal Analysis to Wildlife Management," *World Archaeology* 28(1): 110–25.

Marrinan, R. A. (1986) "Appendix: Faunal Analysis," in R. C. Treat (ed.), *Early and Middle Preclassic Sub-Mound Refuse Deposit at Vistahermosa, Chiapas*, pp. 1–37, Notes on the New World Archaeological Foundation, Vol. 2, Provo: Brigham Young University.

Martinez-Muriel, A. (1989) "Basureros del Formativo Tardio en Don Martin, Chiapas," *Arqueologia 2a. epoca* 1: 61–70.

Masson, M. A. (1999) "Animal Resource Manipulation in Ritual and Domestic Contexts at Postclassic Maya Communities," *World Archaeology* 31(1): 93–120.

McGovern, T. H. (1995) "Human Dimensions of Global Change: A North Atlantic Perspective," *Witness the Arctic* 2(3): 1–3.

McKillop, H. I. (1984) "Prehistoric Maya Reliance on Marine Resources: Analysis of a Midden from Moho Cay, Belize," *Journal of Field Archaeology* 11: 25–35.

———(1985) "Prehistoric Exploitation of the Manatee in the Maya and Circum-Caribbean Areas," *World Archaeology* 16(3): 337–53.

McKillop, H., and Winemiller, T. (in press) "Ancient Maya Environment, Settlement, and Diet: Quantitative and GIS Analyses of Mollusca from Frenchman's Cay, Belize," in K. F. Emery (ed.), *Maya Zooarchaeology: New Directions in Method and Theory*, Los Angeles: Institute of Archaeology, UCLA Press.

Merwin, R. E., and Vaillant, G. C. (1932) *The Ruins of Holmul, Guatemala*, Memoirs of the Peabody Museum of Archaeology and Ethnology, Vol. 3, no. 2, Cambridge, MA: Harvard University Press.

Miksicek, C. H. (1991) "The Natural and Cultural Landscape of Preclassic Cuello," in N. Hammond (ed.), *Cuello: An Early Maya Community in Belize*, pp. 70–84, Cambridge, UK: Cambridge University Press.
Miller, A. G. (1977) "The Maya and the Sea: Trade and Cult at Tancah and Tulum, Quintana Roo, Mexico," in E. P. Benson (ed.), *The Sea in the Precolumbian World*, pp. 97–140, Washington, DC: Dumbarton Oaks.
Minelli, A. (1993) *Biological Systematics: The State of the Art*, New York: Kluwer.
Mock, S. B. (1994) *The Northern River Lagoon Site (NRL): Late to Terminal Classic Maya Settlement, Saltmaking, and Survival on the Northern Belize Coast*, unpublished Ph.D. dissertation, Department of Anthropology, Austin: University of Texas.
Moedano-Koer, H. (1946) "Jaina: un cementerio Maya," *Revista Mexicana de Estudios Antropologicos* 8(1–3): 217–42.
Moholy-Nagy, H. (1963) "Shells and Other Marine Material from Tikal," *Estudios de Cultura Maya* 3: 65–83.
———(1978) "The Utilization of Pomacea Snails at Tikal, Guatemala," *American Antiquity* 43(1): 65–73.
———(1994) *Tikal Material Culture: Artifacts and Social Structure at a Classic Lowland Maya City*, unpublished Ph.D. dissertation, Department of Anthropology, Ann Arbor: University of Michigan.
Morton, J. D. (1987) "A Preliminary Report on the Faunal Analysis of Caracol, Belize," in A. F. Chase and D. Z. Chase (eds.), *Investigations at the Classic Maya City of Caracol, Belize: 1985–1987*, pp. 106–10, Monograph 3, San Francisco: Pre-Columbian Art Research Institute.
Murie, A. M. (1935) *Mammals from Guatemala and British Honduras*, Miscellaneous Publication 26, University of Michigan, Museum of Zoology, Ann Arbor.
Nicholson, R. A. (1993) "A Morphological Investigation of Burnt Animal Bone and an Evaluation of Its Utility in Archaeology," *Journal of Archaeological Science* 20: 411–28.
NSF (2002) *U.S. National Science Foundation Funding Opportunity for "Assembling the Tree of Life" (solicitation NSF 02–074 for Fiscal Year 2002)*, Washington, DC.
Olsen, S. J. (1972) "Animal Remains from Altar de Sacrificios," in G. R. Willey (ed.), *The Artifacts of Altar de Sacrificios*, pp. 243–6, Papers of the Peabody Museum of Archaeology and Ethnology, Vol. 64, no. 1, Cambridge, MA: Harvard University Press.
———(1978) "Vertebrate Faunal Remains," in G. R. Willey (ed.), *Excavations at Seibal, Department of Petén, Guatemala*, pp. 172–6, Memoirs of the Peabody Museum of Archaeology and Ethnology, Vol. 14, no. 1, Cambridge, MA: Harvard University Press.
Olson, G. W. (1969) *Description and Data on Soils of Tikal, El Petén, Guatemala, Central America*, Mimeo 69-2, Department of Agronomy, Ithaca, NY: Cornell University.
Pendergast, D. M., and Savage, H. G. (1971) *Excavations at Eduardo Quiroz Cave, British Honduras (Belize)*, Royal Ontario Museum Art and Archaeology Occasional Papers, Vol. 21, Toronto: Royal Ontario Museum.
Piña-Chan, R. (1968) *Jaina: La Casa en el Agua*, Mexico City: Instituto Nacional de Antropología e Historia.
Pohl, M. D. (1976) *Ethnozoology of the Maya: An Analysis of Fauna from Five Sites in Petén, Guatemala*, unpublished Ph.D. dissertation, Department of Anthropology, Cambridge, MA: Harvard University.
———(1983) "Maya Ritual Faunas: Vertebrate Remains from Burials, Caches, Caves, and Cenotes in the Maya Lowlands," in R. Leventhal and A. Kolata (eds.), *Civilization in the Ancient Americas*, pp. 55–103, Albuquerque: University of New Mexico Press.
———(1990) "The Ethnozoology of the Maya. Faunal Remains from Five Sites in the Petén, Guatemala," in G. R. Willey (ed.), *Excavations at Seibal, Guatemala*, pp. 142–74, Monographs, Vol. 17, no. 3, Cambridge, MA: Peabody Museum, Harvard University.
———(1994) "The Economics and Politics of Maya Meat Eating," in E. M. Brumfiel (ed.), *The Economic Anthropology of the State*, pp. 121–49, Monographs in Economic Anthropology, no. 11, New York: University Press of America.
———(1995) "Late Classic Maya Fauna from Settlement in the Copan Valley, Honduras: Assertion of Social Status Through Animal Consumption," in G. R. Willey, R. Leventhal, A. A. Demarest, and W. Fash (eds.), *The Copan Residential Zone*, pp. 459–76, Papers of the Peabody Museum, Cambridge, MA: Harvard University Press.

Pohl, M. D., and Feldman, L. H. (1982). "The Traditional Role of Women and Animals in Lowland Maya Economy," in K. Flannery (ed.), *Maya Subsistence*, pp. 295–311, New York: Academic Press.

Polaco, O. J., and Guzman, A. F. (1997) *Arqueoictiofauna Mexicana*, Mexico City: Instituto Nacional de Antropología e Historia.

Pollock, H. E. D., and Ray, C. E. (1957) "Notes on Vertebrate Animal Remains from Mayapan," *Carnegie Institution of Washington, Current Reports* 41: 633–56.

Powis, T. G., Stanchly, N., White, C. D., Healy, P. F., Awe, J. J., and Longstaffe, F. J. (1999) "A Preliminary Reconstruction of Middle Preclassic Subsistence Economy at Cahal Pech, Belize," *Antiquity* 73(280): 364–76.

Puleston, D. E. (1974) "Intersite Areas in the Vicinity of Tikal and Uaxactun," in N. Hammond (ed.), *Mesoamerican Archaeology: New Approaches*, pp. 303–11, Austin: University of Texas Press.

———(1983) *Settlement Survey of Tikal*, Tikal Report no. 13, University Museum Monograph no. 48, Philadelphia: The University Museum, University of Pennsylvania.

Pyburn, K. A. (1989) "Maya Cuisine: Hearths and Lowland Economy," in P. McAnany and B. Isaac (eds.), *Prehistoric Maya Economies of Belize*, pp. 325–46, Greenwich, CT: JAI Press.

Reinhard, K. J. (1992) "Parasitology as an Interpretive Tool for Archaeology," *American Antiquity* 57: 231–45.

Reitz, E. J., and Wing, E. S. (1999) *Zooarchaeology*, Cambridge Manuals in Archaeology, New York: Cambridge University Press.

Rick, A. M. (1968) *Mammals from Tikal, Guatemala*, master's thesis, Carleton University, Ottowa, Ontario.

Ricketson, E. B. (1937) "The Artifacts," in O. Ricketson and E. B. Ricketson (eds.), *Uaxactun, Gautemala: Group E—1926–1931*, Washington, DC: Carnegie Institution of Washington.

Ricketson, O. G. J., and Ricketson, E. B. (1937) *Uaxactun, Guatemala, Group E, 1926–31*, Publication 477, Washington, DC: Carnegie Institution of Washington.

Robinson, M. A. (2001) "Insects as Palaeoenvironmental Indicators," in D. R. Brothwell and A. M. Pollard (eds.), *Handbook of Archaeological Sciences*, pp. 121–2, Chichester: Wiley.

Saunders, N. J. (1994) "Tezcatlipoca: Jaguar Metaphors and the Aztec Mirror of Nature," in R. Willis (ed.), *Signifying Animals: Human Meaning in the Natural World*, pp. 159–77, One World Archaeology 16, London: Routledge.

———(1978) "Faunal Findings in Cave Sites in Belize," paper presented at the Annual Meeting of the Society for American Archaeology, April Tucson, AZ.

Scott, R. F. (1979) "A Preliminary Report on Faunal Remains from Colha, Belize," in T. R. Hester (ed.), *The Colha Project, 1979: A Collection of Interim Papers*, pp. 154–6, Center for Archaeological Research, San Antonio: University of Texas, San Antonio.

———(1982) "Notes on the Continuing Faunal Analysis for the Site of Colha, Belize: Data from the Early Postclassic," in T. R. Hester, H. J. Shafer, and J. D. Eaton (eds.), *Archaeology at Colha, Belize: The 1981 Interim Report*, pp. 203–88, Center for Archaeological Research, San Antonio: University of Texas, San Antonio.

Shaffer, B. S., (1992) "Quarter-inch Screening: Understanding Biases in Recovery of Vertebrate Faunal Remains," *American Antiquity* 57: 129–36.

Shaffer, B. S., and Baker, B. W. (1999) "Comment on James' Methodological Issues Concerning Analysis of Archaeofaunal Recovery and Screen Size Correction Factors," *Journal of Archaeological Science* 26: 1181–2.

Shaffer, B. S., and Sanchez, J. L. J. (1994) "Comparison of 1/8″ and 1/4″ Mesh Recovery of Controlled Samples of Small-to-Medium-Sized Mammals," *American Antiquity* 59(3): 525–30.

Shaw, L. C. (1991) *The Articulation of Social Inequality and Faunal Resource Use in the Preclassic Community of Colha, Northern Belize*, unpublished Ph.D. dissertation, Department of Anthropology, Amherst: University of Massachusetts.

———(1995a) "Analysis of Faunal Materials from Ek Luum," in T. H. Guderjan and J. F. Garber (eds.), *Maya Maritime Trade, Settlement, and Population on Ambergris Caye, Belize*, pp. 175–81, San Antonio: Maya Research Programs and Labyrinthos.

———(1995b) "The Importance of Dog in Ritual Feasting in the Maya Preclassic," paper presented at the Annual Meeting of the Society for American Archaeology, April, Minneapolis, MN.

———(1999) "Social and Ecological Aspects of Preclassic Maya Meat Consumption at Colha, Belize," in C. White (ed.), *Reconstructing Ancient Maya Diet*, pp. 83–102, Salt Lake City: University of Utah Press.

Shook, E. M., and Kidder, A. V. (1952) *Mound E-III-3, Kaminaljuyu, Guatemala*, Contributions to American Anthropology and History, no. 53, Washington, DC: Carnegie Institution of Washington.

Sidell, E. J. (1993) "A Methodology for the Identification of Avian Eggshell from Archaeological Sites," *Archaeofauna* 2: 45–51.

Smithe, F. B., and Paynter, R. A. (1963) *Birds of Tikal, Guatemala*. Cambridge, MA: Harvard University Press.

Stanchly, N. (1995) "Formative Period Maya Faunal Utilization at Cahal Pech, Belize: Preliminary Analysis of the Animal Remains from the 1994 Season," in P. F. Healy and J. J. Awe (eds.), *Belize Valley Preclassic Maya Project: Report on the 1994 Season*, pp. 124–49, Occasional Papers in Anthropology no. 10, Peterborough, Ontario: Trent University.

———(in press) "Picks and Stones May Break My Bones: Taphonomy and Maya Zooarchaeology," in K. F. Emery (ed.), *Maya Zooarchaeology: New Directions in Method and Theory*, Los Angeles: Institute of Archaeology, UCLA Press.

Stark, B. L., and Voorhies, B. (1978) *Prehistoric Coastal Adaptation: The Economy and Ecology of Maritime Middle America*, New York: Academic Press.

Steadman, D. W. (1996) "A Chronostratigraphic Analysis of Landbird Extinction on Tahuata, Marquesas Islands," *Journal of Archaeological Science* 23: 81–94.

Steward, J. H. (1955) *Theory of Culture Change: The Methodology of Multilinear Evolution*, Urbana: University of Illiniois Press.

Stuart, L. C. (1935) *A Contribution to a Knowledge of the Herpetology of a Portion of the Savanna Region of Central Petén*, Miscellaneous Publication 29, University of Michigan, Museum of Zoology, Ann Arbor.

———(1958) *A Study of the Herpetofauna of the Uaxactun-Tikal Area of Northern El Petén, Guatemala*, Contributions of the Laboratory of Vertebrate Biology, no. 75, Ann Arbor: University of Michigan.

Tappen, M. (1994) "Bone Weathering in the Tropical Rain Forest," *Journal of Archaeological Science* 21: 667–73.

Teeter, W. G. (2001) *Maya Animal Utilization in a Growing City: Vertebrate Exploitation at Caracol, Belize*, unpublished Ph.D. dissertation, Department of Anthropology, Los Angeles: UCLA.

Thompson, J. E. S. (1974) "'Canals' of the Rio Candelaria Basin, Campeche, Mexico," in N. Hammond (ed.), *Mesoamerican Archaeology: New Approaches*, pp. 297–302, Austin: University of Texas Press.

Trigger, B. G. (1989) *A History of Archaeological Thought*, New York: Cambridge University Press.

Tsukada, M., and Deevey, E. S. (1967) "Pollen Analyses from Four Lakes in the Southern Maya Area of Guatemala and El Salvador," in E. J. Cushing and H. E. J. Wright (eds.), *Quaternary Paleoecology*, pp. 303–31, New Haven: Yale University Press.

Tykot, R. H., van der Merwe, N. J., and Hammond, N. (1996) "Stable Isotope Analysis of Bone Collagen, Bone Apatite, and Tooth Enamel in the Reconstruction of Human Diet: A Case Study from Cuello, Belize," in M. V. Orna (ed.), *Archaeological Chemistry V*, pp. 355–65, Washington, DC: American Chemical Society.

Vail, G. (1988) *The Archaeology of Coastal Belize*, BAR International Series 463, Oxford: British Archaeological Reports.

van der Merwe, N. J., Tykot, R. H., Hammond, N., and Oakberg, K. (2000) "Diet and Animal Husbandry of the Preclassic Maya at Cuello Belize: Isotopic and Zooarchaeological Evidence," in M. A. Katzenberg and S. H. Ambrose (eds.), *Biogeochemical Approaches to Paleodietary Analysis*, pp. 23–38, New York: Kluwer/Plenum.

van Tyne, J. (1935) *The Birds of Northern Petén, Guatemala*, Miscellaneous Publication 27, University of Michigan, Museum of Zoology, Ann Arbor.

Vernon, K. (1993) "Desperately Seeking Status: Evolutionary Systematics and the Taxonomists' Search for Respectability, 1940–1960," *British Journal for the History of Science* 26: 207–27.

Voorhies, B. (1976) "The Chantuto People: An Archaic Period Society of the Chiapas Littoral, Mexico," *Papers of the New World Archaeology Foundation*, pp. 1–147, Vol. 41, Provo: Brigham Young University.

Wharton, J. (1998) "Postclassic Maya Ritual and Staple Faunas of Laguna de On," *Belize*, paper presented at the Annual Meeting of the Society for American Archaeology, April, Seattle, WA.

Wheeler, Q. D. (1995) "Systematics, the Scientific Basis for Inventories of Biodiversity," *Biodiversity and Conservation* 4: 476–89.

White, C. D., Pohl, M. D., Schwarcz, H. P., and Longstaffe, F. J. (2001) "Isotopic Evidence for Maya Patterns of Deer and Dog Use at Preclassic Colha," *Journal of Archaeological Science* 28: 89–107.

———(in press) "Feast, Field and Forest: Deer and Dog Diets at Lagartero, Tikal, and Copan," in K. F. Emery (ed.), *Maya Zooarchaeology: New Directions in Method and Theory*, Los Angeles: Institute of Archaeology, UCLA Press.

Willey, G. R. (1973) *The Altar de Sacrificios Excavations: General Summary and Conclusions*, Papers of the Peabody Museum of Archaeology and Ethnology, Vol. 64, no. 3, Cambridge, MA: Harvard University Press.

———(1990) *Excavations at Seibal: General Summary and Conclusions*, Memoirs of the Peabody Museum, Vol. 14, no. 4, Cambridge, MA: Harvard University Press.

Willey, G. R., Bullard, W. R., Glass, J. B., and Gifford, J. C. (1965) "Animal and Plant Remains," in *Prehistoric Maya Settlements in the Belize Valley*, pp. 523–9, Papers of the Peabody Museam of Archaeology and Ethnology, Vol. 54, Cambridge, MA: Harvard University Press.

Wilson, R. C. L., Drury, S. A., and Chapman, J. L. (2000) *The Great Ice-Age: Climate Change and Life*, New York: Routledge.

Wing, E. S. (1974) "Vertebrate Faunal Remains," in E. W. Andrews (ed.), *Excavation of an Early Shell Midden on Isla Cancun, Quintana Roo, Mexico*, pp. 186–8, Middle American Research Institute Publication no. 21, New Orleans: Tulane University.

———(1975) "Animal Remains from Lubaantun," in N. Hammond (ed.), *Lubaantun: A Classic Maya Realm*, pp. 379–83, Monographs of the Peabody Museum of Archaeology and Ethnology, no. 2, Cambridge, MA: Harvard University Press.

———(1976) "Ways of Going from a Sliver of Bone to a Calorie," paper presented at the Annual Meeting of the Society of American Archaeology, April, St. Louis, MO.

———(1977) "Factors Influencing Exploitation of Marine Resources," in E. P. Benson (ed.), *Dumbarton Oaks Conference on the Sea in the Pre-Columbian World*, Washington, DC: Dumbarton Oaks.

———(1978) "Use of Dogs for Food: An Adaptation to the Coastal Environment," in B. L. Stark and B. Voorhies (eds.), *Prehistoric Coastal Adaptations: The Economy and Ecology of Maritime Middle America*, pp. 29–41, Studies in Archaeology, New York: Academic Press.

———(1981) "A Comparison of Olmec and Maya Foodways," in E. P. Benson (ed.), *The Olmec and Their Neighbours*, pp. 20–8, Washington, DC: Dumbarton Oaks.

———(2001) "The Sustainability of Resources Used by Native Americans on Four Caribbean Islands," *International Journal of Osteoarchaeology* 11: 112–26.

Wing, E. S., and Brown, A. (1979) *Paleonutrition: Method and Theory in Prehistoric Foodways*, New York : Academic Press.

Wing, E. S., and Pohl, M. D. (1990) "Vertebrate Fauna from San Antonio Rio Hondo, Belize, Operation 2 (North)," in M. D. Pohl (ed.), *Ancient Maya Wetland Agriculture: Excavations on Albion Island, Northern Belize*, pp. 187–254, Boulder: Westview Press.

Wing, E. S., and Quitmyer, I. R. (1992) "A Modern Midden Experiment," in W. H. Marquardt (ed.), *Culture and Environment in the Domain of the Calusa*, pp. 367–73, Monograph no. 1, Gainesville, FL: Institute of Archaeology and Paleoenvironmental Studies.

Wing, E. S., and Scudder, S. J. (1991) "The Exploitation of Animals," in N. Hammond (ed.), *Cuello: An Early Maya Community*, pp. 84–97, Cambridge, UK: Cambridge University Press.

Wing, E. S., and Steadman, D. (1980) "Vertebrate Faunal Remains from Dzibilchaltun," in E. W. Andrews I and E. W. Andrews V (eds.), *Excavations at Dzibilchaltun, Yucatán, Mexico*, pp. 326–31, Middle American Research Institute Publication, no. 48, New Orleans: Tulane University.

Wiseman, F. M. (1983) "Subsistence and Complex Societies: The Case of the Maya," *Advances in Archaeological Method and Theory* 6: 143–89.

Woodbury, R. B., and Trik, A. S. (1954) *The Ruins of Zaculeu, Guatemala*, Richmond, VA: United Fruit Company.

Worsaae, J. J. A. (1849) *The Primeval Antiquities of Denmark*, translated by W. J. Thoms, London: Parker.

13
What Did They Do and Where? Activity Areas and Residue Analyses in Maya Archaeology

DANIELA TRIADAN
TAKESHI INOMATA

Maya archaeologists have traditionally been fascinated with the big and beautiful, such as royal tombs and monumental architecture. One of the most exciting areas of development, however, is the recent turn to much smaller matters such as the detailed study of artifact distributions and microscopic residues. Research on activity areas, organic and inorganic residues has arrived comparatively late in Maya archaeology. This is partly due to the strong emphasis in American archaeology on model-building on a grand scale. Earlier developments in the analysis of activity areas and residues can be found in Europe (or in projects directed by European archaeologists) where there was a stronger emphasis on empirical methods (see, e.g., Bethell and Maté 1989; Wells et al. 2000:450 for an overview on soil phosphate analysis; Heron and Evershed 1992; Evershed et al. 2001 for organic residues in ceramic vessels).[1]

The recent focus on the study of activity areas and residue analyses in American archaeology derives partly from the application of European methods and partly from new theoretical developments, especially those in household archaeology. Maya archaeologists in particular played an important role in the evolution of household archaeology (e.g., Hendon 1989;

Rathje 1983; Joyce and Gillespie 2000; Gillespie 2001; Wilk and Rathje 1982). Initial studies followed the theoretical framework of Robert M. Netting (1965, 1993) and Richard R. Wilk (1989, 1991; also Netting et al. 1984), which emphasized households as *activity groups*. Archaeologists addressed the question of what households did through the remains of past activities.

Settlement archaeology became important in the Maya area during the 1960s (e.g., Smith 1962; Willey et al. 1965). Within this framework, researchers not only looked at intrasettlement organization, but also started to focus on individual structures and their immediate surroundings. Single structures as well as groups of structures began to be analyzed to reconstruct social organization on the household level. To this end, the identification of what types of activities people carried out and in what locations became a focus of research. As a result of these studies in the Maya area, courtyards or patio groups are often interpreted as having been occupied by one household (e.g., Hendon 1989; Sheets et al. 1991). On the other hand, some archaeologists argue that individual range type structures were occupied by several households (Tourtellot 1983; Tourtellot and Sabloff 1989). In other cases, the analysis of activity areas shows that one structure was occupied by a single household (Inomata and Stiver 1998).

The evolving emphasis on activity areas and residues in this context was also informed and shaped by other developments in archaeological theory. Scholars came to realize that form does not always correspond with use and/or function. This is particularly true for architecture, as the use of architectural spaces often changes through time. To address this problem, researchers consequently tried to combine data on artifact distributions with architectural forms to interpret their use and functions (e.g., Haviland 1981). Alas, the analysis of artifact distributions is not straightforward either. As formation theory shows, the distribution of artifacts is usually transformed through various modes of abandonment and post-depositional processes (e.g. La Motta and Schiffer 1999; Schiffer 1987). Given these theoretical considerations, effective methods to determine activity areas include the study of artifact assemblages with appropriate considerations of formation processes, as well as the analysis of microscopic and chemical residues that are less likely to be affected by refuse management and abandonment processes.

Most Maya archaeologists now also agree that examining the question of what a *household* did is not sufficient. A household is not a homogeneous entity that collectively carried out activities. Gender studies, in particular, inspired archaeologists to examine the role of individual agents who engaged in different sets of activities and had different identities and statuses (see, for example, Gillespie 2001; Hendon 1997, 1999; Inomata 2001; Joyce

1992, 1993, 2000). Another influential school of thought came from practice theory. Pierre Bourdieu (1977) has argued that large social structures play out and are reproduced through daily practices. Thus, the understanding of past actions on a micro scale is considered to be a critical step for the understanding of social operations on a macro scale.

Defining Activity Areas

In archaeology, we cannot directly observe individuals and their activities. Nevertheless, the study of activity areas may provide an effective way to approach interpretations on the level of individual agents and their practices. Activity areas describe the spatial and functional organization within and around a dwelling. Different lines of evidence are commonly used to define and delineate activity areas, including (1) features that can be linked to specific activities, such as fire pits or mealing bins in the American Southwest; (2) individual artifacts, and especially assemblages or clusters of associated artifacts such as toolkits; and (3) macroscopic and microscopic remains, such as microdebitage, and botanical and faunal remains, as well as chemical residues. Several methodological issues need to be considered when trying to identify and define activity areas. In this paper we focus on distributional analyses of artifact assemblages, as well as the analyses of various organic and inorganic residues in soils and occupational surfaces and on artifacts (see Emery in this volume for a discussion of faunal analyses, Dunning and Beach in this volume for pollen analyses).

Distributional Analyses of Artifact Assemblages

The identification of activity areas through the spatial analyses of artifact *assemblages* is probably most conclusive in situations of rapid site abandonment, which result in *in situ* assemblages, as at the site of Aguateca, Guatemala (Inomata 1997; Inomata and Stiver 1998; Inomata et al. 2002), or Cerén (Sheets 1992, 2002). Our work at Aguateca demonstrates the resolution of interpretation that can be achieved under these rare circumstances.

Aguateca is a Late Classic center located in the southwestern parts of the Petén, Guatemala. Most of its occupation dates to around A.D. 700, and lasted until the early decades of the ninth century. The site is located in a highly defensible position on top of a 60 to 80 m high escarpment, straddling a chasm of equal depth that divides the site center. Toward the end of its occupation, concentric defensive walls were built around the epicenter, guarding access to the royal compound. Despite this effort, Aguateca was fatally attacked, probably in the early 800s, and most of the structures in its center were burned (Inomata 1997). This incident caused the rapid abandonment of its elite residential area and unprecedented *in situ* artifact

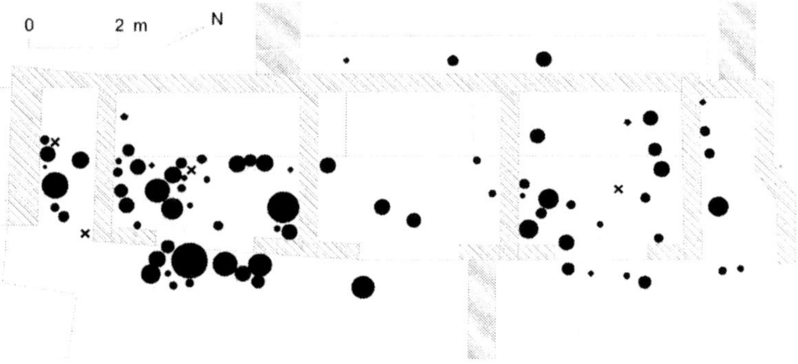

Fig. 13.1 Distribution of ceramic vessels in Structure M8-10 at Aguateca. The sizes of the symbols, except for X, are to scale; X are miniature bottles.

assemblages in theses elite houses (see Inomata and Stiver 1998; Inomata et al. 2002).

The spatial analyses of these assemblages provide crucial information for interpreting the organization of elite households. Figure 13.1 shows the distribution of ceramics in an excavated elite residential structure. The majority of ceramic vessels were found in and around the southern room of the main structure. Based on this distribution, we think that this room was probably used for food storage and possibly food preparation. This pattern of large quantities of vessels in and around one of the side rooms of these elite range structures is consistent at Aguateca and supports the interpretation that the structures were occupied by one household (Inomata and Stiver 1998; Inomata et al. 2002; Inomata and Triadan 2003).

An analysis of the distribution of spindle whorls and figurines in these houses shows a strong correlation with the distribution of ceramics. Spindle whorls indicate spinning and are probably related to weaving and textile work. Ethnographically, most spinning and weaving in modern Maya groups are done by women, and the same was reported by Diego de Landa for the Maya of Yucatán during colonial times (Tozzer 1941:127, 159). In the few archaeological samples—predominantly Late Classic figurines from Jaina—women are the weavers (see Miller 1975:33, Figure 10; Piña Chan 1968:115, Figure 63, 1985:167; Schele 1997:40–1, Figure 25). We thus believe that spindle whorls are evidence of textile fabrication, and that women probably carried out this activity in and around elite houses at Aguateca. The distribution of spindle whorls in conjunction with the ceramics suggests that female members of the elite household occupied a side room of these houses and carried out their daily tasks in these rooms and/or their vicinity. Interestingly, the distributional patterns of ceramic figurines also overlap with those of the ceramic vessels and spindle whorls. This correlation indicates that figurines may have been associated primarily with women and possibly children. Thus, in the case of Aguateca the distributional analysis of the assemblages allows us to not only deduce specific activities that took place in different areas of the residence, but also to make interpretations about the gender of the actors (see also Hendon 1996, 1997, 1999 for a similar interpretation at Copan).

However, even in these admittedly rare situations, formation theory has to be taken into account and artifact assemblages cannot be directly equated with use or function (see Cameron 1993; Inomata and Sheets 2000; Schiffer 1987). *In situ* assemblages reflect the last moment in time before abandonment, and do not necessarily represent the use of artifacts during earlier times of their use life (e.g., Deal 1998). They may also represent storage rather than actual activities.

Residue Analyses

Chemical and microscopic analyses of residues in soils and on artifacts are another approach to identify activity areas. Analyses of soil residues seem to be promising when *in situ* artifacts are absent. These types of analyses were pioneered by Luis Barba and Linda Manzanilla (1987; Manzanilla and Barba 1990; Barba 1994) in the Maya area and further developed by Nicholas P. Dunning (1992, 1994; also Dunning et al. 1997) and later Richard E. Terry and colleagues (Terry et al. 2000; Parnell et al. 2002a, 2002b; Wells et al. 2000; see also Robin 1999, 2002).

In general residues on floors and in soils are organic and inorganic compounds that are fairly stable and preserve in the archaeological record, such as phosphates and heavy metals. High concentrations of phosphates in soils, for example, indicate high organic soil content and may characterize areas of food preparation, cooking, or trash deposition (Manzanilla and Barba 1990; Ball and Kelsay 1992; Dunning 1992:53; Dunning et al. 1997:259–62; Parnell et al. 2002b). Concentrations of heavy metals, such as iron or copper, may indicate lapidary, potter's or painter's workshops (Parnell et al. 2002a). One needs to keep in mind, though, that chemical residues are an accumulation of different activities and interpretations based on these analyses alone may often not be conclusive beyond a very general characterization of the use of an area (see, e.g., Bethell and Maté 1989; Heron 2001 for a critique).

We would like to emphasize that residue analyses at rapidly abandoned sites such as Aguateca and Cerén, where we have almost complete *in situ* assemblages of nonperishable artifacts are particularly important because they provide independent evidence for the identification of activity areas and thus help to interpret the chemical signatures. Also important are ethnoarchaeological studies, where soil samples are taken from locales of known activities (Barba and Denis 1981; Barba and Ortiz 1992; Barba et al. 1995; Fernández et al. 2002; Middleton and Price 1996; Smyth 1991:107–9). The results of these studies will increase the resolution of interpretation if they are applied at gradually abandoned sites, the majority of sites in the Maya area.

Another avenue of chemical determinations is the analysis of residues on artifacts. The identification of pigments on grinding implements, for instance, could provide information about production techniques used by Maya scribes and painters. In the case of rare pigments, it may contribute to the reconstruction of trade and exchange networks.

Residue analyses of ceramics have also gained popularity in Maya archaeology. Organic residues are usually absorbed into the porous fabric of pots or may have been deposited on their surface. If they have not completely deteriorated, these residues may reveal what kinds of food were stored or cooked in those vessels and thus provide important information about prehistoric dietary habits, as well as vessel function (Evershed et al. 1992, 2001; Heron and Evershed 1993; Rottländer and Hartke 1982; Rottländer and Schlichtherle 1979, 1983). It would be intriguing if we could, for instance, establish that cylinder vessels which according to their hieroglyphic texts, were used for cacao (e.g., MacLeod and Reents-Budet 1994:115–9) indeed contained cacao (see Foias in this volume). This was in fact the case for the famous Rio Azul cacao vessel (Hall et al. 1990; Hurst et al. 1989).[2]

However, the tropical environment of the Maya lowlands is not very amenable to the preservation of even the hardiest organic compounds—lipids or fatty acids—and thus it may be hard to identify specific food residues. Shannon Coyston (2002), for example, undertook a study of storage and potential cooking vessels from the sites of Aguateca, K'axob, Cuello, and Cerén. The vessels were from *in situ* contexts in residential structures. Although she found organic residues in all of the samples (in the case of the vessels from Cuello, they were visible charred residues on the vessels' interior), she could not unambiguously identify the original contents of the vessels from Aguateca, K'axob, and Cerén, primarily because of poorly understood degradation processes that had altered the compounds. Isotope analysis of stable carbon and nitrogen on the visible residues of the Cuello vessels suggested that freshwater fish together with some starchy C3 plant were prepared in the pots. Conditions may be somewhat more favorable if vessels come from more sheltered environments, such as sealed tombs, but even in those circumstances the environment is often excessively humid or changeable for organic residues to preserve well.[3]

Interpreting Activity Areas

We also have to ask how much resolution we can obtain in the definition of activities. Often, an activity area does not correlate unequivocally with one activity. Take, for example, the modern bedroom, which in most cases is probably not used exclusively for sleeping. In fact, the concept of the "master suite" implies multiple activities not associated with sleeping, such as watching TV, reading, and so on. Some people may even argue that there are no such things as activity areas. Nonetheless, in most cases we can see *patterns of activities* in a bedroom that are clearly different from those in living rooms or kitchens. Or, in the case of Aguateca, between the center room and side rooms of an elite residential structure. As mentioned above, one of the side rooms of these houses was probably used for food storage and preparation (Triadan 2000). It contains high concentrations of ceramic vessels. The center room, which is almost devoid of artifacts, was probably used for official/political activities of the household head, such as receiving visitors (Inomata and Stiver 1998; Inomata 1997; Inomata et al. 2002). Thus, our goal should not be the identification of activity areas associated exclusively with single activities, but rather an understanding of spatial configurations of activities that comprise both structured qualities and certain idiosyncracies.

Where Do We Go from Here?

The identification of activity areas has come a long way in a relatively short time in Maya archaeology. Detailed distributional analyses of artifact assemblages to reconstruct who did what and where developed out of the focus on settlement archaeology and theoretical frameworks that seek to explain the emergence and internal structure of complex societies; and Maya archaeology has been at the forefront considering these issues. Newer scientific techniques to identify activity areas are, as we have shown, increasingly employed, often in conjunction with artifact assemblages, with the ultimate goal of developing a means to identify activities in situations where such assemblages or even diagnostic features are absent. In fairness, it should be noted that much of the basic research to develop methods to analyze archaeological residues was carried out elsewhere. Hence, it was more a question of eventually applying these methods to Maya cases.

In the Maya area soil residue analyses helped to differentiate agricultural from domestic or other use areas (e.g., Ball and Kelsay 1992; Dunning 1992), as well as to identify activity areas within and around structures (e.g., Barba and Manzanilla 1987; Manzanilla and Barba 1990). However, results must be viewed with caution, because phosphate patterns, for instance, cannot be unambiguously correlated with *specific* activities. They indicate elevated organic contents trapped in surfaces and the soil, but do not necessarily provide unique characteristic signatures that enable us to distinguish between such activities as trash deposition, food preparation, or consumption. Thus, on some level it is questionable whether phosphate analysis alone, without supporting artifactual and/or architectural information or distinct features (such as fire pits), offers a useful resolution. The resolution will probably improve when a larger database of studies for different sites and structures is assembled in the future.

Especially informative have been analyses at rapidly abandoned sites and ethnoarchaeological studies of modern Maya households that provide correlations between soil-chemical patterns and known activities. Broadening this database will lead to a refinement of the interpretation of chemical soil signatures. Another situation where the application of soil phosphate tests may expand in the future is pre-excavation prospecting (see, e.g., Parnell et al. 2001). By using simple phosphate field tests (e.g., Eidt 1973), areas of high phosphate concentrations can be identified and subsequently targeted for excavation. As J. Jacob Parnell et al. (2001) have shown, this should be very helpful in identifying midden deposits and these tests can easily be added to any field regime.

As mentioned above, the elemental analysis of heavy metal concentrations in soils may be useful in identifying special activities and workshop areas. However, we think that ethnoarchaeological studies of ceramic or paint workshops need to be carried out to gain a better understanding on how and in what concentrations metals were deposited in soils and floors by these activities, and how well these deposits preserve over time. So far most ethnoarchaeological studies of soil residues in the Maya area have focused on households of subsistence farmers.

We believe that the research on soil residues in the Maya area is very promising. With the proliferation of these types of studies, we will probably see a lot of the methods become standardized, and it is our opinion that these types of analyses may become routine in Maya archaeology. If the rigorous base-line research that is undertaken today continues, there may be a high potential for the interpretation of household activities at gradually abandoned sites with no characteristic *in situ* artifacts or features, which is the case for the majority of sites encountered in the Maya area.

The analysis of organic residues on ceramics on the other hand, seems to be still quite problematic. Foremost are preservation issues. Because climatic conditions in the Maya area are highly variable (characterized by dry seasons and wet seasons), organic residues do not preserve well and certainly not unaltered. Rolf C. A. Rottländer (1990:39) states the following:

> According to our findings, it appears that a *permanently dry* or a *permanently waterlogged* environment serves well to preserve the fatty material of an archaeological sample, which might otherwise be decomposed by changing water content. Bacterial life and autoxidation is apparently less in an unchanging environment [emphasis added].

Shannon Coyston's (2002) large-scale study on pottery from well-documented, domestic contexts demonstrates these problems. It remains to be seen whether further research on the decomposition of fatty acids will be useful to increase the resolution of the identification of ancient Maya foodstuffs.

As our discussion makes clear, although an enormous amount of progress has been made both theoretically and methodologically, evidence for activity areas should not be interpreted uncritically. However, a thorough and nuanced analysis of what kinds of activities took place and where can provide information on domestic, public, and production activities as well as the organization of space. It may even provide the reconstruction of activities carried out by different members of a household, which in turn informs on the structure of society at large. Thus, research on activity areas combined with residue analyses plays, and will continue to play, a crucial part in the reconstruction of the daily lives of the ancient Maya.

Notes

1. For example, Alfred Lucas (1926, 1934) analyzed organic residues from Egyptian tombs in 1926. Walter Von Stokar (1937, 1938, 1939) analyzed organic residues, including fats and fatty acids. Olaf Arrhenius (1929a, 1929b, 1931) was the first to apply soil phosphate analyses on archaeological sites, and Walter Lorch (1940) used this approach systematically in pre-historic settlements.
2. In the case of Rio Azul, dry residues from the interior of three Early Classic vessels from Tomb 19 contained theobromine, an alkaloid that occurs in significant amounts in cacao beans (Hall et al. 1990; Hurst et al. 1989). More recently, Terry G. Powis and coworkers (2002; Hurst et al. 2002) have analyzed fourteen Preclassic spouted vessels from burials at Colha. In this case, no visible residues were preserved and samples of scraped ceramic powder from the vessels' interiors were analyzed. Three of the vessels contained theobromine (Powis et al. 2002:97–8; Hurst et al. 2002:290).
3. It should be noted that the Rio Azul cacao pot as well as two other pots from that site containing theobromine came from a tomb, and the Preclassic vessels analyzed by Powis and colleagues (2002) were all from burial contexts.

References

Arrhenius, O. (1929a) "Die Phosphatmethode I," *Zeitschrift für Pflanzenernährung, Düngung, und Bodenkunde* Teil A 14: 121–40.

———(1929b) "Die Phosphatmethode II," *Zeitschrift für Pflanzenernährung, Düngung, und Bodenkunde* Teil A 14: 185–94.

———(1931) "Die Bodenanalyse im Dienst der Archäologie," *Zeitschrift für Pflanzenernährung, Düngung, und Bodenkunde* Teil B, 10, Jahrgang: 427–39.

Ball, J. W., and Kelsay, R. G. (1992) "Prehistoric Intrasettlement Land Use and Residual Soil Phosphate Levels in the Upper Belize Valley," in T. W. Killion (ed.), *Gardens of Prehistory: The Archaeology of Settlement Agriculture in Greater Mesoamerica*, pp. 234–62, Tuscaloosa: University of Alabama Press.

Barba, L. (1994) "A Methodology for the Study of Buried Archaeological Sites," in D. A. Scott and P. Meyers (eds.), *Archaeometry of Pre-columbian Sites and Artifacts: Proceedings of a Symposium Organized by the UCLA Institute of Archaeology and the Getty Conservation Institute, Los Angeles 1992*, pp. 353–66, Marina del Rey: Getty Conservation Institute.

Barba, L., and Denis, P. (1981) "Actividades Humanas y Análisis Químicos de los Suelos: El Caso de Usumacinta Viejo, Chiapas," in *Investigaciones Recentes en el Area Maya: 17th Mesa Redonda de la Sociedad Mexicana de Antropología, San Cristobal de las Casas, Chiapas*, Vol. 2, pp. 263–77, San Cristobal de las Casas: Sociedad Mexicana de Antropología.

Barba, L., and Manzanilla, L. (1987) "Estudio de Areas de Actividad," in L. Manzanilla (ed.), *Cobá, Quintana Roo: Análisis de Dos Unidades Habitacionales Mayas del Horizonte Clásico*, pp. 69–115, Mexico City: Universidad Nacional Autónoma de Mexico.

Barba, L., and Ortiz, A. (1992) "Análisis Químico de Pisos de Ocupación: Un Caso Etnográfico en Tlaxcala, Mexico," *Latin American Antiquity* 3(1): 63–82.

Barba, L., de Pierrebourg, F., Trejo, C., Ortiz, A., and Link, K. (1995) "Activités Reflétées dans les Sols d'Unités d'Habitation Contemporaire et Préhispanique du Yucatán (Mexique): Études Chimiques, Ethnoarchéologiques et Archéologiques," *Revue d'Achéometrie* 19: 79–95.

Bethell, P., and Maté, I. (1989) "The Use of Phosphate Analysis in Archaeology: A Critique," in J. Henderson (ed.), *Scientific Analysis in Archaeology*, pp. 1–29, Monograph 5, Oxford University Committee for Archaeology and Archaeological Research Tools 5, Los Angeles: UCLA Institute of Archaeology.

Bourdieu, P. (1977) *Outline of a Theory of Practice*, Cambridge, UK: Cambridge University Press.

Cameron, C. M. (1993) "Abandonment and Archaeological Interpretation," in C. M. Cameron and S. A. Tomka (eds.), *Abandonment of Settlements and Regions: Ethnoarchaeological and Archaeological Approaches*, pp. 3–7, Cambridge, UK: Cambridge University Press.

Coyston, S. (2002) *Noble Chemists and Archaeologists: Chemical Analyses of Food Residues from Ancient Maya Vessels*, unpublished Ph.D. dissertation, Department of Anthropology, McMaster University. Hamilton, Ontario.

Deal, M. (1998) *Pottery Ethnoarchaeology in the Central Maya Highlands*, Salt Lake City: University of Utah Press.

Dunning, N. P. (1992) *Lords of the Hills: Ancient Maya Settlement in the Puuc Region, Yucatán, Mexico*, Monographs in World Archaeology 15, Madison: Prehistory Press.

———(1994) "Ancient Maya Anthrosols: Soil Phosphate Testing and Land Use," in J. E. Foss, M. E. Timpson, and M. W. Morris (eds.), *Proceedings of the 1st International Conference on Pedo-Archaeology*, pp. 203–11, Special Publication 93–03, Knoxville: University of Tennessee.

Dunning, N. P., Beach, T., and Rue, D. (1997) "The Paleoecology and Ancient Settlement of the Petexbatún Region, Guatemala," *Ancient Mesoamerica* 8(2): 255–66.

Evershed, R. P., Dudd, S. N., Lockheart, M. J., and Jim, S. (2001) "Lipids in Archaeology," in D. R. Brothwell and A. M. Pollard (eds.), *Handbook of Archaeological Sciences*, pp. 331–49, New York: Wiley.

Evershed, R. P., Heron, C., Charters, S., and Goad, L. J. (1992) "Chemical Analysis of Organic Residues in Ancient Pottery: Methodological Guidelines and Applications," in R. White and H. Page (eds.), *Organic Residues in Archaeology: Their Identification and Analysis*, pp. 11–25, London: United Kingdom Institute for Conservation, Archaeology Section.

Eidt, R. C. (1973) "A Rapid Chemical Field Test for Archaeological Site Surveying," *American Antiquity* 38: 206–10.

Fernández, F. G., Terry, R. E., Inomata, T., and Eberl, M. (2002) "An Ethnoarchaeological Study of the Chemical Residues in the Floors and Soils of Q'eqchi Maya Houses at Las Pozas, Guatemala," *Geoarchaeology* 17(6): 489–519.

Gillespie, S. D. (2000) "Rethinking Ancient Maya Social Organization: Replacing 'Lineage' with 'House,'" *American Anthropologist* 102(3): 467–84.

———(2001) "Personhood, Agency and Mortuary Ritual: A Case Study from the Ancient Maya," *Journal of Anthropological Archaeology* 20(1): 73–112.

Hall, G. D., Tarka Jr., S. M., Hurst, W. J., Stuart, D., and Adams, R. E. W. (1990) "Cacao Residues in Ancient Maya Vessels from Rio Azul, Guatemala," *American Antiquity* 55(1): 138–43.

Haviland, W. A. (1981) "Dower Houses and Minor Centers at Tikal, Guatemala: An Investigation into the Identification of Valid Units in Settlement Hierarchies," in W. Ashmore (ed.), *Lowland Maya Settlement Patterns*, pp. 89–117, Santa Fe: School of American Research.

Hendon, J. A. (1989) "Elite Household Organization at Copan, Honduras: Analysis of Activity Distribution in the Sepulturas Zone," in A. S. MacEachern, D. J. W. Archer, and R. D. Garvin (eds.), *Households and Communities*, pp. 371–80, Proceedings of the Chacmool Annual Conference 21, Calgary: University of Calgary Press.

———(1996) "Archaeological Approaches to the Organization of Domestic Labor," *Annual Review of Anthropology* 25: 45–61.

———(1997) "Women's Work, Women's Space, and Women's Status among the Classic Period Maya Elite of the Copan Valley, Honduras," in C. Claasen and R. A. Joyce (eds.), *Women in Prehistory: North America and Mesoamerica*, pp. 33–46, Philadelphia: University of Pennsylvania Press.

———(1999) "Multiple Sources of Prestige and the Value of Women in Prehispanic Mesoamerica," in J. E. Robb (ed.), *Material Symbols: Culture and Economy in Prehistory*, pp. 257–76, Occasional Paper 26, Carbondale: University of Southern Illinois.

Heron, C. (2001) "Geochemical Prospecting," in D. R. Brothwell and A. M. Pollard (eds.), *Handbook of Archaeological Sciences*, pp. 565–73, New York: Wiley.

Heron, C., and Evershed, R. P. (1993) "The Analysis of Organic Residues and the Study of Pottery Use," in M. B. Schiffer (ed.), *Archaeological Method and Theory*, Vol. 5, pp. 247–84, Tucson: University of Arizona Press.

Hurst, W. J., Martin, R. A., and Tarka, S. M. (1989) "Authentication of Cacao in Maya Vessels Using High-performance Liquid Chromatographic Techniques," *Journal of Chromatography* 466: 279–89.

Hurst, W. J., Tarka, S. M., Powis, T. G., and Valdez Jr., F. (2002) "Cacao Use by the Earliest Maya Civilization," *Nature* 418: 289–90.

Inomata, T. (1997) "The Last Day of a Fortified Classic Maya Center: Archaeological Investigations at Aguateca, Guatemala," *Ancient Mesoamerica* 8(2): 337–51.

———(2001) "Power and Ideology of Artistic Creation: Elite Craft Specialists in Classic Maya Society," *Current Anthropology* 42(3): 321–49.

Inomata, T., and Stiver, L. R. (1998) "Floor Assemblages from Burned Structures at Aguateca, Guatemala: A Study of Classic Maya Households," *Journal of Field Archaeology* 25(4): 431–52.

Inomata, T., and Sheets, P. (2000) "Mesoamerican Households Viewed from Rapidly Abandoned Sites: An Introduction," *Mayab* 13: 5–10.

Inomata, T., and Triadan, D. (2003) "Where Did Elites Live? Possible Elite Residences at Aguateca, Guatemala," in J. J. Christie (ed.), *Maya Palaces and Elite Residences*, pp. 154–83, Austin: University of Texas Press.

Inomata, T., Triadan, D., Ponciano, E., Pinto, E., Terry, R. E., and Eberl, M. (2002) "Domestic and Political Lives of Classic Maya Elites: The Excavation of Rapidly Abandoned Structures at Aguateca, Guatemala," *Latin American Antiquity* 13(3): 305–30.

Joyce, R. A. (1992) "Images of Gender and Labor Organization in Classic Maya Society," in C. Claasen and M. C. Beaudry (eds.), *Exploring Gender through Archaeology: Selected Papers from the 1991 Boone Conference*, pp. 63–70, Monographs in World Prehistory 11, Madison: Prehistory Press.

———(1993) "Women's Work: Images of Production and Reproduction in Prehispanic Southern Central America," *Current Anthropology* 34 (3): 255–74.

———(2000) *Gender and Power in Prehispanic Mesoamerica*, Austin: University of Texas Press.

Joyce, R. A., and Gillespie, S. D. (eds.) (2000) *Beyond Kinship: Social and Material Reproduction in House Societies*, Philadelphia: University of Pennsylvania Press.

La Motta, V. M. and M. B. Schiffer (1999) Formation Processes of House Floor Assemblages, in P. M. Allison (ed.), *The Archaeology of Household Activities*, pp. 19–29. New York: Routledge.

Lucas, A. (1926) *Ancient Egyptian Materials and Industries*, First Edition, London: Longman Green and Co.

———(1934) *Ancient Egyptian Materials and Industries*, Second Edition, London: Edward Arnold.
Lorch, W. (1940) "Die Siedlungsgeographische Phosphatmethode," *Die Naturwissenschaften* 28: 633–40.
MacLeod, B., and Reents-Budet, D. (1994) "Art of Calligraphy: Image and Meaning," in D. Reents-Budet (ed.), *Painting the Maya Universe: Royal Ceramics of the Classic Period*, pp. 106–63, Durham, NC: Duke University Press.
Manzanilla, L., and Barba, L. (1990) "A Study of Activities in Classic Households: Two Case Studies from Cobá and Teotihuacan," *Ancient Mesoamerica* 1(1): 41–9.
Middleton, W. D., and Price, T. D. (1996) "Identification of Activity Areas by Multi-element Characterization of Sediments from Modern and Archaeological House Floors Using Inductively Coupled Plasma-atomic Emission Spectroscopy," *Journal of Archaeological Science* 23: 673–87.
Miller, M. E. (1975) *Jaina Figurines: A Study of Maya Iconography*, Princeton: Princeton University Art Museum.
Netting, R. M. (1965) "Household Organization and Intensive Agriculture: The Kofyar Case," *Africa* 35: 422–9.
———(1993) *Small Holders, Householders: Farm Families and the Ecology of Intensive, Sustainable Agriculture*, Stanford: Stanford University Press.
Netting, R. M., Wilk, R. P., and Arnould, E. J. (1984) *Households: Comparative and Historical Studies of the Domestic Group*, Berkeley: University of California Press.
Parnell, J. J., and Terry, R. E., Golden, C. (2001) "The Use of In-field Phosphate Testing for the Rapid Identification of Middens at Piedras Negras, Guatemala," *Geoarchaeology* 16(8): 855–73.
Parnell, J. J. Terry, R. E., and Nelson, Z. (2002a) "Soil Chemical Analysis Applied as an Interpretive Tool for Ancient Human Activities at Piedras Negras, Guatemala," *Journal of Archaeological Science* 29: 379–404.
Parnell, J. J., Terry, R. E., and Sheets, P. D. (2002b) "Soil Chemical Analysis of Ancient Activities in Cerén, El Salvador: A Case Study of a Rapidly Abandoned Site," *Latin American Antiquity* 13(3): 331–42.
Piña Chan, R. (1968) *Jaina: La Casa en el Agua*, Mexico City: Instituto Nacional de Antropología e Historia.
———(1985) *Cultura y Ciudades Maya de Campeche*, Mexico City: Editora del Sureste.
Powis, T. G., Valdez Jr., F., Hester, T. R., Hurst, W. J., and Tarka Jr., S. M. (2002) "Spouted Vessels and Cacao Use among the Preclassic Maya," *Latin American Antiquity* 13(1): 85–106.
Rathje, W. L. (1983) "To the Salt of the Earth: Some Comments on Household Archaeology," in E. Z. Vogt and R. M. Leventhal (eds.), *Prehistoric Settlement Pattern: Essays in Honor of Gordon R. Willey*, pp. 23–34, Albuquerque: University of New Mexico Press.
Robin, C. (1999) *Towards and Archaeology of Everyday Life: Maya Farmers of Chan Nòohol and Dos Chombitos Cik'in, Belize*, unpublished Ph.D. dissertation, Department of Anthropology, Philadelphia: University of Pennsylvania.
———(2002) "Outside of Houses: The Practices of Everyday Life at Chan Noohol, Belize," *Journal of Social Archaeology* 2(2): 245–68.
Rottländer, R. C. A. (1990) "Lipid Analysis in the Identification of Vessel Contents," *MASCA Research Papers in Science and Archaeology*, 7: 37–40.
Rottländer, R. C. A., and Hartke, I. (1982) "New Results of Food Identification," in A. Aspinall and S. E. Warren (eds.), *Proceedings of the 22nd Symposium on Archaeometry*, pp. 218–23, Bradford, UK: University of Bradford.
Rottländer, R. C. A., and Schlichtherle, H. (1979) "Food Identification of Samples from Archaeological Sites," *Archaeo-Physika* 10: 260–7.
———(1983) "Analyse frühgeschichtlicher Gefäßinhalte," *Naturwissenschaften* 70: 33–8.
Schele, L. (1997) *Rostros Ocultos de los Mayas*, Singapore: Impetus.
Schiffer, M. B. (1987) *Formation Processes in the Archaeological Record*, Albuquerque: University of New Mexico Press.
Sheets, P. D. (1992) *The Cerén Site: A Prehistoric Village Buried by Volcanic Ash in Central America*, Fort Worth: Harcourt Brace.
———(2002) *Before the Volcano Erupted: The Ancient Cerén Village in Central America*, Austin: University of Texas Press.
Sheets, P. D., Beaubien, H. F., Beaudry, M., Gerstle, A., McKee, B., Miller, C. D., Spetzler, H., and Tucker, D. B. (1991) "Household Archaeology of Cerén, El Salvador," *Ancient Mesoamerica* 1(1): 81–90.

Smith, A. L. (1962) "Residential and Associated Structures at Mayapan," in H. D. E. Pollock, R. L. Roys, T. Proskouriakoff, and A. L. Smith (eds.), *Mayapan, Yucatán, Mexico*, pp. 165–320, Publication 619, Washington, DC: Carnegie Institution of Washington.

Smyth, M. P. (1991) *Modern Maya Storage Behavior: Ethnoarchaeological Case Examples from the Puuc Region of Yucatán*, Memoirs in Latin American Archaeology 3, Pittsburgh: University of Pittsburgh.

Terry R. E. Hardin, P. J., Houston, S. D., Jackson, M. W., Nelson, S. D., Carr, J., and Parnell, J. J. (2000) "Quantitative Phosphorus Measurement: A Field Test Procedure for Archaeological Site Analysis at Piedras Negras, Guatemala," *Geoarchaeology* 15: 151–66.

Tourtellot, G. (1983) "Assessment of Classic Maya Household Composition," in E. Z. Vogt and R. M. Leventhal (eds.), *Prehistoric Settlement Pattern: Essays in Honor of Gordon R. Willey*, pp. 35–54, Albuquerque: University of New Mexico Press.

Tourtellot, G., and Sabloff, J. A. (1989) "Approaches to Household and Community Structure at Sayil, Yucatán" in A. S. MacEachern, J. W. Archer, and R. D. Garvin (eds.), *Households and Communities*, pp. 363–70, Proceedings of the Chacmool Annual Conference 21, Calgary: University of Calgary Press.

Triadan, D. (2000) "Elite Household Subsistence at Aguateca, Guatemala," *Mayab* 13: 46–56.

Tozzer, A. M. (ed.) (1941) *Landa's Relacion de las Cosas de Yucatán: A Translation*, Papers of the Peabody Museum of American Archaeology and Ethnology, Vol. 18, Cambridge, MA: Harvard University.

von Stokar, W. (1937) "Über Fette, Fettsäuren und ihre Auswertung für die Vorgeschichte," *Mannus* 29: 545–9.

———(1938) "Prehistoric Organic Remains," *Antiquity* 12(45): 82–6.

———(1939) "Über die Untersuchung organischer Reste aus paläolithischen Kulturschichten," *Quartär* 2: 147–50.

Wells, E. C., Terry, R. E., Parnell, J. J., Hardin, P. E., Jackson, M. W., and Houston, S. D. (2000) "Chemical Analyses of Ancient Anthrosols in Residential Areas at Piedras Negras, Guatemala," *Journal of Archaeological Science* 27: 449–62.

Wilk, R. R. (ed.) (1989) *The Household Economy*, Boulder: Westview Press.

———(1991) *Household Ecology: Economic Change and Domestic Life among the Kekchi Maya in Belize*, Tucson: University of Arizona Press.

Wilk R. R., and Rathje, W. L. (1982) "Household Archaeology," *American Behavioral Scientist* 25: 617 39.

Willey, G. R., Bullard Jr., W. R., Glass, J. B., and Gifford, J. C. (1965) *Prehistoric Settlements in the Belize Valley*, Papers of the Peabody Museum of Archaeology and Ethnology no. 54, Cambridge, MA: Harvard University.

PART 4
Contemporary Concerns

14
Professional Archaeology and the Modern Maya: A Historical Sketch

JASON YAEGER
GREG BORGSTEDE

Introduction

As Maya archaeology enters the 21st century, it finds itself in the enviable position of being able to look back over more than two centuries of its own history. In this chapter, we look back over that history to examine the discipline's changing relationship with contemporary Maya people, whom most scholars view as the living descendents of the Precolumbian Maya societies we study.[1] We close with some observations and suggestions as to how Maya archaeology might take proactive steps to improve and strengthen this relationship, which we believe will have an ever greater impact on future archaeological research as the area's modern inhabitants grapple with globalization, modernization, and identity politics.

The historiography of Maya archaeology is a relatively new undertaking, and internalist scholarship has dominated the literature. Scholars have assessed the impact of new methodologies and theoretical perspectives on the development of the field (Black 1990; Hammond 1983; Pendergast 1993; Stuart 1992; Willey and Sabloff 1993), and they have examined the roles that individual Western archaeologists and institutions have played in its history (Brunhouse 1975a, 1975b, 1976; Graham 2002; Pendergast 1967; School of American Research 1950; Thompson 1963; Von Hagen 1948, 1950;

Wauchope 1965). Although a few scholars have attempted to situate the field within the larger social, cultural, intellectual, and political economic circumstances that have influenced its development (Schávelzon 1988, 1989; Taylor 1948; Wilk 1985), a comprehensive social history of Maya archaeology remains to be written. This chapter offers a sketch of one aspect of that history: how Maya archaeology, specifically as practiced by archaeologists of the Anglo-American tradition, has interacted with and engaged contemporary Maya people. In addressing this complex and evolving relationship, we employ two frameworks.

First, we break the archaeological project into smaller components. Rather than a monolithic entity understood in abstract terms as the site of data production, we view the project as overlapping, and often interwoven, sets of practices constantly negotiated and sometimes contested over the course of a project's history. We group these practices into four heuristic classes according to the spatial context and logistical content of their constituent practices: 1) construction of the *research design*; 2) implementation of the research design through *fieldwork*; 3) *interpretation* of results; and 4) subsequent *dissemination* of the data and interpretations (Borgstede and Canuto 2000). Although often idealized as a linear sequence, these different categories of practice usually overlap spatially and temporally in actual practice.

Secondly, we draw on observations by Gordon Willey and Jeremy Sabloff (1993), Bruce Trigger (1989), and Thomas Patterson (1995, 1999) to divide the history of Maya archaeology into four broad periods: the Colonial and Antiquarian Period, from the Spanish conquest until the formalization of archaeology as an academic discipline; the Institutional Period, during which archaeology in the United States became embedded in larger academic institutions; the Scientific Period, corresponding to the dominance of the New Archaeology; and the Post-Crisis Period, which emerged out of the crisis in American archaeology marked by the Post-Processual critiques of the 1980s and 1990s. The use of these two frameworks allows us to trace with more nuance the roles that Maya people have played in archaeological research.

Two final points about our goals for this chapter merit emphasizing. First, we have employed the term "historical sketch" in our title to underline the fact that we do not view this chapter as a definitive statement on this complex historical relationship, but rather a first approximation. We hope that some of the salient issues we outline—the broad brush strokes one expects in a sketch—will promote further study and dialogue between archaeologists and non-archaeologists that will add detail, color, and new perspectives to the sketch.

Second, although our analysis is sometimes critical, we are not passing judgment on archaeologists or non-archaeologists, past or present. We do not presume the ability to divine an individual's intentions and motivations, nor do we believe that this kind of psychological approach would be especially productive. Our interest is in the historical structures and circumstances that have conditioned the ways in which professional archaeologists have interacted with contemporary Maya people. Furthermore, given the inherent historical nature of our analysis, we are believe it is inappropriate to judge actions in the past in light of present-day criteria and circumstances.

The Origins of Maya Archaeology: The Colonial and Antiquarian Period (1500s to 1890s)

Our discussion of Maya archaeology begins with the Spanish conquest of the Maya area, despite the fact that Precolumbian Maya historical consciousness entailed an interest in the past that could be considered archaeology (Hamann 2002).[2] In many ways, the foundations for the relationships between Maya groups and Westerners were laid down during the conquest and the early Colonial period. Spanish conquerors and intellectuals had to grapple with the New World they had encountered and make sense of the many differences that existed between themselves and the native inhabitants of the Americas (Pagden 1993; Todorov 1987). Early authors, such as Fuentes y Guzman and Las Casas, despite radically different agendas as apologist for the Spanish colonial enterprise and paternalistic *Defensor de los Indios* respectively, tended to view the native peoples as somehow lesser or inferior, whether due to their unalterable nature or to the socio-economic circumstances that prevented their rise in colonial society.

The Spanish initially recognized native Maya nobility and accorded them positions of political power, but that practice disappeared as Spanish immigration and *mestizaje* obviated the need for power sharing, and an increasingly wide abyss emerged between indigenous peoples and the *peninsulares, criollos,* and *mestizos* of Spanish descent (Farriss 1984). Political and economic structures like *encomienda, repartimiento,* and the *república de indios* institutionalized growing inequalities in Spanish colonial society, which was increasingly structured by racial typologies that defined colonial subjects by percentage of indigenous, European, and African blood. The fundamentally unequal cultural, economic, and political relationships between indigenous and non-indigenous peoples that emerged during the Colonial period have endured into the 21st century, and they have influenced the development of archaeology in the Maya world.

Some of the earliest authors in New Spain wrote about Maya ruins and their relationship to the contemporary Maya people that the Crown was attempting to subjugate (e.g., de Landa 1941), but subsequent generations of historians found little of interest in Precolumbian sites and artifacts. This changed rapidly in the late-18th and early-19th centuries due to the confluence of several factors: the rise of antiquarianism in Europe and the Americas and broader trends in romanticism (Trigger 1989), growing independence movements in the Spanish American colonies (Sued B. 1995), and the increasing dominance of the United States in the Western Hemisphere (Patterson 1995). Although some of these factors were not directly related to Spanish colonialism, the explorations and expeditions that they stimulated were direct products of the colonial milieu.

European antiquarianism spurred King Charles III to send Antonio del Río to explore Maya sites in his colonial possessions in 1787 (del Río 1822). Simultaneously, *criollo* and *mestizo* colonists chafing under Spanish rule, especially following the Bourbon Reforms, drew upon the Precolumbian and indigenous cultures of the Americas to create new identities distinct from the Spanish *peninsulares* (Sued B. 1995; Florescano 1987). Indeed, following independence, the *criollo* leadership of many new states gave their countries indigenous names, beginning with Haiti in 1804 and followed by Mexico, Guatemala, Honduras, and Nicaragua (Sued B. 1995). Despite the continued interest in the Precolumbian past among the intellectual elite of the newly independent Central American republics and Mexico, foreign archaeologists came to dominate archaeological research in those countries.

Over the course of the 19th century, dozens of explorers and adventurers—primarily Americans and Europeans with foreign funding and research agendas—followed in the footsteps of del Río and Juan Galindo, drawing buildings and sculpture and occasionally digging at sites (e.g., Walker and Caddy [Pendergast 1967], Stephens and Catherwood [Stephens 1841, 1843] and Waldeck [1838]). These explorers and their publishers framed their expeditions in culturally constructed notions of exploration and a fetishism of the exotic, themes that drew popular audiences to buy their books in large numbers, and which continue to dominate public views of archaeology today. They were able to carry out their expeditions thanks in part to colonial and related post-colonial political and economic structures in the countries of Mesoamerica and the growing neo-imperialist politics of the United States. The colonial and newly emerged national governments sanctioned the explorations, the U.S. government gave the participants tacit or explicit support, and the expeditions took advantage of economic and political inequalities that existed between foreign explorers and local governments and communities.

Although the earliest Spanish authors acknowledged the link between the modern Maya and the Precolumbian sites they saw and explored, many later authors argued explicitly against that relationship. The failure to associate the contemporary residents of the Maya area with the archaeological sites in that same area can be attributed to multiple factors. The cultural and political disjunctions caused by centuries of colonialism had created a Maya peasantry that seemed to lack the leadership and institutions needed to build great cities. Diffusionism dominated Euro-American intellectual circles at the time, and its proponents posited that developments like metallurgy and writing were unique historical events that happened once and that the cradle of civilization was the Old World (e.g., Smith 1928). In 19th-century North America, the scholarly consensus held that Native Americans did not build the Precolumbian mounds that were ubiquitous in areas being brought under Anglo-American control, a conclusion that provided justification for the relocation of Native Americans to reservations (Patterson 1995). Perhaps unsurprisingly given the broader intellectual and political environment, Mayanist explorers often attributed Maya sites to Egyptians (Rafinesque [Stuart 1989]), Romans (Cabrera 1822; del Río 1822), and other non-indigenous civilizations (LePlongeon 1881). There were exceptions, of course, such as John Lloyd Stephens (1841, 1843), who argued explicitly in two popular accounts of his explorations that the contemporary Maya were the descendents of the people who built Precolumbian cities he visited.

During this period, the contemporary Maya essentially had no voice in the archaeological research process. They did not have access to the American and European intellectual and philanthropic communities within which research expeditions were conceived and funded, and they were divorced from national political structures that sanctioned these expeditions. They lacked the economic resources needed to fund fieldwork, and in many cases had been alienated from the land on which archaeological sites were located. Nor were they part of the academic and public audience to whom researchers directed their publications. Furthermore, because very few of these early explorers associated the Maya with the original inhabitants of Precolumbian sites, there was little reason to consider them in interpretations of the sites or the objects and carvings found therein. Indeed, the only role that the contemporary Maya played in the vast majority of research during this period was as manual labor. During fieldwork, they cleared sites of overgrowth, excavated under the direction of expedition leaders of European descent, and carried equipment, supplies, finds, and sometimes even the researchers themselves (figure 14.1). In this respect, they continued to fill a role that was established in the earliest decades of the Colonial period as the labor that formed the economic backbone of New Spain.

Fig. 14.1 Lithograph of Désiré Charnay, a nineteenth-century archaeologist, borne by a Maya porter. (Courtesy of Museum Library, University of Pennsylvania Museum of Archaeology and Anthropology).

The Institutionalization of Americanist Archaeology (1890s to 1960s)

Between the 1890s and 1920s, the field of archaeology in the United States became increasingly institutionalized through its links to universities, museums, and research institutes. The founders of American anthropology established archaeology courses at universities like Harvard and the University of Chicago, where they provided the formal training that would distinguish certified professionals from the knowledgeable amateurs and dilettantes who had dominated the field in the 18th and 19th centuries (Willey and Sabloff 1993). The professionalization of the discipline not only resulted in the first formalized training in archaeology; it also established criteria for creating knowledge claims about the past that privileged those with access to higher education (Patterson 1995:77). Notions of professionalism were embedded in the praxis of archaeological fieldwork, through which they were passed on to subsequent generations of Mayanist archaeologists. Beginning in the 1950s with Gordon Willey's work at Barton Ramie and subsequently at Altar de Sacrificios, fieldwork became the primary venue for the training of graduate students (Black 1990:258), socializing them in the culture and practice of Maya archaeology.

In the United States, archaeology became situated intellectually and structurally within the four-field anthropology established by Franz Boas, which eschewed comparative studies in favor of detailed studies of the historical trajectories of particular societies (Boas 1896). This intellectual positioning had important consequences for archaeological research, especially in terms of those practices that comprised research design and interpretation. Because of their Boasian heritage, this generation of archaeologists favored conjunctive studies that incorporated archaeology, ethnohistory, and ethnography in the Maya world, a methodology later formalized within archaeology as the Direct Historical Approach (Steward 1942; Wedel 1938) and specific analogy (Ascher 1961). Boasian four-field anthropology and especially historical particularism, together with an ever-growing body of early colonial documents, solidified the perceived cultural and historical links between the modern Maya and Precolumbian archaeological sites in the region. This perception encouraged incorporating the living Maya into archaeological research, but as analogs or sources for interpreting the archaeological record.

The recognition among anthropologists working in North America during this period that Native American societies were changing rapidly led to the birth of acculturation studies (Redfield, Linton, and Herskovits 1936). Like their colleagues to the north, Mayanist scholars began to focus on "salvaging" ethnographic and ethnohistoric data from traditional groups threatened with cultural extinction, the Lacandon being the group thought to be closest to the ancient Maya (Tozzer 1907). During this period, the Carnegie Institution of Washington assembled a multi-disciplinary staff that included some of the most accomplished Mayanist researchers, including Robert Redfield, one of the originators of acculturation studies. The Institution combined ethnographic, ethnohistoric, and archaeological research to better understand Maya culture, with special emphasis on understanding

Precolumbian Maya civilization (Kidder 1937). Their ethnographies were thick descriptions of Maya villages that included ample descriptions of traditional material culture (Redfield and Villa Rojas 1934; Villa Rojas 1945; Wauchope 1938; also Thompson 1930); they correlated native ethnohistories, such as the Popol Vuh and the Annals of the Kakchikels with archaeological sequences (Wauchope 1947); and they combed the archives for early colonial censuses, chronicles, and *visita* documents that could be used to reconstruct Precolumbian Maya civilization (Roys 1939, 1957; Roys, Scholes, and Adams 1940; Scholes and Roys 1948; also de Landa 1941). This research program was founded ultimately on the belief that living Maya populations could play a large role in advancing our knowledge of the Precolumbian past, although trained, professional anthropologists monopolized the privileged mediating relationship between the ancient and modern Maya.

The perceived continuities linking Precolumbian and modern cultures in Mesoamerica and the belief that indigenous cultures would inevitably succumb to pressures of assimilation dove-tailed nicely with political and intellectual currents in Mexico and other parts of Latin America during the middle of the century. Proponents of ethnopopulism and *indigenismo* sought to "preserve what they viewed as the authentic, autochthonous cultures of Indian and other minority communities" (Vargas A. 1995:57; also Sued B. 1995), but in doing so, they created a timeless and folkloric image of indigenous culture that was essentially divorced from the Precolumbian past. This left the latter a fossilized relic, "a dead body that can be partly recovered but never completely revived" (Vargas A. 1995:58).

The disciplinary formalization of archaeology coincided with important changes in the logistical and funding structure of Maya archaeology, which in turn had strong impacts on practices involved with research design. Once funded almost exclusively by direct patronage of wealthy individuals and dilettantes, the turn of the 20th century saw the establishment of well-funded institutions like the Peabody Museum at Harvard, the University of Pennsylvania University Museum, the Field Museum of Natural History, Tulane's Middle American Research Institute, the School of American Research, and the Carnegie Institution of Washington (Black 1990). Although wealthy individuals and companies, such as Marshall Field, Eldridge Johnson, Louis Armour, and the United Fruit Company continued to fund Maya archaeology either directly or indirectly, institutional sponsorship created a stable financial and logistical foundation for unprecedented long-term excavation projects. Simultaneously, of course, it gave sponsoring institutions a strong voice in setting research goals and methodologies. It was in this way that Maya archaeology during this period, perhaps more than ever, found itself linked to some of the structures of neo-colonialism against which anthropology would soon react.

Many of the institutions and individuals sponsoring Maya research were deeply involved in the United States' neo-imperial political policies and its growing economic influence in the region and this involvement guided their sponsorship in some cases. Furthermore, Mayanist archaeologists necessarily depended on the socio-political structures of national and local governments, many of which remained legacies of Spanish colonialism. The neo-colonial aspects of Maya archaeology during this period manifested themselves in several ways.

First, sponsoring institutions and their representative projects provided foreign capital and expertise in exchange for data, including not only information but also valuable archaeological objects and monuments that they removed to foreign museums, albeit generally with the consent of the exporting nations. Although many early research projects carried out restoration work as desired by host governments, the Carnegie's work at Copan was the only project to be co-funded with a national government prior to 1935 (Black 1990:110), and many projects today continue to be funded primarily from abroad.

Second, most Maya archaeological projects during this period did not engage meaningfully with the archaeological communities in the nations where they worked. For example, the contract that the Carnegie Institution signed with the Mexican government for their work at Chichén Itzá stipulated that they hire Mexican archaeologists, but the latter arguably were not fully integrated socially or intellectually into the project (Black 1990:84). In fact, the Carnegie Institution embodied both the proprietary and the paternalistic tendencies of Maya archaeology during this time: their personnel viewed the ancient Maya with "a mixture of romantic imagination, ethnocentrism, and proprietary stewardship" (Hinsley 1989:83), a perspective that left little room for including local archaeologists or local Maya groups in processes of research design or interpretation.

A third way in which Maya archaeology during this period was linked to broader neo-colonial structures had to do with the nature of its patrons. Many of the North American sponsoring individuals and institutions had intimate connections to the U.S. government and powerful U.S. firms that sought to expand their political and economic influence in Central America and Mexico. Although Stephen Black (1990:62) states that "American institutions were granted exploration and excavation concessions on the basis of their solid reputations and their willingness to cooperate with regional governments," the tight connection between structures of U.S. political and economic power and early Maya archaeological research points to the equally important role played by political connections.

The best known Mayanist with direct links to the U.S. government was John Lloyd Stephens, whose first expedition through Central America began as a U.S. diplomatic mission to the confederated Central American republics, but there were several other archaeologists who benefited from their ties to the U.S. government. Steven Salisbury, head of the American Antiquary Society, pushed for E. H. Thompson's appointment to the post of American consul to Campeche and Yucatán, with the condition that he explore Maya ruins for the AAS and Harvard's Peabody Museum (Black 1990:56), and Sylvanus G. Morley worked for the U.S. Naval Intelligence Office in Mexico (Harris and Sadler 2003; Sullivan 1989). In Guatemala, the interpenetration by the United Fruit Company of the Guatemalan government facilitated significant research by archaeologists whom they supported; the company in turn utilized the sponsorship of that research to enhance its prestige in the eyes of the Guatemalan and U.S. publics (Dimick 1948; Schávelzon 1988).

Sponsoring institutions often limited research programs and the political and economic benefits that research brought to host countries to those with governments that were friendly to the United States. The Carnegie Institution of Washington focused its early research in Guatemala, which was a strong ally of the United States government, and later in Chiapas and Yucatán, states that had been antagonistic toward the revolutionary Mexican government (Patterson 1995:60). When political conditions in Guatemala took a turn for the left with the election of Socialist governments in the 1940s and 1950s, established archaeological projects pulled up their stakes. The United Fruit Company stopped funding fieldwork (Black 1990:146–7), as did other institutions. The comments of Percy Madeira, President of the University of Pennsylvania University Museum after the overthrow of the Arbenz government in Guatemala in 1954 make clear the correlation between pro-U.S. governments and U.S. archaeological research: "when President Castillo Armas supplanted the Reds, the writer, who was familiar with Guatemala, revived the [Tikal] project" (Madeira 1964, cited in Black 1990:147).

Simultaneously, national governments were co-opting indigenous sites in nationalist agendas that sought ultimately to incorporate and assimilate diverse indigenous groups within a larger national identity. This tendency was most pronounced in Mexico, where archaeology became "a profession of political faith" (Litvak K. 1986:147) whose goal was "to discover the true roots of Mexico and to proudly exhibit them to the world" (Schávelzon 1990:76). In Guatemala, the Tikal Project not only produced an unprecedented amount of archaeological data; it provided an opening for the Guatemalan national government to reassert and expand its influence in the isolated Petén.

Mayanist archaeologists during this period were not naïve about the importance of the political and economic contexts in which they planned and

Fig. 14.2 Sylvanus Morley, Concepción Cituk, Evaristo Zuluub, and Alfonso Villa Rojas (left to right) at Chichén Itzá in 1935. Cituk and Zuluub were Yucatec Maya leaders during the interwar years in Quintana Roo. (From Sullivan 1989:81, used by permission of Alfred A. Knopf, a division of Random House, Inc.)

carried out their research (figure 14.2). Whether it was using the connections and money of the United Fruit Company to work in Guatemala (Schávelzon 1988), allowing the Chan Santa Cruz Maya to believe that support for their aspirations of independence was forthcoming (Sullivan 1989), or agreeing to invest resources in tourism development, many successful Anglo-American archaeologists proved able politicians in the negotiations by which they secured permission and funding to accomplish their research. Regardless of their personal feelings on the subject, they designed and carried out that research with little explicit discussion of the stake that Maya people and other local communities might have in the structure and nature of archaeological research and in representations of their past.

To summarize, the Institutional Period witnessed a dramatic restructuration of the practice of archaeology in the Maya world. Increasingly, all aspects of the discipline came under the control of academically-trained, full-time archaeologists with the requisite credentials. Research design and interpretation became the privileged domain of these new professionals, who mastered new techniques, methodologies, and theories during advanced studies that were open to a select few. Acceptable and prestigious venues for dissemination of research results narrowed, as archaeology became more technical and focused on specific topics and issues. Sponsoring institutions and individuals exerted enormous pressures on the practice of archaeology, however, often dictating important aspects of research design as well as the logistics of fieldwork. Despite these momentous changes within the discipline, contemporary Maya people remained largely excluded from most components of archaeological practice, save as labor during fieldwork or as objects of analogical reasoning in interpretations of archaeological data.

The New Archaeology and the Scientific Paradigm (1960s to 1980s)

During the early 1960s, Anglo-American archaeology took a turn toward more explicit scientific approaches, epitomized by the New Archaeology (Binford 1964; Watson, LeBlanc, and Redman 1984). Despite the valuable theoretical and methodological contributions that the New Archaeology made to Maya archaeology, it did little to change the nature of the relationships between Maya people and the discipline of Maya archaeology. In fact, we would offer that, in some ways, the scientific epistemology of the New Archaeology actually may have reinforced the trend of non-engagement with local communities. By emphasizing the importance of observational objectivity, New Archaeology downplayed the role of social context in structuring the production of archaeological knowledge. Furthermore, the discipline's goals of creating general covering laws precluded any deep concern for the particularisms of past local contexts; these comprised the "noise" that obscured the signal of cross-cultural generalizations.

This period also witnessed the emergence of significant new funding sources in the 1950s and 1960s, most important among them the Social Science division of the National Science Foundation (Black 1990:140, 144). Although this development allowed some Mayanist archaeologists to distance themselves from politically interested donors and institutions, most archaeological fieldwork continued to be linked to large institutions, directly or indirectly. Furthermore, the very structure and success of foreign research projects, regardless of funding, continued to rely on the international inequalities and regional power structures of postcolonial Mexico and Central America. Archaeologists were not naïve to this reality, nor to the sometimes significant economic and social impacts that their research projects could have on local Maya and non-Maya communities. Regardless, the construction of research designs and their deployment in fieldwork occurred within a scientific discourse of objective and detached empirical research that rarely considered explicitly the social and political contexts in which research occurred.

Some projects during this era did exert a greater effort to meaningfully involve foreign nationals. The Tikal Project, for example, trained a generation of archaeologists in Guatemala, while E. Wyllys Andrews IV and other MARI archaeologists did the same in the Yucatán. In most cases, those who received the most advanced and academically oriented training were members of the educated class, a group to which few Maya men or women belonged at the time, especially in Guatemala. Although many Maya people received technical training that allowed them to make great contributions during fieldwork, the rapid growth of professional archaeological communities during this period in Mexico and Guatemala largely left Maya peoples behind.

Indeed, the increasingly specialized training that professional archaeologists received arguably led to a devaluation of the contributions that local men and women, Maya and non-Maya, made to archaeological fieldwork in the Maya area. This is another case, however, in which we must be careful to not judge the decisions of an earlier generation of archaeologists in light of today's social context. The fact that few projects during this period found ways for Maya people to become professional archaeologists is not surprising given the relative lack of secondary school educational opportunities for Maya people at the time and the paucity of academically trained Maya intellectuals to serve as role models within Maya communities. Both of these factors, of course, have changed considerably in the intervening 40 years.

The Scientific Period witnessed important and dramatic transformations in Anglo-American archaeological epistemology, but we would argue that these did not produce significant changes in the relationships between the field of Maya archaeology and modern Maya peoples. In that respect, this period saw the continuation of trends initiated during the Institutional Period. The contemporary Maya continued to serve as laborers in fieldwork and as modern analogs for interpretation of the archaeological record, but with very few exceptions, they did not actively participate in research design, interpretation, or the dissemination of results.

The Crisis in Anthropology and its Aftermath: Reflexive Approaches and Critical Archaeology (1980s to present)

One of the major turning points in anthropology was what George Stocking (1982) called the "crisis in anthropology," a fundamental awakening of self-awareness and reflexivity that marked the discipline's "reinvention" (Hymes 1972) after its long "Classic Period" (Bennett 1999). The stimulus for this transformation was "an interrelated series of observational, methodological, epistemological, theoretical, ethical, and demographic problems which, articulating with similar concerns in other social sciences, followed hard upon the end of the European colonialism, in the context of postcolonial warfare abroad and radical social upheavals at home" (Stocking 1992:7). The resulting loss of innocence precluded viewing anthropological inquiry as ethically neutral or free from political consequences (Stocking 1992:359).

During the crisis, a critical gaze roved over all subdisciplines of anthropology, manifesting itself as the Post-Processual critique in archaeology. Of particular relevance is the critical strand of Post-Processual archaeology that emerged in the 1980s, the advocates of which are united by their efforts to situate archaeological practice firmly within its social context (Preucel 1995). Mark Leone and others (Leone et al. 1987) have criticized archaeology's scientific epistemology for downplaying the subjectivity of interpretation and largely ignoring the political impact of archaeology outside the academy. Other scholars within this loosely unified movement are exploring the complex relationships between archaeology and nationalism and other forms of identity politics (Arnold 1990; Dietler 1994; Graves-Brown et al. 1995; Jones 1997; Kohl 1998; Kohl and Fawcett 1995; Meskell 2002; Politis and Alberti 1999; Schmidt and Patterson 1995; Trigger 1980). Furthermore, they have initiated explicit discussions of archaeological ethics (Lynott and Wylie 1995; Pyburn and Wilk 1995; Vitelli 1996) and the rights that different constituencies should have over material culture, archaeological sites, and archaeological interpretation (Fuller 1992; Swidler et al. 1997). Among the strongest proponents of a reflexive and engaged critical archaeology is Thomas Patterson (1995:144), who asserts:

> The authority archaeologists possess regarding the meaning and interpretation of certain metanarratives and complex analytical categories—such as primitive cultures, civilization, or societal development—and their silence make it difficult for others to use them in order to understand what is happening in the world. This is especially true when the others who are attempting to formulate understandings of history, class, gender, race relationships, or environmental issues are women, minorities, or oppressed groups, rather than the mainstream media.

Patterson emphasizes that archaeology has a significant impact on society, regardless of whether archaeologists acknowledge that fact.

Paralleling these developments in Anglo-American archaeology is a program of "Social Archaeology" in many Latin American countries. This paradigm seeks a "more refined political analysis of... histories than those routinely carried out in the positivistic paradigm of the United States" (Benavides 2001:355). In its approach, it shares with the Anglo-American critical tradition a concern with the historical and ideological connections between past societies and present ones, a consequent interest in the recursive relationships between the production of archaeological knowledge and the social contexts of that production, and a proactive stance on the use of archaeological knowledge within modern society (Patterson 1994:533–34; also Politis and Alberti 1999).

The critical trends in Post-Processual Archaeology and Latin American Social Archaeology have been relatively slow to appear in the publications or research agendas of North American Mayanist archaeologists. This may be due in part to the fact that Native peoples in Mesoamerica have only recently begun to demand a stronger voice in archaeological research by defining themselves as descendant communities, a process that began much earlier in North America. Furthermore, Anglo-American academics are rarely as directly embedded in national and local political and social contexts as are Latin American archaeologists. We believe, however, that most Mayanist archaeologists today recognize three basic facts about their research. First, archaeology is culturally and politically situated within multiple, complex social contexts. Second, the local communities in which we conduct our fieldwork have a large stake in that research, which directly impacts the very places where they live. And third, our results often have an impact well beyond the confines of academia, one that we can rarely control fully or predict confidently.

The growing awareness of these three facts has led to a more explicit conversation within Maya archaeology about the relationships between archaeologists and indigenous peoples, local communities, and various other constituencies (Ardren 2002; Borgstede 2002; Pyburn and Wilk 1995; also, there have been several recent international symposia that have demonstrated the complexity of these relationships[3]). Although much of the discussion has focused around the relationship between professional archaeologists and local communities (Marshall 2002), this relationship is embedded within a larger archaeological politics, particularly as multiple voices compete in negotiations of Maya culture, history and identity. At issue, ultimately, are the criteria that define legitimate authority in the production and consumption of archaeological knowledge: Whose voices will be heard and why? As the definitions and valorizations of being "Maya" shift with changes in the political conditions in Mesoamerican countries, the development of international tourism and the Mundo Maya, and the growth of pan-Maya and pan-indigenous activism, archaeology is increasingly being deployed by different groups in their representations of ethnic and national identity.

One of the most striking facts to emerge from these discussions is the great diversity among and within the local communities where we work. Local communities vary significantly in size, ethnic composition, wealth, and heterogeneity, and, depending upon the country in which they are located, they have experienced different historical relationships with larger state institutions. Consequently, local communities have very different perceptions about their relationships, historical and otherwise, to the archaeological remains around which they live, and often there is diversity in perception within a given community. To highlight some of these differences, we would like to summarize some observations from two areas of the Maya world, highland Guatemala and lowland Belize.[4]

In highland Guatemala, the historically close ties between archaeology and cultural anthropology increased the impact of the crisis in anthropology. The use of the contemporary Maya as tools for understanding the past was turned on its head with a shift to what would be termed conjunctive research (Carmack and Weeks 1981). Instead of using the modern Maya as analogs to interpret archaeological data, archaeology and the past it documented became a tool for understanding contemporary Maya culture. This subtle but important transformation reflected trends inherent in the crisis in anthropology—a search for relevance, self-critique, and a rapprochement with applied anthropology.

Two large research projects begun in the 1970s reflected the new conjunctive model, the SUNY-Albany project directed by Robert Carmack (1981) and the French project directed by Alain Ichon (Ichon et al. 1996; see also Breton 1994). Both differed from earlier projects in a number of respects. They accorded modern Maya peoples roles as active participants in all four components of archaeological research. The research design of the project included cultural anthropological components focused on local Maya populations, who were also incorporated into the fieldwork as well as the local dissemination of knowledge produced by the research (e.g., Carmack and Morales S. 1983). The projects also specifically sought to understand the social context of archaeological knowledge, if not the archaeological project itself. Importantly, these projects actively reinforced the connections between the archaeological remains being studied and the living Maya in terms of identity and politics. Thus, the arrival of the crisis in anthropology marked a turning point in highland Guatemala in the relationship between professional archaeology and the modern Maya, despite the fact that most archaeological research designs continued to employ a positivist, cultural historical epistemology.

As a result of political instability and warfare, the highlands of Guatemala experienced a long hiatus in research during the 1980s and early 1990s. This absence of recent fieldwork has promoted two different views of highland archaeology. First, the western highlands are viewed as a cultural backwater with little to contribute to our understandings of broader developments in Mesoamerica, contrary to A.V. Kidder's (1940) assertion that the western highlands contained answers to key questions in Maya prehistory. This unfortunate misperception has been perpetuated by a lack of investigations in the region. Second, researchers believe that the western highlands remain unstable in the 21st century, if not nationally, then in terms of local issues such as crime and internal community politics. Both of these perceptions about the western highlands are used to justify the lack of archaeological attention to a region with the densest modern Maya population in Latin America. By ignoring the region, however, archaeologists implicitly de-valorize the descendant communities' histories as being peripheral to developments elsewhere in Mesoamerica and limit occasions for collaboration and involvement by not working in, and with, descendant communities.

The Southern Maya Lowlands present strikingly different social and political landscapes than the highlands, and this difference is reflected in the relationships between Maya communities and Maya archaeology. One striking aspect of the cultural landscape in many parts of the lowlands is the disjunction that many Maya people perceive between themselves and the inhabitants of Precolumbian sites (e.g., Maurer 1997). Until quite recently, most archaeological projects in the lowlands relied heavily on modern Maya people for labor, but made little effort to include them in project research decisions nor did Maya people constitute an important audience for a project's results. Despite this, many projects had significant impacts on local communities, Maya and otherwise. They provided wages for at least some members of local communities, and many projects incorporated significant consolidation and development components, the goal of which was to increase tourism, creating new opportunities for local economic growth. The design of these projects almost always remained in the hands of foreign and national archaeologists and tourism and development professionals, despite the fact that such development can have a very significant and not always welcome impact on local communities.

This situation has begun to change, especially during the last decade. Many lowland projects now disseminate the results of their projects to local communities and other constituencies through public lectures, tours for school groups and tour guides, traveling exhibits and permanent displays, and popular publications and newspaper articles. In Belize, the legal conditions for an archaeological permit established by the Department of Archaeology (2002: Section 17) mandate that permit holders convey "the nature, ethics and morals of their archaeological research to the local community." Although the primary interpretation of project data generally remains in the hands of professional archaeologists, the wide-spread dissemination of those results in different media creates a possibility for multiple and continuing interpretation by different groups. Furthermore, presentations like those mandated by the Belize government create a dialogic space where local communities can engage archaeologists in discussions of research design and interpretation.

Into the Next Millennium

The close relationship that exists between archaeology and socio-cultural anthropology in the United States causes many developments in one field to recursively impact the other. It is therefore likely that some of the changes that socio-cultural anthropology underwent following its crisis will be mirrored by post-crisis changes in archaeology. Stocking (1992:15) observed that the focus of ethnography "moved from problems of ethics and responsibility (Rabinow 1977), to those of 'ethnographic authority' (Clifford 1983) and the creation of ethnographic texts (Geertz 1988; Marcus and Cushman 1982), to the 'poetics and politics' of ethnography (Clifford and Marcus 1986), and more recently to the consideration of specific regional traditions in relation to general theoretical developments in the discipline (Fardon 1990)."

We believe that Maya archaeology is following a broadly similar progression. Questions of archaeological ethics and the responsibilities of archaeologists to descendant communities are becoming important (McAnany 1995:167–8; Pyburn and Wilk 1995).[5] As discussed above, these ethical considerations necessarily lead us to related epistemological questions of archaeological politics and the role of archaeology in the representation and construction of Maya history and identity, which in turn entail issues of authenticity and archaeological authority. This is likely to be especially true in the post-war context of political and economic reform in Guatemala (Warren and Jackson 2002).

As the relationship between professional archaeology and living Maya peoples grows in salience and importance, it becomes critical that we construct appropriate frameworks for understanding various aspects of that complex relationship. In some analyses, a perspective that takes in the entire field of Maya archaeology proves useful. One such approach draws on deconstructionist critiques of the Anglo-American academic tradition to critically assess Maya archaeology as practiced in across various spatial and social contexts (e.g., Castañeda 1996; Hervik 1998). These universal critiques are valuable because they reveal weaknesses—and strengths—that are widely shared across Maya archaeology, and they can thus inform the reflexive assessment of our discipline and help guide the construction of an "engaged" Maya archaeology.

One of the criticisms of such analyses, however, is that their practitioners—archaeologists, anthropologists, and sometimes Maya activists—must necessarily generalize, and this sometimes leads to essentialization of Maya archaeology and Maya culture and identity alike. Our emphasis on the role of social context in guiding our discipline leads us to advocate analyses of Maya archaeology that are sensitive to the wide variety of contexts within which archaeology is practiced, which are conditioned by the distinct historical experiences of Maya peoples in different countries of Mesoamerica and differences in the archaeological agendas of various national governments. Increasingly, important aspects of research design are conditioned by local and national constituencies, whether constructed as "Maya" or otherwise. The complexity of these negotiations and the constituencies that claim a legitimate voice within them is particularly clear in the Guatemalan case, where various Maya communities, from the local (geographical) to the ethnic (linguistic) to the national and international (Pan-Maya) have different interests and agendas with regard to archaeology (Borgstede 2002). This variability within just a single portion of the "Maya world" suggests that different contexts may require different theoretical as well as pragmatic approaches. Clearly, universal analyses must be complemented by considerations of specific regional traditions.

These contextual differences must be taken into account when attempting to develop any theoretical approach to the social context of Maya archaeology. The variability of situations and contexts precludes any overarching paradigm that would be universally applicable to all archaeological projects in the Maya area; archaeologists must develop their own procedures and methodologies based on the contingencies of local conditions and communities. Simply put, an approach that works in one place can be wholly irrelevant for another. Therefore, we suggest that archaeologists instead grapple with the issue at a broader level: how can archaeologists create context-sensitive strategies to explicitly incorporate local social conditions and people in pragmatic decision-making processes? The advantage of shifting debate into this arena is that various publics outside archaeology can be involved in the research design, and the concept of social context moves from an implicit, non-debated topic to being an arena of legitimate research.

Finally, although we have focused this chapter on understanding Maya archaeology from the perspective of the Anglo-American tradition of academic archaeology, we close with a brief consideration of the place of the Maya in defining Maya archaeology. Maya people have developed multiple national and international avenues for advancing their agendas on a variety of issues, including the goals and nature of archaeological research (Cojtí Cuxil 1995). Although there is no unified or monolithic Maya voice, the ever-stronger Maya agenda of self-representation precludes the notion that anthropology can speak for Maya groups. Instead, we must seek to incorporate sometimes disparate Maya perspectives into our academic discourse (Montejo 2002). This is particularly relevant in archaeology, where Anglo-American academics have rather jealously guarded their interpretive authority and have been relatively sheltered from local social and political developments.

This shift toward greater engagement with Maya people, which we believe is inevitable and welcome, will entail significant changes in the practices of archaeological research, and it will be neither simple nor easy. For example, many Maya groups want Anglo-American archaeologists to document historical connections between living Maya groups and archaeological sites, especially sacred sites, in order to protect those sites and guarantee Maya access to them (figure 14.3; see Cojtí Cuxil 1995; Ivic, this volume). Regardless of the wishes of the archaeologist, this kind of research readily lends itself to identity politics, as it highlights continuities between societies past and present that are then easily translated into an essentialized unity (Bernbeck and Pollock 1996; also Fischer 1999).

As an additional example, control over sites, particularly sacred places but also economically important sites, is contested by foreign and national

Fig. 14.3 Cultural conferences have become common in Guatemala, such as the Primera Feria Hemisférica de Educación Indígena in 2001. The conference brought together educators and cultural leaders, including Minister Lux de Cotí (center), from throughout the Maya region to meet with indigenous educators throughout the Americas. An important issue was the role of education in cultural preservation, including archaeological sites. (Photo by Antonio Silvestre).

archaeologists, various state institutions, and diverse Maya groups in an arena of shifting alliances and power relations. The creation of national legislation to regulate and authorize decisions about archaeological resources reveals just how hotly contested this territory is. By making archaeologists, particularly foreign archaeologists, responsible for issues of access, protection, and stewardship of Maya sites, the 1996 Guatemalan Peace Accords greatly narrow the role of the state in the archaeological endeavor. The Belize Department of Archaeology guidelines, in contrast, establish that the Belizean government holds the ultimate responsibility for management of the nation's cultural resources and their development. Ultimately this issue of authority and control, along with other concerns of Maya leaders and protagonists, will be decided not in the academy but through formal and informal negotiations in the local contexts in which archaeology takes place. These will involve foreign and national archaeologists, state institutions and their representatives, and multiple local, national, and international constituencies who can claim a legitimate voice.

We would like to conclude with our belief and hope that the new millennium will witness important and far-reaching changes in the practice of archaeology in the Maya world. What we have outlined in this final section are a few of the issues that have recently crested the horizon; there are others that we have not discussed and many that we surely cannot foresee. Although far from forming a coherent picture, jointly they point toward an emerging new vision for Maya archaeology, one that is conjunctive and holistic, one that meaningfully engages with the various voices and publics interested in the practice of archaeology. Our hope is that the emergence of this new vision for Maya archaeology will be an inclusive, explicit process of academic and non-academic co-operation and collaboration that respects and values both the procedures and policies of archaeological inquiry and the rights and concerns of Maya descendant communities and other constituencies who are invested in Maya archaeology.

Acknowledgments

The authors thank Stephen D. Houston and Robert J. Sharer for inviting us to present an earlier version of this paper in the symposium "Continuity and Contention: Maya Archaeology at the Millennium" at the 100th Annual Meeting of the American Anthropological Association, Washington, DC. We have benefited greatly from our on-going discussions about public archaeology and descendent communities with Traci Ardren, Karla Silvestre, Marcello A. Canuto, Richard Leventhal, K. Anne Pyburn, and Richard Wilk. Traci Ardren, Minette C. Church, T. Patrick Culbert, Richard Leventhal, and Thomas Patterson all provided helpful feedback on an earlier draft of this paper. All of the abovementioned individuals have given us much to think about in terms of the complex issues that this paper addresses; we take full responsibility for the analysis and opinions expressed in this chapter, however.

Notes

1. We recognize that by framing our analysis in terms of these two categories we risk reifying and essentializing two complex and historically contingent social groups. Historians of archaeology have outlined some of the regional, socio-economic, and intellectual divisions that have characterized Anglo-American archaeology (Kehoe 1998; Patterson 1999, 2001; Trigger 1989) and that inherently place limits on generalizations about "professional archaeologists". Nonetheless, we believe that this broad category remains valid for this study because the ways in which Mayanist archaeologists have understood and interacted with the contemporary Maya have been conditioned largely by aspects of professional preparation shared widely among Anglo-American archaeologists.

   The term "Maya" presents greater difficulties. Contemporary or "living" Maya peoples are often distinguished from the "ancient" or Precolumbian Maya. The academic division of labor that traditionally defined the fields of archaeology, history, and cultural anthropology naturalizes this artificial dichotomy, thus reifying a schism between the past and the present and emphasizing discontinuities between the ancient and modern Maya. Many Maya people and some Mayanist archaeologists contest this distinction, a position articulated most strongly by the current Pan-Maya movement in Guatemala (Cojtí Cuxil 1995).

   Furthermore, the modern Maya people who reside in Mexico and Central America are far from a homogeneous group. Although the popular culture and scholarly literature often essentializes the Maya (see critiques by Ardren [in press]; Hervik [1998]; Pyburn [1998]), modern Maya peoples reflect diverse cultural traditions, live in urban and rural environments, and have occupations that range from directors of universities and national politicians, to artisans and subsistence farmers. Thus, despite the expanding influence of globalizing forces on Maya identity (Fischer 2002) and the emergence of pan-Maya activism (Fischer and Brown 1996; Warren 1998), a unifying definition of Maya identity or culture remains elusive. Individual Maya people have varying political, economic, and cultural concerns, concerns that influence their understanding of and interest in Maya archaeology. Although this diversity has had little impact on the practice of Maya archaeology historically, it is now becoming important, although the complexities of this topic are beyond the purview of this chapter.
2. Byron Hamann (2002) has discussed Mesoamerican conceptualizations of the past, the importance of which is reflected in practices like the burial of Olmec and Teotihuacan artifacts in the Aztec Templo Mayor (Matos M. 1988) and the deposition of Classic-period jades in the Sacred Cenote at Chichén Itzá (Proskouriakoff 1974). Furthermore, indigenous historical consciousnesses have continued to act as powerful structuring forces throughout the colonial and modern periods (Bricker 1981; Farriss 1987; Gossen 1996). Despite these facts, indigenous Maya views of history have not contributed significantly to the practice of Maya archaeology.
3. Symposia that have specifically discussed the ethical dimensions of the relationship between archaeologists and modern Maya peoples have included "The Social Context of Maya Archaeology," organized by M. A. Canuto and G. Borgstede for the Annual Meeting of the American Anthropological Association in San Francisco in 2000, "Towards a More Ethical Mayanist Archaeology," organized by Marvin Cohodas, Avexnim Cojtí Ren, Lix Lopez, and Wendy Porter at the University of British Columbia in November 2002, and "Owning the Past, Building the Future: Archaeology, Cultural Property, and Maya Identity in Post-war Guatemala," organized by Edward F. Fischer and Arthur A. Demarest for the 101st Annual Meeting of the American Anthropological Association, New Orleans, 2002.
4. Our focus on highland Guatemala and lowland Belize reflects the specific field experiences of the authors. Yaeger has conducted archaeological fieldwork in Belize since 1990, most recently directing a multi-disciplinary study of the incorporation of Yucatec Maya immigrants into British Honduras during the decades following the Caste War in Yucatán. Borgstede has

directed a community-based archaeological project in the western highlands of Guatemala since 1999.

5. Some projects that have actively sought to incorporate the concerns of local communities in their research designs are those of Traci Ardren (2002) and Scott Fedick and Jennifer Mathews in Mexico, Anabel Ford (Ford and Montes 1999) and K. Anne Pyburn in Belize, and Greg Borgstede (2000, 2002) and Arthur Demarest in Guatemala.

References

Ardren, T. (2002) "Conversations about the production of archaeological knowledge and community museums at Chunchucmil and Kochol, Yucatán, Mexico," *World Archaeology* 34(2):379–400.

———(in press) "Where are the Maya in ancient Maya archaeological tourism? Advertising and the appropriation of culture," in Y. Rowan and U. Baram (eds), *Marketing Heritage*, Walnut Creek, Calif.: AltaMira Press.

Arnold, B. (1990) "The past as propaganda: Totalitarian archaeology in Nazi Germany," *Antiquity* 64:464–78.

Ascher, R. (1961) "Analogy in archaeological interpretations," *Southwestern Journal of Anthropology* 17:317–25.

Belize Department of Archaeology, Ministry of Tourism and Culture (2002) "Conditions for archaeological permits," Document on file, Belmopan.

Benavides, O. H. (2001) "Returning to the source: Social archaeology as Latin American philosophy," *Latin American Antiquity* 12(4):355–70.

Bennett, J. W. (1999) "Classic anthropology," *American Anthropologist* 100(4):951–56.

Bernbeck, R., and Pollock, S. (1996) "Ayodhya, archaeology, and identity," *Current Anthropology* 37(1):S138–S142.

Binford, L. R. (1964) "A consideration of archaeological research design, *American Antiquity* 29(4):425–41.

Black, S. L. (1990) *Field Methods and Methodologies in Lowland Maya Archaeology*, unpublished PhD dissertation, Harvard University.

Boas, F. (1896). "The limitations of the comparative method in anthropology," *Science* 4:901–8.

Borgstede, G. (2000) "Archaeological Investigations in Jacaltenango, Guatemala," paper presented at the 65th Annual Meeting of the Society for American Archaeology, Philadelphia.

———(2002) "Defining the descendant community in a non-Western context: The Maya of highland Guatemala," *Teaching Anthropology* 9(1):27–9.

Borgstede, G., and Canuto, M. A. (2000) "The importance of the social context of Maya archaeology: An introduction," Paper presented at the 99th Annual Meeting American Anthropological Association, San Francisco.

Breton, Alain (ed.) (1994) *Representaciones del espacio político en las tierras altas de Guatemala*, Cuadernos de Estudios Guatemaltecos 2, Guatemala: Piedra Santa.

Bricker, V. (1981) *The Indian Christ, The Indian king: The Historical Substrate of Maya Myth and Ritual*, Austin: University of Texas Press.

Brunhouse, R. L. (1975a) *Pursuit of the Ancient Maya: Some Archaeologists of Yesterday*, Albuquerque: University of New Mexico Press.

———(1975b) *Sylvanus G. Morley and the World of the Ancient Mayas*, Norman: University of Oklahoma Press.

———(1976) *Frans Blom, Maya Explorer*, Albuquerque: University of New Mexico Press.

Cabrera, P. F. (1822) *A Critical Investigation and Research into the History of the Americans*, London: Henry Berthoud.

Carmack, R. (1981) *The Quiche Maya of Utatlan*, Norman: University of Oklahoma Press.

Carmack, R., and Morales S., F. (eds.) (1983) *Nueva Perspectivas sobre el Popol Vuh*, Guatemala: Piedra Santa.

Carmack, R., and Weeks, J. M. (1981) "The archaeology and ethnohistory of Utatlan: A conjunctive approach," *American Antiquity* 46:323–41.

Castañeda, Q. E. (1996) *In the Museum of Maya Culture: Touring Chichén Itzá*, Minneapolis: University of Minnesota Press.

Clifford, J. (1983) "On ethnographic authority," *Representations* 1:118–46.
Clifford, J., and Marcus, G. (1986) *Writing Culture: The Poetics and Politics of Ethnography*, Berkeley: University of California Press.
Cojtí Cuxil, D. (1995) *Ub'aniik ri una'ooj uchomab'aal ri Maya' tinamit. Configuración del pensamiento político del pueblo Maya, 2da. Parte*, Guatemala: Cholsamaj.
de Landa, Diego (1941) *Landa's relación de las cosas de Yucatán*, Translated by A. M. Tozzer, Papers of the Peabody Museum of Archaeology and Ethnology no. 18, Cambridge, MA: Harvard University.
del Río, A. (1822) *Description of the ruins of an ancient city, discovered near Palenque*, London: Henry Berthoud.
Dietler, M. (1994) "'Our ancestors the Gauls': Archaeology, ethnic nationalism, and the manipulation of Celtic identity in modern Europe," *American Anthropologist* 96(3):584–605.
Dimick, J. M. (1948) "Zaculeu, a highland Maya restoration and study," *El Palacio* 55:201–09.
Fardon, R. (ed.) (1990) *Localizing Strategies: Regional Traditions of Ethnographic Writing*, Washington: Smithsonian Institution Press.
Farriss, N. M. (1984) *Maya Society under Colonial Rule: The Collective Enterprise of Survival*, Princeton: Princeton University Press.
———(1987) "Remembering the future, anticipating the past: History, time, and cosmology among the Maya of Yucatán," *Comparative Studies in Society and History* 29(3):566–92.
Fischer, E. F. (1999) "Cultural logic and Maya identity: Rethinking constructivism and essentialism," *Current Anthropology* 40:473–99.
———(2002) *Cultural Logics and Global Economics: Maya Identity in Thought and Practice*, Austin: University of Texas Press.
Fischer, E. F., and Brown, R. M. (eds) (1996) *Maya Cultural Activism in Guatemala*, Austin: University of Texas Press.
Florescano, E. (1987) *Memoria mexicana: Ensayo sobre la reconstrucción del pasado: Época prehispánica-1821*, Mexico: Editorial J. Mortiz.
Ford, A., and Montes, J. A. (1999) "Medio ambiente, uso de la tierra y desarrollo sostenible: La Reserva Arqueológica de El Pilar para la Flora y Fauna Mayas de Belice y Guatemala," *Mesoamérica* 20:31–50.
Fuller, N. J. (1992) "The museum as a vehicle for community empowerment: The Ak-Chin Indian Community Ecomusuem Project," in I. Karp, C. M. Kreamer, and S. D. Lavine (eds), *Museums and Communities*, pp. 327–65, Washington: Smithsonian Institution Press.
Geertz, C. (1988) *Works and Lives: The Anthropologist as Author*, Stanford: Stanford University Press.
Gossen, G. H. (1996) "Maya Zapatistas move to the ancient future," *American Anthropologist* 98(3):528–38.
Graham, I. (2002) *Alfred Maudslay and the Maya: A Biography*, Norman: University of Oklahoma Press.
Graves-Brown, P., Jones, S., and Gamble, C. S. (eds.) (1995) *Cultural Identity and Archaeology: The Construction of European Communities*, London: Routledge.
Hamann, B. (2002) "The social life of pre-sunrise things: Indigenous Mesoamerican archaeology," *Current Anthropology* 43(3):351–82.
Hammond, N. (1983) "The development of Belizean archaeology," *Antiquity* 57:19–27.
Harris, C. H., and Sadler, L. R. (2003) *Archaeologist was a Spy: Sylvanus G. Morley and the Office of Naval Intelligence*, Albuquerqe: University of New Mexico Press.
Hervik, P. (1998) "The mysterious Maya of National Geographic," *Journal of Latin American Anthropology* 4(1):166–197
Hinsley, C. M. (1989) "Revising and revisioning the history of archaeology: Reflections on region and context," in A. Christenson (ed), *Tracing Archaeology's Past: The Historiography of Archaeology*, pp. 79–96, Carbondale: Southern Illinois Press.
Hymes, D. H. (ed.) (1972) *Reinventing anthropology*, New York: Pantheon.
Ichon, A., Douzant-Rosenfeld, D., and Usselman, P. (1996 [1988]) *La cuenca media del Río Chixoy*, Cuadernos de Estudios Guatemaltecos 3, Guatemala: Piedra Santa.
Jones, S. (1997) *The Archaeology of Ethnicity: Constructing Identities in the Past and Present*. London: Routledge.
Kehoe, A. B. (1998) *The Land of Prehistory: A Critical History of American Archaeology*, London: Routledge.

Kidder, A. V. (1937) "A program for Maya research," *Hispanic American Historical Review* 17(2): 160–9.
———(1940) "Archaeological Problems of the Highland Maya," in C. L. Hay et al., *The Maya and Their Neighbors,* pp.117–38, New York: Dover.
Kohl, P. L. (1998) "Nationalism and archaeology: On the constructions of nations and the reconstructions of the remote past," *Annual Review of Anthropology* 27:223–46.
Kohl, P. L., and Fawcett, C. (eds.) (1995) *Nationalism, Politics, and the Practice of Archaeology,* Cambridge: Cambridge University Press.
Leone, M. P., Potter, P. B., and Shackel, P. A. (1987) "Toward a critical archaeology," *Current Anthropology* 28(3):283–302.
LePlongeon, A. (1881) *Vestiges of the Mayas, or, facts tending to prove that communications and intimate relations must have existed, in very remote times, between the inhabitants of Mayab and those of Asia and Africa,* New York: John Polhemus.
Litvak King, J. (1986) *Todas las piedras tienen 2000 años,* Mexico: Editorial Trillas.
Lynott, M. J., and Wylie, A. (eds.) (1995) *Ethics in American Archaeology: Challenges for the 1990s,* Washington: Society for American Archaeology.
Marcus, G. E., and Cushman, D. (1982) "Ethnographies as texts," *Annual Review of Anthropology* 11:25–69.
Marshall, Y. (2002) "What is community archaeology?" *World Archaeology* 34(2):211–9.
Matos Moctezuma, E. (1988) *The Great Temple of the Aztecs,* New York: Thames and Hudson.
Maurer, K. E. (1997) *Ancient Images, Modern Visions: Representations of Maya Identity in Belize,* unpublished PhD dissertation, University of California-Los Angeles.
McAnany, P. A. (1995) *Living with the Ancestors: Kinship and Kingship in Ancient Maya Society,* Austin: University of Texas Press.
Meskell, L. (2002) "The intersection of identity and politics in archaeology," *Annual Review of Anthropology* 31:279–301.
Montejo, V. D. (2002) "The multiplicity of Maya voices: Mayan leadership and the politics of self-representation," in K. Warren and J. Jackson (eds.), *Indigenous Movements, Self-Representation, and the State in Latin America,* pp. 123–148, Austin: University of Texas Press.
Pagden, A. (1993) *European Encounters with the New World: From Renaissance to Romanticism,* New Haven: Yale University.
Patterson, T. C. (1994) "Social archaeology in Latin America: An appreciation," *American Antiquity* 59(3):531–37.
———(1995) *Toward a Social History of Archaeological Thought,* New York: Harcourt Brace.
———(1999) "The political economy of archaeology in the United States," *Annual Review of Anthropology* 28:155–74.
———(2001) *A Social History of Anthropology in the United States,* New York: Berg.
Pendergast, D. M. (1967) *Palenque: The Walker-Caddy expedition to the ancient Maya city, 1839–1840,* Norman: University of Oklahoma Press.
———(1993) "The center and the edge: archaeology in Belize, 1809–1992," *Journal of World Prehistory* 7(1):1–33.
Politis, G. G., and Alberti, B. (eds.) (1999) *Archaeology in Latin America,* London: Routledge.
Preucel, R. W. (1995) "The Postprocessual condition," *Journal of Archaeological Research* 3(2):147–75.
Proskouriakoff, T. (1974) *Jades from the Cenote of Sacrifice, Chichén Itzá, Mexico,* Memoirs of the Peabody Museum of Archaeology and Ethnology vol. 10, no. 1, Cambridge, MA: Harvard University.
Pyburn, K. A. (1998) "Consuming the Maya," *Dialectical Anthropology* 23(2):111–29.
Pyburn, K. A., and Wilk, R. R. (1995) "Responsible archaeology is applied anthropology," in M. J. Lynott and A. Wylie (eds), *Ethics in American Archaeology: Challenges for the 1990s,* pp. 71–76, Washington: Society for American Archaeology.
Rabinow, P. (1977) *Reflections on Fieldwork in Morocco,* Berkeley: University of California Press.
Redfield, R., Linton, R., and Herskovits, M. J. (1936) "Memorandum on the study of acculturation," *American Anthropologist* 38:149–52.
Redfield, R., and Villa Rojas, A. (1934) *Chan Kom: A Maya village,* Carnegie Institution of Washington Publication 448, Washington: Carnegie Institution of Washington.
Roys, R. L. (1939) *The Titles of Ebtun,* Carnegie Institution of Washington Publication 505, Washington: Carnegie Institution of Washington.

———(1957) *The Political Geography of the Yucatán Maya,* Carnegie Institution of Washington Publication 613, Washington: Carnegie Institution of Washington.

Roys, R. L., Scholes, F. V., and Adams, E. B. (1940) *Report and Census of the Indians of Cozumel,* Contributions to American Anthropology and History vol. 6, no. 30, Carnegie Institution of Washington Publication 523, Washington: Carnegie Institution of Washington.

Schávelzon, D. (1988) "Arqueología y política en Centroamérica: Las excavaciones de Zaculeu y su contexto histórico (1946–1950)," *Mesoamérica* 16:335–59.

———(1989) "History of Mesoamerican archaeology at the crossroads: Changing views of the past," in A. Christenson (ed), *Tracing Archaeology's Past: The Historiography of Archaeology,* pp. 107–12, Carbondale: Southern Illinois University Press.

———(1990) *La conservación del patrimonio cultural en América latina,* Facultad de Architectura, Diseño, y Urbanismo, Universidad de Buenos Aires, Buenos Aires.

Schmidt, P. R., and Patterson, T. C. (eds.) (1995) *Making Alternative Histories: The Practice of Archaeology and History in Non-Western Settings,* Santa Fe: School of American Research Press.

Scholes, F. V., and Roys, R. L. (1948) *The Maya Chontal Indians of Acalan-Tixchel,* Carnegie Institution of Washington Publication 560, Washington: Carnegie Institution of Washington.

School of American Research (1950) *Morleyana; A Collection of Writings in Memoriam Sylvanus Griswold Morley, 1883–1948,* Santa Fe: School of American Research and the Museum of New Mexico.

Smith, G. E. (1928) *In the Beginning: The Origin of Civilization,* New York: Morrow.

Stephens, J. L. (1841) *Incidents of Travel in Central America, Chiapas, and Yucatán,* New York: Harper.

———(1843) *Incidents of Travel in Yucatán,* New York: Harper.

Steward, J. H. (1942) "The direct historical approach to archaeology," *American Antiquity* 7(4):337–43.

Stocking, G. W. (1982) "Anthropology in crisis? A view from between the generations," in E. A. Hoebel, R. Currier, and S. Kaiser (eds), *Crisis in Anthropology,* pp. 407–19, New York: Garland.

———(1992) *The Ethnographer's magic and other essays in the history of anthropology,* Madison, WI: University of Wisconsin Press.

Stuart, G. E. (1989) *The Beginning of Maya Hieroglyphic Study: Contributions of Constantine S. Rafinesque and James H. McCulloh, Jr.,* Research Reports on Ancient Maya Writing 29, Washington: Center for Maya Research.

———(1992) "Quest for decipherment: A historical and biographical survey of Maya hieroglyphic investigation," in E. Danien and R.J. Sharer (eds), *New Theories on the Ancient Maya,* pp. 1–62, University Museum of the University of Pennsylvania Monograph 77, Philadelphia: University Museum Press.

Sued Badillo, J. (1995) "The theme of the indigenous in the national projects of the Hispanic Caribbean," in P.R. Schmidt and T.C. Patterson (eds), *Making Alternative Histories: The Practice of Archaeology and History in Non-Western Settings,* pp. 25–46, Santa Fe: School of American Research.

Sullivan, P. (1989) *Unfinished Conversations: Mayas and Foreigners between Two Wars,* Berkeley: University of California Press.

Swidler, N., Dongoske, K. E., Anyon, R., and Downer, A. S. (eds.) (1997) *Native Americans and Archaeologists: Stepping Stones to Common Ground,* Walnut Creek: Altamira Press.

Taylor, W. W. (1948) *A Study of Archeology,* Memoirs of the American Anthropological Association no. 69, Menasha: American Anthropological Association.

Thompson, J. E. S. (1930) *Ethnology of the Mayas of Southern and Central British Honduras,* Field Museum of Natural History Anthropological Series vol. 17, no. 2, Chicago.

———(1963) *Maya Archaeologist,* Norman: University of Oklahoma Press.

Todorov, T. (1987) *The Conquest of America,* New York: Harper and Row.

Tozzer, A. M. (1907) "Survivals of ancient forms of culture among the Mayas of Yucatán and the Lacandones of Chiapas," in *Proceedings of the XVth International Congress of Americanists,* vol. II, pp. 283–88, Quebec.

Trigger, B. G. (1980) "Archaeology and the image of the American Indian," *American Antiquity* 45:662–76.

———(1989) *A History of Archaeological Thought,* Cambridge: University of Cambridge Press.

Vargas Arenas, I. (1995) "The perception of history and archaeology in Latin America: A theoretical approach," in P. R. Schmidt and T. C. Patterson (eds), *Making Alternative Histories: The*

Practice of Archaeology and History in Non-Western Settings, pp. 47–68, Santa Fe: School of American Research.

Villa Rojas, A. (1945) *The Mayas of East Central Quintana Roo*, Carnegie Institution of Washington Publication 559, Washington: Carnegie Institution of Washington.

Vitelli, K. (ed.) (1996) *Archaeological Ethics*, Walnut Creek: Altamira Press.

Von Hagen, V. W. (1948) *Maya Explorer: John Lloyd Stephens and the Lost Cities of Central America and Yucatán*, Norman: University of Oklahoma Press.

———(1950) *Frederick Catherwood, Architect-Explorer*, New York: Oxford University Press.

Waldeck, J. F. (1838) *Voyage pittoresque et archeologique dans la Province d'Yucatán, pendant les années 1834 et 1836*, Paris: F. Ditot-frere.

Warren, K. B. (1998) *Indigenous Movements and Their Critics: Pan-Maya activism in Guatemala*, Princeton: Princeton University Press.

Warren, K. B., and Jackson, J. E. (eds.) (2002) *Indigenous Movements, Self-representation, and the State in Latin America*, Austin: University of Texas Press.

Watson, P. J., LeBlanc, S. A., and Redman, C. L. (1984) *Archeological Explanation: The Scientific Method in Archeology*, New York: Columbia University Press.

Wauchope, R. (1938) *Modern Maya houses: A study of their Archaeological Significance*, Carnegie Institution of Washington Publication 502, Washington: Carnegie Institution of Washington.

———(1947) "An approach to the Maya correlation problem through Guatemala highland archaeology and native annals," *American Antiquity* 13:59–66.

———(1965) *They Found Buried Cities*, Chicago: University of Chicago Press.

Wedel, W. R. (1938) *The Direct-Historical Approach in Pawnee Archaeology*, Smithsonian Institution *Miscellaneous Collections* vol. 97, no. 7, Washington, D.C.

Wilk, R. R. (1985) "The ancient Maya and the political present," *Journal of Anthropological Research* 41:307–26.

Willey, G. R., and Sabloff, J. A. (1993) *A History of American Archaeology, 3rd edition*, New York: W. H. Freeman.

15
We Have Never Been Post-modern: Maya Archaeology in the Ethnographic Present

K. ANNE PYBURN

I want to reconsider the use of the word "post" to describe the state of social science at the dawn of the new millennium. Speaking at an academic conference on post-colonialism, aboriginal activist Bobby Sykes commented, "What? Post-colonialism? Have they left?" (quoted in Tuhiwai Smith 1999). I don't think we are really post anything; the results of the conquest and enslavement of first peoples continue into the present day, both as echoes of the past and in new and terrible forms. In fact, as Linda Tuhiwai Smith (1999:14) notes, many aboriginal people view post-colonialism "as the convenient invention of Western intellectuals which reinscribes their power to define the world."

Even though there is now extensive documentation of just how far-reaching the repercussions of colonialism have been, most archaeologists are still very unclear about what colonialism has to do with the pursuit of science or how we ought to change what we do. A few of us have considered that our basic assumptions about the reliability of empirical data may be questionable, but just how the testing of academic models has repercussions in the political present is mysterious. Deliberate attempts to be relevant, laudable though they may be, are not the archaeology we were trained to do and they are not science. Why should our research into the distant, romantic, mysterious, irrelevant past be anyone's business but our own? *We* do not have an agenda; all we want is to know, to solve mysteries, to satisfy our natural curiosity about the spectacular culture of the Maya as it existed before Europeans arrived.

The problem is that science is not separable from the cultural matrix that generated it (Toulmin 2001). The questions that arouse our interest, the explanations that satisfy our curiosity, the reconstructions that seem convincing have to do with both empirical data and the cultural context within which the archaeologist transforms the material record into data. In other words, our natural curiosity is cultural, and one archaeologist's empirical facts are another archaeologist's biased sample. We all follow an agenda of one sort or another; the only question is whether or not we make it explicit.

My title is a reference to Bruno Latour's book "We Have Never Been Modern" (1993) in which he discusses the failure of modernism to make and enforce the desired division between nature and culture, to construct a scientific process untainted by humanism and not susceptible to bias or political pressure. Archaeologists have struggled as hard as any scientists to fulfill this quest. Most of us are not post-modern because we are still overwhelmed with the impossible task of being modern—we hold to a standard of objectivity beyond what recent philosophers of science tell us is possible or even desirable.

Steven Toulmin comments, "Even now it takes a sophisticated analysis to convince many behavioral scientists that their theories rest on value assumptions which, if not always explicit, are nonetheless unavoidable" (2001:205). But the result of what Toulmin calls the separation of rationality from reasonableness, or what Latour calls the failure to deal with hybrids between nature and culture, is an inability to apprehend how our part in a cultural sphere affects our perception of data and our reception by others. And unless we see it, we are not going to be able to take any responsibility for it.

Thirty years ago Clifford Geertz (1973:346) commented as follows on anthropologists: "Know what he thinks a savage is and you have the key to his work." This is pretty much still the case for archaeologists. Certain reductionist beliefs about the Maya appear to have resonance in the collective psyche of Western academics, because they are particularly impervious to data. These include the idea that soil types and hydrology inspire complex society, the concept of chiefdoms, the belief in the ubiquity and rigidity of patrilineal descent, the assumption of iconographic continuity in time and space, the equation of houses with households, the supposition of gender dualism, and the emphasis on extensive agriculture, to name only a few. All these ideas have been challenged with real old-fashioned empirical data collected by card-carrying archaeologists, but none have been dethroned.

Nor will they be until we take a closer look at where such theories come from. As long as we refuse to examine the social context that keeps such constructions alive, our perception will continue to be influenced by factors outside our awareness. The issue of the social context of archaeology is not a stand against science; it is a desire for better science and more responsible interaction with the present. It is time for us to look carefully at who we archaeologists are as an anthropological question and to take an equally ethnographic perspective on who our audience might be. The archaeology of the twenty-first century is going to be about engagement, but before we can get on with it, we have a bit of housekeeping to do. Most of us are not quite ready to deal with the ethnographic present. Echoing Latour, but borrowing from Tuhiwai Smith's admonition to her fellow cultural anthropologists in 1999, I would agree that "there can be no postmodern for us until we have settled some business of the modern" (Tuhiwai Smith 1999:34).

Although I think an ethnographic study of Mayanist archaeologists that describes us as a group in terms of the usual demographic and cultural variables would be very interesting and point out a great deal of consistency between our *habitus* (Bourdieu 1977:80) and our research designs, I simply want to argue that we come to our discipline with a set of assumptions and prejudices which sit right alongside our knowledge of the relevant literature when we develop a research design. I do not point this out as a failing: I emphasize it as a perfectly ordinary aspect of being human that, as social scientists, we are equipped to use to our advantage.

In her essay entitled "Feminism as Method: What Scientists Get That Philosophers Don't," philosopher of science Lisa Lloyd (1995) makes this point very clearly. She shows how an overtly feminist perspective, a theoretical bias, if you will, has actually enhanced the practice of science. It has done this by forcing practitioners to be explicit about their perspective, consistent about their models, and extremely careful about ruling out competing hypotheses, because by displaying their bias, they invite and facilitate criticism. In other words, researchers in any field have biases: committing yourself to one openly does not make you less objective and it can make you more consistent and even more honest.

For archaeologists, entanglement with the political present is certainly neither new nor undocumented. What is new and important is the movement to acknowledge this entanglement and take some responsibility for it by developing an intentional and planned engagement (Cohodas et al. 2003). Here is where the serious housework needs to come in, because gender equality, nation building, economic development, and ethnic pride are not programs that can be built on good intentions. The desire to help people does not translate into responsible engagement any more than liking women makes you a feminist. This sort of archaeology takes a new kind of effort, an increased sense of humility, a huge amount of time, and some sophisticated anthropology.

We are at a dangerous crossroads in Maya archaeology. Most of us who are in positions to run projects, and have an impact on the political present with our research designs and our behavior in the field, were trained in the pure anti-applied approach to anthropology of ten to twenty years ago (we learned what our advisors had learned in graduate school). A lot has happened in cultural anthropology since then, and it takes some effort to catch up with current information and ideas about culture change and human rights. If we go out into the world armed with good intentions, backed up with a culture concept designed by Emile Durkheim or George Peter Murdock, we are going to be unnecessarily out-of-touch.

The danger is that overconfidence, fueled by a sincere desire to help, will do damage. Most countries with Maya populations are economically underdeveloped and any help we provide is eagerly appreciated. In fact, compared to other parts of the world, the citizens of much of Latin America have shown an amazing tolerance and generosity of spirit toward archaeologists. But local people and city officials are not likely to have anthropological knowledge of the downside of "ethnic pride" or the infrastructure implications of tourist development. These are quick fixes that can make us feel like heroes, at least in the short term. But there is an anthropological literature on culture change, and as anthropologists, we have both the responsibility to be aware of it and to teach what we know. Not to make the decisions about health care and economic development—but to inform the decision makers.

Returning to my housework metaphor, I think this means we are not quite ready for company. Although the needs and wishes of local people and descendant communities must figure large in the archaeology of the next century, we archaeologists are not quite ready to meet them. We clearly have good intentions, and I doubt there is an archaeologist of the Maya who does not admire Maya culture, past and present, far beyond the admiration of any ordinary person. Nevertheless, in our very enthusiasm to do something big and good, to make up for errors of the past, and of course to outdo each other, we run the risk of promotions that will backfire on the archaeological record, as when angry communities destroy monuments to spite local factions or even drive archaeologists away; that will backfire on us, as when our disciplinary factions result in political factions outside the discipline that undermine our credibility with local communities and scholars (Tierney 2001); and that will backfire on the people we meant to help, as when economic development results in increasing the distance between rich and poor (Meskell 1998). As any development anthropologist knows, such fallout cannot always be prevented, but if we can foresee it, we can at least try to do better.

We do need input from outside the discipline, and Maya people should certainly be asked to help us identify areas that need work and places we might try to help, but I do think we need to make some home improvements before we run out into the world and start doing good. I would like to suggest that we rethink our science with an eye to engagement before we dive head first into development work. After all, archaeology is what we are really trained to do. I think if we clean up our approach to the past, we can make a more successful transition to the present.

By cleaning up our approach I only mean we should take a step back from our research and ask ourselves "What exactly am I trying to find out about the past?" This is a question that we need to answer in at least two ways. First of all, the proximate answer is likely to be that we are interested in something pretty specific, such as "was the pottery made by specialists" or "did the stone tools get imported from another community" or "is this the same verb that has been identified at Palenque." But as social scientists we embed these specific investigations in larger research programs that we hope will contribute to a larger picture of the ancient world. And this is where the question becomes crucial. Are we reinforcing a picture of the past that has the potential for bad political repercussions in the present? Can we honestly say it would compromise our intellectual freedom to take another approach or ask another question?

For example, might an uncritical focus on the power of elites and the glory of kings reinforce a world view among our admirers and students that we do not actually believe in or want to promote? Might the perpetuation of a model that organizes world cultures into a historical trajectory which posits the natural evolution of hierarchical states reflect more of the political present that it teaches about the past? Is it really scientific or desirable to provide this uncritical validation for the status quo? Once you get started, it is easy to come up with similar questions about the way we approach gender, labor, technology, and other facets of past societies. Are we asking questions in such a way that the ascendancy of a particular sort of political economy is always confirmed?

The perspective I describe sounds like political radicalism because I am suggesting that we approach our work with an eye to the subversive inclinations we all indulge. Whether we are employed by universities, museums, or government contracts, we are all teachers, and teaching is the most subversive of all employment situations. Nobody teaches without an agenda; nobody designs an exhibit, or writes a guidebook, lecture, or textbook without wanting to instill his or her ideas in an audience. In fact, since we are not really politicians, ethnographers, or development anthropologists (which is not to say that we cannot take on these roles as we learn more about the social context of our work), I would like to propose that we can most responsibly approach both the past and the present as teachers.

If we think about what we can teach the world with our discoveries, a more positive framework for both research and development becomes clear. Questions about the past may be directed toward issues that can open up people's minds about the possibilities of the present. A focus on the ancient elites who rose to control Tikal through economic and political connections to Teotihuacan (rather than providing another TV special on the ancient rich and famous) might suggest how social hierarchy can operate to disenfranchise local people who might originally have expected to benefit. This suggests that tourist development strategies that depend on a great deal of foreign capital may not really help the local people of the Mundo Maya, but instead create a greater divide between rich and poor—a problem that might be hypothesized to have affected the Maya Classic period. In this vein, I have argued that the sustainability of Maya smallholders is an example that can be used to teach about the efficiency and superiority of small farms in the present day, an argument with a clear and unvarnished political agenda (Pyburn 1996; Mortensen and Pyburn, forthcoming).

If we approach the social context of our research as teachers, I think we will get a better response and a better result. Teaching is subversive. To do it well, you have to know your students well enough to communicate with them in terms they can understand. You have to have clear goals, so you can make it apparent exactly what information and what perspective you have to impart and so you can objectively evaluate performance. And although we may feel proud of the expertise that allows us to teach, teachers are also humble; the goal of the class is not to keep the students in school forever, but to give them the tools to use on their own. We also are humble about what we do not know—we do not teach outside our areas of expertise.

Archaeologists of the Maya know a huge amount about the ancient past and a reasonable amount about human behavior in general as it occurs in the huge sweep of time. This gives us good things to teach with, important points to make. As anthropologists, we also have an intellectual commitment to the possibility of cross-cultural understanding. It has been the life work of most of us to establish an understanding of the past; it should be child's play for us to establish cross-cultural understanding in the present.

I am not suggesting that living people—whether Maya, Navajo, cowboys, or politicians—need to be taught lessons by arrogant archaeologists; teaching is not self-absorbed pontificating. A real teacher teaches what he or she knows and is honest and humble about what he or she does not know. And to teach effectively, it is necessary to work very hard at continuing to learn.

It is a very great mistake for archaeologists to try to tell living Maya people what to do to solve the problems of the modern world system. But we can be proud of what we do know about the origin and effects of the world system, and other sorts of system, and to offer our knowledge as appropriate for combination with the many other sorts of information that must go into policy decisions in the present day.

In conclusion, I have said that, as scientists, we need to be aware of the sociopolitical agendas we contribute to with our research and be braver about addressing the issues we really believe in. And I have said that, as archaeologists, we are best prepared to face the political present as teachers with ideas and information based on our study of the past that are relevant to policy decisions. We are not qualified to make those decisions or to dictate the future, but knowledge is power and we can use it to make a difference.

References

Bourdieu, P. (1977) *Outline of a Theory of Practice*, Cambridge, UK: Cambridge University Press.

Cohodas, M., Cojtí Ren, A., Lopez, L. and Porter, W. (2002) *Towards a More Ethical Mayanist Archaeology*, http://ethical.arts.ubc.ca/Introduction.html

Geertz, C. (1973) "The Cerebral Savage: On the Work of Claude Levi-Strauss," in C. Geertz (ed.) *The Interpretation of Cultures*, pp. 345–359, New York: Basic Books.

Latour, B. (1993) *We Have Never Been Modern*, Cambridge, MA: Harvard University Press.

Lloyd, L. (1995) "Feminism as Method: What Scientists Get That Philosophers Don't," *Philosophical Topics* 23: 37–68.

Meskell, L. (ed.) (1998) *Archaeology under Fire: Nationalism, Politics and Heritage in the Eastern Mediterranean and Middle East*, London: Routledge.

Mortensen, L., and Pyburn, K. A. (forthcoming) "The Future in the Past: The Development Potential of Archaeological Settlement Patterns," in R. Agurcia (ed.), *Essays in Honor of George Hasemann*, Copan, Honduras: Asociacion Copan.

Pyburn, K. A. (1996) "The Political Economy of Ancient Maya Land Use: The Road to Ruin," in S. Fedick (ed.), *The Managed Mosaic: Ancient Maya Agriculture and Resource Use*, pp. 236–47, Ogden: University of Utah Press.

Tierney, P. (2001) *Darkness in El Dorado: How Scientists and Journalists Devastated the Amazon*, New York: W. W. Norton.

Toulmin, S. (2001) *Return to Reason*, Cambridge, MA: Harvard University Press.

Tuhiwai Smith, L. (1999) *Decolonizing Methodologies: Research and Indigenous Peoples*, London and Dunedin: Zed Books, University of Otago Press.

16

The Sacred Place in the Development of Archaeology in Guatemala: An Analysis

MATILDE IVIC de MONTERROSO

In Guatemala, evidence of sacred places within the frame of Pre-Hispanic origins, religion and spirituality can be traced as far back as 3,500 years. Maya people who survived the Spanish Conquest retained many of their cultural traits, including native spiritual elements. Gradually, these cultural elements have become more relevant, such that by the end of the twentieth century their role was that of revindication for indigenous people. The "Accord on Identity and Rights of the Indigenous People," part of the Peace Accords signed in 1995 between the Guatemalan government and representatives of the National Revolutionary Unity of Guatemala (URNG) that went into effect in 1996, included indigenous people's claim to use and manage sacred places. This received national and foreign political support, as well as government recognition. During the 1999 National Referendum, however, these claims were rejected by a majority of voting Guatemalan citizens (see Warren 2002).

My three-year research on the subject involving sacred places in Guatemala highlights the complexities and difficulties of the subject. Lack of communication between the parties involved has resulted in misinformation, mistrust, and uncoordinated action. Simply obtaining the documentation needed to study this phenomenon was made difficult by a lack of publications, political interests, and fanatical attitudes. Presently, some leaders of the popular indigenous movements are taking extreme positions regarding sacred places. This could make revitalization movements a serious limitation in the development of archeological projects in Guatemala in the future. Because of the latter, I believe that in research and information dissemination about sacred places, the building of bridges—and not walls—is necessary. In this research, an analysis of relevant Peace Accords concerning sacred places, as well as the progress in or difficulties of their enforcement, is presented. At the same time, it is expected these ideas will reach institutions and persons involved in development in Guatemala as well as leaders of both local and foreign indigenous religious and popular organizations.

Prior to presenting the above-mentioned analysis, it is necessary to highlight three important aspects related to the concepts of sacred places, spirituality, and indigenous people. First, in Guatemala, there are archaeological sites not considered sacred places. Chivacabé, San Rafael, and the like, are sites with paleontological findings that are not being claimed by indigenous populations. There are sacred places that are not archaeological sites; these are known among the natives as altars (among the better known are Cerro El Baúl, Cerro María Tecún, and Laguna Chicabal). And there are sacred places that at the same time are archaeological sites (e.g., Iximché, Gumarcaaj, and Zaculeu). This last group includes mostly highland sites that nearby indigenous people have held in reverence since at least the nineteenth century. Second, indigenous people prefer the terms "spirituality" and "spiritual guide" instead of religion and priest because the latter in each case implies the existence of a hierarchy. Third, in the signed accords, three groups called "indigenous people" were united: the Maya, Xinca, and Garifuna. The ancestors of the first two groups are indigenous to the area now known as Guatemala, whereas the Garifuna grew out of a mix of African and Caribe-Arahuac peoples who had begun expanding their territory along the Atlantic coast by the end of the eighteenth century. By the nineteenth century, they had arrived in Livingston and Puerto Barrios, Guatemala (González 1995:402–3). Unfortunately, the Xinca are almost extinct and the Garifuna are not indigenous to Guatemala, so the term "indigenous people" in the Peace Accords in essence refers to Maya people.

Origin and Development of Sacred Places in Guatemala

By means of archaeological, epigraphic, and ethnohistoric data, we know that in the Pre-Hispanic period, the Maya people gave sacred status to geographical features such as mountains, caves, and lagoons. Under Maya cosmology such places had special characteristics. Here people could perform rites that allowed them to communicate with their dead ancestors and with the gods. Equally sacred were temples and other places where Maya people once buried their dead. Because the dead were often buried under the floor of Mayan dwellings, these locations were likewise considered sacred.

It is believed that some of the archaeological significance of places, rites, and objects, mostly obtained by epigraphy, was transmitted to Maya intellectuals by workshops held by epigraphers from the United States and Guatemala. This remains as a case study for anthropologists (Christenson 2001:19). In addition, the ethnohistorical interpretations of the *Popol Vuj* have to be considered in the context of present-day Mayan spirituality. In the 1970s, the Maya activist and intellectual Adrián Inés Chávez started workshops for the revitalization of Maya culture using the *Popul Vuj* (Secaira 2000).

With the Spanish Conquest, Pre-Hispanic civilization was lost but not indigenous culture. Some elements of ancient religion survived, transmitted from one generation to another, their rituals performed in secret. As the Maya population from the lowlands was virtually extinguished, the recognition of sacred places and the observance of the rituals associated with them survived primarily in the highlands region. During the Colonial period, the syncretism of the Catholic religion with the native one began. Even today, however, there are still unexpected elements of indigenous culture to be found. For example, in the area surrounding Lake Atitlán, we can still find places dedicated to the Lord of Hunting (Brown and Romero 2002:771–6).

By the end of the eighteenth century, which included the Enlightenment and its interest in the past, a dichotomy of interests had arisen at archaeological sites: those of European investigators and those of the indigenous population whose spirituality focused on sacred sites. The end of Spanish control in Guatemala by 1821, together with the diminished power of the Catholic Church and the administrative disorder of the young Guatemalan nation, signified to indigenous peoples that they had more room to express their beliefs. It is possible that, from this point, some people living around archaeological sites in the highlands began to openly conduct rituals at those archaeological sites they considered sacred. Perhaps in the future historical archaeology will confirm this hypothesis.

During most of the twentieth century, community spiritual guides continued in this tradition. But the 1990s were particularly noteworthy, as the leaders of Maya popular organizations made sacred places, including many archaeological sites, centerpieces of their revitalization movements. It is worth mentioning that several Maya activists are linguists who are familiar with a hypothesis of Terrence Kaufman (1976). Kaufman affirms that all the Maya populations descend from a single linguistic family. The claim to archaeological sites from the lowlands to the highlands is derived from this hypothesis.

The Maya organizations have made it clear from where their movement was derived: The 1945 Political Constitution of the Republic of Guatemala legislated their indigenous rights, but these were not enforced [Comisión para la Definición de Lugares Sagrados or Commission for the Definition of Sacred Places (CDLS) 1998:4]. The decades of the 1960s and 1970s were characterized in Guatemala by turbulent social currents. The beginnings of the Maya movement also took place during this time.

During the thirty years of armed conflict in Guatemala, Maya communities were victimized by political murders and systematic attacks on their culture. Many political and religious leaders were killed. However, in the 1990s, groups defined as Maya popular organizations played a deciding role in the Assembly of the Civil Society. It was in the Assembly of Civil Society that the Accord on the Identity and Rights of the Indigenous People, which formed part of the Peace Accords, was proposed. In 1996, the Guatemalan government and representatives of the URNG signed the Peace Accords (Secaira 2000:35).[1]

Analysis of the Signed Accords

In the Peace Accords, the contents relating to sacred places appear under Sections C and D (see Appendix). Basically, the compromises agreed to by the Guatemalan Government in 1995 can be summarized as follows:

Section C

1. Allow the performance of native spirituality in public and in private realms.
2. Reform Article 66 of the Political Constitution of the Republic of Guatemala so that the state recognizes, respects, and protects the various forms of spirituality.
3. Recognize the historical value and actual significance of the temples and ceremonial centers as part of the indigenous people's heritage.

Section D

It is divided in two parts: (1) temples and ceremonial centers located in archaeological areas protected by the government, and (2) sacred places.

Temples and Ceremonial Centers

1. Ratifies that under the constitution temples and ceremonial sites of archaeological value are part of the national cultural heritage.
2. Recognizes the right of the indigenous people to participate in the conservation and management of the archaeological sites.

3. Makes a commitment to promote the legal means for redefining the government entities in charge of archaeological sites.

Sacred Places

1. Recognizes the existence of other sacred places where spiritual rituals are usually performed and that have to be preserved; agrees to create a commission combining government- and indigenous-organization representatives to define these places and the regime for preserving them.

These commitments can be analyzed through two key events: results of the 1999 National Referendum and creation of the CDLS, according to Acuerdo Gubernativo 261-97 enacted on May 20, 1997, and its modifications contained in Acuerdo Gubernativo 84-98, 536-98, and 387-2001.

With regard to temples and ceremonial centers, it is important to note that the rights of indigenous people to the cultural patrimony were ratified by the signing of the Peace Accords in 1995 and 1996, and by Covenant 169 of the International Labor Organization. However, the results of the 1999 National Referendum made it impossible to include the indigenous people's claims in the Political Constitution of the Republic of Guatemala. But the Peace Accords are in force and have international support.

With the administrations of both Presidents Alvaro Arzú and Alfonso Portillo, archaeological sites are now open for spiritual guides to hold native ceremonies. Abaj Takalik, Kaminaljuyu, and Tikal are the best examples of these new cases. On November 2002, the Minister of Culture, Otilia Lux de Cotí, who is a Maya, inaugurated new altars in some of Tikal's squares to accommodate Mayan visitors' ceremonies. Other groups of different religious and philosophical currents have taken advantage of this situation, as cases of New Age and "black magic" rites have been reported by staff managing archaeological sites. These situations seem to be related to urban settings in the neighborhood of archaeological sites.

The first CDLS was established in 1997. It was an integrated panel, with four spiritual guides from the National Permanent Commission for Spirituality (CNPE), and four government representatives, two of them with a background in archaeology. However, its activities stopped with the change of government administration in 2000. The second commission has been appointed to function from the last part of 2001 to December 2004. Ten government representatives are part of it, among them the Maya Cultural Vice-Minister Virgilio Alvarado Ajanel, a lawyer who advises Minister Lux de Cotí, an anthropologist from the Latin American Social Science Faculty (FLACSO), and a philosopher at the Rafael Landívar University. With regard to spiritual guides, there are eight Maya representatives and five deputies, three Maya, one Garifuna, and one Xinka. On behalf of the

Coordination of Maya Popular Organizations of Guatemala (COPMAGUA), there are five Mayan representatives and two deputies, also Maya. There are no archaeologists in this second commission.

During the negotiation process that led to the formation of the first commission, the most important issue was the inclusion of archaeological sites from all parts of Guatemala and the listing of traditional sacred places such as mountains, lakes, and highlands sites. Due to the lack of formal, published reports of the meetings of this first commission, there are some unclear points. According to some sources, the Maya organizations' proposal was too ambitious and it included a large portion of the Guatemalan territory. Nevertheless, it seems that the counterproposal from the government representatives was never presented in writing, and the negotiations stopped.

It is important to point out that some of the government representatives in this first commission had been working in the area of Petexbatún. This area was suffering substantial looting caused by Maya and Ladino communities who had recently been uprooted from their homes and had settled in Petén as a result of government policies. This situation made government representatives question whether the assumed sacredness of lowland sites was only part of the political discourse of the spiritual guides and was not present among the beliefs of indigenous people living near the sites. The1994 and 1995 publications by Demetrio Cojtí, presently Vice-Minister of Education, presented unfavorable concepts about archaeology and the work carried out by Guatemalan archaeologists. This, along with the valid perception of existing deterioration and looting in most archaeological sites, certainly created a communications barrier with the indigenous representatives. Looting of archaeological sites has increased in the last twenty years in part due to the meager budget assigned to the Ministry of Culture.

From that first commission only a photocopied document dated October 29, 1998, is known. Both the government and indigenous groups claim to be the authors. The document contains several definitions of what constitutes sacred places. The most important ones are the following:

> Since its existence is known, the Maya, Xinca and Garifuna have identified special places where the energy that fills their spirit and gives fullness to its physical wellbeing flows. In these places communication with the Superior Being, Builder and Shaper of the Universe, and with the ancestors is established, according to their vision of the cosmos.... The Ancient Maya and Xinca Cities are Sacred Places, and the burials that exist in their structures complement the sacred area. (CDLS 1998:4)

The document establishes that the sacred places should remain in the control of indigenous peoples, through their spiritual guides and local leaders (CDLS 1998:4, 14.). An interesting fact is that this document was presented at the National Congress on Cultural Policies Guidelines held in April 2000 by the Ministry of Culture headed by the Mayan Otilia Lux de Cotí. The opinions of the spiritual guides reflected the contents of the above-mentioned document. These opinions, the mandates of the Political Constitution, and the commitments agreed on in the Peace Accords are the basis for the Ministry of Culture's policies from 2000 to 2004.

As an outcome of the second CDLS, a document that unified the criteria used to define sacred places was produced, dated March 2002, with the support of Dr. Linda Asturias de Barrios, Director of the Identity Project of the Ministry of Culture and the United Nations Development Program. The same elements presented by the first CDLS definition are included, although the use of "sacred spaces" provides a broader frame of reference and the dimension of the "future" was added. The following is the definition of sacred places as developed by the second commission:

> Considered as sacred places are the spaces where cosmic energy meets for the communication with the Ajaw (Creator and Builder) and with the ancestors, where the practice of spirituality from the beginnings of the Maya, Garifuna, and Xinca's people was, is, and will be performed. (These places are) for example: villages, ancient cities, temples, actual and future ceremonial centers, water sources, lakes, rivers, lagoons, hills, and others, natural and historic, or built by the human being (CDLS 1998:16).

During this meeting, a spiritual guide added that sacred places exist "in sacred objects, such as books, artifacts of stone, clay, jade, bone and others that posses cosmic energy" (CDLS 2002:32.) According to a source, this second commission prepared a draft to reform legislation related to cultural patrimony, but after three attempts on the part of the author, it was not possible to obtain the document.

Present Repercussions

Upon evaluation of the present situation, it is evident that the results of the 1999 National Referendum have not precluded the fulfillment of some of the Peace Accords, particularly those related to spirituality and those allowing management of sacred places by indigenous peoples. Different approaches have been taken to accomplish this and changes are evident in three, sometimes closely linked, sectors: government, Maya organizations, and other civil society organizations.

Government Sector

Actions taken by Otilia Lux de Cotí, Minister of Culture, are establishing foundations for issues such as cultural interaction and tolerance, decentralization, and community participation in the management of archaeological and sacred places. Evidence of this is the support given to the second CDLS.

Also, in 2001 the Ministry of Culture hired consultants to create a program of shared management of archaeological sites making use of the World Bank's funding. Recommendations were made in this study to start a pilot program in the highlands where there is community identification with a site, and where there are legally established local authorities. It suggested taking into account successful cases where the state-delegated management of natural patrimony to civil society organizations, as well as those situations in which there was adequate management of communal forests by Maya from the eastern highlands of Guatemala (Núñez and Ivic de Monterroso 2001; Secaira 2000).

Mayan Organizations Sector

Both the Maya popular organizations as well as some groups of spiritual guides have unified criteria and efforts in the CDLS to achieve control of sacred places. However, in 2002, a brief survey by Marcelo Zamora, Luisa Escobar, and Karla Cardona done in places of worship located in the highlands in Chimaltenango, Totonicapán, Huehuetenango, and Sololá indicated that several spiritual guides ignore the existence of this commission and do not feel represented by it. In fact, notwithstanding the lack of legislation and support demanded by the commission, in the eastern highlands there are cases of sacred places that are not archaeological sites but are managed based on common law (Secaira 2000).

Added to the above are three important cases: (1) Purchase of land containing the archeological site Cahyup, in Baja Verapaz, by a spiritual guide and his group; it is not known, however, whether leaders are legally requesting management of the site. (2) Legal authorization by Government Decree of 2001 to manage Chixukub' in Cobán, Alta Verapaz, to a group of Maya Q'eqchi', whose leader is also a member of the second CDLS. (3) Proceedings done by the Tz'utujil association Gran Señor Tepepul to establish a community museum south of Chuitinamit, Atitlán, Sololá; the exhibition of archaeological vessels recovered from Lake Atitlan for community development and income from tourism is sought.

Other Sectors from the Civil Society

Representatives of Non-Governmental Organizations (NGOs) and other aspects of civil society involved in these processes include the Fundación Defensores de la Naturaleza, an organization with ten years of experience in the management of natural resources, which is requesting control of the cultural patrimony in Sierra del Lacandón Park, Petén, from the Ministry of Culture. This includes Piedras Negras and other less-known archaeological sites. Also included in this sector are development and community participation components in archaeological projects, such as Cancuén, which includes the purchase by Vanderbilt University of the property next to the site, and community development activities by Guatemalan and French archeologists at La Joyanca, Petén.

Final Comments

This analysis clearly shows that different situations inform an approach to sacred places that are archaeological sites, as well as those which are not. In the case of the former, the Political Constitution of Guatemala as well as the Peace Accords state that archaeological sites are part of the national cultural patrimony and, as such, belong to the state. The possibility of including indigenous people in its administration will necessarily occur with shared management, one part of which will be the government.

There are several opinions in all sectors involved, and they cannot be presented as a unified perspective. During the present research, I have heard archaeologists speak in favor of projects that include community development programs, and in support of communities managing sites because of the benefits it would bring to the involved communities, and because it is evident the state does not have the necessary resources. Other archaeologists believe that this is a more complicated and longer-span process than an archaeological project, for which there is already insufficient funding available. They also consider development to be a government responsibility.

On the other hand, among the Maya, some are open to having young people involved in the archaeological discipline. Others perceive a contradiction between their spirituality and the handling of the remains of their ancestors, even though archaeology is a much more broadly defined field. Some oppose tourism and the "folklorization" of their ancestry, whereas others see it as a strategy for survival.

There are also government representatives opposed to community participation in the management of archaeological sites. They consider shared management to be unconstitutional. It is ironic that some of them are opposed to authorizing research projects unless the institution proposing the project is also committed to providing permanent protection to the site. This is, in fact, another way of shared administration.

Commitments acquired by the Guatemalan government influence the development of archaeology with regard to indigenous peoples' participation and to a possible redefinition of the role of public institutions in charge of archaeological patrimony. Therefore, the following are some issues that have been proposed: First, project directors and archaeological parks' managers should be prepared for and open to the performance of Mayan rituals. It is necessary for the Ministry of Culture to prepare clear guidelines to support park managers and to establish limits for their use. Second, the Ministry of

Culture needs to again include representatives of the field of archaeology in the decision-making process affecting the future of the archaeological patrimony of Guatemala. It is important to take advantage of experience gained by archaeologists working in the Atlas Project,[2] the Department of Pre-Hispanic Monuments, and the Abaj Takalik National Project. Archeologists of the latter project have succeeded in negotiating with the spiritual guides. Third, a thorough knowledge of the Peace Accords, as well as other relevant laws regarding the administration of cultural patrimony, is necessary in order to clarify each sector's area of influence. Fourth, it is important to reach consensus, perhaps suggesting that shared management begin in some of the many highland sites that are disappearing because of high levels of looting and deterioration. Here, there is still a link between community members and sites, which are considered part of the communities' background or ancestry. The lowlands region has a more complicated situation because most of the Maya and Ladino communities surrounding the sites have been recently established as a result of government policies supporting communities uprooted during the armed conflict. The issue of sacred places in Guatemala needs urgent and concrete actions in the present. As the debate over their use, future, and management continues, our national patrimony continues to be destroyed and damaged in an irreversible manner.

Acknowledgments

I would like to thank Mauricio Monterroso, Carolina Monterroso, Dave Mitchell, Héctor Escobedo, and Mireya de Weller for their valuable comments and great help with the English translation of this article.

Addenda

A version of this chapter was presented at the XVI Symposium of Guatemalan Archeology in July 2002. On November 15 of the same year, the Minister of Culture Otilia Lux de Cotí issued Decree Number 525-2002. It has eleven articles enumerating rules on access to the sites and the performing of spiritual rites. According to Article 1, the spiritual guides and their followers can enter without restrictions archaeological sites defined as sacred places by Maya cosmology. This applies only to sites under Ministry jurisdiction. Participants of these activities have to abide by normal guidelines of respect, hygiene, security, and cleanliness for the conservation of these places. Article 3 of Decree Number 525-2002 establishes that for the present Decree

> Sacred Sites are those spaces—monuments, parks, complexes or archaeological centers—[that are] considered source of cosmic energy, life and knowledge, for

> the spiritual communication with the Superior Being or Ajaw and its cohabitation with nature, for strengthening and linking the present with the past and the future.

In addition, Article 8 exempts the spiritual guides and their followers from an admissions fee to archaeological sites.

Article 9 establishes that each spiritual guide must identify him or herself with a card provided by the Ministry of Culture's Specific Unit of Sacred Places.

Finally, in Article 10 it is indicated that where a sacred altar exists, a ground-level platform for the celebration of ceremonies will be built by the General Direction for Cultural and Natural Patrimony. Its location will be indicated by the spiritual guides or Ajq'ibjab' (Ministerio de Cultura y Deportes 2002).

Appendix: Accord on Identity and Rights of the Indigenous People*

Article C. SPIRITUALITY

1. Maya spirituality's importance and specific characteristics are recognized as an essential component in Mayan cosmology and in the (act of) transmission of their values, as well as that of the other indigenous people.
2. The Government is committed to enforce respect of the performance of this spirituality in all its expressions, specifically the right to practice this spirituality publicly and privately, through its instruction, practice and observance. The importance of due respect to indigenous spiritual guides, its ceremonies, and its sacred places is also recognized.
3. The Government will promote before National Congress a reform to Article 66 of the Political Constitution of Guatemala in order to establish the State's recognition, respect, and protection of the various spiritual practices of the Maya, Garifuna and Xinca people.

Article D. TEMPLES, CEREMONIAL CENTERS, AND SACRED PLACES

1. Historical value and present influence of the temples and ceremonial centers as part of the Maya and other indigenous people's cultural, historical and spiritual heritage is recognized. Temples and ceremonial centers located in State protected zones due to its archaeological value.
2. According to the Political Constitution of the Republic, temples and ceremonial centers of archaeological value are part of the national cultural patrimony. As such, they belong to the State and must be protected. It should be assured in this context that this principle

is not jeopardized in the case of temples and ceremonial centers of archaeological value that are located or discovered in private property.

3. The right of the Maya, Garifuna, and Xinca people to participate in the conservation and administration of these places is recognized. To guarantee this right, the Government is committed to promoting legal actions, together with the participation of the indigenous people, that assure a redefinition of the State's entities in charge of enforcing this right.
4. Ruling for the protection of ceremonial centers in archaeological zones will be modified so that the practice of spirituality is made possible and so that it cannot hinder it. The Government, together with the spiritual indigenous organizations, will promote access regulations to those ceremonial centers that will guarantee the free practice of spirituality within the conditions of respect required by the spiritual guides.

Sacred Places

The existence of other sacred places that must be preserved and where indigenous spirituality, specifically Maya, is traditionally performed is recognized. To that effect, a commission formed by Government representatives, indigenous organizations, and of spiritual guides, to define these places as well as their conservation regime.*

Notes

* From 1997 Peace Accords, pp. 30–34. Acuerdo sobre Identidad y Derechos de los Pueblos Indigenas 1995: 30–34, trans. by author.

1. It is also important to mention the reactions that various indigenous groups on the continent had to the 500-year commemoration of the discovery of America by Christopher Columbus. The groups organized meetings to share ideas about rights and claims, and when the Peace Accords were drafted and signed in 1996, these ideas were in the leaders' agendas.
2. This project is attempting to catalog all archaeological sites in Guatemala and create an archaeological atlas of the country. It is directed by the archaeologist Juan Pedro LaPorte in Guatemala.

References

Acuerdo Gubernativo No. 261-97 (1997) Guatemala City.

Acuerdo Gubernativo No. 387-2001 (2001) *Diario de Centro América Tomo CCLXVII* Guatemala City Número 50.

Acuerdo sobre Identidad y Derechos de los Pueblos Indígenas (1995) Programa de Naciones Unidas para el Desarrollo (PNUD), Guatemala City: Editorial Saqb'e y Editorial Cholsamaj.

Brown, L., and Romero, L. A. (2002) "Lugares sagrados para ritos de cacería," in J. P. Laporte et al. (eds.), *XV Simposio de Investigaciones Arqueológicas en Guatemala*, pp. 771–82, Guatemala City: Museo Nacional de Arqueología y Etnología.

Christenson, A. (2001) *Art and Society in a Highland Maya Community: The Altar Piece of Santiago Atitlan*, Austin: University of Texas Press.

Cojtí Cuxil, D. (1994) *Políticas para la revindicación de los mayas de hoy (Fundamento de los Derechos Específicos del Pueblo Maya)*, Guatemala City: Editorial Cholsamaj y Seminario Permanente de Estudios Mayas.

———(1995) *Configuración del pensamiento político maya, 2ª parte*, Guatemala City: Editorial Cholsamaj y Seminario Permanente de Estudios Mayas.

Comisión para la Definición de Lugares Sagrados (CDLS) (1998) *Propuesta de los Guías Espirituales sobre Lugares Sagrados, redacción, ordenamiento y agregados al documento de consulta de la Comisión para la Definición de Lugares Sagrados*, unpublished manuscript.

———(2002) *Foro de Unificación de criterios para la definición de los lugares sagrados*, Ministerio de Cultura y Deportes, Guatemala City.

González, N. (1995) "Los garífuna," in J. Lujan (ed.), *Historia General de Guatemala, Tomo III, Siglo XVIII hasta La Independencia*, Guatemala City: Fundación para la Cultura y el Desarrollo.

Kaufman, T. (1976) "Archaeological and Linguistic Correlations in Mayaland and Associated Areas of Meso-America," *World Archaeology* 8, 1: 101–18.

Ministerio de Cultura y Deportes (2001) *Políticas Culturales y Deportivas*, Guatemala City: Editorial Nojib'sa.

Ministerio de Cultura y Deportes (2002) Acuerdo Ministerial 525-2002, 15 Nov 2002, Diario de Centro América, Guatemala City.

Núñez, O., and Ivic de Monterroso, M. (2001) *Lineamientos para la implementación de un programa de coadministración de sitios arqueológicos y/o de aquellos lugares que por sus características puedan ser objeto de la misma*, unpublished manuscript.

Secaira, E. (2000) *La conservación de la naturaleza, el pueblo y el movimiento maya, y la espiritualidad en Guatemala; Implicaciones para conservacionistas*, Guatemala City: Proarca/Capas/AID, la Iniciativa de Uso Sostenible de la Unión Mundial para la Naturaleza, el Fideicomiso para la Conservación de Guatemala y Nature Conservancy.

Warren, K. B. (2002) "Voting against Indigenous Rights in Guatemala: Lessons from the 1999 Referendum," in K. B. Warren and J. E. Jackson (eds.), *Indigenous Movements, Self-Representation, and the State in Latin America*, pp. 149–80, Austin: University of Texas Press.

PART 5
Conclusion

17
Continuities and Changes in Maya Archaeology: An Overview

T. PATRICK CULBERT

The time during which I have worked in Maya archaeology has been remarkably exciting, a period marked by great progress and stunning changes in methods and ideas. When I entered graduate school in the mid-1950s, the criticisms of Clyde Kluckhohn (1940) and Walter Taylor (1948) remained a topic of frequent conversation. But the ruling paradigm was still the Morley–Thompson (Morley 1946; Thompson 1954) model of slash-and-burn farmers of low population density, vacant ceremonial centers and, gentle priest leaders without egos. Sylvanus Morley (1946:262) revealed the attitude toward the inscriptions:

> The Maya inscriptions treat primarily chronology, astronomy. . . . and religious matters. They are in no sense records of personal glorification and self-laudation like the inscriptions of Egypt, Assyria and Babylonia. They tell no story of kingly conquests, recount no deeds of imperial achievements; they neither praise nor exalt, glorify nor aggrandize, indeed they are so utterly impersonal, so completely nonindividualistic, that it is even probable that the name-glyphs of specific men and women were never recorded upon the Maya monuments.

The First Revolution

All of this was to change very rapidly. Gordon Willey, as he so often did, led the way. The introduction of settlement pattern studies in the project at Barton Ramie (Willey et al. 1965) was of the towering significance that

Jerry Sabloff and Wendy Ashmore (2001) attribute to it. I once asked Gordon whether the Kluckhohn–Taylor criticisms had been influential in his decision to study house platforms at Barton Ramie and he replied no, that it had been Julian Steward's cultural ecology approach that influenced him. In the heady days of the late 1950s and 1960s, a series of large projects in the Maya lowlands—the Pennsylvania Tikal Project, the Dzibilchaltun Project, and Willey's projects at Altar de Sacrificios and Seibal—took Maya archaeology in new directions.

The new directions involved little change in methodology. We already knew how to map; it was simply that almost nobody had mapped *all* structures. We knew how to excavate and only minor changes were necessary to excavate house platforms. The results, of course, were to completely change our understanding of ancient Maya society. A key point in this change was the seminar on the Classic Maya collapse at the School of American Research in 1970 (Culbert 1973). The idea was to gather a group of scholars who had taken part in the major projects of the 1960s. We had amassed an enormous amount of new data, but most of it was still unpublished. To marshall a group familiar with these data and focus on a single problem would not only provide the chance to communicate in the seminar sessions, but also result in getting summaries of some key data being put into print. Gordon Willey, Richard Adams, Jerry Sabloff, and I served as a planning committee, and seven other scholars agreed to participate.

The seminar sessions, under the incisive leadership of Willey, proved breathtaking. One of the first tasks was to consider what sort of society had collapsed. All of us had had previously sensed some of the defects of the then standard model of ancient Maya society. In our week of discussions at the seminar, putting our ideas together was like building a jigsaw puzzle that provided the outline of a new concept of Maya Classic society. Features of the Morley–Thompson model crumbled almost instantly.

Most of the 1960s projects had included mapping of substantial areas within site centers, although rural surveys were still in short supply. It was undeniable that population densities in the Late Classic far exceeded those suggested earlier on the basis of the assumption that the Maya could have done nothing other than long-fallow slash-and-burn agriculture. Maya centers had been urban areas rather than vacant ceremonial centers. Although little ecological work had been done at the time, the population figures made clear that the Maya must have had alternatives that could support larger populations than those possible through slash-and-burn farming.

Population figures over time were also available and showed that from a small population beginning in most sites during the Middle Preclassic, there was steady growth to a Late Classic peak. Then the demographic devastation of the collapse occurred, reducing populations by staggering amounts within the space of a century or a little more. The population loss was by no means contemporaneous, for the Pasión River sites continued into a thriving Terminal Classic before they, too, were devastated. It was also clear that the Postclassic population in the central Petén was miniscule in comparison with that of Late Classic times, and was concentrated almost entirely in lakeside and island settlements along the string of lakes at the heart of the area. Although household analysis did not figure heavily in the seminar, we at least were learning about the kinds of houses of non-elite Maya and the artifacts they used.

Another part of the Morley–Thompson model came asunder with Tatiana Proskouriakoff's 1960 article, which revealed in only twenty-one pages the key to understanding Maya inscriptions. Even in that single paper, it was clear that much of the inscriptions were devoted to royal records. With this evidence, gentle priest leaders disappeared to be replaced by hereditary rulers as bloodthirsty and egomaniacal as the kings we know and love from elsewhere in history. With the work of Proskouriakoff and an increasing number of other scholars who followed her lead, the histories of site after site became available. When Yuri Knorosov (1958) showed the way to read the inscriptions in Maya, expertise in Maya linguistics was added to the tools needed to understand the Classic Maya.

More Recent Changes

The study of Maya inscriptions has perhaps moved and changed more rapidly through time than any other branch of Maya studies. Progress in readings and the addition of data from an ever-increasing number of sites have added to our knowledge of the Classic Maya. The Maya historical records have helped clarify archaeological finds. For example, the meaning of the strong artistic and artifactual evidence of Teotihuacan contacts in the Maya lowlands in the Early Classic became clearer when specific events and the Mexican-style names of such major players as Spearthrower Owl were deciphered.

I have often jealously claimed that epigraphers have an advantage over archaeologists. For epigraphers, a new inscription or the decipherment of a single phrase can cause a breakthrough, whereas comparable advances for archaeologists are likely to demand years of painstaking research. An excellent example of an epigraphic breakthrough is the change in our understanding of intersite political structure occasioned by the decipherment by Simon Martin and Nikolai Grube (2000) of a few expressions indicating hierarchical relations between rulers of different sites. At the time when the seminar that resulted in *Classic Maya Political History* (Culbert 1991) was held, the opinion was overwhelmingly in favor of small-scale independent polities, based on the suggestion that possession of an emblem glyph was ipso facto a sign of political independence (Mathews 1991). Within a year or two of the circulation of Martin and Grube's unpublished first paper (1994), the opinion had almost unanimously swung to a political model of a few superpowers that, in some way or other, held sway over other sites.

There is still a tension between two polar attitudes toward the inscriptions. At one extreme are what I call the "skeptics" who believe that the inscriptions are such biased political propaganda that we have little to learn from them. At the other extreme are the "literalists" who accept whatever the Maya said as exact fact. There are few Mayanists at either extreme and most of us fall somewhere between. The differences between us along the continuum are useful because they act as a system of checks and balances.

As the archaeology of the Maya has continued to evolve, I am struck by the emergence of new themes in the last several decades. One is the importance of technological breakthroughs. The revolution after World War II was marked less by changes in methodology than by new questions being asked. More recently, the development of new technologies has created access to data that we could not have imagined in the 1950s. Many of these involve physical and chemical testing, especially in the use of isotopes. Isotopic studies of bone and teeth and sourcing studies of obsidian and ceramics have opened new vistas. They tell us things about diet and the movement of both artifacts and individuals through space.

Despite these other technological breakthroughs, there has been little advance in our methods of absolute dating. Accelerated Mass Spectrometer (AMS) has made it possible to obtain radiocarbon dating for much smaller fragments and has improved precision in machine counts. But we are still faced with the problems of carbon from large trees, parts of which far predate the contexts in which they are found. In addition, contextual control of even short-lived species is often problematic. Even today's precision is not sufficient for many of our problems. Attempts to tie the hypothesized drought in the lowlands to the Maya collapse (Hodell et al. 1995) are, to my mind, extremely tenuous. Whether a drought was a factor in the collapse depends a great deal on whether the drought occurred in A.D. 700, 750, or 800, and I do not believe the dates allow us to be that specific.

In addition, it appears that attempts to use hydration rates of obsidian for dating are exceedingly dubious. Geoffrey Braswell (in this volume) calls the present model "badly flawed" and is pessimistic about whether obsidian hydration can ever be made reliable, an opinion that is now shared by most Mayanists.

Another recurring theme in the articles in this volume is the necessity of multidisciplinary collaboration in research. We need the expertise of specialists in technical fields such as zooarchaeology, osteology, paleobotany, sourcing, and isotope analysis (Emery this volume; Wright this volume). We also need collaboration between archaeologists, art historians, epigraphers, ethnohistorians, and ethnographers. This diversity is a source of strength because specialists not only supply expertise, but also bring different approaches and viewpoints. It is important that specialists be built into projects—at least large projects—from the beginning. The days are over when an archaeologist at the end of a project might think, "I've got some bones here; I wonder if there's anybody who could look at them?" We must also face the fact that there will, and should continue to be, small projects where a large range of specialists simply cannot be afforded. A firm focus on what questions are to be asked and on research design will be necessary for all projects.

Another growing theme in Maya archaeology is an appreciation of the diversity of Maya culture both through time and through space. As Nicholas Dunning and Timothy Beach (in this volume) point out, we now know much more about the great environmental diversity in the Maya lowlands and the multiple ways in which the Maya affected it and adapted to it. We have learned to expect diversity up and down the social scale of the Maya and no longer feel bound to interpret social structure of the lower classes as some sort of miniature replica of the structure of royal families. Diversity is also expected between sites of the same size in close proximity to large centers and those in rural hinterlands. Similarly, regional differences are to be expected. What we need in the future are more data to show us the details of this expectable diversity.

What Have We Learned?

We have learned a great deal more about the Maya in the last several decades, thanks both to the new technological developments and to the amassing of large quantities of new data. At the level of the individual, Lori Wright (in this volume) speaks of the possibility of life histories based on new isotopic methods. At the level of the household, Daniela Triadan and Takeshi Inomata (in this volume) speak of the potential for residue analysis to show activity areas. These studies will be aided by the remarkable data provided by the burned structures at Aguateca (Inomata et al. 2002) and Cerén (Sheets 2002) (marginal to the Maya area, but of obvious relevance). It is now possible through isotope analyses to speak of Maya diets, with implications both for gender and social class differences. Much more data for small communities are now available although we have not come far in understanding local economies. There are hints, however, both from earlier and more recent studies, that local production systems were probably the result of part-time specialization and outside the range of state control.

At a larger scale, great amounts of new data from settlement surveys are available. Particularly noteworthy are the results of the Proyecto Intersitios of the Instituto de Antropología e Historia de Guatemala that, under the direction of Vilma Fialko (1996, 2000, 2001), has completed strip surveys between Tikal, Nakum, Yaxha, and Naranjo. It continues to be obvious that a hierarchy of sites of different sizes and complexities existed, but the mechanisms by which these sites were integrated into a single system are still not clear. Marcello Canuto and William Fash (in this volume) suggests a new level of community analysis that would help to bridge the gap between the lower levels of settlement structure and the large ceremonial and administrative centers.

For the uppermost levels of Classic Maya society, we know vastly more than two decades ago. Both inscriptions and art provide data about the great sites and their royal families. The lines of numbered rulers maintained for centuries at major sites were not dynasties in a genetic sense. There are obvious instances in which "outsiders" broke lines of succession. Robert Sharer and Charles Golden (in this volume) clarify the issue by stressing that it is the institution of kingship at a particular site which is critical. A strict genetic line could sometimes be broken without disrupting the legitimacy of succession to the institution of kingship.

The political machinations of rulers have become much clearer through the inscriptions. Peaceful mechanisms, such as currying the favor of nonroyal elites within a site or arranging marriages with royal lines at other sites, are obvious. Power alliances between sites, especially in the critically important institution of warfare, can be seen. The struggle between the two great powers, Tikal and Calakmul, continued for several centuries and drew in polities from across the Southern Lowlands (Martin and Grube 2000). We still do not understand the mechanisms and degree of control involved when a ruler at one site acknowledged an overlord. It seems not unlikely that there will be diversity in these features depending on such factors as the relative sizes of sites, the distances between them, and the political strength of individual rulers.

Technical studies as well as the signing of some great works of art help with understanding the production and distribution of elite goods. The sourcing of ceramics by Neutron Activation Analysis (NAA) shows movement of the most outstanding styles over great distances, perhaps as gift exchange and perhaps for use in feasting (Antonia Foias in this volume).

All political events and mechanisms are surrounded by ceremony and couched in terms of religious significance. Both ancestors and gods are invoked in establishing legitimacy, and attention to such ideological and symbolic factors is steadily increasing in frequency.

What should our interaction be with the broader worlds of anthropology and history and the role of comparisons with other societies? In their excellent article, Sharer and Golden (in this volume) criticize the borrowing of whole models from other societies into which the Maya are then crammed. As an example, they cite the wave of weak state models applied to the Maya that has faded into obscurity with multiple evidence that the Maya were not, infact, a weak state. They effectively demonstrate the failure of the Classic Maya to fit the segmentary state and galactic polity models that have been applied to them. They suggest that "holistic models derived from a culturally specific context should not be applied cross-culturally" (42). Instead, the appropriate procedure is to build a model based on the Maya data and then look for specific attributes of this model that can be found in other societies. I could not agree more wholeheartedly.

Contemporary Concerns

This volume's final section "Contemporary Concerns" raises a series of challenging issues. The essence, as I understand it, is to caution archaeologists of today and the future to be conscious about the impact of what we are doing on levels all the way from the local areas in which we work to the world audience. Part of the emphasis is on the living Maya who, as descendants of the people we study, have a right to a primary voice in our activities. But the issues are far broader and concern our interactions with local workers and communities, colleagues in the countries in which we work, and government institutions concerned in one way or another with archaeology.

I will not deal with interactions with living ethnic Maya because I have not worked with Maya since the late 1950s, and that was a different time and different Maya culture (Tzeltal). Equally important, however, are our relationships with the local people of the Petén. Many of them have Maya names and no hesitation in speaking of recent ancestors who still spoke Maya, but they do not identify with communities where people still speak Maya and wear native dress.

In the chapter by Jason Yaeger and Greg Borgestede, there is an excellent analysis of the constituencies that have interests in archaeological projects in the Maya area and the ways chosen to communicate with them. This could well serve as an example for archaeologists to consider. There is, however, a point in Yaeger and Borgstede's section on the New Archaeology (1960s–1980s) with which I must disagree strongly. They suggest that ". . . the increasingly specialized training that professional archaeologists received arguably led to a devaluation of the contributions that local men and women Maya and non-Maya made to archaeological *fieldwork* (271)."

In fairness to those of us involved in fieldwork at the time, I must simply say that this is untrue. When the Pennsylvania Project was inaugurated at Tikal in the mid-1950s, a group of *chicleros* and *milperos* was recruited as workers. Their skills developed very rapidly, and they were treated with great respect by archaeologists who recognized, as Yaeger and Borgstede note, that they exceeded many of the students and archaeologists in their skills and experience.

An issue that is often neglected in the heated discussions of the ethics of Maya archaeologists is the economic contribution that employment makes to local people. I am particularly proud of the way that the Pennsylvania Tikal Project and the Proyecto Nacional Tikal supported their workers. Many of them worked for these projects and the Tikal National Park for their lifetimes, experiencing both security of employment and more financial support than they could have gained in their traditional occupations. Now, when I return, I occasionally meet the children of these workers. They have had far more education than was available to their parents and have middle-class jobs. Our workers used their improved financial status to educate their children and provide them opportunities that would probably not have been possible without archaeological fieldwork. I do not believe that we were unethical, as the Cohodas seminar would claim, nor would our workers agree that we were unethical. A very significant contribution has been the creation of whole communities of specialists in archaeological fieldwork as at Succotz in Belize or in Dolores, El Petén, where Juan Pedro Laporte has trained a group of workers whose skills are avidly sought by projects.

K. Anne Pyburn's article asks that we be aware of our biases and the impacts our research may have all the way from the local to the international level. In addition, we must consider the issue of relevance. When I began to work at Tikal in 1960, I believe that we considered that, at best, there was a vague utility for educated people to know something about the past. There was clearly a bias in the profession against "popularizers" who would give newspaper interviews or write for a general audience. This existed in a context in which anthropology was on the crest of a wave: students came to classes in droves and academic jobs were available in profusion. As the crest began to wane, however, this exclusivity was not an adaptive attitude for the profession. When I was a member of the Society for American Archaeology Executive Board (SAA) in the 1970s and thereafter cochair of the SAA's committee on archaeological employment, we had to face this issue and realize that communication with the public was critical for the profession.

Even in the early days in Tikal, however, we were well aware of the impact of the project on local people and the national government. As already noted, we valued and were concerned for our workers. On the national level, we were delighted when the Guatemalan government supported the project by providing free flights on Aviateca Airlines and even more delighted when they decided to increase support to help the project continue five years longer than we had originally anticipated. I continue to believe that this was good for us and for archaeology as well as for the country of Guatemala.

But relevance and political significance are relative. I would be hard pressed to argue with any except an archaeological audience that my still-continuing work with Tikal ceramics is relevant to the world at large. And it would be a very strange political system in which it had any political significance. My more recent work on population, subsistence, and the Classic collapse I am convinced *is* relevant because I consider this another example of the dangers that face the planet's future. In addition, work with my NASA colleagues using satellite imagery to identify microecological zones is even more directly relevant because such research can be used to trace the progress of deforestation and to help preserve the Maya Biosphere Reserve. Moreover, this is very directly political because there are a variety of constituencies whose interests in the lands of the reserve are in conflict.

I believe that our ethical responsibilities are quite clear. We have responsibilities to our workers. We must listen to their concerns, respect and learn from them, and support them financially to the extent possible. We have responsibilities to our colleagues in Maya countries, and to the institutions and governments of those countries. It is important for us to remember that when we work in these countries, we are there as guests and outsiders. For us to engage in social archaeology as Latin Americans do *within* their own countries (except if we do so under the guidance of and in direct collaboration with colleagues in the countries concerned) could carry us to and often over the brink into Yankee imperialism. As our Guatemalan colleague, Hector Escobedo, has put it, "Internationalist efforts can only exist in an atmosphere of mutual respect and solid regard for Guatemalan norms, needs and expectations."

References

Culbert, T. P. (ed.) (1973) *The Classic Maya Collapse*, Albuquerque: University of New Mexico Press.

———(ed.) (1991) *Classic Maya Political History*, Cambridge, UK: Cambridge University Press.

Fialko, V. (1996) "Yaxhá y Nakum: Jerarquías y patrones de asentamiento en sus espacios intersitios," *Mayab* 10: 14–24.

———(2000) Sangre, Sudor y Lagrimas: Investigaciones arqueológicas en los Centros Urbanos Menores ubicados en la periferia este de Tikal (Uolantun, El Corozal, Chalpate), Vol.11, manuscript on file, PRONAT-Triángulo, Instituto de Antropología e Historia, Guatemala City.

———(2001) "Investigaciones arqueologicas en la cuenca del rio Holmul entre Tikal y Nakum, Parte 2," paper presented at XV Simposio de Investigaciones Arqueologicas en Guatemala, Museo Nacional de Arqueologia y Etnologia, July Guatemala City.

Hodell, D. A., Curtis, J. H., and Brenner, M. (1995) "Possible Role of Climate in the Collapse of Classic Maya Civilization," *Nature* 375: 391–4.
Inomata, D., Triadan, D., Ponciano, E., Terry, R. E., and Eberl, M. (2002) "Domestic and Political Lives of Classic Maya Elites: The Excavation of Rapidly Abandoned Structures at Aguateca, Guatemala," *Latin American Antiquity* 13: 305–30.
Kluckhohn, C. (1940) "The Conceptual Structure in Middle American Archaeology," in C. L.Hay et al. (eds.), *The Maya and Their Neighbors*, pp. 41–51, New York: D. Appleton-Century
Knorosov, Y. V. (1958) "The Problem of the Study of the Maya Hieroglyphic Writing," *American Antiquity* 23: 284–91.
Martin, S., and N. Grube (1994) "Evidence for Macro-political Organization amongst Classic Maya Lowland States," unpublished manuscript.
———(2000) *Chronicle of the Maya Kings and Queens*, London: Thames and Hudson.
Mathews, P. (1991) "Classic Maya Emblem Glyphs," in T. P. Culbert (ed.) *Classic Maya Political History: Hieroglyphic and Archaeological Evidence*, pp. 19–29, Albuquerque: University of New Mexico Press.
Morley, S. G. (1946) *The Ancient Maya*, Palo Alto: Stanford University Press.
Proskouriakoff, T. (1960) "Historical Implications of a Pattern of Dates at Piedras Negras, Guatemala," *American Antiquity* 25: 454–75.
Sabloff, J. A., and Ashmore, W. (2001) "An Aspect of Archaeology's Recent Past and Its Relevance in the New Millennium," in G. Feinman and T. D. Price (eds.), *Archaeology at the Millennium: A Sourcebook*, pp. 11–32, Nerw York: Kluwer/Plenum.
Sheets, P. D. (2002) *Before the Volcano Erupted: The Ancient Cerén Village in Central America*, Austin: University of Texas Press
Taylor, W. W. (1948) *A Study of Archaeology*, Memoirs of the American Anthropological Association, 69, Menasha, WI: American Anthropological Association.
Thompson, J. E. S. (1954) *The Rise and Fall of Maya Civilization*, Norman: University of Oklahoma Press.
Willey, G. R., Bullard, W. R., Glass, J. B., and Gifford, J. C. (1965) *Prehistoric Maya Settlements in the Belize River Valley*, Papers of the Peabody Museum of Archaeology and Ethnology, no. 54, Cambridge, MA: Harvard University.

Index